MATTERS OF SEX

Matters of Sex

Katharine Bement Davis and America's First Sexual Revolution

Anya Jabour

A WASHINGTON MEWS BOOK

New York University Press

NEW YORK UNIVERSITY PRESS
New York

WASHINGTON MEWS BOOKS
An Imprint of
NEW YORK UNIVERSITY PRESS
New York
www.nyupress.org

Library of Congress Cataloging-in-Publication Data
Names: Jabour, Anya author
Title: Matters of sex : Katharine Bement Davis and America's first sexual revolution / Anya Jabour.
Description: New York : New York University Press, [2026] | Includes bibliographical references and index.
Identifiers: LCCN 2025054924 (print) | LCCN 2025054925 (ebook) | ISBN 9781479838868 hardback | ISBN 9781479838875 ebook | ISBN 9781479838882 ebook other
Subjects: LCSH: Davis, Katharine Bement, 1860–1935 | Women sexologists—United States | Women social reformers—United States | Women—Sexual behavior—United States | LCGFT: Biographies
Classification: LCC HQ18.32.D38 J33 2026 (print) | LCC HQ18.32.D38 (ebook)
LC record available at https://lccn.loc.gov/2025054924
LC ebook record available at https://lccn.loc.gov/2025054925

This book is printed on acid-free paper, and its binding materials are chosen for strength and durability. We strive to use environmentally responsible suppliers and materials to the greatest extent possible in publishing our books.

The manufacturer's authorized representative in the EU for product safety is Mare Nostrum Group B.V., Doelen 72, 4831 GR Breda, The Netherlands. Email: gpsr@mare-nostrum.co.uk.

Manufactured in the United States of America

10 9 8 7 6 5 4 3 2 1

Also available as an ebook

This book is dedicated with deepest thanks to Katharine Bement Davis's great-niece, Francie Garber Pepper, who proudly carried on the family legacy of strong women working to make the world a better place.

When she cleaned out her mother's closet, Francie Garber Pepper discovered a treasure trove of original source material, including an unpublished memoir, family correspondence, and personal memorabilia, belonging to her great-aunt, Katharine Bement Davis. Exclusive access to these materials made this book possible. Sadly, Francie passed away before this book's publication. Here, Francie waves from a boat near the family's vacation home in the Georgian Bay, "St. Helena," named for Davis's sister, Helen Alling Davis. Courtesy Helen Garber.

CONTENTS

Katharine Bement Davis called herself "a busy woman." Indeed, Davis was a true trailblazer. Throughout her long life—from 1860 to 1935—she fought for women's equality in the workforce, at the ballot box—and in the bedroom. Courtesy Frances Garber Pepper.

Introduction

"A Busy Woman"

At the time of her death in 1935, Katharine Bement Davis was recognized as "one of the outstanding women of our times." As one editorial explained, "Dr. Davis in a time when many avenues were closed to women demonstrated her ability to accomplish great things."[1]

Indeed, Davis was a true trailblazer. A quintessential "new woman"—as social commentators labeled the first generation of women to pursue higher education and professional careers—Davis, born in 1860, blazed her way through—and often pioneered—most of the professional fields open to women in turn-of-the-century America.

One of the first women in the United States to earn a PhD, Davis went on to become the first superintendent of New York's Reformatory for Women at Bedford Hills. Subsequently, she became the first female commissioner of correction for New York City, where she quelled a riot and instituted reform. She spent the final decade of her career directing the Bureau of Social Hygiene, a privately funded think tank committed to combating commercialized sex and curbing the spread of sexually transmitted infections.[2]

While there, she conducted research for the world's first comprehensive study of female sexuality. Decades before Alfred Kinsey launched his celebrated studies of human sexuality, Davis published *Factors in the Sex Life of Twenty-Two Hundred Women*, which remains one of the most thorough investigations of female sexuality ever conducted. In the process, she both exemplified and advanced the shift from Victorian to modern womanhood.[3]

Importantly, Davis did not only blaze new trails for herself. At every stage of her career, she also advanced equality for women as a group. At Bedford Reformatory, she provided educational and recreational opportunities for the inmates; she also hired a cohort of highly educated women to work as physicians and psychologists. While she tackled what some called "a man's job" as commissioner of correction, she also advocated women's voting rights as an officer of the national suffrage organization.[4]

Finally, Davis made it her mission to investigate what she called "matters of sex." By publishing the results of her extensive study of women's sexual desires and experiences—and by collaborating with birth-control advocates, free-speech activists, and civil rights lawyers—she not only redefined the parameters of "normal" female sexuality in modern America but also advanced the nation's "first sexual revolution" in the 1920s. By funding both "the scientific study of sex" and the burgeoning birth-control movement, Davis also paved the way for the second (and now better-known) sexual revolution of the 1960s and 1970s and laid the groundwork for ongoing civil rights struggles.[5]

"Greatest Women"

Contemporary accounts consistently identified Davis as one of the greatest women of her generation. Davis's membership in that august group—which included luminaries such as Nobel Peace Prize winner Jane Addams, "The Yellow Wallpaper" author Charlotte Perkins Gilman, and US Children's Bureau chief Julia Lathrop—mattered. The impressive generation of "new women" who came of age in the Gilded Age—especially those who were native born, white, and well-to-do—enjoyed unprecedented opportunities to seek higher education, pursue professional careers, and demand political rights.[6]

Davis took full advantage of these expanding horizons. Born and raised in New York, she worked as a schoolteacher to earn money to attend Vassar College. She subsequently ran a model home at the World's Fair in Chicago, which led to a position as a settlement house worker in Philadelphia. After becoming one of the first women in the nation to earn a PhD at the coeducational University of Chicago, she returned to New York to pioneer new fields for women as a prison reformer and public health expert.[7]

At the same time that she supported herself as a single woman, Davis advocated for women's rights as an outspoken suffragist and an active participant in local, state, and national politics. Although her

PhD was in political economy, she gained a national reputation as a sociologist for her statistical studies of the "social evil," as contemporaries labeled sex work. She parlayed that expertise into a position at the helm of a Rockefeller-funded agency, the Bureau of Social Hygiene, dedicated to the suppression of both the sex trade and sexually transmitted infections. During World War I, she collaborated with both the federal government and women's organizations to promote "social hygiene," as pioneers dubbed the early sex education movement.[8]

Finally, Davis turned her attention away from "the social evil" toward the sex life of "normal" women, publishing the world's first large-scale study of women's sexuality in 1929. *Factors in the Sex Life of Twenty-Two Hundred Women* boldly redefined women's sexuality by demonstrating that "average" women—not just sex workers or sexual deviants—experienced sexual desire, engaged in sexual activity, and enjoyed sexual satisfaction.[9] At the same time that she conducted her revelatory study, Davis also lent her expertise to ongoing campaigns to legalize birth control, promote sexual education, and challenge censorship. She thus became not only a gatherer of sexual information but also an advocate for sexual freedom.[10]

Still more remarkably, Davis did all this in the shadow of the Comstock Laws—a set of interlocking federal bans and state laws that severely limited Americans' access to accurate information about both sex and birth control—and now threaten to do so once again. Named for the mutton-chopped moralist, Anthony Comstock, the original federal statute, "An Act for the Suppression of Trade in, and Circulation of, Obscene Literature and Articles of Immoral Use," adopted just as Davis entered her teens, defined both printed material and material objects dealing with sex, contraception, and abortion as obscene and made the distribution of such material through the US mail a federal crime.[11]

By the time Davis was an adult, the Comstock Laws had come to refer not only to the original Comstock Act of 1873 but also to so-called mini–Comstock Laws at the state level and to US Customs restrictions on the importation of sexual information and contraceptive devices from abroad. As a special inspector for the US Postal Service, Comstock zealously enforced anti-obscenity laws by prosecuting—one might say persecuting—female physicians, free-speech advocates, feminist activists, and family-planning proponents until his death in 1915, just as

Davis took the reins of New York City's law enforcement, first as commissioner of correction and then as the founder and first head of Gotham's Parole Board.[12]

The Comstock Laws did not die with their original advocate and avid enforcer, however. Rather, it took decades of concerted effort by feminist activists, supportive physicians, free-speech advocates, and civil rights lawyers to curtail the power of the Comstock Laws. As an educator, a researcher, and an activist, Davis did her best to combat what critics called "Comstockery."[13]

During her career as a corrections official, Davis was obliged to uphold New York State's "mini–Comstock Laws," even supervising the prison sentences of both Emma Goldman and Margaret Sanger for distributing contraceptive devices and disseminating birth-control information in defiance of the law. But after leaving public office to work at a privately funded think tank—and even more so, after her controversial research led her to lose her job—she challenged both the Comstock Laws and the "conspiracy of silence" they fostered by investigating women's sexual desires and experiences, establishing a national agency dedicated to the study of human sexuality, advocating legal and effective birth control, and providing scientifically sound sex education—all with the aim of promoting what she called "a sane outlook" on "matters of sex."[14]

"Fundamental Facts"

In some ways, Davis—a country schoolteacher turned corrections official—might seem an unlikely candidate for her trailblazing role as a sexual savant. She devoted the first half of her professional career to policing women's sexuality, not promoting it. While her undergraduate studies in the natural sciences and her graduate work in the social sciences gave her the tools to conduct statistical analysis, she initially used her expertise to study female convicts at Bedford Reformatory. Her conclusion that the "fundamental fact" about "women delinquents" was that they were "women who lead sexually immoral lives" did little to foreshadow her future as an advocate of sexual liberation. Nor did her repeated clashes with birth-control advocate Margaret Sanger, who emerged as an outspoken adversary of the law-and-order Davis during her term as commissioner of correction for New York City, when she supervised the fiery activist's imprisonment for distributing contraceptives in defiance of the law.[15]

In the course of her wartime work promoting both sex education and woman suffrage, however, Davis became convinced that the best way to promote women's equality and challenge the sexual double standard was to dispel sexual ignorance. Even as sex suffused popular culture, she pointed out, a powerful "taboo" on open and informed discussions of sexuality led to "distorted views, baffled speculation, and unfortunate experiences."[16]

Davis insisted that only by obtaining accurate information could Americans achieve a rational understanding of "all matters pertaining to sex." To this end, she founded the nation's first agency dedicated to "the scientific study of sex" and launched the world's first large-scale study of "normal" women's sexuality.[17]

Davis dedicated nearly a decade to her monumental study of women's sexuality, which she referred to as her own "special piece of work."[18] *Factors in the Sex Life of Twenty-Two Hundred Women* was notable not only as the first comprehensive study of women's sexuality conducted by a woman but also as the first published study of "normal" women's sexuality—what Davis described as the study of "the woman who was not pathological mentally or physically and who was capable of adjusting herself satisfactorily to her social group." Her revelations that "average" women—white, well-educated, and well-to-do—used birth control, engaged in masturbation, and had lesbian relationships shocked a generation of Americans struggling with the shift from Victorian to modern ideas about sexuality. In particular, the study challenged prevailing beliefs about female "passionlessness": the idea that "proper" women did not experience sexual desire or enjoy sexual activity. Instead, Davis's data demonstrated that women were sexual beings.[19]

Davis's landmark study redefined "normal" women's sexuality by providing statistics on "average" women's behavior. In addition, Davis centered women's own experiences by including personal narratives as well as statistical tables in her study. Proclaiming that women's sexuality was an important subject, Davis pioneered the scientific study of sex in

Factors in the Sex Life of Twenty-Two Hundred Women, released in 1929, was not only the first major study of women's sexuality conducted by a woman but also the first published study of "normal" women's sexuality. Katharine Bement Davis dedicated nearly a decade of her life to her magnum opus, which both documented and drove the nation's "first sexual revolution." Photo by Isa Tumble.

America decades before Dr. Alfred Kinsey gained acclaim as the "father of the sexual revolution."[20]

If Kinsey was the father of the sexual revolution, Davis was its foremother. By conducting her study during the turbulent 1920s, Davis both documented and drove profound shifts in sexual attitudes and behavior in early twentieth-century America. By redefining "normal" female sexuality, she both advanced the nation's first sexual revolution and paved the way for the second. Finally, Davis not only detailed "matters of sex" but also demonstrated that sex matters.[21]

An "Unadorned Story"

Davis impressed her contemporaries as one of the greatest women of her generation—no mean accomplishment for a generation that included first lady Eleanor Roosevelt, birth-control advocate Margaret Sanger, and investigative journalist Ida Tarbell. As one of Davis's many admiring friends expressed it, "She is a wonderful woman, the greatest in her field. Her influence for good is immeasurable! It is all beyond computations what she has accomplished in her useful, crowded life! To find a woman of such grasp, such a fund of expert knowledge, and yet find the heart of the woman beating so high with youth, and enthusiasm and love of humanity is a wonderful example of what a human mind may achieve!"[22]

And yet, when Davis turned her attention to writing a book about her life—what she called an "autobiographical biography" since she worked with a collaborator to write it—she was unable to find a publisher. Writing to Paul Kellogg, editor of the social work journal *The Survey*, in 1933, she explained her dilemma. She had "hoped and expected" that Harper Brothers, which had published her sex study, would take on the project, but the press turned her down, explaining that "they could not afford to take it as they were stocked up with biographies." Next, she approached Appleton's, with whom her ghost writer had a prior relationship, but that publishing house also rejected her book. Completely overlooking her record as a pathbreaking sex researcher and characterizing her instead simply as a social worker, the press opined that "I was too little known to make it likely to be a profitable undertaking." Davis was deeply disappointed. "I feel very down in the mouth," the would-be autobiographer admitted.[23]

Davis continued to seek a publisher as well as an explanation for her failure. Wondering if there was "something wrong with the writing," she asked Kellogg to read her opening chapter, "A Warning to Prospective Readers," in which she cautioned her imagined audience not to expect either romance or scandal—the typical fare of celebrity biographies, then and now. Instead, she explained, what she had to offer was "the plain, unadorned story of the life of a busy woman, told in words of one syllable."[24]

Although "the life of a busy woman" covered many important topics, Davis's matter-of-fact presentation "in words of one syllable" did not make for riveting reading. Kellogg wrote in an internal memo to himself that he found her first chapter "discouragingly apologetic." In fact, in his opinion, the entire book, as described in a detailed chapter-by-chapter description Davis sent him, "doesn't sound like a very beguiling possibility for a publisher in hard times!"[25]

Beyond the lackluster opening, Davis's autobiographical biography had other shortcomings, among them the lack of a narrative arc. Although the book description asserted that the manuscript would be more than "a recital of her accomplishments," the draft chapters often read this way, with little explanation of how or why Davis moved from one endeavor to another. As Davis herself remarked, "My life has been an extremely 'logical' one—i.e., one thing has just led to another."[26]

Kellogg suggested that Davis rethink her chronological approach and consider instead a thematic one. "Granted that biographies are not any too popular in hard times," he wrote, "it might be worth while for you to consider recasting the book . . . so that it will be less of an autobiography and more of a fresh charge of observation, philosophy and experience."[27]

While it is not clear that Davis ever considered rewriting her life story in the way that Kellogg suggested, she understood that she needed to provide more reflection in the manuscript. In the detailed description she sent Kellogg, either Davis or her amanuensis—Jean Henry Large, the author of a popular "Girl Scouts" series of books for young readers as well as President Henry Hoover's sister-in-law—suggested that the book might be presented as a metonym for women's evolving role in national life. Her life, noted the description, could be seen as "an account of the transition period of women's development in this country, bridging the gap between the early suffrage leaders, who fought and suffered for women's rights[,] and the modern women who with increasing rapidity are entering every field of activity." Since Davis belonged to both groups, "her life appears as a symbol of the best in woman's new position in the world." But, perhaps because of what Davis described as her "unusual lack of introspection," the incomplete draft manuscript did not fulfill this promise.[28]

Either due to discouragement over poor publication prospects or because of her declining health, Davis never completed the final two planned chapters—those covering her years at the Bureau of Social Hygiene and what she regarded as her "special piece of work" on women's sexuality.[29] But this was not the only barrier to publication.

Some years after her death, a Vassar College classmate, Caroline Furness, read portions of the unfinished manuscript. She remarked, "I read many of the chapters but they did not satisfy me. I talked to her . . . sister Charlotte about it, and we both agreed the kernel was not there. . . . As they were, they told the bare facts but did not show why they were epoch making." Davis's sister Helen agreed, opining that it would take "a master hand" to "do something with what material we have."[30]

While I don't claim to be "a master hand," I have spent the past several years contemplating why Katharine Bement Davis deserves a biography and exploring the importance of the epochal events of her eventful life. As detailed in the acknowledgments, I have benefited from access to materials held in both private hands and public collections, which greatly enriched my understanding of Davis's life and legacy.

And yet, after spending years researching Davis and reflecting on her life, I still found it difficult to find the essential "kernel" of her story, in part because of the lack of materials documenting her interior life. Valuable as her "autobiographical biography" was in providing an overview of her illustrious career, it offered disappointingly few insights into her personal motivations. Her book description indicated that retirement offered "time at last for some introspection!" But even when she had time for reflection, Davis avoiding doing so, writing, "I took things as they came, as a matter of course, and never considered my own motives or the influences that spurred me to action."[31]

"A Remarkable Woman"

Even after I determined that Davis's most important legacy was her pathbreaking study of "normal" women's sexuality, then, I still found myself stymied by a lack of insight about why a woman who spent the first half of her career policing women's sexuality dedicated the final decade of her professional life to promoting it.

Davis did not complete the chapter of her memoirs in which she would have addressed the study. Given the lack of reflection in the rest of the manuscript, even if she had written this chapter, she might not have addressed this issue. Moreover, there appears to have been a virtual conspiracy of silence on the sex study in the contemporary media, probably due to behind-the-scenes activity by Davis's employer, prudish philanthropist John D. Rockefeller Jr., and his media-shy and misogynist colleagues. Finally, the few small stashes of personal correspondence included in her family's private collection offer few clues about this dramatic shift in Davis's perspective.

Of course, the lack of personal information is not unusual for women of Davis's generation, who often zealously guarded their private lives even when—indeed, often especially when—they were eager to record their professional successes and their political achievements. For Davis, an unmarried woman who wrote extensively about women's sexuality—including prostitution, masturbation, and lesbianism—professional success required cloaking her personal life, for any revelations that she had the type of "romances" that she publicly disavowed in the opening chapter of her autobiography would have damaged both her personal reputation and her professional standing beyond repair.[32]

And yet, Davis's personal life helps explain her professional achievements. While her family of origin inspired her to defy convention and encouraged her to achieve greatness, her chosen family—a family of female friends—shaped and supported her decision to do so by conducting a pioneering study of women's sexuality and dedicating herself to promoting women's sexual freedom.

"Unusual Early Cultural Advantages"

While her "autobiographical biography" offers some bread crumbs to follow, other sources—including a few small caches of family correspondence, the diaries and photographs of family friend May Bragdon, and public records about both family members and female friends—proved essential to understanding these influences on Davis's life and work.

Throughout her life, Davis had the advantage of membership in an affectionate and supportive family. In her memoirs, Davis highlighted the example of her grandmother, abolitionist and feminist Rhoda Denison Bement. Grandmother Bement, who lived with the Davis family, thrilled and inspired Davis and her siblings with true stories about her daring work as a "conductor" on the Underground Railroad and her historic participation in the nation's first women's rights convention at Seneca Falls. Throughout her adult life, Davis honored her grandmother's legacy by using her full name on all professional correspondence and the monograph "KBD" on her personalized stationery.[33]

Although Davis consistently highlighted her "Bement" legacy, her entire family helped her achieve her aspirations and become "a remarkable woman" like her grandmother. Rhoda Denison Bement's daughters carried on the family tradition of independent womanhood. Her older daughters, Anna and Rhoda, both worked as schoolteachers in New York's common school system, serving as role models for Davis, who would devote ten years of her life to teaching school. Her youngest daughter, Frances—destined to become Davis's mother—also demonstrated women's abilities. At age seventeen, Frances achieved a reputation for bravery and quick thinking when, while on a steamship bound for Detroit, she spied another ship engulfed in flame. When Frances's ship came within reach, many of the female passengers were in "hysterics." But the teenager "kept her head and was able to give valiant service to the unfortunates." At her wedding, "some of those she nursed" presented her with a silver cake-basket engraved, "Presented to Frances Bement for services rendered." Many decades later, the Davis family still used the cake-basket for "festive occasions."[34]

When Frances Bement married Oscar Davis, she gave up her surname but kept her strong spirit. In her memoirs, Davis fondly recalled her parents' unstinting love and support; she also noted that both her father's paid professional work and her mother's unpaid domestic labor sustained the growing family, which eventually included five children: Katharine (b. 1860), Charlotte (b. 1861), Hamilton (b. 1864), Helen (b. 1871), and Frank (b. 1875). Their commitment to their children was constant, even as they moved frequently—from Buffalo to Dunkirk and finally to Rochester—in search of financial stability.[35]

Frances and Oscar supported their children in emotional as well as material ways. As Davis noted in a chapter overview for her "autobiographical biography," she enjoyed "unusual early cultural advantages."[36] Like other parents of future feminists, the Davises were a civic-minded and hard-working couple who valued personal achievement and public service. The Davises also encouraged their children in their interests and took pride in their accomplishments.[37]

Growing up, young "Kitty," as she was then known, displayed a "marked degree of curiosity and creative instinct." Her parents encour-

Katharine Bement Davis's mother, Frances, displayed the same sort of initiative and courage that Davis would develop when, as a teenager, she rescued refugees from a burning steamship. Many years later, Davis would perform a similar service after a devastating earthquake in Sicily. For her efforts, Frances received a commemorative cake-basket, still cherished by family members. Photo by Wendy Magee, courtesy of John Pepper.

aged these qualities, indulging their firstborn's "continual desire to experiment." While her native curiosity encouraged her to pursue scientific study, Davis also shared her family's love for the written word—and their wicked sense of humor. A devoted reader, she also was an aspiring writer, fond of composing verse (especially humorous limericks) as well as writing and producing her own plays.[38]

The Davises also supported female ambition, encouraging their daughters as well as their sons to pursue their dreams. For instance, while Oscar had no musical inclinations and limited financial resources, he cheerfully funded his daughter's music studies; even though Frances disapproved of Kitty reading "potboiler" novels, she invited the neighbors to attend the original plays the youngster scripted, based on forbidden reading material. The Davises' support promoted their daughters' achievements. While Davis would become the most well known of her siblings, her sisters also pursued both higher education and professional careers. Helen, who graduated from the Boston Normal School of Gymnastics, taught gymnastics at the Rochester YWCA before holding a series of leadership positions in the Young Women's Christian Association (in which Frances Davis also was active). Charlotte worked as a stenographer and secretary for the US Postal Service for nearly two decades before ill health led her to curtail her career.[39]

Although Davis confessed that she found it difficult to identify important influences on her life, engage in "character analysis," or offer a "philosophic basis" for her career, the three sisters' success stories suggest that their family life imbued them with tremendous confidence and determination. For Davis, who greatly admired her grandmother's "fighting spirit," this meant that she was always ready to engage in what she called "a good fight" for what was right. As she noted in her memoirs, "I have always felt that it was much more fun to argue a cause when you had an audience which contained a goodly proportion of people who were opposed to you."[40]

In short, her family's unwavering support and feminist principles molded Davis into a woman whose "versatility, adaptability, ingeniousness, objectiveness, unfailing energy and ability for intense concentration" instilled in her "the power of leadership and pioneering spirit, shown in the fact that frequently she has been the first woman in certain undertakings, and sometimes the only woman."[41]

The diaries and photographs of a family friend, May Bragdon, reveal that the Davis family was fun-loving as well as feminist. A dedicated diary keeper and enthusiastic amateur photographer, Bragdon spent a great deal of time at the Davises' Rochester residence, where she recorded good times and high jinks. Bragdon also documented the family's vacations in the "Thirty Thousand Islands" of Canada's Georgian Bay, where they enjoyed staying at the cottage Helen built on her own island, "St. Helena," and spending time outdoors with family and friends. As Bragdon put it, "Saint Helen reigns supreme, and all her guests are happy."[42]

Along with the rest of her family, Davis also enjoyed the natural surroundings of her native New York. While living in an apartment over-

Katharine Bement Davis grew up in a supportive family that imbued her with the confidence to pursue her goals and the willingness to engage in "a good fight" for her principles when necessary. Davis remained close to her family throughout her life. This photograph by family friend May Bragdon shows (*left to right*) Katharine Bement Davis, Charlotte Davis, Helen Alling Davis, Mary Mosher, Hamilton Davis, and Howard Mosher near "St. Helena," the family's vacation home in Canada's Georgian Bay. "Kate, Chat, Helen, Mary M. Hamilton & Mr. M.," August 4, 1903, May Bragdon Diaries, Rare Books, Special Collections, and Preservation, University of Rochester River Campus Libraries.

looking the Hudson River on Riverside Drive, she engaged in a playful debate about poetry with her sisters, who dared her to return to her roots by resuming her attempts at poetry. Davis accepted the challenge, writing a piece titled "Clouds" about the clouds of smoke rising from the New York Central Railroad that was printed (anonymously) in an African American newspaper, the *New York Age*. Subsequently, she composed several more poems about life on Riverside Drive. One year, as a Christmas gift, she collected the poems, under the title "From My Window," and had them privately printed and bound with a charming cover featuring a woodcut of the view from her window, depicting a stone bench overlooking the Hudson River, courtesy of her friend and colleague Dr. Robert L. Dickinson, a progressive gynecologist and birth-control advocate. The poems are some of Davis's most reflective writing, revealing her longing for the snowy scenery of her childhood home even as they expressed admiration for the very different landscape along the Hudson River.[43]

Davis remained close to her family throughout her life. She exchanged affectionate letters with her parents and siblings and made frequent visits to the family home during her parents' lifetime. (Oscar passed away in 1908; Frances followed in 1915.) In later life, Davis shared a residence with her sisters, first in New York City and then, after retirement, in California. She also hired Charlotte as her own personal secretary and collaborated with Helen in social reform. Davis also maintained a close relationship with her brothers, Hamilton and Frank. She had an especially important relationship with Frank's daughter after his wife's premature death. Davis and her sisters shared responsibility for rearing their motherless niece, named Frances after their own mother. Frances even lived with her aunts while attending high school in New York City in the 1920s.[44]

Shortly before her retirement, Davis, a long-time renter, purchased a "garden apartment" in Jackson Heights. The purchase may have been intended to provide the Davis sisters with both a close community and financial security as they entered old age. According to one profile published at the time, in addition to "staging daily experiments . . . in the kitchen of her cozy Jackson Heights apartment," Davis enjoyed visiting with her neighbors and attending club meetings. Yet, later that year, when Helen—the only sister still pursuing her profession—accepted a position at the YWCA's Asilomar conference center in California, Davis happily relocated with her sisters. "We are three old maids and we have lived together for many years," she told a reporter, adding, "Now I feel as if I were going to heaven."[45]

Designed by the renowned architect Julia Morgan, the lovely arts and crafts campus on the western tip of the Monterey Peninsula, with its rustic buildings, wooded grounds, and ocean views, must have reminded the Davis sisters of their beloved family vacation home in Canada's Georgian Bay, where they had enjoyed boating, fishing, and hiking decades earlier. For the sisters' first Christmas in their new home, Davis penned a poem, printed on the reverse side of a postcard featuring a sketch of a shingled one-story cabin surrounded by tall pine trees. Titled

"Our Redwood Home in the West," Davis's verses praised the glorious view, the abundant wildlife, and the deep quiet.[46]

After Asilomar's closure due to financial difficulties during the Great Depression, Davis and her sisters moved to what her college friend Caroline Furness described as "a cunning little Spanish house within easy sight of the Bay of Monterey and the ocean," close enough to Asilomar for the sisters to continue to enjoy the delightful vistas and ocean breezes they had so relished during their time there.[47]

One key to Davis's extraordinary career, then, may be traced to her family of origin. Many women of Davis's generation found that the "family claim" frustrated female ambition. Davis was fortunate instead to experience a "family culture" that fostered female achievement.[48]

The "Female Salt Spoon"

Female friendship, as well as family ties, sustained Davis throughout her life. As she explained in her memoirs, "I have always been friendly with boys and men. I like them, [and] we have been good chums." But while Davis always got along well with men—her insubordinate subordinates at the Bureau of Social Hygiene would be the only notable exception to this rule—her most significant relationships, outside of her own family, were with other women.[49]

Davis formed her most important friendship after leaving the family home in Rochester to return to her childhood home, Dunkirk, to work as a schoolteacher. While there, she met Ella Lapham, a graduate of Vassar College and a resident of nearby Fredonia. Lapham, who shared Davis's enthusiasm for both literary pursuits and outdoor activities, immediately became "Kate's particular chum," as May Bragdon expressed it.[50]

Lapham supported Davis's ambitions, introducing her to women's rights gatherings and encouraging her to attend Vassar College. Nearly inseparable during Davis's ten-year tenure as a schoolteacher, the two women maintained their close relationship until Lapham's premature death in 1917, exchanging frequent visits and letters—although the latter, unfortunately, have not survived. Despite this gap in the historical record, it is clear that Lapham helped Davis pursue higher education and new professional opportunities. It also seems likely that this close relationship contributed to Davis's decision to include same-sex relationships in her pioneering study of women's sexuality.[51]

While Davis never seems to have formed another romantic relationship, she had many female friends. She forged close ties with her classmates at Vassar College, where she found a community of like-minded women who shared her intelligence and ambition. She remained in contact with several of them—including Mary Swain Wagner and Caroline Furness—for the rest of her life. At Vassar, Davis also benefited from her contact with the all-female faculty, forging an especially important relationship with historian Lucy Maynard Salmon, who became both a professional mentor and a personal friend.[52]

After graduating from what was originally called "Vassar Female College"—for the rest of her life, Davis treasured a "little female salt spoon" that "disappeared" from the dining hall—Davis surrounded herself with supportive female friends for the rest of her life. At the University of Chicago, she lived at Foster Hall, a women's residence hall, where she developed lasting friendships with her fellow "Fosterites," who cheered her on through her graduate studies. Several of Davis's fellow graduate students became both lifelong friends and professional collaborators. Jessie Taft and Clara Weidensall both worked closely with Davis at Bedford Reformatory, while Mary Harris, at Davis's urging, assumed the superintendency of the Blackwell's Island women's workhouse during Davis's tenure as New York City's commissioner of correction.[53]

Davis enjoyed close relationships with other women throughout her life. At Bedford Reformatory, where she hired a cohort of highly educated women to assist her in studying and rehabilitating wayward women, she formed lifetime friendships with her colleagues. Even when a devastating earthquake interrupted a much-needed European vacation, she corresponded with what she called "my dear Bedford family"; after moving to New York City to become commissioner of correction, she frequently visited Bedford's "Hilltop" campus. At her retirement party in 1928, former Bedford staffer Agnes Crowley averred, "I shall always treasure my Hilltop memories of Miss Davis' visits on weekends as most interesting and inspiring occasions."[54]

While Davis maintained her relationships with college friends, fellow graduate students, and reformatory colleagues, she found new friends wherever she went. During World War I, she developed an extensive network of fellow reformers who shared her interest in social hygiene; she also had an active social life in New York City. Fellow Riverside Drive resident Blanche Boring Snow first met Davis through her wartime collaboration with her husband, Dr. William F. Snow, combating venereal disease. Snow recalled being "very much in awe" of Davis at their first meeting, when Davis struck her as "a very cold, businesslike, marvellously accomplished lady." But, Snow confessed, after Davis kept her company at the wharf while waiting for Dr. Snow's ship to set sail, "I had to revise my first idea, finding you sympathetic and understanding." Still later, encountering Davis at a birthday party, Snow was astounded to find her leading "a comb orchestra," composing humorous verse, and being "the life of the party." Yet even though Snow described Davis as "full of fun," she also insisted, "you're sentimental, too, Don't deny it." Snow closed her admiring missive, "So you see, I'm still a little bit in awe of you, but this is so tempered by affection that half the time I forget all about it."[55]

Female friendships both sustained and shaped Davis's study of female sexuality. During her tenure at the Bureau of Social Hygiene, Davis developed a close working relationship with her longtime secretary, Ruth Topping, who accompanied Davis to Europe to gather information about social hygiene efforts there. The pair subsequently collaborated on compiling *Factors*; they continued to correspond until Davis's death. Davis also worked closely with Marie Kopp, a researcher who coauthored the book's chapters on same-sex relationships and later conducted studies of contraceptive effectiveness at Margaret Sanger's birth-control clinic.[56]

While Davis conducted research for her sex study, she also formed alliances with rival birth-control advocates Mary Ware Dennett and Margaret Sanger. Davis's early discoveries about women's desire to control their fertility prompted her to develop closer relationships with both Sanger and Dennett, while her study subjects' determination to limit family size—even when that meant defying the law to acquire contraceptives or obtain abortions—spurred her to support their efforts to overturn the Comstock Act and legalize birth control.[57]

Despite a rocky start that pitted the law-and-order commissioner of correction against the fiery activist, Davis and Sanger reconciled in the 1920s, when Davis funneled bureau funds to Sanger's new birth-control clinic (where collaborator Marie Kopp conducted her research). The two former antagonists became firm friends. Throughout the decade, they carried on a cordial correspondence, exchanged holiday cards, and occasionally met for lunch. Davis also joined forces with Sanger and others in efforts to legalize the distribution of contraceptives as a member of the Committee on Maternal Health, which regarded the illegal status of birth control as a dire threat to women's welfare. In 1929, Davis praised Sanger's published collection of desperate women who wrote to her seeking contraceptive information and cheered on her efforts to overturn the Comstock Laws, even as she shared details of her own declining health, which prevented her from seeing Sanger in person.[58]

Davis's relationships with Sanger and Dennett and her sex research were mutually reinforcing. Davis and Dennett likely met in New York's suffragist circles in the 1910s, when both held office in the National American Woman Suffrage Association. During World War I, their shared commitment to pacifism further cemented their relationship. But what really drew the two women together was their shared interest in sex education.[59]

Davis's sex survey revealed women's painful lack of information about the facts of life. These findings in turn fueled her commitment to sex education—what she called "correct and timely instruction in the matter of sex." In 1929, when Dennett faced charges of violating the Comstock Act for circulating her sex education pamphlet, *The Sex Side of Life*, Davis came to her aid. In addition to raising funds for Dennett's defense, Davis corresponded with her lawyer about the case, which culminated in a victory for free speech and birth control as well as for Dennett herself.[60]

"Perfect Little Ladies"

For Davis, political commitments and personal connections were closely intertwined. Her relationships with women not only sustained her throughout her life but also shaped her approach to the study of women's sexuality. While she had many female friends, professional colleagues, and political allies, Davis does not seem to have had a romantic relationship after Ella Lapham's premature death in 1917. She never shared a residence with a romantic partner, instead making her permanent home with her sisters (and occasionally her niece). But she was well acquainted with many women who chose to share their lives with other women. Perhaps the first lesbian Davis ever met, as well as the one who was most open about her romantic relationships, was a fellow Rochester resident, May Bragdon.

Soon after Davis left Rochester to take charge of St. Mary's Settlement House in Philadelphia, her sisters, Helen and Charlotte, joined a group of single, self-supporting women they called the "Perfect Little Ladies." As a group, "the Perfects," as they called themselves, avoided marriage and motherhood in favor of female companionship and fun-filled gatherings. Many also engaged in gender-bending activities (such as cross-dressing) and same-sex relationships (both fleeting romances and long-term partnerships). The group's photographer and chronicler, family friend May Bragdon, not only documented Davis's relationship with Lapham but also dreamed of a similar attachment. After a series of romantic misadventures and a passionate affair that she described as her "Venus time," Bragdon eventually settled into comfortable domesticity in Rochester with Edyth Allen, with whom she lived for at least twenty years.[61]

Despite Davis's disavowal of any romantic entanglements in her memoirs—"you will find no love stories at all in this tale of my life," she warned prospective readers—it seems likely that both her own relationship with Ella Lapham and the same-sex relationships she observed firsthand shaped her candid approach to women's sexuality in her magnum opus. Indeed, one could read Davis's sex study, with its lengthy chapters on women's lesbian relationships, as a belated tribute to her lost love.[62]

"To Do the Next Thing"

Davis's lifelong curiosity—channeled, in adulthood, into the social sciences—may be just as compelling an explanation. In the 1890s, when Davis traveled throughout Europe to study Bohemians—Czech-speaking people from the former Kingdom of Bohemia—she also probably became familiar with the pioneering work of physicians and psychologists in the field that would later become known as sexology.[63]

In the early twentieth century—while "bohemians" of a different sort converged in Greenwich Village and established a radical feminist organization, Heterodoxy, which became a "hotbed" for challenges to conventional social and sexual mores—Davis began to conduct her own studies of women's sexuality. While serving as superintendent of Bedford Reformatory, she completed a statistical survey of sex workers confined there, included as an appendix to a larger study of commercialized sex in New York City. Davis's contribution became an unexpected bestseller, prompting her to request that her study be printed as a pamphlet to meet popular demand.[64]

Davis does not seem to have fostered relationships with New York City's new bohemians during her tenure as commissioner of correction. Indeed, she may have purposely made her first New York City home with her sisters in Midtown Manhattan rather than in Greenwich Village to avoid being associated with the radical elements—anarchists, Wobblies, and free-speech activists—and the sexual outlaws—from free lovers to effeminate "fairies"—who congregated there—and who sometimes ran afoul of the law and ended up in the institutions she oversaw.[65]

However, her wartime work promoting "social hygiene" convinced her that Villagers' open discussions of women's sexuality had merit. During World War I, Davis was appalled to discover the depths of women's ignorance about their own bodies. The international conference of women physicians—including Heterodoxy feminists—that she organized at the war's conclusion reinforced her commitment to gathering reliable information about sex and reproduction. Davis credited Dr. Max J. Exner—affiliated with both the American Social Hygiene Association, which fostered close ties with the Bureau of Social Hygiene, and the YMCA, the male counterpart of the YWCA—with encouraging her to undertake the study. However, her contact with biology professor Clelia Mosher, then wrapping up another pioneering study of women's sexuality (not published until many decades later) and with the outspoken feminists of Heterodoxy—who prided themselves on being women who did unexpected things—also may have inspired Davis to undertake her own sex survey.[66]

Davis's enduring commitment to bettering women's lives also may explain her determination to reassess women's sexuality. After all, she took up this project soon after the conclusion of a successful campaign for women's suffrage. With women's political rights secured, she turned to promoting women's personal satisfaction. Ultimately, since Davis refused to reveal her motivations, we have to be satisfied with measuring the impact of her work.

That impact was important. When Davis shifted her focus from imprisoned prostitutes to "normal" women, she radically reoriented the study of women's sexuality. At the same time, she brought her statistical expertise to bear on the study of human sexuality, thereby anticipating the direction of future sex research. Davis's large-scale study, relying on detailed questionnaires completed by thousands of research subjects, profoundly challenged conventional views of women as lacking sexual passion. Moreover, by including controversial subjects such as contraceptive use, same-sex relationships, and auto-erotic practices in a study of "average" women, Davis redefined "normal" women's sexuality.

Davis's pioneering study garnered less attention than it deserved. Deeply uncomfortable with her findings—which validated women's sexuality on its own terms, apart from marriage and motherhood—her male coworkers and competitors forced her into retirement and did their best to suppress her study. They only partly succeeded, persuading Rockefeller to dismiss her from her post but not to withdraw his support for her research. However, Davis's detractors did ensure that Davis would not get the recognition she deserved. Although the Bureau of Social Hygiene funded Davis's study, the media-shy agency also limited publicity for it. In addition, the bureau probably played a role in the mysterious disappearance of the completed questionnaires, preventing future researchers from using Davis's data.

Davis's massive study proffered a fundamental reassessment of women's sexuality and laid the groundwork for the work of her successors. However, her revelations about women's sex lives attracted far less attention than that of later sex researchers who followed in her footsteps, such as Dr. Alfred Kinsey and his all-male research team in the 1940s and 1950s and the husband-and-wife team of Richard Masters and Virginia Johnson in the 1960s and 1970s. Whereas these researchers gained wide acclaim and popular recognition both at the time of their publications and in subsequent treatments in film (*Kinsey*) and on television (*Masters of Sex*), Davis and her research have attracted limited attention. Indeed, Davis's obituaries often failed to mention her sex study. Even those that did devoted far more attention to her work as the first superintendent of New York's female reformatory, her disaster relief work in Italy, her tenure as New York City's first female commissioner of correction, or her role in promoting "social hygiene" and sex education during World War I.[67]

Both the virtual disappearance of Davis's sex study and her failure to find a publisher for her life story probably contributed to her relative obscurity for decades following her death in 1935. But obscure does not mean unimportant. In the decades following the publication of *Factors*, experts in a variety of fields, ranging from sociology to sexology, cited Davis's pathbreaking study. As the field of women's history developed in the late twentieth century, researchers repeatedly returned to Davis's research for reliable information about women's sex lives in the past, especially regarding contraceptive use and same-sex relationships. In the early twenty-first century, scholars of the history of sexuality turned to *Factors* to understand not only American women's self-reported sexual behavior but also evolving understandings of sexual desire.[68]

Davis herself also has received some attention in the past few decades. Although nobody has undertaken a full-scale biography, several scholars have written about both her record as a prison reformer and her career as a sex researcher.[69] Recently, Australia-based social media sensation Esme Louise James, who hosts a TikTok series on the history of sex, featured Davis in her provocative exploration of human intimacy, *Kinky History*. In addition, US scholar Rebecca Davis included a brief discussion of Davis in her sweeping study of sexuality in America, *Fierce Desires*.[70]

Still, for the most part, in both scholarly and popular books, Davis has been relegated to the footnotes rather than being the focus. Indeed, there is a bit of a "Where's Waldo?" quality to her frequent, but fleeting, appearances in print. In a recent Google search, "Katharine Bement Davis" appears in nearly five thousand books—most of them devoted to women's history or human sexuality—but most of these appearances are footnotes, with only a few more extended discussions of Davis's record as a progressive reformer and sex researcher. This book shifts the focus to "a busy woman" whose many "firsts" included being the first sex researcher who was committed to understanding women's sexuality on its own terms.

Davis's research remains relevant today as Americans continue to engage in debates about both sexual diversity and reproductive rights. Nearly a century after the publication of her pioneering study of women's sexuality, it is finally time for Davis to receive the attention she—and her work—deserve.

Davis's impressive career encompassed multiple professional identities, from schoolteacher to social worker, from suffragist to sexologist. Her professional trajectory, from policing women's sexuality to promoting women's sexual equality, still surprises audiences today. Even when invited to reflect on the twists and turns of her long and eventful life, the always-pragmatic Davis offered few explanations. She told reporter Rhoda E. McCulloch that "to be willing and ready to do the next thing, and after that the next thing, was a far better use of time and energy than to dream about distant mountain peaks of great deeds of the future"—or, apparently, than to reflect on her own remarkable transformations.[71]

The *Woman's Journal* described her as "a woman of action," not reflection, after Davis, in a conversation with journalist Mabel Eichel, characterized her career trajectory as "but a logical sequence of events":

> "If," she says, with a twinkle in her blue eyes, "you are searching for some altruistic motivating impulse in my life, as a reason for my entrance into sociological fields, you will not find it. It's been largely a process of evolution. I like to create, and most of the things I have done have called for creative instinct. I'm probably a good deal of an experimentalist also. I always like to try a thing once. Even when I was very small I got myself spanked for doing things I had been warned not to do, because I wanted the experience of doing them."[72]

And yet, Davis's contemporaries called attention to one constant in her varied career: her commitment to women. The *New York Age*, an African American newspaper, ran a story shortly after Davis's retirement in 1928 under the headline "Woman's Work for Women," noting that "her labors in this work for the relief and rehabilitation of womanhood have known no limits of race or color." Rather, her "lifework for the redemption of womanhood" had no boundaries.[73]

This long-overdue biography of "a busy woman" explores how Katharine Bement Davis translated her lifelong commitment to women's welfare into a powerful and provocative investigation of "matters of sex" during America's first sexual revolution.

1

"To Work for an Ideal as Well as for a Living"

When Katharine Bement Davis joined the ranks of "New Women," the first generation of American women to pursue higher education and professional careers, by gaining admission to Vassar College in 1890, some of her classmates regarded the newcomer with skepticism. As one classmate recalled, "When 'K. B. Davis' joined the class of '92 in our junior year, none of us suspected her of being a genius. Her appearance was unimpressive and she stated with unassuming frankness that she was thirty years old and 'had taught' to earn money for a college education."[1]

Yet Davis quickly gained acceptance as part of "a galaxy of brilliant young women," as another classmate put it—appropriately for a student who both lived and worked in the campus observatory.[2] By the time she graduated with honors just two years later, Davis had become a popular member of the college community and had taken full advantage of the many opportunities offered at one of the nation's first women's colleges. Along the way, she gained a reputation for "keen intelligence, a capacity for swift action, and an unswerving and indomitable energy."[3]

During her time at Vassar, Davis excelled in her coursework, gaining admission to the honor society and earning the respect of both her classmates and her professors. She also enjoyed a rich social life that introduced her to such campus traditions as cross-dressing dramatic performances and same-sex romances, known as "smashes." Most importantly, Davis's college career paved the way for her professional future. As a college student, Davis studied science, specializing in nutrition. As she later explained, there were two essentials to human survival: food and sex. She spent the first half of her professional career studying the first; she would spend the second half studying the second.[4]

Young "Kitty" Davis approached the world with wide-eyed curiosity. An anecdote about her childhood reveals that even as a girl, she was determined to understand the world around her. On one occasion, when a family friend took her for a ride in his carriage, "she inquired the name and use of every part of the carriage." As this account concluded, "This habit of going to the very bottom of things was to be of great use to a woman who was to have hard problems to settle in her public life." Courtesy Frances Garber Pepper.

A Circuitous Road for a Curious Child

Katharine Bement Davis's road to Vassar College was a circuitous one. Even as a young child, "Kitty" Davis was intensely curious about the world around her. Early photos depict her as wide-eyed and solemn-faced. While her sober expression was somewhat misleading—she also was playful, humorous, and occasionally rebellious—her unblinking gaze in family photos accurately captured her intense interest in the world around her. On one occasion, when a family friend took her for a ride in his carriage, "she inquired the name and use of every part of the carriage. By the time they reached home, her companion felt as if he had been put through a severe examination; but Katharine knew all about the carriage." As this account concluded, "This habit of going to the very bottom of things was to be of great use to a woman who was to have hard problems to settle in her public life."[5] Indeed, throughout Davis's long and eventful life—including her dogged pursuit of higher education, her ten years as a schoolteacher, her time as an inner-city social worker, her innovations as a corrections officer, her work on behalf of woman suffrage, and her pathbreaking research on female sexuality—the "habit of going to the very bottom of things" would prove to be essential to her success.

Strong family ties and supportive familial relationships provided Kitty Davis with a firm foundation for her future career. The oldest of five children, Kitty grew up in a loving family with limited financial resources. Kitty's parents, Frances Bement and Oscar Davis, met and married shortly before the Civil War. They welcomed their firstborn into the world on January 15, 1860, at the home they shared with Frances's widowed mother, Rhoda Denison Bement, in Buffalo, New York. Kitty's grandmother had braved excommunication from the Presbyterian church in Seneca Falls, New York, for her outspoken antislavery opinions. She subsequently served as a "conductor" on the Underground Railroad and helped organize the nation's first official women's rights convention. Her example as "a woman who had always had a hand in any new movement to make the world better" would be a lifelong inspiration for Davis.[6]

In later years, Davis attributed both her high ideals and her "fighting spirit" to her grandmother's influence: "She was the kind of person who was quite ready if occasion arose to fight, bleed and die in a cause in which she believed; and, if she believed in a cause, she believed in it hard. It is to her unconscious influence that I am sure I owe many of the beliefs which have stayed by me but which she never definitely taught me."[7]

While Grandmother Bement's influence was a constant, Kitty's childhood was somewhat unsettled. "My father was never a man with a large salary," she reflected in her memoirs. Oscar Davis's quest for secure, well-paid employment led to several moves. In 1860, when Kitty was born in Buffalo, his occupation was listed as "Flour & Feed." When Kitty was three years old, however, the Davises moved to Dunkirk, fifty miles southeast of Buffalo, on the shores of Lake Erie.[8] In Dunkirk, Oscar sought to support the growing family as an employee of the Lake Shore and Southern Michigan Railroad. The rapidly expanding railroad system had begun to rival the Erie Canal as the primary source of transportation in the Empire

State. Initially, the railroads flourished, and so did the Davis family fortunes. By 1870, after a decade of renting, the family—which had expanded to include Charlotte (born in 1861), Hamilton (born in 1864), Helen (born in 1871), and Frank (born in 1875)—had purchased a home of their own. But in 1877, the Great Railroad Strike derailed Oscar's career.[9]

In dire economic straits, the Davises sold their home and moved one hundred miles away to Rochester, New York, on the shores of Lake Ontario. There, Oscar took advantage of the city's centrality to commerce to make a new start, first as a mercantile agent and then as an insurance agent. Finances remained tight, however. The Davis family moved frequently in an attempt to find rented quarters that were both commodious enough to accommodate a large family and affordable enough to match their limited resources. While Oscar struggled to increase his income, Frances pinched pennies. As Davis proudly recalled in her memoirs, her mother found creative ways to meet the family's needs by raising a flock of chickens and gathering fruit from the orchard—even when this caused a kerfuffle with the landlord, a Briton known locally as "Lord Oliphant." When Lawrence Oliphant "sent word" that he intended to take the ripening fruit for himself, Frances Davis wrote "a pretty saucy letter" pointing out that there was no such stipulation in the lease. "Mother was not afraid even of a lord!" Davis exclaimed. "She reminded him that we were not living in England and that our place was not a part of an English estate and stated that she proposed to use the fruit for family purposes." And, Davis proudly concluded, "She did!"[10]

While Davis praised her parents' dedication and determination, the family's peripatetic lifestyle and insecure finances no doubt contributed to her early awareness that she would need to support herself, rather than depending on either her father or a husband. At the same time, however, Davis was determined to make a difference. As she later put it, her lifelong aspiration was "to work for an ideal as well as for a living."[11]

"We Had Very Good Times"

Despite frequent moves and financial difficulties, the Davis home was a happy one. Oscar and Frances granted their children—boys and girls alike—considerable freedom. "Our childhood home was always a center for neighborhood good times," recalled Davis, adding, "Mother allowed us to do almost anything outside of breaking our necks; and so we had very good times."[12]

Indeed, Frances and Oscar Davis did not merely indulgently look on as their high-spirited children engaged in high jinks; they joined in the fun themselves. Family friend and frequent visitor May Bragdon often commented on the gaiety of spontaneous gatherings at the Davis home, in which family members—"all as entertaining as ever"—related humorous anecdotes, told wry jokes, sang sentimental songs, posed amusing riddles, and composed humorous verse.[13]

While the Davises were permissive by the standards of the Victorian era, they did discipline their children. If progressive in their parenting, Kitty's parents were—fortunately, according to Davis—ignorant of "psychology and psychiatry and behaviorism" and thus unaware of "the terrific dangers that lie in bringing up children." Ironically, given that Davis would devote much of her adult life to the behavioral sciences, when reflecting on her childhood, she later mused, "Life was much more simple" before adults became concerned about "the terrible inferiority complex that might develop if a child were spanked." Rather, in her childhood, "it was the way of the world for children to be spanked if they were naughty," explained Davis. "All of my playmates were spanked on occasion, and we took it as a matter of course and, so far as I can remember, didn't hold it against our parents. I know I didn't, for I always knew in the back of my head that I deserved it."[14]

If curiosity killed the cat, as the old adage goes, for Kitty, it sometimes led to corporal punishment. "I very well remember the last spanking I received," Davis recalled. One Saturday—baking day—eight-year-old Kitty went into the kitchen, where she spied "a row of fresh loaves of bread, a batch of cookies, a nice cake, and, most beautiful of all, four shiny rich brown pumpkin pies. I can see them now, without even shutting my eyes!" Fired by a desire to know what would happen, she seized a knife and "proceeded to decorate the top of a pie by cutting gashes in a pattern which greatly improved its appearance." Her "horrified" mother, entering the room, chastised her for doing "such a dreadful thing!" The incident might have ended there, except that Frances, misjudging her daughter's determination, "proceeded to add somewhat rashly, 'If you ever do such a thing again, I shall shut you up in a closet until your father comes home and then will have him spank you!'" The moment her mother left the room, strong-willed Kitty "picked up a knife, and cut another!" Her mother followed through on her promise, and her father did spank her. "It didn't hurt so much, so far as I can remember, but it must have been effective," she mused in her memoirs, "for it was the last time my father ever used that method of punishment." But rather than quenching Kitty's curiosity or leading to lasting psychological problems, the incident became an amusing anecdote in her memoirs—one she used to criticize the trend toward psychoanalysis in the 1930s. "Furthermore," she concluded, "I do not recall any feeling of inferiority on my part. I knew, well enough, I deserved it!"[15]

As a girl, Kitty soothed her hurt feelings (and sore hindquarters) with the thought that she was following the example of her grandmother, who "inherited the fighting spirit of her ancestors." As an adult, Davis would continue to challenge authority to satisfy her insatiable curiosity—sometimes at great cost, as when she lost her job at the Bureau of Social Hygiene for conducting a then-shocking study of sex.[16]

Davis learned leadership early. The Davis family home was a lively, even rambunctious household, with five exuberant children eagerly engaged in a variety of activities, both indoors and outdoors. As the oldest, Kitty took the lead in the children's play, ranging from building forts from kindling to writing and directing "potboiler" plays based on her "surreptitious" reading of sensational novels and adventure stories.[17]

A voracious reader, Kitty was often "deeply absorbed in a book." While she read classics, such as works by Charles Dickens, she also enjoyed adventure tales, such as Sir Walter Scott's *Talisman* (which briefly inspired her to daydream about becoming a foreign missionary, before she realized the difficulty of learning Arabic). Her reading of works by women writers—including the prolific American author Mary Jane Holmes, who wrote moral fiction; British author Charlotte Mary Yonge, who wrote heroic medieval tales; and unnamed authors of sentimental and sensational fiction—inspired her to try her hand at both writing her own stories and producing them as plays on the nearest stage: her family's parlor.[18]

One of her earliest efforts highlighted both Kitty's unquenchable enthusiasm and her gender-bending tendencies. "Grace Clifton: Or the Lost Lover of Diamond Lake" traced the tale of "the lover who goes to sea and disappears and his friend cuts him out in his best girl's affections." The play was full of action as well as romance. Kitty played "Eugene, the villain of the piece," while her younger sister Charlotte played "Arthur Merton, the lover." At the play's climax, the sisters acted out a duel with toy pistols. "My paper-caps refused to explode at the critical moment," Davis recalled, but undeterred, "in a stage aside I said, 'Die,—anyway'!—and Charlotte dropped to the ground."[19]

Although her mother sometimes disapproved of Kitty's choice of reading material—behind her mother's back, Kitty borrowed dime novels from the family's maid, then read them behind closed doors in the kitchen—the entire family participated in the plays, supporting Kitty's creativity and fostering her leadership. Grandmother Bement donated her shawl to decorate the set, and Kitty's younger siblings played supporting roles in the original melodramas in which Kitty herself always played a starring role. On holidays, the Davises opened their home to the neighbors, who paid a small entry fee, donated to charity, for the privilege of attendance. Decades later, Davis would call upon the winning combination of good works and amateur theater when she served as the first superintendent of the state's female reformatory in Bedford Hills.[20]

"My Life Work"

Kitty enjoyed music as well as theater. Even though her family was "not a musical one," and her father was "never a man with a large salary," as she later recalled, she convinced him to pay for piano lessons with the organist at the family's Presbyterian church, Harriet Heyl. Since Davis's hands were "too small" for her to master "rapid octave passages" and her family was "not well off," this might have been a short-lived experiment. But then the music teacher, less than two years her student's senior, invited Kitty to attend the opera with her in the big city of Buffalo, only fifty miles distant, but seemingly a world away, from the rural village of Dunkirk.[21]

It was a pivotal moment in young Kitty's life. In addition to granting her the chance "to hear a really truly grand opera"—"Lucia Di Lammermoor," with prima donna Claire Louise Kellogg—the invitation meant that Kitty would spend the night at the home Harriet shared with her parents and brother near the Dunkirk train station, since the pair would return to town very late at night. The visit initiated a closer relationship with Harriet—the first of many female friendships that would sustain

Davis throughout her life. Davis, who cautiously avoided calling attention to her same-sex relationships in her memoirs, nonetheless offered clues to the importance of this association with the statement, "Her friendship was quite influential in my life." Given that many likely lesbians of the era recalled important early relationships with older women—often teachers or mentors—Davis's friendship with Heyl may have been even more influential than she acknowledged.[22]

Kitty's relationship with Harriet also launched the younger girl's lifelong study of languages, since Harriet's parents were German immigrants and German was the only language spoken in the Heyl home, where Davis spent "a great deal" of time, especially enjoying Sunday evenings gathering around the piano in the parlor and singing "German folk-songs."[23]

Most of all, at the time, Kitty's Buffalo adventure and Dunkirk sleepover was a thoroughly enjoyable experience, reminiscent of a scene in the turn-of-the-century novel *Anne of Green Gables* in which the orphaned Anne Shirley feels tremendously honored at the invitation to sleep in a real "spare room." In language that will sound familiar to readers of that roman á clef, Davis later pronounced, "The thrill was something that I shall never forget."[24]

Kitty's early exposure to classical music and her admiration for her music teacher shaped the rest of her life. With Harriet Heyl's enthusiastic encouragement—and her father's financial support—she threw herself into the study of music "heart and soul," learning the pipe organ well enough "to play all the music for a Sunday morning service, including the Prelude and the Recessional" at Dunkirk Presbyterian Church.[25]

"Alas!" Davis later declared, she did not have the keyboard skills or the vocal range necessary to become either an "accomplished pianist" or "an opera singer." Nonetheless, when Dunkirk hosted a six-week summer music institute, Kitty seized the opportunity to study "base [*sic*] and harmony, the history of music, musical forms, etc."[26]

Fourteen-year-old Kitty was in her element at the institute. Even though she was the youngest participant, she excelled, especially in composition. Her talents were unmistakable, and the teenager was justly proud of her achievements: "With what thrills of pride did I see a hymn I had composed written on the blackboard for the whole Institute to sing," she gushed. With her music teacher's enthusiastic encouragement and her father's generous financial support, Kitty attended the institute—now held in nearby Fredonia—for two more years, even though this meant the additional cost of boarding. "At last, I thought, I had found my life work," she mused. "I would become a great composer. I knew I couldn't earn a living at it,—certainly not at first,—school teaching would have to do that for me. . . . But I'd do it in my leisure hours until I had won a name for myself."[27]

Davis's ambition, coupled with her awareness that she would need to support herself, was evident in these youthful dreams. So, too, was her admiration not only for Harriet Heyl but also for her mother's sisters: single, self-supporting schoolteachers who served as important role models for the aspiring career woman. Most importantly, however, Kitty's friendship with her music teacher not only fired her ambition for a professional career but also provided her with a pathway to success.[28]

When, in 1877, Harriet announced her intention to attend Cornell University, a coeducational institution that had opened in 1868, Kitty immediately exclaimed, "I would go, too!" When financial reversals forced her family to move to Rochester the year after her third summer music institute, she concluded that "music was a lost cause, so far as a career was concerned. But the desire for a college education did not pass, and that was one thing in which I was finally successful." Music remained "an opportunity for self-expression" throughout Davis's life, as well as "a source of recreation for my staff and a means not only of recreation but of development for young women under my charge" when she became superintendent of Bedford Reformatory. But education became the defining force in her entire life.[29]

"Higher Learning"

An inquisitive child, a voracious reader, and a keen observer, Kitty had always done well in her studies. When she was still a toddler, learning her ABCs at home under her mother's tutelage, she and her parents passed by Dunkirk's "intermediate" school on a neighborhood walk. As Davis recalled, "There was a picket fence around the school yard, in which the pupils were enjoying the recess. Attracted by the noise of the games, I went up to the fence, grasped a picket in each hand and put my nose between the pickets as far through as it would go. So entranced was

I at what I saw that it was with difficulty I was pried away and persuaded to go on. Mother used to say laughingly that I showed thus early in life my attraction to the higher learning!"[30]

While Kitty was a good student, she was no goody-two-shoes. Once she attended the schoolhouse she had regarded with so much awe, she stood out more as the class clown than as the class brain. She frequently ran afoul of her beleaguered teacher, who found young Kitty's behavior—which included vaulting over the long recitation desks rather than making her way sedately down the aisle—extremely trying. Corporal punishment did nothing to curb Kitty's antics. Rather, the pleasure she took in unladylike behavior and making others laugh far outweighed her concern about her conduct report. As she recalled, at the conclusion of each school day, the teacher took a roll call for students' conduct. Perfect conduct entitled pupils to call out, "Ten!" Although Kitty's decorous seatmate, Addie, always earned a perfect ten, she never did.[31]

Unquenchable Kitty took pride in her rebel status. She recalled overhearing some classmates discussing the conduct reporting system: "Said one, 'I wouldn't be as good as Addie H. for anything, but I'd just as soon be as good as Kit Davis.'" In her memoirs, Davis demonstrated no regrets for lost points or physical punishment. Instead, she whimsically noted that her own youthful misbehavior was excellent preparation for a career as an educator. "Many years later, when I became a school teacher, I remember I felt rather glad that I had not been such a dreadfully good child in school," she reflected. "It seemed to me that I could understand and sympathize better with my pupils than if I had been 'as good as Addie H.'"[32]

Despite occasional misbehavior, Kitty did well in school, especially excelling in mathematics, although she always struggled with spelling. After the family's 1877 move to Rochester prompted her to give up her dreams of becoming a professional musician and she redirected her ambitions toward attending college, the seventeen-year-old became more serious about her studies. Now known as "Kate," she was the first—and, for a while, the only—girl in the "classical" course at Rochester's Free Academy, which required students to study Greek. However, Kate was as charismatic as ever, and she soon recruited another girl into the classical course. As classmate Carrie A. Page later recalled, "When I discovered that she was taking Greek, I immediately acquired a taste for Greek." The girls took to their studies with gusto, determined not to be outdone by the boys in their class. They were successful; many years later, one of their most famous classmates, the theologian Walter Rauschenbusch, remarked that they "set the pace for the boys."[33]

While Kate took her studies more seriously in high school than she had in her younger years, she remained a bit of a class clown. After the class completed their first Greek book, they decided to hold a funeral for it. Drawing on her musical training, Kate composed appropriate music for the occasion, much to her classmates' delight. "I do not think I ever heard a more dirgelike air," Carrie reminisced.[34]

Book funerals notwithstanding, Kate and Carrie made the study of ancient languages fun. They "became ambitious to talk Greek," located a book on Greek conversation, and practiced phrases—sometimes during class. One day, frustrated with their disruptive chatter, the instructor ordered them to "keep still or go out." Inspired rather than quelled by this directive, after school, the girls purchased a large sheet of paper, paint, and a paintbrush and set to work. The next day, arriving before anybody else, they displayed their artwork at the front of the classroom. When their teacher and fellow students arrived, "they greeted, amid shouts of laughter," a Latin motto, in bold capital letters, that translated as: "KEEP STILL, OR GO OUT."[35]

"A Name for Myself"

While teenaged Kate was clearly a hit with her classmates—male and female—her universal popularity did nothing to incline her toward marriage. Without explaining her logic, Davis evidently never considered marrying. Even in her earliest memories, when she dreamed of making "a name for myself" as a missionary or a musician, she anticipated supporting herself rather than depending on a husband's income, and she declared her intention of defining her own destiny rather than fusing her identity with a man's.[36]

Many years later, during a "social hygiene" lecture delivered during World War I, Davis whimsically reflected on her many friendships—but never flirtations—with men: "The friendly companionship between young men and women Dr. Davis commended as one of the charms of life, but she asked the girls to let their mothers know all about their friends. 'And don't carry flirting to familiarity. Some girls,' she added indulgently, 'can't help flirting; it's just the look out of the eye. As for me,' she said, humorously, 'I sometimes envy the flirt, for I should be about as awkward at it as an elephant!'"[37]

Despite her avowed awkwardness at mating rituals and her assertion that "I was never the sort with whom men were always falling in love," Kate received at least two marriage proposals during her time in western New York. However, she turned both men down, noting that she had no desire to become a farmer's wife, although she was sorry to miss the chance to become a mother. "I have always loved babies," she commented in her memoirs, adding that as a girl, she had planned to have six children: three girls and three boys.[38]

Again, many years later, Davis humorously reflected on her life choices. When serving as New York City's commissioner of correction, she jested that she would like to hire a husband to accompany her to the social occasions to which male public officials brought their wives, who ably assisted them in their work. But while she thought a husband would be a fine companion for vacations and a useful accessory for her career, she remarked, she had no interest in a permanent relationship. "Would it be possible to engage one for the coming four years?" she joked.[39]

While she never regretted her choice to avoid marriage, Davis did express sorrow at missing her chance at biological motherhood. But, like many of her contemporaries, she practiced social motherhood instead. Throughout her life, Davis would "borrow" other people's children, starting with the son of her Presbyterian pastor, "a beautiful baby" whom she took for regular outings "in his baby-carriage." Davis maintained her fondness for children for the rest of her days. While working at Bedford Reformatory, she would take a special interest in her charges' children; with her sisters, she would share responsibility for rearing her niece, Frances, who lost her own mother when she was very young.[40]

Late in life, half humorously, half defensively, Davis defended her life choices in response to an alumnae survey conducted prior to her thirty-year college reunion: "First, I am still an old maid; therefore, I cannot write interesting things about my husband and children, [and] how I have treated him and how I have raised them. First and last, however, I have had a good deal to do in the way of looking after other people's husbands and children."[41]

"The Struggle of Life"

By the time she reflected on her choices to avoid marriage, remain childless, and dedicate her career to "other people's husbands and children," decades had passed since Davis rejected marriage proposals in favor of higher education. But it was no easy road. When she graduated from Rochester's Free Academy in 1879, Kate delivered a commencement address, "More Light," that compared the universe to "a huge potato bin" and described people as "potatoes stored therein." Kate used this humble analogy as inspiration, asserting that "those who sought the light always came out ahead in the struggle of life."[42]

Kate's potato analogy was prescient, for she would spend nearly a decade struggling toward the light of higher education. It took more than good grades and fierce determination to attend college; it took money, too. Tuition, room and board, textbooks, and school supplies all added up, and the Davis family was unable to foot the bill. Disappointed but undaunted, Kate did what many intelligent and ambitious women did at a time when few professional opportunities were available to them: she taught school.[43]

Initially, "Miss Kate B. Davis" taught all ages and all topics as a country schoolmistress in a one-room schoolhouse. Like many schoolteachers then and now, she sought creative solutions to budget shortfalls. "Miss Davis" used her experience in drama and music to fill the gap, putting on theatrical productions to raise funds to purchase school supplies. Thanks to her civic-minded parents' connections in their former community, however, ambitious Kate soon acquired a post teaching high school science in her home town, Dunkirk. She advanced quickly, partly because of her willingness to take on challenges. When a need arose for a college-prep trigonometry course, she volunteered to teach it, although she had never studied the subject. With just three days' head start, she managed to usher her students through college entrance examinations the following spring.[44]

Although Kate demonstrated her seriousness of purpose at Dunkirk Academy, she also displayed her trademark insouciance. The schoolgirl who had horrified her teacher—and entertained her classmates—with her unladylike antics now became a schoolmistress who scandalized parents—and delighted pupils—by adopting split skirts and riding a bicycle, the quintessential symbol of women's liberation in Victorian America.[45]

"Kate's Particular Chum"

While living and working in Dunkirk, New York, Davis met Ella Lapham, a resident of nearby Fredonia. Ella was destined to become "Kate's particular chum," as a family friend expressed it.[46] Kate, who so enjoyed theater, met Ella through the subscription Shakespeare courses the Vassar alumna taught to support her aging parents. Despite a ten-year age difference, the two soon became fast friends, spending most of their free time together. They also joined a variety of clubs, including a mixed-gender outdoor club, which sponsored hiking and boating excursions, as well as numerous single-sex clubs dedicated to self-improvement and social reform.[47]

Kate's participation in the burgeoning women's club movement gave her the opportunity to continue her studies. She taught a wide array of subjects at Dunkirk Academy, including botany, geology, biology, chemistry, and astronomy, as well as trigonometry. But she also studied literature and history as a member of the Fredonia Shakespeare Club and the Dunkirk Literary Society. Structured study in the club setting, which dedicated each year to a different topic and required members to deliver research reports, allowed noncollegiate women in nineteenth-century America to pursue what later generations would call continuing education. Kate studied and lectured on an impressive range of topics, including scientific education in England, religious conflict in Ireland, Elizabethan literature, and United States history. Kate's club curriculum kept her in the habit of serious study, which was extremely important for an aspiring college student.[48]

Women's clubs also offered an entrée to social reform. By the time Kate met her in 1885, Ella Lapham was an established force in the Association for the Advancement of Women, an early women's rights organization. Lapham, who had graduated from Vassar College in 1876, may have joined the organization at the behest of the college's celebrated astronomy professor, Maria Mitchell. However, she soon became a leader in her own right, not only advocating women's higher education but also speaking on women's need for greater professional opportunities and equal political rights.[49]

Ella's commitment to women's equality surely strengthened her bond with the intelligent and ambitious Kate, who also became a leader in local women's rights organizations. After causing an uproar in the Dunkirk school district by threatening to resign if her supervisors refused to increase her salary (they did), Kate became a founding member of the Dunkirk chapter of the Women's Educational and Industrial Union. As an officer of the organization, she promoted "the educational, industrial, and social advancement" of women at local, state, and national meetings. In 1890, she attended a meeting of the General Federation of Women's Clubs, an umbrella organization for clubwomen whose aims, as the featured speaker put it, amounted to nothing less than "the complete emancipation of American women."[50]

For Kate Davis, "complete emancipation" demanded higher education. Although Davis had intended to follow in Harriet Heyl's footsteps by attending coeducational Cornell University, Ella Lapham encouraged her to pursue admission to her own single-sex alma mater instead. Ella also helped Kate study for Vassar College's entrance exams, even inviting her to live with her in Fredonia while she did so to avoid the distractions of a small-town schoolteacher's busy social life. Accordingly, Dunkirk Academy's "Miss Davis" spent a year residing with Ella and her parents in Fredonia. In 1890, after a year devoting her Saturdays to working in the chemistry laboratory of the Fredonia State Normal School and her evenings to studying French, Kate tested into the junior class and enrolled at Vassar College as a "Special," or nontraditional, student, shortly before her thirtieth birthday. After postponing her college dream for more than a decade, Kate approached Vassar College with "zeal," according to her closest friend.[51]

"The Development of the Whole Woman"

For young women in Victorian America, Vassar College offered unprecedented opportunities. Founded in 1861, it was one of the first women's colleges worthy of the name. Davis praised Vassar as a "pioneer institution, which offered to women, the most advanced opportunities of its time for higher education." Like the other "Seven Sisters" colleges, Vassar created space for women to foster their intellects, nurture their talents, forge lasting relationships, and explore career opportunities. As Davis emphasized, the college was dedicated to "the development of the whole woman, mind, body, and spirit."[52]

When Kate arrived at Vassar College, located on the outskirts of Poughkeepsie on the banks of the Hudson River more than three hundred miles from her birthplace, she found herself in what many of her contemporaries described as a perfect paradise. One Vassarian waxed ecstatic in her first letters home, exclaiming,

> This is the loveliest place I ever saw in my life. I never imagined it could be so beautiful. The college grounds are nearly a square mile in extent and full of the prettiest places and scenery that one could think of. . . . There are lots of big evergreen trees of all kinds, and cedar hedges, and in the spring there are oceans of daisies. . . . The college is a five story brick building, perfectly immense and all covered with woodbine which has nearly all turned scarlet and yellow and which makes the building look very lovely. Then there are several other quite large buildings, the Laboratory, Music Hall and Observatory. There is the most beautiful little lake of almost still water, surrounded by these gorgeous colored trees.[53]

The brick building this student described was Main Hall, where Kate, like most Vassar students, lived during her first year. Many first-year students filled their personal journals and family correspondence with detailed descriptions of their dorm rooms and in-depth discussions of their roommates. Kate left no such record, perhaps because she was burdened by academic "conditions" and took weekly placement examinations "every Saturday morning as regularly as I ate my breakfast," as she later recalled. Within a year, however, she was able to take her place alongside her classmates as a full-fledged senior and a member of the honor society, Phi Beta Kappa.[54]

When Davis graduated from Vassar College in 1892, she joined the ranks of "new women," the first generation of American women to pursue higher education and professional careers. Davis's time at Vassar provided her with scientific training and familiarized her with same-sex relationships, setting the stage for her pathbreaking study of women's sexuality. Archives and Special Collections, Vassar College Library (Photo File 11.33).

"Higher Things"

In her first year at Vassar, Kate studied astronomy with Mary Whitney, who had succeeded the college's celebrated feminist activist and astronomy professor, Maria Mitchell. "Maria Mitchell had for years been one of my great women," Davis reflected. "To work in her observatory was in itself an experience."[55]

During her second year, therefore, Kate was delighted to accept a work-study position in the college's astronomical observatory. The observatory position was a plum post. Although there was neither heat nor plumbing, and only a coal stove for warmth, the semicircular room, fitted like a ship's cabin, boasted several windows, offering views of the new gymnasium. Behind a pillar supporting the telescope, a "gangway"—a cross between a ladder and a stairway—led to the upper level, where Mary Whitney lived.[56]

Vassar student Caroline Furness, who lived and worked at the observatory the year before Kate did, penned a detailed description of the living quarters there, accompanied by a sketch indicating the placement of each item of furniture and decor. "We feel very happy in our room," she confided to her sister. "It is especially pleasant in the evening when the gas is lit [and] the lamp sends such a pleasant glow over the room—the ceilings are rather low, and that adds to the coziness of the room."[57]

The most attractive feature of life in the observatory, however, was the ready access it offered to intimate association with a beloved member of Vassar's faculty. At Vassar, as at other women's colleges, college students regarded female faculty as role models as well as intellectual guides. Furness, who idolized Mary Whitney, cherished every moment she spent with her. As she put it, "It is so pleasant to live with people who care for all the higher things, are interested in all that goes on in the world, and read every thing that is worth reading."[58]

Kate and her roommate, Mary Swain Wagner, also enjoyed exploring "higher things" in the upper reaches of the observatory. "An astronomer's life may be a happy one but it certainly is not always comfortable, especially in the winter time when a brass telescope may freeze one's eye-lids," remarked Wagner. "But for the hours of exposure to the cold there was always a great compensation in store for the amateur observers—a whole hour perhaps in Professor Whitney's own room with hot chocolate and wafers for material comfort, and Browning or Lowell for a mental feast—and then down the 'gang-way' to bed." Davis cherished her time in the observatory. In her memoirs, she wrote, "I look back to this year as a most happy one."[59]

Associating closely with faculty members and discussing great ideas left an indelible mark, inspiring college students to follow in the footsteps of their faculty mentors. "Undoubtedly Katharine Davis absorbed somewhat the spirit of the place—simple living and high thinking," Wagner concluded. Indeed, Davis, who would dedicate her entire life to intellectual pursuits, paid special attention to this experience in her memoirs. "I've always been thankful for this year in the Observatory and the friendship with Miss Whitney to which it gave rise," she remarked.[60]

"A Constant Finding of Congenial Spirits"

Kate clearly relished her time at Vassar College, eventually becoming a loyal alumna—and a college trustee—who maintained a meaningful connection with her alma mater for the rest of her life. After a decade of teaching, despite her "advanced years," Kate quickly established herself as a star student—appropriately for one who both lived and worked in the campus's observatory.[61]

It was no easy task for a "Special" student to become a star student at one of the Seven Sisters. Vassar's demanding curriculum included modern and classical languages, science and mathematics, philosophy and history, and literature and rhetoric, as well as health and hygiene. To graduate in just two years, the former schoolteacher took a heavy course load in addition to fulfilling her duties in the observatory. Her college roommate joked that she was known as a "cloudy-night friend" since she could be enticed away from her instruments only on nights when she could not see the stars. However, she also insisted that Kate was not a "dig," or a student who was so serious about academic pursuits that she had no interest in recreational activities. Rather, like her classmates, Kate also enjoyed extracurricular activities and informal socializing. As one of her contemporaries expressed it, "There is lots of fun mixed in with the work here, I tell you."[62]

As she had been in high school, Kate was quite popular in college. If her age and background did not initially impress all of her classmates, her frank manner and enthusiastic attitude soon made her a universal favorite. "She joined in our most childlike amusements with zest and humor," her classmate Amy Reed remarked favorably, "and responded to any friendly advance with such good will that she rapidly became 'one of us.'"[63]

In keeping with her history of mild rebellion, Kate was a frequent hostess for Vassar's illicit evening entertainments, known as "spreads." Her parties were especially notable among a population that rated their members according to their skill at hosting gatherings. The observatory resident went well beyond the usual homemade candy and popcorn to prepare a full meal, including a tossed salad and a steak as fine, her roommate opined, as that served at the well-known fine-dining restaurant, Delmonico's. She even cleaned up afterwards![64]

Vassar, like other women's colleges in Victorian America, had many cherished traditions. Among these were elaborate celebrations of Valentine's Day. At Vassar, as at other all-female campuses, same-sex romances, known as "crushes" or "smashes," were commonplace. Not surprisingly, then, Vassar Valentine's Day celebrations revolved around same-sex relationships. Students exchanged both humorous and sentimental poetry, often decorating their handmade cards with elaborate pen-and-ink or watercolor drawings. Perhaps because of her relationship with Ella, Kate seems to have had no special friendship at Vassar. Nonetheless, she was a popular author and fortunate recipient of numerous valentines. "At the approach of Saint Valentine's Day she could compose the 'lovingest' verses of all," her roommate recalled. Kate also received copious "effusions of love" from Vassar freshmen and sophomores, who traditionally developed crushes on juniors and seniors.[65]

Kate's familiarity with college crushes and same-sex smashes—as well as her friendship with Ella Lapham—may have predisposed her toward her candid discussion of same-sex relationships in her later studies of women's sexuality. In her 1929 magnum opus, *Factors in the Sex Life of Twenty-Two Hundred Women*, Davis would reveal the prevalence of same-sex attraction and sexual activity among white, well-to-do, well-educated women, challenging prevailing ideas about homosexuality as sexual perversion.[66]

The testimonials that Davis included in an article drawn from her research may have reflected the experiences of her Vassar classmates. One respondent, who "always preferred girls to boys," explained that this preference increased when she attended a women's college, where "there was a constant finding of congenial spirits, with considerable expression of affection by kissing and embracing."[67]

At Vassar College, students had ample opportunities to find "congenial spirits." Vassar students enjoyed an endless round of social activities, both school-sanctioned and student-led. Amateur theatricals were especially popular, including both formal events sponsored by the college's dramatic society, "The Phil" (short for Philalethian), and "hall plays" staged by individual classes. Vassar's aspiring thespians devoted

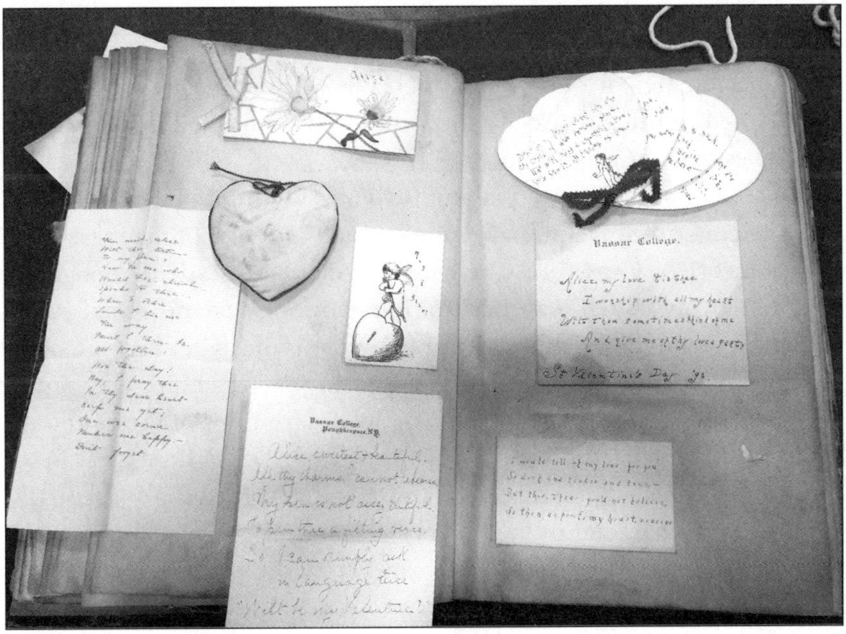

In the Victorian era, female collegians celebrated same-sex romance. On Valentine's Day, Vassar students vied with one another to compose the best verses and produce the prettiest cards for the objects of their admiration. Vassarians prized such tributes and preserved them in their scrapbooks. According to her roommate, Katharine Bement Davis received copious "effusions of love" from younger students and used her versifying skills to "compose the 'lovingest' verses of all." Photo by Anya Jabour, Scrapbook 232, Alice Robbins Martin, VC 1892, Special Collections, Vassar College.

themselves wholeheartedly to the theater, spending weeks memorizing lines, building sets, and assembling costumes in advance of each one-time-only performance. While not all students took to the stage, Vassarians' accounts indicate that nearly everybody was an active participant in the flurry of preparations and the follow-up celebrations. Students carefully planned their wardrobes to attend the theater—even if the theater in question was simply a student parlor—and those not playing roles helped with decorating. Afterward, actors and audience members alike enjoyed "a delightful spread."[68]

For college women, amateur theatricals provided not only a break from their studies but also a chance to try on different personas, envisioning themselves, if only for an evening, living in a different time and place, and assuming a different role in society. In particular, acting in plays offered ample scope for playing with gender. Students played both male and female parts to popular acclaim, although Kate's roommate complained of the "absurd" school rules that prohibited those playing male roles from wearing trousers.[69]

Vassar students enjoyed playing with and poking fun at both social conventions and conventional gender roles. Comedies of manners were special favorites. Cross-dressing heightened college students' delight in simultaneously copying and critiquing gender roles and social rules. Student scrapbooks included many photographs of amateur actors, playing both male and female roles, engaged in playful banter and genial disagreement, and students wrote lengthy descriptions of their prowess at playing "men's parts."[70]

As a girl, Kate wrote, directed, and acted in original plays, usually taking on the character of the male villain. As a schoolteacher, she produced and directed both dramatic and comedic performances. As a member of several women's clubs in western New York, she performed in both theatrical and musical entertainments. While her busy schedule may have prevented her from joining "The Phil," one can imagine that she took to Vassar's dramatic scene like a duck to water.[71]

Musical events also were a regular feature of Vassar student life. During Kate's time at Vassar, a "Banjo and Glee Club" flourished, offering students the opportunity to put on their own musicales and perform popular songs in addition to attending classical concerts.[72] As a teenager, Kate had studied music seriously for several years, becoming proficient at playing the piano and organ as well as taking classes in vocal harmony and musical composition. Although her studies were cut short by her family's financial reversals, music would remain a mainstay in her life. Shortly before matriculating at Vassar College, she was the accompanist for a musical performance at a fundraiser for the Dunkirk Women's Educational and Industrial Union. In later years, she would direct the music program at Bedford Reformatory. Although there is no record of her participation, it seems only logical that she would have been a regular at musical events at Vassar, even if her rigorous academic schedule prevented her from practicing and performing.[73]

Outdoor activities also abounded. Some of these were school related. All Vassar students were required to exercise for an hour each day, which might include walking the extensive grounds or boating on the lake in good weather or using the gymnasium equipment or the swimming pool in bad weather. In addition, students spent time in the woods and fields near campus collecting botanical samples for classroom purposes. However, many Vassarians voluntarily spent additional time engaged in physical activities. Students reported not only exploring the extensive campus but also taking long rambles in the countryside. Others took advantage of the proximity of Vassar Lake, rowing or skating, depending on the season. A tennis craze swept campus in the 1890s, and sporty students filled their scrapbooks with cleverly designed scorecards from both singles and doubles tournaments. In winter, many Vassar students enjoyed skating and sleigh riding.[74]

Kate likely was an enthusiastic participant in all such vigorous activities. Prior to enrolling at Vassar, she had belonged to an outdoors club, which sponsored "long tramps" in the wilds of western New York. Having grown up on the shores of Lake Erie and Lake Ontario, she also enjoyed water sports in all seasons, including boating and skating. She no doubt would have agreed with a fellow student's assessment of Vassar's environs: "This is just a grand place!"[75]

"Duty of Women to Women"

Activism was another important aspect of student life. Although the college banned suffrage activities during Davis's time there, many faculty members were committed feminists who encouraged students to promote women's rights. Weekly talks by reformers, missionaries, and settlement workers inspired students to take up social reform, with a special focus on what one speaker called the "Duty of Women to Women."[76] Reinforcing the centrality of engaged citizenship, one of Kate's faculty mentors, history professor and suffrage supporter Lucy Maynard Salmon, hosted salons every Friday to discuss current events.[77]

With her strong ties to the Young Women's Christian Association (YWCA), Kate must have been pleased to find that the organization had a strong presence at Vassar College. Kate's mother was active in the "Autumn Chapter" of the Rochester YWCA, and her sister Helen worked as a gymnasium instructor at the Rochester YWCA before moving on to state and national leadership. Kate herself had founded the Dunkirk

At Vassar College, as at other women's colleges in the Victorian era, female faculty fostered strong ties with their students. History professor Lucy Maynard Salmon and her partner, librarian Adelaide Underhill, frequently hosted students in the home they shared near campus. A suffrage advocate, Salmon would become an important mentor to Katharine Bement Davis, helping launch her career as a "scientific reformer." Lucy Maynard Salmon Papers, Special Collections, Vassar College.

YWCA while teaching at Dunkirk Academy. At Vassar, the student chapter of the organization held weekly meetings and hosted regular social events. In addition, each Christmas, Vassar students dressed dolls to send to the New York College Settlement under the auspices of the YWCA.[78] In the years to come, Davis would lead a settlement house and collaborate with her sister in the YWCA's wartime campaign to combat sexually transmitted infections and promote sexual education. Vassar's emphasis on women's activism, moral reform, and settlement work profoundly shaped Davis's future.

"Scientific Knowledge"

In 1892, "Katharine Bement Davis," as the new college graduate now called herself, graduated with honors from Vassar College. She gave a commencement address titled "The Missing Term in the Food Problem," a discussion of the chemistry of cooking. The subject might seem arcane to modern ears. Indeed, even at the time, Davis apparently thought it necessary to defend her choice of topic, explaining, "Nothing can be of more vital interest than those investigations which have to do with the production, preparation, and consumption of food." Moreover, she asserted, "The importance of this term of the food problem,—the preparation of the food,—cannot, it seems to me, be over estimated." Davis argued that a better understanding of food preparation had scientific, economic, and nutritional benefits. She concluded, "A scientific knowledge of cooking . . . will make cheap dishes tasteful and tempting, and put tempting dishes within reach of all. In this greatest good to the greatest number we ought all to be able to rejoice."[79]

Davis's choice of topic would prove to be prescient. Her interest in producing affordable, tasty, and healthy dishes may have reflected her own experience—when she was a girl, her mother raised chickens and picked fruit in order to feed the family on a limited budget—but it also put her at the cutting edge of a new professional field for educated women then known as "domestic science," pioneered by Vassar alumna Ellen Swallow Richards.[80]

Later diluted into the type of high school "home ec" classes that some of today's readers may remember and regard with disdain, in the late nineteenth century, domestic science offered one of the only opportunities for women scientists to pursue their professional goals. It also was closely allied with the burgeoning settlement house movement and with the emergence of the field that we now call public health. In the decades to come, Davis would explore all of these aspects of domestic science. More broadly, she would become an enthusiastic advocate of using science to solve social problems.[81]

It was perhaps only fitting, therefore, that on her graduation day, Davis crossed paths with industrialist John D. Rockefeller Jr., a trustee of the college who was on campus to pledge his support for a new residence hall for Vassar students. Although Davis had no way of knowing it at the time, this moment presaged a long and productive relationship with the wealthy philanthropist in their shared pursuit of public health. Ultimately, Davis's relationship with Rockefeller would facilitate her pioneering sex research under the auspices of the Bureau of Social Hygiene.[82]

For Katharine Bement Davis, as for other "new women" of her generation, attending college was an important step on the path to independent womanhood. As she reflected in her memoirs, "Perhaps it is because for years I wanted to go to college so badly and worked so hard for it that I have always cared so much about it." While Davis may have worked longer and harder for a college education than some of her peers, like most early women graduates, she regarded her college years as "an outstanding part of my life," one that supplied her with both useful knowledge and "lasting friendships."[83]

But like many other "New Women," even as she donned the traditional white gown for commencement ceremonies, she must have wondered, "What next?" Attending college was still a rarity for American women, but career possibilities were even fewer than educational opportunities. Fortunately, this new woman from New York had both the intellectual prowess and the sturdy resolve necessary to pioneer new professional pathways. In addition, her college roommate praised both her people skills and her problem-solving abilities: "Her success in dealing with all kinds of people may lie in her strong power of intuition which is almost a sixth sense, enabling her to grasp a problem and solve it before the rest of the world realizes that the problem exists."[84]

2

"A Scientific Reformer"

The summer of 1893 was a momentous one for the city of Chicago, which had won the honor of hosting the World's Columbian Exposition. It also offered an extensive array of exciting experiences for the thousands of Americans who flocked to the fair to exclaim over the electrical lights and walkways, to congratulate themselves on the progress evident in the fair's technological exhibits, to revel in the exotic "ethnic" villages on the Midway, and to tantalize the senses with side shows featuring suggestive dancers and skilled sharpshooters. Fairgoers also were intrigued by a unique living exhibit: a model home designed to show how a working-class family could live on five hundred dollars a year, prepared and presented by recent college graduate and budding domestic scientist Katharine Bement Davis. Vassar classmate Amy Reed described the scene:

> In the summer of '93, her astonished classmates found her at the World's Fair in Chicago running a Workingman's Model Home as part of the New York State exhibit. There in the blazing heat a family of five were living on an income of $500 a year in a house costing $1,000 to build and $300 to furnish. The menus were posted on the walls, the clothing hung in the closets, and through the four rooms streamed a crowd of visitors, to whom K. B. Davis explained that you could feed a workingman's family on fifty-four cents a day but that it was a grave question whether you ought to do so.[1]

Although the model home was open to the public only for a few months—June through October—it was an important innovation on several fronts. It shaped and promoted the nascent fields of domestic science and social work, which emerged as new professional opportunities for educated women at the turn of the century, thereby offering both a justification for women's higher education and an avenue for women's professional pursuits. It also shaped Katharine Bement Davis's professional trajectory for the next several years by establishing her expertise as a domestic scientist and her identity as "a scientific reformer" who would spend the rest of her life using science to improve society.[2]

"Right Living"

Initially, Davis followed a fairly traditional course of action after completing her college degree: she taught school. Shortly after graduation, she accepted a position as a high school science teacher at Brooklyn Heights Seminary. While grateful to have a job, Davis did not relish the setting, which she described as "absolutely without laboratory or opportunity for experimental work." However, the job had other benefits. The position was part-time—Davis taught only four hours a day—and the location offered her the chance to pursue graduate-level education at a time when attending graduate school was even more of a rarity than attending college for American women.[3]

As a case in point: Columbia University did not admit women. However, a sympathetic chemistry professor there invited Davis to work in his laboratory. With his support and guidance, Davis daily risked detection by the "disapproving Dean" to conduct experiments on the chemistry of foods. Her unofficial graduate-level research built upon her prior chemistry studies and furthered her expertise in domestic science.[4]

After delivering her commencement address at Vassar College, Davis continued to promote the field of domestic science and establish her own place in the vanguard of the discipline by publishing a lengthy article in the *Vassar Miscellany* touting the merits of scientific housekeeping. While in days past, she conceded, housewifery had "stifled rather than encouraged mental effort," as a new century dawned, the scientific study of the home and its operations meant that housekeeping now required "the highest faculties of the mind." Moreover, she insisted, the emergence of domestic science was intertwined with the rise of women's higher education. Now that women had proven their abilities *beyond* the home, it was time for them to apply their newly acquired educations *to* the home. "The time is past when it is necessary for a woman to show that she *can* do a thing," she pronounced. "To-day she *may* do anything she can." Davis optimistically predicted,

"Not only has the 'Women's Century' dawned, but we hope the 'Housekeeper's Century' as well."[5]

By insisting that homemaking was an honorable calling, Davis both challenged and confirmed the notion that women's place was in the home. She challenged prevailing ideas about home-bound femininity by insisting that women could and should pursue higher education and professional careers. Davis positioned domestic science as a refutation of claims that collegiate women emphasized theory over utility, because nobody could "condemn as wasteful of energy such studies as will lead to better ways of living." Thus, she argued that domestic science was ideally suited to collegiate study. "For the college woman there is no other field which seems to me to offer so wide an opportunity for original work," she declared, because so many disciplines could be applied to the demands of daily life. At the same time, she confirmed traditional ideas about women's domestic nature by assuming that most women would devote their lives to homemaking because of the primacy she attached to home life. Ultimately, she insisted, "Our health, our happiness, our success in life depends upon our right living."[6]

An "Interesting Sociological Experiment"

Davis's specialty in domestic science not only offered a practical justification for women's education but also allowed Davis to highlight women's contributions to American society at the World Columbian Exposition, better known as the World's Fair. In spring 1893, at the recommendation of Vassar history professor Lucy Maynard Salmon, Davis won a post in charge of an innovative "living exhibit" at the fair known as the "Model Workingman's Home."[7]

Because Davis specialized in scientific study at Vassar, Salmon might seem like an unlikely mentor. Indeed, Davis had never taken a class with the history professor. However, the two had other shared interests. Salmon was known for her innovative approach to the study of history. At the time when she and Davis met at Vassar, she was working on a pathbreaking book on domestic service. Salmon's research on domestic labor dovetailed with Davis's emerging specialty in domestic science. The two women's shared commitment to social reform and woman suffrage further strengthened their relationship. Thus, when Salmon's proposal for a model home gained approval from the New York State fair planning authorities, she knew just the right person to plan, prepare, and present the project. Salmon suggested that Davis use her "scientific knowledge" to spearhead this "interesting sociological experiment."[8]

It was an excellent opportunity for everybody concerned. For Davis, operating the model home was a chance to explore professional horizons beyond the high school classroom. By definition, Davis's position at the World's Fair was a temporary one, designed to last only for the duration of the fair. But much more was at stake than a six-month job. Not only Davis's own future but also the professional options available to educated women like her hung in the balance. While increasing numbers of women attended college in the closing decades of the nineteenth century, their professional options were extremely limited. As Davis recalled, in her youth, "school teaching was practically the only occupation open to girls." Indeed, except for teaching, women had made few inroads into the established professions. Law, medicine, and the clergy remained extremely hostile to women.[9]

However, graduate programs in the emerging social sciences—sociology, economics, and political science—had begun to accept female applicants. Graduates from these programs pursued newly professionalized careers in "charities and corrections," which brought together women's traditional work as caretakers with their new expertise in statistical analysis. Some schools, such as Columbia University and the University of Chicago, had begun to take the first tentative steps toward establishing entirely new fields of study intended to prepare women for professional careers in social work and domestic science. While these programs were in their infancy in the 1890s, interested observers understood that if a few intrepid women could demonstrate their abilities in these areas, then new opportunities would open up for many more women. Davis was destined to become one of these professional pioneers.[10]

The World's Fair was an ideal venue to advocate for professional opportunities for educated women. Billed as a commemoration of the four hundredth anniversary of Christopher Columbus's "discovery" of America, the World's Columbian Exposition celebrated Western "progress." As one might expect from such an event, the fair unabashedly espoused colonialism and imperialism. It also condoned racism and promoted white supremacy by excluding African American exhibitors and by literally sidelining colonized peoples, relegating them to ethnic "villages" on the Midway. But for white women, the fair offered an unprecedented opportunity to display women's accomplishments and demand women's rights. A Woman's Building, designed by a female architect, featured exhibits showcasing women's accomplishments, while a week-long World's Congress of Representative Women at the fair hosted more than five hundred speakers who highlighted women's contributions to social progress.[11]

Vassar women played a prominent role in what amounted to a national and international conversation on women's role in society, industry, and politics. In addition to exhibiting in the Woman's Building and participating in the Women's Congress, Vassarians planned buildings and exhibits for individual states.[12] The Workingman's Model Home especially exemplified "the college spirit."[13] As the *Vassar Miscellany* explained, the living exhibit highlighted the importance of women's college education as "the very foundation of a well-balanced, wholesome life."[14]

Hired only weeks before the fair was scheduled to open, Davis moved quickly to plan every aspect of the model home, intended to demonstrate how a family of five—a male breadwinner, a female homemaker, and three young children—could live on an annual budget of five hundred dollars. While in Davis's imagined family both parents had previously earned wages, the wife now devoted herself full-time to caring for her home and family. As with her broader discussions of domestic science, Davis's "ideal" scenario both lauded the value of women's unpaid work inside the home and asserted the necessity of having a full-time homemaker. Insisting that an efficient housekeeper was "as truly earning as if she brought actual dollars and cents into the family treasury," she also suggested that the absence of a devoted housewife might be disastrous, "for there is no real economy in a home where the children are uncared for, the house untidy, the food unpalatable and innutritious."[15]

Davis's commentary was unintentionally ironic, given that in the vast majority of working-class households at the time, it simply was not financially feasible for a single wage earner to support a family of five. Rather, most families among the working poor relied upon multiple sources of income from all family members. Davis used more accurate information when it came to furnishing the home and feeding and clothing its residents. She consulted with the US Bureau of Labor Statistics to calculate annual income and monthly rent and with both American and German physiologists, chemists, and statisticians to determine nutritional demands. Finally, to make decisions about clothing needs, she consulted with "women in various stations in life, as school teachers, clerks, servant girls and wash women." On the basis of these conversations, she took into account not only the clothing needs of each family member but also the presumed ability of the housekeeper to "turn," or remake, clothing and the commonplace reliance on hand-me-downs for younger children.[16]

Located at the southern portion of the fairgrounds, the model home was a one-and-a-half-story frame structure, with a living room, kitchen, and bathroom on the first floor and three bedrooms on the second floor.[17] Davis described the home in idyllic terms: "In appearance it resembled hundreds of the cottages one sees scattered throughout New York and New England; white, with green blinds, little porch with vines and hanging baskets, window boxes of green-painted pine, and flower beds filled with inexpensive but cheery flowering plants."[18]

Davis designed and decorated the home with an eye to both beauty and utility. For instance, she chose paint rather than wallpaper because it was less expensive, but also because she deemed it more sanitary. She made careful color choices for the walls and floors and used remnants of fine Brussels carpeting sewn together to make an attractive striped rug in coordinating colors.[19]

She purchased the home's furnishings and the family's clothing at local shops, "just as the workingman's wife . . . would have to do." In the home, she posted the prices for each item of clothing and each piece of furniture, as well as sample menus. After weeks of planning, she moved into the house to give personal tours and to conduct what she saw as the most important part of the exhibit. Living in the house with the designated "family"—actually a widow with three children and an unmarried man who worked as a guard at the fair—she personally prepared "three square meals a day" for the home's official residents.[20]

Davis's experiment attracted a good deal of interest. Fairgoers flocked to the house to watch Davis knead bread while answering rapid-fire questions from onlookers. Davis must have had some interesting conversations with the visitors who "thronged the house" from June through October. Some questioned the premise of the experiment, pointing out that the budget made no allowances for expenses for education, health care, or recreation. Others pointed out that many families, for all their best efforts, could not earn five hundred dollars a year. Davis defended the experiment by pointing out that it was "obviously ridiculous" to expect a short-term experiment to solve "all the social and industrial problems of the day." Rather, she insisted, the value of the exhibit lay in "the stimulation of thought along these lines."[21]

Davis did comment on the false assumption that a typical working family could live on a typical working man's wage. "I believe in fair wages for a fair day's work," she told the Women's Educational and Industrial Union, adding that she supported the aims of labor unions, which sought to increase workers' income, even though her own efforts focused on "the question of reducing the outlay rather than of increasing the income."[22]

More specifically, Davis focused on "the topic of foods . . . from a scientific standpoint bringing out the relation of nutrition to cost." At the model home, she offered hearty plain fare such as Boston baked beans, liver and onions, and beef fricassee. Minimizing waste by using scraps for soups, she boasted that of more than four hundred pounds of food purchased, only eleven pounds, mostly meat bones and potato parings, were thrown away.[23]

The family, examined by a physician both before and after the month-long experiment, did well on this diet. Ultimately, Davis considered "the food experiment" a success. She pointed out, "The less we spend for food the more we can spend for those things which can minister to the higher needs of ourselves and others."[24]

Davis's work at the World's Fair had important implications for public policy. Despite her careful study of the subject and her announced sympathy with the aims of the labor movement, her commentary on the model home also revealed both her class privilege and her condescending attitude toward working-class Americans. At the same time that she advocated fair wages and better living conditions, for instance, she also positioned herself as the expert who could teach others how to live better. This was, of course, the purview of the domestic scientist. Establishing her own expertise meant evaluating other people. Thus, she declared, "In order to attain to the highest conditions of living it is necessary not only that the workingman earn a fair wage but that he and his be educated sufficiently to distinguish between the necessary and the unnecessary, the cheap and the shoddy; that which is truly worth having from that which gives only temporary pleasure."[25] While Davis's commentary on fair wages was a call for social justice, her discussion of "educating" working people to make wise choices framed living conditions as a matter of individual merit. Not at all unique to Davis, this tension would continue to inform well-meaning reformers' approaches to the plight of the poor for generations to come.

The model home also had important repercussions for Davis's professional trajectory. Davis's work at the World's Fair established her reputation as "a scientific reformer," as one laudatory account put it. While contemporary observers cast this topic as a "scientific" one, it also was an economic one. Although Davis initially emphasized the scientific importance of her work, ultimately, the economic aspects of the project would appeal to her more, leading her to study economics, rather than science, as a graduate student. Before Davis's path took her to graduate school, however, it led into the settlement house movement, which united efforts to address social and economic problems under one roof.[26]

"Social Democracy"

One of Davis's visitors at the model home was Susan Wharton, an officer of the Philadelphia College Settlement. Impressed by Davis's "little house," she invited Davis to interview for the vacant position of head worker at the Philadelphia settlement house, also known as the St. Mary's Settlement. Although she was familiar with college settlements "only in theory," Davis was intrigued by the opportunity "to experiment with humans instead of with chemical compounds." Turning over day-to-day operations of the model home to her sister Helen, she relocated to Philadelphia in fall 1893.[27]

Settlement houses—so called because they were based on the premise that well-educated, well-to-do, and well-meaning people should "settle" among their less-privileged neighbors to learn about and address their most pressing needs—proliferated in turn-of-the-century cities on both sides of the Atlantic. The original settlement house, located in the United Kingdom, was Toynbee Hall; Jane Addams, founder of the most celebrated settlement house in the United States, Chicago's Hull House, modeled her settlement on Toynbee Hall, with one notable difference. While Toynbee Hall was founded and run by men, Hull House was designed and operated by women. Indeed, while male-led and mixed-gender settlement houses existed in the United States, most American settlements were spaces for college-educated women to establish their place in US society and politics at a time when women's professional opportunities and political rights were extremely limited. Like many other college-educated women of her generation, Davis sought a meaningful calling in settlement work. As her closest companion, Ella Lapham, explained, she had "a longing to mingle more intimately in the world's activities, to find a field where she could plan as well as execute, to deal not only with preparations for life, but with life itself."[28]

A women's organization paved Davis's path into settlement work. The dual goals of helping others—a quintessentially feminine pursuit—and promoting women's status—an essentially feminist goal—came together in the College Settlements Association, established by the Seven Sisters Colleges in spring 1890. One of the association's "chief aims" was "to bring all college women within the scope of a common purpose and a common work."[29] Settlement work offered collegiate women an approved pathway into public service: "There can be no better training school than Settlement life for the women coming out of college, eager to do helpful service but ignorant of where to take hold."[30]

For Davis, part of the appeal of settlement work appears to have been its similarity to college life. St. Mary's Settlement, she wrote in the *Vassarion*, brought back "pleasant reminiscences of college days," as settlement residents retained "college customs," such as sharing outerwear with "communistic spirit," cooking—and sometimes burning!—simple meals, dropping in on one another unannounced, "doubling up" when necessary, and even putting on dramatic productions of Victorian novels such as "The Colonel's Opera Cloak," part of a popular "No Name Series" of books semi-anonymously authored by well-known women writers, including Louisa May Alcott.[31]

Davis clearly relished her time at the settlement, which included elaborate birthday celebrations, late-night conversations, and "characteristic nicknames." Davis especially enjoyed the opportunity to continue her association with like-minded women, although she was careful to point out that settlement life was not entirely "one-sided." While life at the settlement included "comradeship with the young men connected with the various clubs and classes," the centerpiece was women's camaraderie. "There is an unconventionality and freedom which perhaps is only possible in a family of young women," Davis reflected. For Davis, the settlement also offered the opportunity to live with Ella Lapham, who was listed as an official "visitor" in 1893 or 1894; it seems likely that this was one of the examples of "doubling up," or sharing rooms (and even beds), that Davis had in mind when she penned her piece for the Vassar publication.[32]

While Davis enjoyed "a jolly time" at St. Mary's, there was serious work to be done, too. The association's dual mission—to promote "social democracy" in American cities and to provide women from "the cultured classes" with a meaningful career—was rife with internal contradictions.[33] Davis, who frequently lectured and wrote about social democracy and settlement work, embodied these contradictions. She spoke eloquently about the concept of social democracy. "Members of social settlements are social democrats and really believe in social democracy," she declared. "We think it is possible for persons to establish themselves on an equal plane of friendship who have been born in different social positions."[34] But almost in the same breath, she indicated that she saw herself as superior to people who occupied "different social positions." Less than a year into her new position, she told one reporter, "I have seen a remarkable improvement in the moral and sanitary conditions of the neighborhood."[35]

Ideally, social democracy meant that settlement workers and neighborhood residents encountered one another as equals and learned with and from one another. When Davis reflected on the "fundamental principle" of settlement work, she explained, "The settlement residents come into a community simply as neighbors," getting to know the residents and taking their cues from them about what services to offer. At the same time, however, settlement workers assumed that they knew better than the residents how to go about improving conditions. Indeed, the very nature of settlement work, in which "individuals who have received advantages at the hands of society" ventured into slums and ghettos "to contribute to the social welfare of their community," nearly ensured this would be the case. Certainly, when Davis first moved into the St. Mary's

Street neighborhood, while she saw a crying need for public playgrounds and social services, she also opined that "the people who lived in the district had not the faintest notion of how to go to work to improve their conditions." Therefore, Davis and her crew of college graduates had to take charge: "It was up to the settlement residents through their connection with the life of other sections of the city to get these things."[36]

If settlement workers sometimes fell short of the ideals of social democracy, they made a good-faith effort to tailor social services to community needs. As Davis explained, there was no set agenda for settlement work; "it all depends." As head worker, Davis's first order of business was simply to "make friends" with her new neighbors.[37] This was an uphill battle for Davis, who had little in common with local residents. South Philadelphia was home to a mix of African Americans and Eastern European Jews, and "the two groups had practically nothing in common." Given that she had little to no previous contact with either Black Americans or Jewish people, perhaps it should not be surprising that Davis characterized her new neighbors in terms of prevailing stereotypes. "Our Negro neighbors were mostly day laborers, ignorant, with little knowledge of or desire for better things," she opined. While she had a higher opinion of the neighborhood's European immigrant population, a language barrier hindered communication.[38]

Rather than taking her cues from local residents, then, Davis and her colleagues—like Jane Addams and other residents of Hull House—started by conducting a "careful study" of the neighborhood, noting the number and location of public buildings, schools, saloons, and "disorderly houses." Davis was shocked at the conditions she studied: "Very few of the public schools had kindergartens. In our district there was no public library, no playgrounds or recreation centers for young people; there were open gutters for sewage; no proper tenement house laws or enforcement of what there were."[39]

There was no set template for settlement work, but because turn-of-the-century cities suffered from common problems—and because settlement workers shared similar values—most settlement houses engaged in similar programs. They provided immediate assistance to neighborhood residents and directed them to appropriate agencies where they existed. They offered educational and cultural opportunities by hosting reading rooms, social clubs, and drama troupes. They established parks and playgrounds for neighborhood youth and hosted day nurseries and kindergartens for the children of working mothers. They worked with city authorities to improve sanitation and enforce building codes. Many settlement houses cooperated with labor unions by providing space for union meetings and facilitating reading groups dedicated to discussions of economic theory. Finally, most settlements engaged in what would come to be called applied sociology by conducting statistical analyses of the neighborhoods in which they were located and using the data collected to advocate for new public policies, ranging from offering vaccinations against contagious diseases to providing "mothers' pensions" for impoverished single women and their children.[40]

Davis's work at the St. Mary's Settlement typified turn-of-the-century settlement work. Davis and the house's official residents—five college-educated women—initially spent a great deal of time making referrals to charitable agencies and healthcare facilities. As she recalled, "We became a sort of clearing house. Our neighbors treated us as if we were a combination of city directory, encyclopedia, and clearing house of public charities, an official authority on all public and private questions."[41]

The settlement also quickly became a social hub. The house was "constantly active," hosting classes, clubs, and concerts. Girls could attend a Reading Club or the "Daisy Chain," intended for "amusement and instruction." The latter group, mostly composed of adolescent workers, set their own agenda. In her memoirs, Davis recalled that during her four years at the settlement, the members first chose to study French, then English literature, then American literature, and finally cooking. "I was much amused by the progression from the purely cultural to the practical aspects of life," she reflected.[42]

Boys could choose from a Boys' Club for Improvement, a Boys' Business Club, or a group for "small boys" called "The Little Helpers." But by far, Davis's favorite boys' organization was a group originally formed for military drills that dubbed themselves the "Davis Cadets." This club's activities extended far beyond its original mission, however. In addition to performing drills for settlement fundraisers and political rallies, the Cadets doubled as a dramatic troupe. After performing "Julius Caesar" to great acclaim, they produced "Pinafore," with the boys playing both male and female roles. Davis humorously recalled the difficulty she experienced enforcing "proper modesty" and preventing the young thespians from showing off their frilly undergarments: "The boys were so proud of the embroidery on the ruffles their dresses concealed that they had to be constantly scolded to keep them from displaying it throughout the performance."[43]

Not surprisingly given her background as a teacher, Davis emphasized educational opportunities for all ages. "A campaign of education was carried on all the time," she remarked.[44] For very young children, the settlement provided drop-in recreational and educational activities in an on-site gymnasium and kindergarten, both innovative approaches to education intended to counter the limitations of urban life. For children who had limited exposure to the natural world, Davis and her staff provided trips to the city zoo and color pictures of birds and insects. (On a more practical level, youngsters also got a midday meal "at the nominal charge of one cent.") In cramped cities, children had few opportunities to engage in physical activities unrelated to wage earning; in addition to the indoor gymnasium, the settlement ultimately provided both a park and a playground for this purpose.[45]

The settlement also provided educational opportunities for older children, who often ended their formal schooling early in order to earn money to support their families. Reflecting her interests in innovative pedagogy and political economy, Davis took a special interest in introducing young people to what she called "the mysteries of political economy, in order to bring about municipal reform." Boys and girls alike discussed "the machinery of politics," then formed clubs to monitor public services and engage in local politics. For instance, one club was in charge of determining whether the contracts for street cleaning in their district were completed satisfactorily; finding they were not, club members learned how to make complaints to city officials.[46]

The settlement also offered adult classes, ranging from basic English instruction to a lecture series on economics and politics. By her own admission, Davis learned as much from these classes as did neighborhood residents. As she later recalled, the "working men" of the neighborhood—many of them Russian and German Jews with socialist, communist, or even anarchist views—were "better informed than I was on matters of economics and politics." At their request, Davis invited faculty from the University of Pennsylvania to lecture on a variety of topics, including labor organization and arbitration, socialism and social insurance, and "The Single Tax."[47]

For Davis, these lectures and the lively discussions they provoked were a revelation. "I was greatly abashed that in spite of the fact that I had been to college, and in spite of the fact that a great majority of our audience could neither read nor write English, they seemed to know so much more about these things than I did," she recalled, adding, "It was this sort of thing that inspired in me a desire to really learn something of political economy and political science."[48]

Life at the settlement also provided Davis with cultural education. A significant proportion of the local population was Jewish, inspiring Davis to learn Yiddish so that she could read the neighborhood newspapers. (Her diligence also impressed her new neighbors favorably.) But becoming familiar with Jewish customs meant more than acquiring language skills. Although Davis had learned to recognize the sign designating certain butchers as kosher, she initially failed to comprehend the intricacies of Jewish dietary law. Her first fall at the settlement, when she invited members of the Daisy Chain to dine there, she was baffled when the guests carried on a pleasant conversation but ate nothing. Afterward, when she asked the club president about this, she was startled to learn that the meal was "unclean" because, even though the food itself was kosher, it had been prepared in the same kitchen and served on the same dishes as nonkosher food.[49]

"City Housekeeping"

Davis's experiences at the settlement challenged her sense of social superiority, forcing her to reexamine her assumptions about both herself and her new neighbors. Settlement work also reinforced her commitment to social reform, public policy, and political activism. A hallmark of Davis's settlement career was translating social experiments into public policy. During Davis's four-year tenure at the settlement, she worked with the Free Library of Philadelphia to establish a branch library in the neighborhood, convinced the Department of Education to assume responsibility for running the settlement kindergarten, and persuaded the Board of Health to appoint a female physician and settlement resident as medical inspector.[50]

Davis was not alone in using women's activism as the basis for social reform. Indeed, she often lectured on settlement work as "city housekeeping." Framing women's public engagement as city housekeeping, municipal housekeeping, or social housekeeping was a common tactic among women activists in turn-of-the-century America. By arguing that modern life required women to apply their skills as homemakers and caretakers to the "larger family" of city dwellers, female reformers "domesticated politics" and established a unique "women's political culture" that justified their entry into public life and, ultimately, into party politics. As Davis explained this then-popular concept, "city housekeeping" simply meant "the extension of the activities which have been carried on by women in the home to the larger field of the community in which she lives."[51]

One of the ways that "city housekeepers" framed civic life as comparable to home life was to suggest that women would "clean up" corrupt politics. Along these lines, at the same time that she gave classes on domestic science at a local girls' school and lectured on domestic service to women's groups, Davis made what she called "my debut into practical politics." At the time, Philadelphia, like other major American cities, was rife with political corruption designed to keep one political party in power; that party then rewarded its loyal voters with patronage in the form of political office and government contracts. Davis compared Philadelphia's political "machine" to New York's infamous Tammany Hall, although whereas Gotham was ruled by Democrats, the City of Friends was dominated by Republicans. But the result was the same: "Graft was rampant and it was difficult for those who were interested in reform to make any headway."[52]

A particular problem in Philadelphia was illegal voting. Casting extra ballots on behalf of deceased or disqualified registrants was so easy that the saying went that even the city's cats and dogs were registered voters. At the request of a group of independent (male) voters, Davis transformed the settlement into "headquarters" for a house-to-house canvass, conducted by settlement residents and their supporters, intended to determine the actual number of eligible voters, remove false registrations, and encourage voting among qualified residents. Due to a provision in the city charter that permitted women to run for positions on school boards, the campaign expanded to include women's candidacy for these positions.[53]

With the enthusiastic support of the Davis Cadets, who sported badges reading, "Women Want Women on the School Board," Davis herself ran for political office during this campaign. Davis enjoyed her first foray into electoral politics. "It was fun to see a parade of our College Settlement youths, with torchlights and banners bearing my name," she recalled. Though "of course we were defeated"—an outcome Davis accepted as inevitable—she later reflected that "this was a good political beginning" for someone who would later hold public office and advocate for women's suffrage.[54]

The campaign highlighted corruption in city politics and presented women as the "good government" alternative to business as usual. As a later account by a fellow suffragist explained, "She was beaten by an Italian saloon-keeper. An amusing fact which gives some idea of how much a woman of her caliber was really needed in that City of Brotherly Love was that when the vote was counted it was found that her precinct had polled seven more votes than it was entitled to!"[55] The political campaign thus offered Davis an opportunity to spread the gospel of social housekeeping and promote the cause of women's suffrage. It also reinforced her commitment to both civil service and political engagement. As she explained, "Although our candidates were defeated, the value of the experience was left, and it is well worth the hard work given to obtain it. We learned more of certain neighborhoods than we had ever known before and realized to the full the need of municipal work by enlightened men and women."[56]

"The Housing of the Poor"

Davis's work at the settlement introduced her to political activism and allowed her to rehearse arguments in favor of women's suffrage. The centerpiece of Davis's settlement work, however, was housing reform. When Davis assumed her new role as head worker of the St. Mary's Settlement, the neighborhood was the heart of the city's growing African American population, but it also was an area plagued by severe overcrowding, unspeakable filth, and violent crime. Black residents, unable to find housing elsewhere due to racial discrimination, paid high rents for cramped tenements filled with the odor of the open gutters, where raw sewage flowed through the streets and alleyways.[57]

The area also was a hotbed of crime. According to Davis, the "ramshackle tenements" in the neighborhood—formerly single-occupancy residences that had been hastily and inadequately converted into multifamily dwellings—were "occupied by disorderly characters, drunkards, and even criminals." At one building near the settlement house, there were nightly "drunken quarrels," resulting in at least one fatal stabbing.[58]

The adoption of new housing laws, which resulted in the condemnation of the buildings, only exacerbated an already terrible situation. As landlords washed their hands of responsibility for buildings they could not rent, renters moved out of the abandoned buildings, landlords refused to maintain them, and "disreputable characters" squatted in the shuttered buildings.[59]

Frustrated with the slow pace of reform, one night, Davis targeted a condemned building that had become a magnet for the city's most desperate—and dangerous—elements. She recruited "a few of her young women assistants, and they went forth by night and broke every window in that house, so that it was no longer habitable." To ensure that the building would no longer attract transients, Davis and her workers also lit a bonfire to destroy all the furniture they found there. While Davis's friends gleefully told this story to demonstrate that "she was capable of practical deeds when occasion demanded," her actions probably only worsened the housing situation. As Davis reflected in her memoirs, "Perhaps I was cruel, [for] hoboes have to sleep; but so did I, and I could not do my work when kept awake night after night."[60]

Not all of Davis's housing-related activities involved demolition. Building on her experience at the World's Fair, Davis also experimented with model housing in Philadelphia. After transforming the previously run-down tenement on St. Mary's Street into "a pleasant home," the organization purchased four other tenements, which were "put in good sanitary condition" and rented as "model homes" to local residents. Davis also worked closely with the Civic Club to study and promote model tenements, although she lamented that "there has been comparatively little done here as yet."[61]

Like the model home at the World's Fair, model tenements in major cities tended to emphasize individual effort more than social engineering. But Davis's interest in housing reform ultimately led her to a more sophisticated understanding of the structural causes of shabby housing. In 1896, Davis published a three-part story on "The Housing of the Poor" in the *College Settlement News*. In this series, she asserted that it was incumbent on public officials—city authorities in this case—to address the problem of slums. In particular, she suggested that the city needed to enact and enforce regulations limiting occupancy (to avoid overcrowding) and requiring "necessary conveniences" (meaning indoor plumbing). Once such conditions were established, she explained, philanthropists could provide model housing to serve as an example of what was possible, offering not only comfortable and sanitary housing for individual families but also communal libraries and children's playgrounds. Finally, offering several such projects in Philadelphia as an example, Davis insisted that they had "proved profitable" and thus served as a pattern for investors as well as reformers.[62]

"A Clear Understanding of the Problem"

Davis's interest in addressing housing problems, especially those that plagued Philadelphia's Black residents, led to a close association with pioneering African American sociologist W. E. B. Du Bois. It also allied her with the settlement house movement's emerging emphasis on applied sociology, the use of statistical analysis to understand and address social problems. Finally, it led her out of settlement work entirely and prompted her to pursue a graduate degree at the University of Chicago.

In 1896, the Harvard-trained sociologist W. E. B. Du Bois launched a comprehensive study of Black Philadelphia. Taking up residence at St. Mary's Settlement, Du Bois designed detailed questionnaires and conducted a door-to-door canvass of five thousand households. Pioneered at Hull House, the "distinctly scientific work" of collecting statistical data had quickly become a distinguishing feature of settlement work. By hosting Du Bois and supporting his project, Davis demonstrated her unusual commitment to African American welfare and interracial cooperation. She also strengthened her association with social science as well as with social reform.[63]

Du Bois, like Davis, was not favorably impressed by his new neighborhood. "Murder sat on our doorsteps, police were our government, and philanthropy dropped in with periodic advice," he sourly commented in his autobiography. Indeed, Du Bois's magisterial study, *The Philadelphia Negro*, published in 1899, confirmed many of Davis's initial observations. He described what he called an "almost unbelievable . . . depth of poverty and degradation" and condemned the "crime, filth, and poverty of the district." However, like Davis, he came to see these problems as a result of public policy rather than moral failings. A major contributing factor to the problems he observed, he opined, was the city's failure to enforce housing regulations. He quoted one housing inspector who alleged that in some of the alleyways, not a single dwelling could pass inspection "without being condemned as prejudicial to health."[64]

Davis's association with Du Bois reinforced her interest in understanding the social and economic underpinnings of inequality in Gilded Age America. As she explained in a lengthy and laudatory review of *The Philadelphia Negro*, "Any attempt at solving a problem should be preceded by a clear understanding of what the problem involves." In the case of Black Americans, she echoed Du Bois's findings, the majority were concentrated in the most poorly paid occupations: day labor and domestic service. This was, she averred, not due to lack of individual enterprise. Rather, African Americans' limited employment resulted from both "historical" factors, such as lack of skilled work experience, and contemporary ones, specifically, "the prejudice of the whites." Davis, who supported labor organizing, also pointed out that unions excluded African Americans, effectively excluding them from skilled occupations. Finally, she called attention to the discriminatory practices of landlords, which restricted Black renters, even those with means, to the least desirable neighborhoods. Davis's comments indicated how far she had come, in just four years, in understanding individual problems in social context.[65]

Inspired both by the worker-led study groups and by Du Bois's sociological studies at the settlement house, Davis decided to pursue graduate-level studies in political economy: the creation and distribution of wealth. Only with this knowledge, she had become convinced, could she effectively address the underlying issues that plagued American cities and their residents.

Davis's settlement house years not only inspired her to study the social sciences but also changed her approach to her subject matter. Initially, Davis came to settlement work with an attitude of both individual and class superiority. Her innate leadership ability and her assumptions of cultural superiority helped her to achieve far more than most women—even well-to-do, well-educated, white women—were able to do in the Victorian era. Her take-charge attitude drew comment. One European settlement visitor christened her "Czarina" because, he said, of her remarkable ability to get things done. Less obliquely, Davis's own mother, when complimented on her eldest daughter's "executive ability," responded, "Oh! That is nothing. It only means that she likes to boss a job."[66]

While Davis never lost her desire or ability to be in charge, she also learned humility during her time at the settlement house. Moreover, she acquired a deeper understanding of the structural underpinnings of economic inequality, a subject she would continue to probe in graduate school. When she returned to Chicago to pursue graduate study, she did so with the lessons from settlement life fresh in her mind, ready to learn with and from others.

A Female "Fellow"

Like many other pathbreaking women academics, when she decided to pursue a PhD, Davis set her sights on attending the University of Chicago, which not only was one of the nation's first coeducational research universities but also was at the forefront of the new social sciences. Fortunately for the self-supporting Davis, the university—like Vassar, a beneficiary of the philanthropy of industrialist John D. Rockefeller Jr.—not only admitted women to all academic departments but also offered them fully funded positions, known as fellowships. Davis entered the Department of Political Economy as the first female "fellow"—and the only woman student—in fall 1897.[67]

Davis's decision to turn away from domestic science toward political economy reflected not only her own settlement house experiences but also ongoing developments in higher education. Political economy was a new discipline, part of a suite of social sciences that developed in response to—and also fueled—the Progressive Era impulse to use scientific methods to study and address social problems. These fields attracted ambitious women for a variety of reasons. To begin with, many such women were interested in social reform. In addition, as new disciplines, the social sciences, unlike the natural sciences, welcomed women

After graduating from Vassar College, Davis designed a model home at the World's Fair of 1893, served as head of a settlement house in Philadelphia, and completed a PhD in political economy at the University of Chicago. A family friend, May Bragdon, captured this image of a determined Davis ready to pursue graduate studies. Photograph Album, "Photographs of Friends," Box 8, Folder 1, Bragdon Family Papers Addition, D.255. Rare Books, Special Collections, and Preservation, University of Rochester River Campus Libraries.

as students. Finally, studying social science provided women with professional opportunities beyond the schoolroom, usually in the nascent field of social work.[68]

While it was more common for women to study sociology than to probe political economy, the all-male faculty in the University of Chicago's economics department had a reputation for encouraging female students—although they were not, as Davis and her contemporaries learned only later, especially interested in helping female graduates establish academic careers. Moreover, while other women at the University of Chicago were in the process of establishing new departments dedicated to domestic science and social work, these female-friendly fields (complete with female faculty) did not yet exist when Davis decided to pursue a doctorate. Finally, Davis, always somewhat of a maverick, probably relished the thought of defying convention and subverting expectations. Thus, while her interest in studying political economy stemmed from her settlement house experiences, her decision to pursue a doctorate in the subject also cemented her sense of herself as a woman of many "firsts."[69]

Before beginning graduate school, Davis returned to Rochester. There, she visited her family, who remained extremely supportive of her ambitions. She also reunited with Ella Lapham, whose example and encouragement had initiated Davis's pursuit of higher education.

Davis and Lapham had remained in close contact throughout Davis's tenure at the settlement house. At some point in 1893 or 1894, Lapham was a "visitor" at the settlement, meaning that her stay lasted less than a month.[70] She then returned home to New York, where she lived with her parents and completed her master's degree at Vassar (probably from afar). However, the two women spent time together whenever Davis made one of her frequent visits to the family home. In 1896, mutual friend May Bragdon recorded in her diary, "Miss Lapham has just taken her second degree at Vassar (she's a B.A., A.M. now)[.] She's a demure little thing & Kate's particular chum. Lives in Fredonia. Kate goes there for vacation & Charlotte & Helen are thinking of riding down there with her—on their wheels."[71]

In 1897, before relocating to Chicago, Davis again returned to Rochester. While there, she hosted a "Pedro Party" (Pedro was a card game similar to bridge); visited the "dog pound" (Davis was an animal lover); and indulged in "phosphate etc." (phosphates were drinks purchased at soda fountains). She also enjoyed bicycle rides with her sister Helen, her brother Frank, and their friend May. (After winning a newspaper prize, Davis had purchased a new Spaulding the previous summer; while she had previously sported split skirts, by the mid-1890s, the fashion-conscious cyclist instead struggled with "a 'floppy' dress.")[72] Relaxing with her family and friends refueled Davis for the next stage of her academic and professional career.

"The Only Woman"

"The fall of 1897 found me at the University of Chicago," Davis later wrote. While she enjoyed the companionship of fellow "Fosterites," as the women who resided in Foster Hall were known, she was "alone in my glory in political economy." Indeed, while Davis's graduate studies would familiarize her with the statistical methods necessary to understand the structural underpinnings of economic inequality, they also would remind her of the ongoing limitations posed by gender inequality. Initially, she recalled, the male fellows "had not favored the innovation of a woman in the department," and Davis, as "the only woman" studying political economy, "hesitated" to use the department's library. After one fellow invited her in, however, she joined them, "and from then on I had a beautiful time. There were some awfully nice boys there."[73]

Despite this inauspicious beginning, Davis enjoyed the give-and-take of departmental seminars and productive relationships with faculty members. The department's fiscal conservative, J. Laurence Laughlin, suspected Davis of "leanings toward something too liberal," and whenever she made a point in class, he would cry out, "There it sticks up his head!" While Davis claimed not to be perturbed by Laughlin's attitude, she also remarked that she did not get anything out of his classes that she could not get out of textbooks. She had a more congenial relationship with the department's avowed socialist, Thorstein Veblen, who "made one think." For her "minor subject," against Laughlin's advice, Davis completed coursework in sociology, working especially closely with Albion Small, who was known for his interest in public policy and municipal reform and whose students conducted community studies similar to those completed at settlement houses. In the sociology department, as well as in Foster Hall, where she lived during her time at the university, Davis found community among other women students. Some of them, like Sanskrit scholar Mary Harris, became lifelong friends.[74]

For her thesis topic, in keeping with the settlement house tradition, Davis drew inspiration from the local situation, choosing to conduct a comparative study of "Bohemians," Czech-speaking people who formerly resided in the kingdom of Bohemia. After Bohemia was absorbed into the Austro-Hungarian Empire, these people became dispersed throughout the multinational, multicultural, multilingual crownlands as well as immigrating to the United States, especially Chicago. Drawing on her domestic science background as well as her training in political economy, Davis decided to write her dissertation on "Standards of Living of Bohemians Under Three Forms of Government: Feudalism, Imperialism and Democracy."[75]

Davis's comparative study required her to visit three major Central European cities: Berlin, Vienna, and Prague. With the support of a prestigious fellowship from the New England Women's Educational Association, during the 1898–1899 academic year, she spent a semester each at the University of Berlin and the University of Vienna. As she later recalled, this gave her the unique opportunity of meeting the professors who had written the work she had studied in the classroom.[76]

The academic fellowship also gave Davis—whose family could not afford to send her on a "grand tour" of Europe—a chance to travel overseas. Ella Lapham served as her witness on her passport application, which described the thirty-eight-year-old Davis as five feet three inches tall, with blue eyes and brown hair, an "oval" face with a "square" forehead and a "dimpled" chin, a "snub" nose and "good teeth," and a "light brown" complexion.[77]

Following in the footsteps of American women such as popular novelist Louisa May Alcott and Transcendentalist thinker Margaret Fuller, Davis made the most of her first opportunity to travel abroad. In fall 1898, before classes commenced in Berlin, she met her sisters, Helen and Charlotte, who had sailed separately for Europe with family friend May Bragdon. (May's diaries indicated that the trio had been planning this trip for an entire year.) After sightseeing with her sisters in Holland, where they walked until their feet ached, Davis spent a month at a boardinghouse in Blankenburg, dividing her time between exploring the countryside and working with a language tutor. Between her living situation, her sightseeing, and her studies, she recalled, "Life was one long German lesson."[78]

Davis's intensive language study prepared her to take a full courseload at the University of Berlin that fall, where she once again found herself the only woman studying taxation, statistics, and finance. Undaunted, she studied with Gustav Schmoller, a leader of the German historical school of economics. Although Schmoller disavowed the label "socialist," his heterodox approach to economics emphasized careful study of actual conditions, as opposed to classical theory. He also emphasized

When she won a competitive fellowship to study in Europe for her final year of graduate school, Katharine Bement Davis made the most of her opportunity to travel abroad, meeting up with her sisters, Helen and Charlotte, as well as with a family friend, May Bragdon. After sightseeing with her sisters, Davis boarded with a German family and worked with a language tutor to prepare herself to study at the University of Berlin. Davis—whose friendship with her music teacher, Harriet Heyl, had introduced her to German language and culture—later recalled her first visit to the country: "Life was one long German lesson." Bragdon Family Papers Addition (D.255), Series VII, Box 8, Folder 2, Rare Books, Special Collections, and Preservation, River Campus Libraries, University of Rochester.

applied research, arguing that economists should use their expertise to design social and economic policies to address the problems resulting from industrialization and urbanization. Davis probably chose to work with Schmoller because he influenced American sociologists and social reformers she admired, including her former colleague W. E. B. Du Bois and her sociology professor, Albion Small. She also took several courses with other members of the faculty, but what stood out in her memories was her "running argument" with a fellow student over whether the United States was a "Kultur Staat" or a culturally coherent nation, over glasses of beer (for him) and water (for her). (He argued that it was not; she argued that it was.)[79]

Between terms, Davis visited Venice with an American friend, taking "just a peek" at the Dolomite Mountains along the way. After a "delightful" railroad trip over the mountains, Davis settled into a boardinghouse near Vienna's military barracks, which afforded her the opportunity to watch the soldiers march each morning, "often to the tune of a Sousa march." Reflecting her fondness for music—and her indifference to men—Davis recalled that the first time she heard them coming, "I rushed from the table with my napkin in my hand and waved it frantically from the open window." Thinking the American intended "a personal salute," the leader "threw me a kiss." With her usual wry wit, Davis concluded, "He did not guess that my salute was for Sousa."[80]

At the University of Vienna, Davis once again found herself the only woman in the Department of Political Economy. Davis had hoped to study with Eugen Ritter von Bohm-Bawerk, a "great authority on finance," whose neoclassical orientation was more similar to Laughlin's than Schmoller's. Indeed, Bohm-Bawerk critiqued Karl Marx's theory that capitalists benefit by exploiting workers, arguing instead that workers benefited from industrial employment. Whether because she was inclined to agree with him, or because she enjoyed vigorous debate, this made Davis eager to learn from him. "I had been much interested in his ideas on capital and the theory of value, and I wanted to learn more," she explained. However, his appointment to the Ministry of Finance took him out of the classroom.[81]

"Greatly disappointed," Davis had to satisfy herself with courses with other faculty members. "My university work was entirely under Professor Phillipovitch," she recalled. Davis, never a spelling bee champion, misspelled Eugen Philippovich's name, but the Austrian-born lawyer and economist "was very good to me," even inviting her to a dinner at his house at which she met Bohm-Bawerk, who later invited her to his own home. Nonetheless, Davis did not enjoy her coursework in Vienna as much as in Berlin, although she did enjoy the company of her fellow students and afternoon coffee in the outdoor cafes.[82]

Davis's status as the lone woman in her graduate programs at both the University of Berlin and the University of Vienna reinforced her sense of herself as a bold pioneer. She took pride in her ability to hold her own in debates with her classmates. In her memoirs, she pointed out that while she was at the University of Berlin, the school conferred its first doctorate on a woman. She also recalled—with a mix of amusement and embarrassment—the occasion on which, during a dinner party, she inadvertently joined the men in the library, where they had retired for drinks and cigars after dinner, rather than accompanying the other women to the salon, as was the local custom. Although "very much absorbed" in a discussion about the differences between American and European universities, when she realized her faux pas, Davis hastily repaired to the salon, only to find that "the conversation was devoted almost exclusively to "Kinder, Kuche, and Kirche" (literally, children, kitchen, and church, the German equivalent of what Americans called "woman's sphere"). While Davis was perfectly capable of participating in the women's chatter, she reflected, she found the men's conversation much more interesting.[83]

"I Was Never Beautiful"

While Davis occasionally ran afoul of gender conventions, she enjoyed the company of nearly everybody she encountered in Europe. Although she "lived in mortal terror" of being called upon to read aloud in Professor Schmoller's seminar on taxation in the Middle Ages, which required reading archaic Latin, she fondly recalled "an old gentleman," a statistics professor whose name she could not remember. Once again "the only woman" in the class, Davis was touched by the elderly professor's unusual courtesy. The other professors simply "came briskly to the platform, bowed, and said 'Meine Herren' [my gentlemen], and were off!" By contrast, she recalled, "My nice Statistics man was one of the most courteous gentlemen I ever met. He came into class, began with a very polite bow to me: 'Geeherte Dame' [dear lady] he would say, then 'und meine Herren.'"[84]

Davis also got along well with her all-male classmates. She even "taught some of them to open the front door for me," which she counted as "a great achievement." She explained, "These street doors certainly required two-girl power, and boys were not accustomed to open them for their fellow women students," who had only recently been admitted to the university.[85]

During her time in Europe, Davis also fostered friendships with the few other female students there. (Indeed, only her lack of confidence in her language skills prevented her from accepting an invitation to speak about a pet topic, bathroom plumbing, at the women's student union!) However, most of her interactions were with men, and most of them were positive. In an anecdote that highlighted both her easy relationships with men and her lack of interest in them as romantic prospects, she reflected,

> The only time in my life that I was ever spoken to on the street by a man who should not, was on my way home one night [in Berlin] from one of those [evening] seminars [with Professor Schmoller]. I was standing on the corner by the University, waiting for a streetcar to take me home. When I got to Berlin I had bought my winter outfit there, thinking it unnecessary to buy it in the United States and carry it across the ocean; so my clothes were German. The man approached from the rear, and before he had actually looked at me remarked that a young girl ought not to be out alone at night, and might he come along with me? I turned around and looked at him very severely over my glasses, which I wore at the time, and said in a stern tone, "Was?" [What?] He recognized then that he was not addressing a young girl and turned and fled.

Taking pride in her ability to deflect unwelcome attention, Davis also disparaged her physical appearance, adding, "The fact that I was never beautiful was a factor when I went around the slums of Philadelphia and later New York at all hours of the night without ever attracting attention." Indeed, the aspiring professional's always pleasant, but never flashy, appearance would serve her well throughout her professional career. During her time in Europe, Davis—who enjoyed eating as well as preparing hearty fare—gained twenty pounds, transforming her from a slim girl to a sturdy woman. For the rest of her life, Davis projected a matronly persona that helped forestall potential criticisms of her unorthodox activities.[86]

"Bohemian Labor"

In addition to her formal coursework at the University of Vienna, Davis pursued other opportunities to learn about European economics, politics, and culture. Even amidst her busy schedule, she found time for a few social engagements that doubled as social-scientific research—and tripled as social reform. For instance, she visited a "Workmen's House" and spent an afternoon at "Prof. Menger's Library." The "Workmen's House"—which may have been either a model neighborhood built in the 1880s by the Association for Workers' Housing to allow working people to become homeowners or a public housing project launched in 1895 to honor the fiftieth anniversary of Emperor Franz Joseph's reign—would have appealed to Davis because of her interest in housing reform. Anton Menger, a recently retired law professor, had a famous collection of socialist literature; Davis's visit to his library indicated Veblen's enduring influence on Davis as well as the instructive interactions she had with socialists at the Philadelphia settlement house.[87]

Both Davis's formal studies and her informal explorations highlighted her eagerness to study challenging—and controversial—subjects. By choosing to study Bohemians in the 1890s, Davis placed herself at the epicenter of complex political and cultural conflicts in Central Europe. During its relatively brief existence, from 1867 to 1918, Austria-Hungary was home to a diverse population that spoke different languages and practiced different religions. Despite its official motto, "indivisibly and inseparably," the Austro-Hungarian Empire, which also controlled Croatia, Slavonia, Bosnia, and Herzegovina, was rife with divisions. Czech speakers, dissatisfied with their inferior social status, had launched a cultural revival that culminated in the creation of the Czech National Theatre in Prague in the 1880s. German-speaking Austrians, who were politically and culturally dominant, opposed the Czech national movement as well as a Czech-Slovak cultural movement in Hungary that united Czechs and Slovaks beginning in the 1890s—and, in the aftermath of World War I, would lead to the creation of Czechoslovakia.[88]

These developments profoundly shaped Davis's time in Europe. Of particular importance for an international student, the University of Vienna itself had split into two parts, one German and one Czech, in the 1880s. Dissatisfied with the faculty at the University of Vienna, Davis sought out Czech University economics professor Albin Braf, an advocate of Czechoslovakian independence. (Importantly for Davis's studies, Braf's wife, Libuse, not only was named for a Czech folk heroine but also was the daughter of Baron Frantisek Ladislav Rieger, a prominent Czech politician, whose wife, Marie, also was a Czech cultural leader.)[89]

Tensions between German speakers and Czech nationals affected Davis's recreational activities as well as her intellectual pursuits. Davis, who made a point of attending the opera—especially works by Wagner—in each of the European cities she visited, was surprised at the extent of the "bad feeling between the Germans and the Czechs" and the existence of separate opera houses for Czech- and German-speaking residents.[90]

"Bad feeling" was not confined to educational or cultural institutions. The rise of Czech nationalism coincided with the emergence of a powerful labor movement. In the 1890s, at the same time that Czechs and Slovaks were collaborating in a cultural movement, trade unionists and their allies were gaining power in the Social Democratic Party. Trade unionism increased rapidly in Austria in the 1890s, and electoral reforms in 1897 allowed Social Democrats to gain political representation. Davis had a front-row seat to these historic events, as well as to the violence associated with the resistance posed to the Social Democratic Party and its allies by the National Socialist Party and its supporters.[91]

Thanks to Professor Braf, who "brought me books and pamphlets on the subject of Bohemian labor," Davis became intimately familiar with trade unionism in turn-of-the-century Central Europe. Braf also introduced Davis to local labor leader (and future Czech politician) Jan Cerny, whom she described as "an interesting young man, very much concerned with the labor movement." Through Cerny, who invited her to accompany him to union meetings, Davis met other labor organizers, including an American expatriate, a former teacher who had been dismissed from her post for union organizing. Davis also fostered connections to local labor leaders on her own by dining "at workingmen's restaurants."[92]

"Workingmen's restaurants" were not the safest place to be at the time. Central European cities in the 1890s experienced significant labor unrest that pitted striking laborers, strikebreakers, and state authorities—ranging from the city police to the imperial army—against one another. Conflicts over labor often intersected with tensions between Social Democrats and National Socialists and between German nationalists and Czech activists. In Vienna, a German nationalist youth group formed gangs that roamed the streets and attacked both Social Democrats and Czech nationalists.[93]

Whether because of her innate sense of justice, her support for workers' rights, or her identification with underrepresented groups, Davis sided with the underdogs. In a letter to her mother, she described a workers' demonstration protesting what she called "a most unjust, unscientific and ridiculous Election Reform Law which the Clerical party has forced thro' the legislature to strengthen its power." Davis's views were shaped not only by her own allegiances but also by the political leanings of Professor Philippovich, who had organized a meeting of the Association for Social Policy in 1895 and founded the Social Democratic Party in 1896. She added, "That party had better look out—If it goes a little further something will happen—Prof. P. said to me the other day that the feeling was such that there might be another revolution—if the government hadn't such good cannon!"[94]

To complete her European studies, Davis made a side trip to Prague. The city, located in the heart of the former kingdom of Bohemia, was now a part of Austria-Hungary, which had absorbed the original homeland of Czech-speaking people (as well as several other former nations and kingdoms). It also was an epicenter of political strife, labor unrest, and ethnic conflict. Davis, who befriended and boarded with labor leader Jan Cerny while staying in Prague, wrote in her memoirs, "Serious fighting between the students often took place on the streets, resulting now and then in grave injuries."[95]

From Prague, Davis made a sojourn into the countryside to visit an estate still run on feudal principles. Again, Professor Braf used his connections to help the American student by introducing her to his father-in-law, wealthy landlord and Czech politician Frantisek Ladislav Rieger. While Baron Rieger proudly declared that, unlike in previous generations, each tenant family had their own room, Davis found the conditions wanting. After observing the cramped and cold cottages in which estate workers lived and noting that the young men and women who tended and herded the estate's cattle spent many nights in shacks, barns, and stables, Davis gained a new perspective on the living conditions of Czech immigrants to American cities: "After seeing the way these people lived I could understand why the Bohemian population in Chicago, with which I had been somewhat familiar, did not complain of what, to us[,] seemed intolerable living conditions."[96]

"It Was Very Gay"

Finally, in summer 1899, Davis returned to Vienna to wrap up her coursework and to enjoy some long-postponed sightseeing. During her semester at the University of Vienna, in addition to her official studies, Davis—perhaps dreaming of a future trip to the Mediterranean—also took private Italian lessons. Small wonder, then, that she had little time for "dissipations"—although her penny-pinching ways and strong work ethic also played a role in her decision to focus on her studies. Only during her last two weeks in the city—after purchasing a ticket on "one of the slower & cheaper lines"—did Davis, who described herself as a "blankety blanked idiot" for bungling her original travel arrangements, spend time sightseeing. With the promise of supplementary funds from her brother Frank and both her coursework and her language lessons drawing to a close, she finally took some time to enjoy herself, ending her workday at 4:30 in the afternoon so that she had time to visit museums, galleries, parks, and gardens—and even attend the ballet.[97]

By that point in her journey, her small wardrobe was so ragged, she confided to her mother, that "I have to sew myself up every time I dress." While she had allowed "the Baroness"—presumably the wife of Baron Rieger—to persuade her to order "a beautiful evening gown & a nice street dress," she confessed, "when I go out in the latter I feel like a whited sepulcher" because of the shabby state of her undergarments, and "it took a whole morning (nearly) to mend the lining of my winter coat to be respectable on the boat." Davis's humorous comments on her clothing reveal both her keen fashion sense and her practical abilities, demonstrating that when she planned her Workingman's Model Home at the World's Fair to include the housekeeper's ability to "turn" clothing, she showcased her own expertise and experience.[98]

Still watching her budget despite the promised funds from her family, Davis did very little shopping in Europe, instead donning "my cotton shirt waist & old skirt" for everyday wear. But she did enjoy sightseeing. She praised the "beautiful flower beds" and the "tunnels of green" trimmed trees surrounding the emperor's summer palace. She also listened to a live band in the city's public park, where she "watched 'gay Vienna' promenade & sit at little tables & eat & drink." Finally, she enjoyed an outdoor festival during which "the trees are filled with colored electric lights, so it looks like a fairy land." After watching "perfect crowds of people" promenading the streets enjoying live music, fine dining, and colorful confetti, she concluded, "It was very gay, & quite came up to one's ideas of frivolous Vienna."[99]

After Vienna, Davis proceeded to London, where she spent a month at the British Museum conducting research for her thesis and "looking up such other things as I had on my mind." She also squeezed in a week of sightseeing in France and Switzerland before returning to the United States.[100]

While "gay" did not mean then what it means now, Davis's European sojourn offered her the opportunity to observe—and perhaps even experience—queer community and culture. All the places Davis visited displayed recognizable gay subcultures, nurtured self-aware queer identities, and even developed nascent civil rights movements in the late nineteenth century. Moreover, Davis's time in Europe coincided with the emergence of the discipline of sexology, or what she later would dub "the scientific study of sex." Although it would be decades before Davis would incorporate these insights into her research, the timing of her European travels was fortuitous indeed for a woman who would dedicate the latter half of her career to studying sex.

Berlin, where Davis spent fall 1898, was not only the epicenter of a burgeoning gay rights movement but also the birthplace of a modern queer identity. Despite—or perhaps because of—the German empire's 1871 adoption of Paragraph 175, which criminalized sodomy, Germany became the focus of efforts to decriminalize homosexuality. While this movement ultimately did not succeed, the ongoing controversy functioned as a queer consciousness-raising movement, raising public awareness about LGBTIQ+ people and instigating an international discussion about gay rights. From the 1860s forward, German authors and activists introduced terminology to define sexual identities (such as "homosexual," "heterosexual," and "bisexual"), defy the gender binary (suggesting the existence of a "third sex"), and describe "same-sex" relationships.[101]

Meanwhile, queer culture flourished in "Gay Berlin"—and so did conversations about and conflicts over queer rights. By the time Davis arrived in Germany in fall 1898, the debate was in full swing. After a sex scandal involving a night watchman named Heinze in 1891, Kaiser

Wilhelm II pushed for the adoption of the Heinze Law, which—much like the Comstock Act that would be adopted in the United States two years later—censored public performances and published works that addressed a wide range of sex-related topics, ranging from contraceptives to homosexuality. Unlike the Comstock Act in the United States, however, the Heinze Law elicited public outcry from many sectors of the population, including members of the Social Democratic Party; artists, authors, and attorneys; and ordinary German citizens, who ultimately blocked the proposed statute. By establishing that texts about sex could not be censored if they had scientific or educational merit, these debates made Germany a mecca for publications about sex—with profound consequences for at least one American visitor.[102]

While important, Berlin was not the only European center for queer culture. Paris was another. During her time in Paris, Davis—who had studied French, although she never spoke it well—would have had ample opportunity to observe the burgeoning lesbian subculture in fin-de-siècle Paris, constructed by both American expatriates and Parisian sophisticates. Moreover, given the crossover between queer culture and theater circles, it seems unlikely that Davis could have been entirely ignorant of cultural developments in the Belle Epoque (1871–1914), especially during the 1890s, also known as the "Gay Nineties."[103]

London, where Davis spent her final month abroad, was less welcoming to people who might now identify as LGBTIQ+. Indeed, in 1895, the playwright Oscar Wilde, after enduring three trials for the crime of sodomy, began his two-year sentence of hard labor in the Reading Gaol.[104] He was released shortly before Davis arrived in Europe; one wonders if Davis, who so loved theater, read about his much-publicized series of trials (or reveled in his much-beloved comedies of manners) while she spent a month "looking up such other things as I had on my mind" in the British Museum in summer 1899.[105]

There is no evidence that Davis participated in the queer subculture that flourished in European cities at the turn of the century, although plenty of her contemporaries took advantage of European sojourns to flaunt convention.[106] Nonetheless, the timing of Davis's travels certainly makes it seem likely that her early exposure to the rise of queer culture and a burgeoning civil rights movement informed her later research and writing about women's same-sex relationships.

"Things of the Body" and "Things of the Mind"

In August 1899, after an eventful year in Europe, Davis boarded a ship to return to the United States. While she shipped most of her luggage ahead of her, she hand carried her most "precious" belongings: a black velvet evening gown custom made in Vienna and "the manuscript notes intended for my thesis." Reflecting on the stereotype that higher education defeminized women, she humorously remarked, "You see, University women can care for things of the body as well as for things of the mind."[107]

Body and mind were timely topics during Davis's European sojourn. Although Davis did not comment on this in her memoirs, her studies abroad put her in the right place at the right time to become intimately acquainted with an academic area of expertise that would become both her life work and her lasting legacy.

In the late nineteenth century, Europe was the epicenter of the emerging scholarly subfield of sexology—what Davis would later call "the scientific study of sex." In the 1880s and 1890s—while Davis was first studying and then teaching natural sciences, running a social settlement, collaborating with progressive sociologists, and studying the new social sciences—European scholars established sexuality as a legitimate field of scientific inquiry.

Not all sexologists celebrated or even accepted people who might now identify as queer but then called—variously, and with different levels of scorn, pity, and empathy—"hermaphrodites," "inverts," "urnings," or "intermediaries." But they established the legitimacy of the study of sex, including the study of sexual diversity, with profound implications for future generations—and for one female scientist.

Medical men—and they were all men, most of them only interested in studying men, and many of them profoundly misogynistic—were at the forefront of this field. Among these, the German-born Richard von Krafft-Ebing, who relocated to Austria in 1885, led the way. His monumental study, *Psychopathia Sexualis* ("Sexual Psychopathy"), first published in 1886, established his reputation as the world's first sexologist. (The book was translated and reprinted frequently; the seventh edition appeared in 1893, the same year that Davis welcomed many European visitors to her model home at the World's Fair.) Krafft-Ebing's work stigmatized sexual diversity and gender variance at the same time that it documented a wide range of sexual practices. Nonetheless, many people who might now define themselves as LGBTIQ+ eagerly read his work, seeking validation for their own experiences.[108]

Decades later, Davis—who might well have met Krafft-Ebing during her time in Austria—would cite his writings extensively in her study of American women's same-sex relationships. The fact that she read his work in the original German, rather than in translation, suggests that she may have become familiar with his writing at the same time that she described life as "one long German lesson."[109]

While Krafft-Ebing characterized same-sex desire as a form of sexual psychopathy, other European sexologists not only investigated sexual variation but also promoted civil rights. One such scholar was Berlin physician Magnus Hirschfeld, destined to become Europe's leading advocate for gender-affirming treatment and legal protections for transgender and gender-nonconforming Germans. In 1897—just a year before Davis crossed the Atlantic—Hirschfeld founded the Scientific Humanitarian Committee. The committee promoted *Sexualwissenschaft*, or the interdisciplinary study of sexuality, through the publication of the *Jahrbuch fur sexuelle Swischenstufen* (Yearbook for Intermediate Sexual Types). In addition, as reflected in its motto, "*Per scientiam ad justitiam*" (Through science to justice) the committee was committed to advocating for queer rights. Although Hirschfeld would not publish his most significant theories on "sexual intermediaries"—people who transgressed the gender binary, either by changing gender or by combining traits considered "masculine" and "feminine"—until the 1900s, he republished all the writings of Karl Heinrich Ulrichs, the (in)famous "Urning" who coined nonjudgmental terms to describe sexual diversity and "outed" German public figures, in 1898, the year that Davis arrived in Europe.[110]

Since Hirschfeld attended the World's Fair in Chicago in 1893, it is tempting to think that the two might have connected (or reconnected) during Davis's lengthy stay in Berlin. Unfortunately, the destruction of most of Hirschfeld's correspondence, as well as his library, by Nazis in 1933 makes it impossible to confirm this theory—although by the time she published *Factors*, Davis was intimately familiar with Hirschfeld's writings, citing, among other things, his 1899 article on "The Objective Diagnosis of Homosexuality," published during her time in Europe.[111]

It is also difficult to document Davis's association with British sexologist Havelock Ellis in the 1890s, although by the 1930s, they would clearly be familiar with one another's work. Ellis published his first work on sexology with Oxford-educated literary critic and cultural historian John Addington Symonds, who explored the celebration of male homosexuality in ancient Greece—and introduced the word "homosexual" into the English lexicon—in an 1873 study, *A Problem in Greek Ethics*. (One wonders if Davis, who studied classics at Rochester's Free Academy in the 1870s, was familiar with this work!)[112]

Subsequently, Symonds collaborated with Ellis on a sympathetic study of same-sex love, *Sexual Inversion*, possibly as a response to Berlin-based physician Albert Moll's critical discussion of the subject, published in German with a foreword by Krafft-Ebing in 1891 as *Die Contrare Sexualempfindung* (The Contrary Sexual Instinct). The same work appeared in French as *Les Perversions de L'instinct Genital: Etude sur L'inversion Sexuelle* (Perversions of the Genital Instinct: Study of Sexual Inversion) in 1893—the year that Davis was working at the World's Fair. (Davis would cite a later version of Moll's work in her own scholarship, although she dedicated more attention to other, more sympathetic, sexologists.)[113]

While Symonds died before the book was published, and his executors blocked the English-language version of *Sexual Inversion*, Ellis took advantage of the outcome of the Heinze controversy, which determined that works with literary or scientific merit could not be censored, to publish a German-language version, *Das Kontrare Geschlechtsgefuhl* (variously translated as "The Contrary Sexual Sentiment," "The Contradictory Sentiment of Gender," or "The Contrary Sexual Feeling") in 1896.[114]

While there is no solid evidence that Davis read this work at the time, she probably would have found Ellis's scholarship especially compelling because he—unlike many of his male colleagues—did not overlook women. Over the next four decades, Ellis would publish widely on many aspects of human sexuality. Unlike most male sexologists, he devoted significant attention to female sexuality, addressing topics ranging from autoeroticism (masturbation) to sexual periodicity (fluctuations in sexual desire and behavior related to the menstrual cycle)—both topics that Davis would take up in her own study of women's sexuality thirty years later.[115]

If Davis would have been attracted by Ellis's inclusive scholarship, he would have been interested in her intellectual development. Ellis was a generous interlocutor as well as a prolific author. In addition, unlike many of his contemporaries, he took women seriously as scholars as well as subjects. His correspondence includes a lengthy exchange with an American expatriate researcher, Alice Withrow Field. Ellis not only encouraged Field to publish her observations on women's status and social welfare in Russia but also offered practical tips on how to do so. He also invited her to visit him at his home to discuss their shared interests, which included sexuality, gender, contraception, and eugenics. Finally, he shared advance copies of his books with her and enthusiastically praised her publications. It seems likely that Ellis may have had a similar relationship with Davis, although none of the cataloged collections of his extensive writings include references to her.[116]

It seems especially likely that Ellis and Davis were acquainted because of their shared interest in the subject of lesbianism, which he addressed in *Sexual Inversion*. Like many commentators then and since, Ellis conflated same-sex desire and gender nonconformity, assuming that women who desired women must be "mannish" and that men who desired men had to be effeminate. In this formulation, an invert was a person whose tastes were those of the other sex but whose desires were for a person of the same sex. Based on a small sample of case studies (including his own wife), Ellis theorized that inversion could be either innate ("born that way") or acquired ("became that way").[117]

Contemporary readers found these ideas empowering and reassuring. One of the subjects in Davis's study, a bookkeeper who found even "the thought of sex relations with men . . . very repugnant" but whose emotional relationships and sexual experiences with women "have given happiness as long as they lasted," almost certainly read Ellis. Davis's case study explains that the bookkeeper, who read every book she could find on the subject of "sexual inversion" and discussed them with "people who have had similar experiences," described herself as a "congenital invert."[118]

Davis, whose own life closely resembled that of many of her study subjects, may well have read Ellis's work before or during her European sojourn, although she cited a 1902 American edition in *Factors*. While Davis, an indefatigable researcher, referenced a wide range of scholarship—including obscure authors who published only in German—she gave Ellis pride of place, citing his *Sexual Inversion* first in her lengthy discussion of scholarship on "Homosexuality."[119] Ellis would return the favor by endorsing *Factors* and citing Davis's magnum opus in his later publications.[120]

Whether or not Davis met luminaries like Richard von Krafft-Ebing, Magnus Hirschfeld, or Havelock Ellis during her time in Europe, the work of these social scientists would profoundly influence her own future scholarship. So, too, would the contemporary writings of natural scientists.

At the same time that sexologists pondered the varieties of sexual desire and gender identity, natural scientists also probed the causes of human variation. These men—and they were still all men!—pioneered the fields that would become known as genetics (the study of how traits are passed down from one generation to the next through genes) and endocrinology (the study of how chemical messengers called hormones—secreted in the endocrine system, a series of glands located in the brain, pancreas, adrenals, and ovaries and testes—produce so-called secondary sex characteristics such as breasts and body hair, regulate essential bodily tasks such as proper digestion, and regulate the body's reaction to stress, such as the "fight-or-flight" response). Some—but by no means all—of these scientists also disrupted the prevailing intellectual and moral binary of "good/natural" versus "evil/unnatural" by demonstrating that sex, gender, and sexuality all displayed "natural" variation.[121]

In the process, they also laid the groundwork for distinctions between sex (a "biological" category that could be defined in several ways: by reproductive capacity, or the ability to fertilize or produce an egg; by body shape, such as the hip-to-waist ratio; by genetic composition, such as the chromosomal patterns XX, XY, XXY; or by hormones, such as estrogen and testosterone); gender (the social significance of sex, or the appearance, behavior, and roles associated with "biological" sex); and sexuality (individuals' sexual desires, experiences, and/or identities).[122]

From childhood, Davis, who helped her mother tend extensive gardens, was intrigued by "the wonderful work of [American botanist Luther] Burbank with plants" as well as "the breeding of fine animals, horses, chickens, and the like," an interest she attributed to her "farmer ancestors." As a college student, Davis often "compared chemical compounds to people," wondering what accounted for marked differences in appearance, personality, and interests even within families. Finally, as her late-in-life interest in "hunting ancestors" indicated, she was endlessly fascinated by "the subject of heredity," wondering which of her "genes" accounted for her own life course. Thus, it seems safe to assume that she would have followed these developments closely.[123]

Davis was born just a year after British naturalist Charles Darwin shared his theory of natural selection, or "survival of the fittest," in his 1859 book *On the Origin of Species*. Darwin's scholarship inspired other scientists to search for answers about natural variations. For instance, Austrian monk Gregor Johann Mendel, who conducted experiments with pea plants in the 1850s and 1860s, is sometimes known as the "Father of Genetics," although it took decades—and the work of scientists in Germany, Holland, and England—for the term to develop.[124]

Meanwhile, British physiologists Ernest Starling and William Bayliss joined forces at University College in London in 1899, just as Davis was wrapping up her European studies. Davis returned to the United States before the pair's research into pancreatic secretions demonstrated the existence of what Starling would name "hormones" in 1905. In addition to establishing a new field of study, endocrinology, Starling and Bayliss paved the way for a new scientific understanding of how bodily secretions defined biological sex—with profound implications for both pioneering sexologists and transgender patients.[125]

Despite Hirschfeld's optimistic motto, "through science to justice," scientific discoveries would prove to be a double-edged sword for social justice. In the 1880s, British polymath Francis Galton built upon his cousin Charles Darwin's work on evolution by establishing the field of eugenics, advocating "improving stock" by "judicious mating"—in other words, using selective breeding to perpetuate certain traits, protect "good breeding stock," and produce desirable offspring.[126] In the decades to come, prominent eugenicists on both sides of the Atlantic would devise a variety of flawed measures, from measuring human skulls to testing "mental age," to determine who should—and who should not—reproduce. These developments would result in dire consequences for many groups of people, including ethnic minorities, people with disabilities, and LGBTIQ+ individuals. But at the same time that some scientists used new information about heredity as a weapon against "undesirable" people, others used scientific discoveries to promote queer rights. In her own lifetime, Davis would do both, initially becoming an enthusiastic advocate of eugenics, and later becoming an even more avid proponent of sexology.[127] First, though, she had to complete her degree program.

"K.B.D., Ph.D."

Back in Chicago, Davis spent one more year in the classroom before taking her final oral exams in spring 1900. She felt "rather shaky" about her oral examinations because of tensions between the political economy and sociology departments—an academic rivalry heightened by gender politics. But "after a long afternoon, the ordeal was over," and she passed with honors. Despite her "bedraggled appearance" afterward—necktie askew, collar wilted, and her cap over one ear—she and her fellow "Fosterites" celebrated at Foster Hall with an enormous cake with "K.B.D., Ph.D." emblazoned on it in icing. At age forty, Davis had finally achieved the doctorate she would proudly include on all of her publications and correspondence for the rest of her life.[128]

Three years later, family friend May Bragdon revealed how important Davis's degree was to her when she engaged in a playful debate with her siblings—Charlotte, Hamilton, and Helen—about a banner Bragdon constructed of leaves to welcome Davis and her mother back to their vacation home in the Georgian Bay. Bragdon's composition read, "Welcome Mother & Kate." She explained, "The family criticised [*sic*] it freely . . . and decided it should be 'Katherine' [*sic*] instead of 'Kate,' but I refused (It was lovely as it was) but offered to add 'Ph.D.'—which they scorned." Ultimately, however, Kate was "delighted" with the welcome; "She never missed the 'Ph.D.,'" commented Bragdon with satisfaction. Indeed, it was while on vacation with her family and friends, more than any other time, that Davis let down her guard and enjoyed "quite jolly" good times. The cumbersome clothing of the era notwithstanding, Davis and her friends and family hiked, fished, and sailed, even braving "Hamilton's unfinished bridge" to explore the entire area.[129]

Davis's doctoral studies, focused as they were on Czech-speaking workers, bore little resemblance to her later studies on women's sexual-

Katharine Davis was ambitious and driven, and much of her life was defined by her work. But she had a playful side, too, as revealed in this photo taken by family friend May Bragdon. Davis and her friends and family relished their time at the family's vacation home in Canada's Georgian Bay, where they hiked, fished, and sailed and generally had a "quite jolly" time. "Hamilton's bridge," August 4, 1903, May Bragdon Diaries, Rare Books, Special Collections, and Preservation, University of Rochester River Campus Libraries.

ity. However, her thesis was unusual in at least one important way: unlike most of her counterparts, Davis recognized that women, as well as men, were an important part of the labor force. Moreover, Davis's graduate studies not only imbued her with skills in statistical analysis but also with the confidence to challenge received wisdom.[130]

Even before completing her PhD, Davis authored an article in the leading academic journal in her field critiquing the Austrian head statistician's analysis of workers' wages. Specifically, she called attention to "a certain carelessness in his handling of statistics" because he failed to distinguish between wages with board and wages without board. Davis concluded, "This illustrates the dangerous character of statistics as a basis for economic deduction, unless one takes some pains to see that the facts match the figures." For the rest of her professional career, Davis would attempt to match facts and figures.[131]

For Davis, as for most other women of her generation, a PhD did not lead to a faculty appointment. Instead, Davis once again relied on her connections with women reformers to obtain a professional position, this time as the superintendent of New York's newest female reformatory. Although gender discrimination barred Davis from a career in academia, her high-profile work at the World's Fair, her practical experiences at the settlement house, and her top-notch training in the social sciences all prepared her to take full advantage of new opportunities for "new women" in turn-of-the-century America as "a scientific reformer," as one journalist described her. Perhaps most importantly for her professional trajectory, Davis's specialization in statistical analysis would serve her well in her future studies of female sexuality.

3

"God Bless Miss Davis!"

In 1914, the *American Magazine* ran an unusual feature: "an amazing autobiography" by a former inmate of New York State's Reformatory for Women at Bedford Hills. In this article, entitled "Taming My Rebel Soul," a self-proclaimed "bad girl" offered her account of her confinement at the reformatory, her initially fraught relationship with Superintendent Katharine Bement Davis, her leadership of the "Terrible Ten" in a rebellion against reformatory rules, and, finally, her complete reform thanks to Superintendent Davis's patience and persistence.[1]

The anonymous author of the piece initially scoffed at the notion of reform. As the daughter of a notorious gambler and the niece of a murderous moonshiner, she came from "a stock which held the law in disregard." True to her heritage, she explained, she displayed an "adventuresome disposition" that led her to engage in "any sort of mischief to break the monotony" of daily life, culminating in "a perfect frenzy of rebellion" that led to a hasty marriage to a career criminal and her own collusion with a gang of thieves and tricksters. When a judge sentenced her to a three-year indeterminate sentence at Bedford, the twenty-one-year-old vowed to emerge from the institution even more wicked than she entered it. "Reform—rats!" read a caption beneath an illustration of the fashionable flapper juxtaposed with the straitlaced superintendent.[2]

Superintendent Davis, as was her wont, invited the new arrival for a personal interview. The newest reformatory resident was determined not to be impressed. Describing Davis as "a very ordinary and commonplace little woman," she dismissed her as "not at all formidable or awe-inspiring." Davis's mild blue gaze and inquiring head tilt, rather than disarming her guest, convinced her that she could lie with impunity, and she responded to her intake interview with "a most picturesque string of lies." When Davis carefully recorded her replies in a notebook, she was satisfied that she had "put one over" on the superintendent.[3]

Whether Davis was fooled or not, she followed standard procedure by classifying the new arrival and assigning her housing accordingly. Either despite or because of her mendacious replies in her interview, she was assigned the "middle" grade, meaning that she was placed in a single room in the Reception Hall, originally designed as a prison but now mostly converted into single rooms. While pleasant enough, rooms in the former prison building lacked the homelike atmosphere of the reformatory's two-story "cottages," reserved for "first" grade girls. But they were far superior to the block of disciplinary cells, complete with barred doors and windows, reserved for "the institution's incorrigibles."[4]

All too soon, a disagreement with a matron won the rebellious newcomer a place in the disciplinary cell block, commonly known as "The Prison." The newcomer's rebellious spirit was inflamed, rather than quelled, by a diet of bread and water, the standard punishment for troublemakers. She and her compatriots, dubbing themselves the "Terrible Ten," initiated "a reign of terror such as Bedford had never known." Sleeping during the daytime, they spent the nights screaming, howling, and shaking the barred gates to their cells. The resulting "pandemonium" not only kept the other residents of the building awake but could be heard at Bedford Station, a mile and a half distant. For nine nights, the "hideous bedlam" continued. Throughout, Superintendent Davis served the inmates their meals of bread and water, entirely disregarding the "veritable volley of abuse" that came her way. Against her will, the ringleader felt "a twinge of compassion" for her.[5]

On the tenth night, the Terrible Ten spontaneously suspended their campaign and "decorously retired like human beings instead of hyenas." The next morning, to their surprise, the superintendent delivered a full breakfast, thanked them for their good behavior, and offered them the privilege of outdoor work. For the rebel band's ringleader, working in the garden was a genuinely life-changing experience. She "gloried" in the "earthly paradise" of Bedford's vegetable gardens. Much to her own surprise, she soon won a promotion to a higher grade for good conduct, earning a spot in one of the cottages, where she enjoyed decorating her private bedroom, eating well-prepared meals in the dining room, and reading and playing games in the recreation room. "Wondrous to relate," she shamefacedly admitted, "I had come to the conclusion that being bad didn't pay!"[6]

As a "cottage girl," the former "bad girl" now enjoyed the privilege of participating in the cultural activities that Superintendent Davis had instituted at the reformatory. When Davis offered her the opportunity to write, direct, and star in the annual Christmas play, she jumped at the chance. The resulting performance was a smash hit; the budding playwright was especially pleased that her own mother traveled thousands of miles to be in the audience. After congratulating her on the play's success, however, Davis informed her that in addition to the charge on which she had been incarcerated, nine other indictments were still pending.[7]

Superintendent Davis offered the Bedford inmate a unique opportunity. To prevent another arrest and sentence, Davis promised to parole her out of state, in her mother's custody, if only the former ringleader could maintain a perfect record for the next six months. "I do this because I have confidence in you," the older woman explained. With these words branded on her conscience, "the worst girl in the place" became a model citizen. At the end of that time—after two and a half years at Bedford—as she departed the reformatory to begin her new life, she found herself exclaiming, "God bless Miss Davis!"[8]

For Davis—who read the article prior to its publication and described it as "practically photographic in its accuracy"—the remarkable reformation of this "rebel soul" was a compelling validation of her entire program at Bedford Reformatory. Davis especially called attention to this "beautiful illustration" of the importance of the indeterminate sentence, which allowed Davis to keep inmates for up to three years and thereby gave her time to develop a positive relationship with even the most recalcitrant offenders. But the account also highlighted several of Davis's other innovations at Bedford, including the adoption of the "cottage system," the classification of inmates, the importance of outdoor labor, and the value of cultural opportunities.[9]

Because the "rebel soul" was white, her account did not highlight one of Davis's most significant policies: racial integration. However, the author's emphasis on her "stock" reflected a relatively new program at Bedford: the psychological testing and mental evaluation of inmates. By the time this account was published, Davis's frustration with incorrigible inmates and repeat offenders had led her to adopt eugenicist explanations for their behavior, including blaming faulty heredity for criminal behavior. Indeed, by the time subscribers to the *American Magazine* read this story, Davis had moved on from Bedford Reformatory to a new position at the helm of New York City's corrections system. That post, however, built upon Davis's remarkable record as the inaugural superintendent of New York State's newest experiment in penal reform.

"Good Will to Woman"

When Katharine Bement Davis arrived at Bedford Reformatory on January 1, 1901, it was not only the year that was new. It was a new century, and Davis was the new superintendent of a new institution that was, in itself, the product of new ideas about the best solutions to urban crime. Indeed, when Davis alighted from the horse-drawn wagon that carried her from Bedford's train station to the site of the reformatory, the buildings there were still under construction. Davis brought a cot, a washbowl, and a water pitcher to allow her to camp out in the unfinished Administration Building; because the heating plant was not yet operational, she carried a hot brick to bed to keep warm at night. Undaunted by these primitive conditions, Davis immediately arranged to have her piano delivered, and music quickly became a staple of reformatory life.[10]

Although it was only a two-hour train ride north of Brooklyn, Bedford Reformatory, nestled in the rolling hills that gave the nearby village of Bedford Hills its name, was a very different world from New York City, and intentionally so. New York State's newest reformatory, like similar institutions founded at the turn of the century, reflected new approaches to rehabilitating, rather than punishing, lawbreakers.

Bedford was designed for youthful female offenders, a group that feminist activists and prison reformers considered most capable of—and in need of—reform. Removed from the corrupting influences of city life while serving an indeterminate sentence of up to three years in an idyllic rural setting, the theory went, so-called wayward women had the opportunity for a fresh start. Bedford's official motto was, "Forgetting the things which are behind and reaching forth to the things which are before."[11]

Bedford fused progressive ideas about penal reform with Victorian ideals of proper womanhood. Like similar institutions founded in turn-of-the-century America, Bedford was a product of the women's prison reform movement. Beginning in the late nineteenth century, women reformers justified female leadership of separate institutions based on Victorian assumptions about elite white women's moral superiority and their commitment to uplifting their fallen sisters at the same time that they adopted progressive ideas about prison reform.[12]

Katharine Bement Davis was the perfect choice to lead Bedford Reformatory, a brainchild of the Victorian era that came of age in the Progressive Era. In many ways, Davis exemplified new womanhood and personified the progressive impulse. She was a highly educated, self-supporting, professional woman. She also had acquired expertise in the new social sciences. While her coursework in economics—and, to a lesser extent, sociology—had not emphasized the criminal justice system, her excellent study habits enabled her to easily pass the civil service examination required to assume the position of superintendent. Indeed, her entire preparation for the exam consisted of reading completed on the train ride from Chicago to Albany, just a week before completing the requirements for her PhD at the University of Chicago. "Of course she passed," commented one acquaintance. "Given a week and Miss Davis would be ready for almost any undertaking."[13]

Davis's lack of experience in the prison system was an advantage, in that it practically guaranteed that she would adopt an innovative approach to her work. In her memoirs, Davis wrote that she accepted the appointment on the understanding that she was an educator first and foremost. Before taking the job, the former schoolteacher announced, "My only interest in accepting the superintendency is my desire to make an educational institution of it. I have no desire to be the warden of a prison." Drawing on her own college experience, the Vassar alumna explained that her goal was to make Bedford "to its inmates what an ideal college is to a college student, a stepping stone towards a happier and more useful life."[14]

Davis was a new woman committed to making Bedford Reformatory a shining example of penal reform in the Progressive Era. But as a daughter of the Victorian era, she also embraced traditional ideas about ideal womanhood and women's sexuality. Throughout her time at Bedford—and beyond—Davis upheld Victorian ideals of sexual behavior. Rejecting the sexual double standard that condemned women's sexual activity outside of marriage but excused men's moral lapses, Davis consistently called for a single sexual standard, which she defined as "the so-called woman's standard, imposing chastity and continence outside of the marriage relation on both men and women."[15]

While Davis condemned the sexual double standard, her charges found themselves at Bedford because of it. Bedford's inmates—girls and women between the ages of sixteen and thirty—were confined for a variety of reasons, ranging from minor offenses to serious crimes. But according to a study Davis conducted of women sent to Bedford from New York City courts between 1901 and 1913, while only a minority (40 percent) had been arrested as "common prostitutes," the vast majority (nearly 70 percent) had been arrested for "other offenses" against the public order, such as public intoxication or disorderly conduct. While not technically crimes, these behaviors violated both city ordinances regulating social order and prevailing standards of feminine propriety. Davis considered such conduct offenses to be "directly related to prostitution."[16] Indeed, Davis unequivocally asserted that "the fundamental fact" about "women delinquents" was that they were "women who lead sexually immoral lives."[17]

Davis's emphasis on policing women's sexuality reflected a Progressive Era panic about prostitution. At the turn of the century, when Davis took charge at Bedford, reformers in major cities throughout the nation—including New York—campaigned to shut down so-called red light districts and supported efforts to crack down on street prostitution. Meanwhile, new federal laws targeted sex trafficking, then known as "white slavery." While many feminist activists hoped to improve women's lives by eradicating the sex trade, the resulting policies often led, instead, to increased policing of women's sexuality. Meanwhile, men's sexual behavior was neither stigmatized nor criminalized. In short, while activists like Davis frequently condemned the sexual double standard, in practice, their efforts all too often reinforced it.[18]

Davis's mission at Bedford, therefore, was to use modern methods to promote Victorian morality. She undertook this challenging task with her characteristic zeal. With "good will to woman" and "an apparently exhaustless source of cheerful energy," as journalist Ida Tarbell put it, Davis aimed to make Bedford Reformatory "as hopeful an institution as there is in this country."[19]

"Right Living"

As a brand-new institution, Bedford was the ideal setting for Davis's grand experiment in transforming "moral weaklings" into moral women. Arriving at the unfinished campus only months before admitting the first inmate, Davis immediately set about transforming the physical environment. Under her guidance, Bedford's bucolic campus soon became the ideal setting for moral reform. Featuring handsome red-brick buildings, accessed by winding pathways and arranged attractively around well-kept lawns, Bedford's extensive grounds also encompassed pastures, a stream and pond, vegetable gardens, and pens and outbuildings for livestock, all linked by concrete walkways and stairways poured by the inmates, who also tended the gardens and cared for the animals.[20]

Assigning inmates responsibility for tending this idyllic institution was an essential aspect of Davis's program of moral reform. While using inmate labor to fulfill institutional needs was common practice at the time, Davis's decision to assign women outdoor work was highly unusual—and effective. Visitors praised the "lovely" landscape and marveled at the bloomer-clad "farmerettes" who maintained the grounds, a task that included maintaining manicured lawns, tending productive gardens, grading the hilly site, constructing outbuildings, building roads and walkways, and caring for livestock. Inmate labor allowed Davis to develop an attractive—and productive—campus at minimal cost. But more importantly, Davis regarded what one journalist dubbed "heavy work for women" as beneficial to Bedford's inmates. "The results of the out-door work are good appetite, sound sleep and improvement in general health and consequently in self-control, all of which is an important step toward moral regeneration," she declared in one annual report.[21]

In keeping with her longstanding commitment to housing reform, and consistent with emerging trends in corrections, Davis also regarded proper housing as essential to moral reform. When Davis first stepped foot on the Bedford campus, it was home to a three-story Prison Building, "a gloomy, prison-like structure" with barred windows and bleak cells; an unfinished Administration Building; a laundry room; and four individual "cottages": two-story brick buildings equipped with a kitchen, living room, dining room, and individual bedrooms to accommodate up to thirty residents. Davis promptly renamed and remodeled the Prison

As the inaugural superintendent of New York State's Reformatory for Women at Bedford Hills, a two-hour train ride north of New York City, Davis presided over a bucolic campus that was the ideal setting for moral reform. Inmates lived in comfortable red-brick "cottages" and established an "earthly paradise" by grading the hilly site, maintaining manicured lawns, tending productive gardens, constructing outbuildings, building walkways, and caring for livestock. Photograph of Outside Buildings at New York Bedford State Reformatory for Women, MSS 16A/7/23/3/63, Howard League for Penal Reform Collection, Modern Records Centre, University of Warwick. Reproduced with permission from the Howard League for Penal Reform.

Building, converting most of the cells in the new "Reception Building" into "light and airy" bedrooms. However, the focus of Davis's building program was on the individual cottages.[22]

During Davis's tenure, she supervised the construction of four additional cottages, each tailored to the needs of a particular group of inmates. Davis was especially proud of the Honors Cottage, where residents who had proved amenable to reformatory rules were allowed to practice limited self-government. Because so many of Bedford's inmates arrived while expecting, another important innovation was the establishment of a separate cottage for pregnant women, new mothers, and their infants. Davis also designated separate cottages for the use of the youngest inmates and for "return girls" (released inmates sent back to Bedford for parole violations), thereby separating first-time offenders from repeat offenders.[23]

The cottage system was the quintessential expression of penal reformers' optimistic outlook. Widely adopted in institutions for juvenile offenders, the cottage plan called for "dependent and delinquent" youth to be housed in homelike cottages rather than in prisonlike barracks. This setup was especially well suited to all-female institutions, where inmates performed all necessary domestic labor. Reformers like Davis regarded such activities as both cost-effective and gender-appropriate. Visitors and journalists alike praised the "homelike" system at Bedford, calling attention to the cottages' well-appointed common areas, featuring prints by the old masters, and to the comfortable private rooms, which inmates decorated to suit their own tastes. Under the supervision of cottage matrons, Bedford inmates imbibed Victorian morality in the process of practicing conventional femininity.[24]

At Bedford, the cottage plan also served another important purpose. Individual cottages were essential to Davis's classification system, which she considered an important prerequisite to moral reform. The typical Bedford inmate was the daughter of a working-class family beset by tragedy and poverty; fewer than half had both parents living, and surviving parents held poorly paying jobs. Prior to incarceration, the majority of inmates either had contributed to the family economy or had supported themselves. With little education or training, most worked as domestic servants or factory operatives, occupations characterized by limited job security, low pay, and long hours. While the economic circumstances and family backgrounds of Bedford's inmates were fairly consistent, the reformatory population represented significant racial and ethnic diversity. Throughout Davis's tenure as superintendent, the majority of Bedford's inmates were US-born whites, but roughly half of these were first-generation Americans. Approximately one in four inmates was an immigrant; and nearly one in five inmates was Black.[25]

The presence of African Americans set the stage for one of Davis's most important innovations. At the time, most private "houses of refuge" excluded African Americans entirely, and most public institutions were racially segregated. However, Davis, who prided herself on her abolitionist ancestry, insisted on full racial integration. At Bedford, white and Black inmates lived, ate, studied, worked, and played together. For Davis, this was a question of conscience. "I come of good New England Abolition stock," she declared, "and my theory and practice are dictated by principle." Insisting "morality is not a question of color," Davis condemned racial segregation itself as "immoral."[26]

Rather than separating inmates by race, Davis sorted them on the basis of age and background as well as her own estimation of their ability and character. (Later, she also would use intelligence testing and psychological evaluations to classify new arrivals.) All new inmates met with the superintendent both in small groups, over tea and cakes served on the best china and silverware, and individually, when Davis queried them about their background and their aspirations for the future.[27]

On the basis of this initial assessment, Davis assigned new arrivals to a "grade." Housing accommodations, classroom instruction, work assignments, and recreational opportunities all depended upon an inmate's classification. "First grade" inmates, or "cottage girls," not only had the privilege of living in comfortable cottages rather than in the former prison building but also took more advanced classes and had more recreational opportunities; for instance, only cottage girls could perform in Bedford's dramatic and musical programs.[28]

To encourage inmates to abide by the rules, Davis ran the reformatory on a reward system. She insisted that "everything should depend entirely upon the girl's response to the incentives for right living which were placed before her." Compliant inmates could earn promotion from one "grade" to the next, with corresponding improvements in housing and increases in privileges. Especially well-behaved inmates could gain admission to the Honors Cottage, where they practiced limited self-government. The ultimate reward, of course, was early release. Bedford inmates served an indeterminate sentence of up to three years, but most completed their sentence on parole. Davis believed that her system was "in accordance with the best reformatory methods" because it encouraged inmates to be on their best behavior. She was especially proud that "girls from both races" earned elected positions in the Honors College and left Bedford to become "self-respecting, upright citizens." "Right living," not race, determined inmates' place at Bedford.[29]

Davis adopted enlightened policies in response to religious diversity as well as racial diversity. In turn-of-the-century America, private organizations concerned with the welfare of children and youth were predominantly Protestant; many such organizations either excluded Catholics and Jews entirely or aggressively attempted to convert their charges. As the head of a public institution, however, Davis took a different path. Due to the predominance of immigrant and first-generation Americans, Bedford inmates demonstrated great religious diversity, with significant Catholic, Protestant, and Jewish populations. To accommodate different faiths, Bedford offered weekly services for both Catholics and Protestants, led by local priests and ministers. In the absence of a nearby synagogue, Davis enlisted Jewish women—beginning with the delightfully named Rosetta Stone—to conduct Sabbath School classes for Jewish inmates. Finally, since Bedford's budget covered only three visits per month from outside religious leaders, the Presbyterian-raised superintendent led ecumenical services once a month.[30]

"To Fit Them for Life"

At Bedford, moral improvement was not limited to religious services. Rather, Davis's plan for moral redemption relied upon a "daily regimen" that did not allow time for "sullen introspection." Each inmate would have "a half day of work and a half day of study, with plenty of outdoor exercise interspersed, and sufficient recreation to keep up her spirits."[31] Davis established a comprehensive program that included academic coursework, manual labor, cultural programming, and recreational opportunities. During the week, Bedford's inmates divided their days between classroom instruction and so-called industrial training, a catch-all term for work experience that included domestic, agricultural, and industrial labor. Davis was not alone in offering a mix of academic and industrial instruction, which by the early twentieth century was considered best practice in institutional settings. However, her emphasis on integrating these different aspects of Bedford's curriculum into a coherent whole set the reformatory apart.

As in other aspects of life at Bedford, inmates' academic studies depended upon their classification. While those in the intermediate and highest grades studied advanced subjects such as geography, history, and composition, those in the lower grades did remedial work in reading, writing, and arithmetic. However, all classroom instruction had to take inmates' generally low levels of preparation into account. The majority of Bedford's inmates had not completed grammar school (or sixth grade), and a significant proportion were illiterate.[32]

Davis adopted an innovative approach to classroom instruction that emphasized "hands-on" learning adapted to the inmates' needs. As the former schoolteacher explained, Bedford's curriculum, instead of relying on textbooks, focused on "real objects, . . . local interests, current events, etc., and all suited to the needs of this class of pupils."[33] This approach accommodated inmates' low levels of preparation, but it also reflected pedagogical innovations by renowned philosophers such as John Dewey, whom Davis may have met at the University of Chicago. Davis's methods also anticipated the theoretical perspectives of influential educators such as Maria Montessori, whose research on learning disabilities Davis may have learned about because of Montessori's work with juvenile delinquents. Both Dewey and Montessori emphasized experiential learning: learning from life. However, Davis herself indicated that she used the curricula developed at southern Black schools, such as Hampton Institute and the Tuskegee Institute, as a model. This meant that job preparation—or "learning for work"—was a key aspect of Bedford's curriculum. "Few, if any, of our pupils will ever attend school after leaving us," Davis opined. "Our effort is, then, not to train them to pass examinations nor to enter higher grades, but, so far as possible to fit them for life."[34]

Regardless of its intellectual origins and utilitarian justifications, the Bedford curriculum emphasized connections between life and lessons. For instance, what would come to be called "nature study" formed a significant component of Bedford's curriculum, allowing students to study botany and biology firsthand—and outdoors. English composition classes focused on writing letters home, while advanced mathematics classes calculated the acreage of Bedford's garden plots. As Davis explained, "An effort is being made to coordinate more closely the school and industrial work, so as to enable the pupils to see the direct connection between what they receive in the schoolroom and their daily life."[35]

Bedford's curriculum also included physical education classes. As with the emphasis on experiential learning, the focus on physical health

At Bedford Reformatory, Davis implemented modern methods of moral reform. Her innovative approach included experiential learning, outdoor work, and racial integration. For instance, after calculating the square footage to be covered, a racially mixed group of inmates constructed concrete steps on the hilly campus. Photograph of Prisoners Working Outside at New York Bedford State Reformatory for Women, MSS 16A/7/23/3/66, Howard League for Penal Reform Collection, Modern Records Centre, University of Warwick. Reproduced with permission from the Howard League for Penal Reform.

reflected progressive reformers' ideas about the deleterious effects of urban life and the beneficial effects of vigorous exercise. As a veteran of the settlement house movement, Davis was well acquainted with these theories, which regarded physical strength as a prerequisite to moral fortitude. Because so many of Bedford's inmates were in poor health, their systems weakened by drink, drugs, and disease, Davis considered the physical education program to be essential to their regeneration. At Bedford, physical education took a variety of forms, ranging from "Swedish" calisthenics to folk dancing to outdoor sports, such as basketball. In addition to movement classes and organized sports, Bedford's wellness program included courses in health and hygiene, prefiguring Davis's later commitment to public health and sex education.[36]

In addition to formal classroom instruction, all Bedford inmates devoted half of each weekday to "industrial" training. While an emphasis on vocational preparation was common in Progressive Era institutions, Davis's commitment to outdoor activities was unusual and reflected her conviction that outdoor work was a form of moral regeneration. Convinced of the value of outdoor work, Davis herself led multiple work projects.[37]

To encourage inmates to undertake heavy physical labor, Davis adopted the "Tom Sawyer" method of doing it first and making it fun. When confronted by a lack of funds to construct walkways between Bedford's buildings, for instance, she "sallied forth in quest of a contractor . . . and learned from him how to mix concrete." After "seeing their Superintendent having such a fine time mixing mud pies on such a grand scale," Davis's memoirs explained, the inmates "begged to help."[38]

Because there were never enough staff to supervise outdoor work, however, most inmates' "industrial" work was domestic work, such as cooking, laundry, sewing, knitting, and rug making. As at similar institutions, inmates produced most of the items used in institutional life. Bedford records include long lists of the items that inmates sewed, including sheets, pillowcases, nightgowns, dresses, and even "sanitary napkins"![39]

As in other areas, hands-on learning reinforced classroom instruction. After the completion of a new classroom building in 1910, Bedford offered coursework in "domestic science" as well as household work assignments. This reflected practical considerations as well as Davis's own keen interest in domestic science. Because many parolees worked as domestic servants or assisted their families with household tasks, Davis averred, "There is no branch of training which we can give to our women which positively benefits so large a number as training in domestic service and home-making."[40]

Davis was keenly aware, as she put it, that "our success as a reformatory institution will depend in large measure on our ability to so train our inmates as to enable them to earn an honest livelihood when they leave us." While Davis's advocacy for domestic science reflected her own interests, she recognized that not every woman was suited, "by nature or taste," to domestic service, and she was always on the lookout for ways to add variety to Bedford's industrial program. She hoped that working in the reformatory's state-of-the-art steam laundry and using knitting machines to mass-produce stockings would prepare Bedford inmates for industrial jobs, for instance. She also offered "special employment" and specialized training in typing and nursing to select inmates.[41]

Despite their varied work experience at Bedford, however, the vast majority of Bedford's parolees were placed in domestic service. With some chagrin, Davis noted in one annual report that "it is far easier to place a woman in service when she goes out on parole than to find any other occupation for her." Demand for domestic servants from Bedford was so high that Davis kept a waiting list, but due to a discriminatory job market, "it has been extremely difficult to find openings in other occupations, no matter how competent we may believe the girl to be."[42]

From "Wayward Women" to "Wholesome Women"

Bedford's classroom instruction and industrial training were generally consistent with those provided at other turn-of-the-century institutions, although Davis's emphasis on vigorous outdoor activities and her enthusiasm for varied occupational training set Bedford apart. Less common, however, were Bedford's extensive cultural programming and abundant recreational opportunities. However, for Davis, these enrichment activities were essential to "enlightened and effective treatment" of female offenders. Only by providing recreational and cultural opportunities as well as coursework and job training, she believed, could she transform so-called wayward women into what she called "healthier, more wholesome, and more efficient women."[43]

At Bedford, weekdays were devoted to academic and industrial subjects. However, in the evenings, on weekends, and for holidays, Bedford's inmates—at least those in the advanced "grades"—could attend a variety of educational and entertaining activities, such as illustrated lectures and classical concerts. Bedford hosted an impressive variety of visiting lecturers, including Vassar College astronomy professor Mary Whitney, British suffragist Sylvia Pankhurst, and African American sociologist W. E. B. Du Bois. (While there is no record of inmates' responses to the lectures on astronomy and African Americans, Davis told one fellow suffragist that with only one exception, Bedford's population opposed women's voting as "*unladylike*"!)[44]

In addition, Bedford inmates enjoyed a variety of recreational activities. Outdoor pursuits included picnics and berry-picking excursions, while indoor recreation included birthday parties and social dances. Davis, an outdoors enthusiast herself, argued that such activities provided not only "immediate pleasure" and "pleasant memories" but also moral benefits. "We believe it to be an important part of our duty to teach them how to amuse themselves in a harmless way—so far as possible to have some resources within themselves," she insisted.[45]

While official reports emphasized organized activities and structured schedules, life at Bedford also included unstructured time and informal recreation. Davis loved both animals and children, and Bedford had plenty of both. During her time at Bedford, Davis kept three dogs, a St. Bernard named Duke (short for "The Duke of Bedford"), "a lively little dog" named Joker, and a German Shepherd called "Attila the Hun." Reformatory residents were especially fond of Duke, who roamed the campus at will, sometimes showing up in photographs alongside work crews constructing concrete pathways and stairways.[46]

Davis also had cats—lots of cats. A grainy photo of Davis cuddling a kitten accompanying an article about her time at Vassar suggests that she adored cats even as a college student. She "acquired" the reformatory's first cat soon after arriving at Bedford; after this first cat gave birth to a litter in Davis's closet, the staff named her "Mother."[47]

According to Davis's memoirs, "'Mother' was a cat of character as well as a friendly animal." On one occasion, when Davis stood to deliver her monthly sermon, "up walked 'Mother' and sat on the chair Dr. Davis had just vacated." The inmates watched in rapt attention as the

Katharine Bement Davis loved animals. At Bedford Reformatory, in addition to stock animals—all beloved and christened with clever names by Davis's all-female staff—there were generations of dogs and cats. The first dog was a St. Bernard dubbed the "Duke of Bedford," known as Duke. In her memoirs, Davis humorously recalled that when the actual Duchess of Bedford joined the throng of European visitors to the celebrated reformatory, "a conspiracy was formed to keep the dog, Duke, out of the picture." Under ordinary circumstances, however, Duke roamed the campus at will. Photograph of Prisoners Working Outside at New York Bedford State Reformatory for Women, MSS 16A/7/23/3/66, Howard League for Penal Reform Collection, Modern Records Centre, University of Warwick. Reproduced with permission from the Howard League for Penal Reform.

attention-seeking feline took center stage: "From there she jumped to the reading desk. Thus far, the girls comported themselves with marvelous dignity, and barely smiled. The cat looked solemnly about. Then turned and looking up into Dr. Davis' face yawned slowly, broadly. A spontaneous burst of laughter followed this incident. Dr. Davis unceremoniously picked up kitty and handed her to one of the girls and the services went on."[48]

In addition to dogs and cats, Bedford had stock animals, which also became beloved pets. Bedford staffer Mary Farley (a Rochester friend Davis hand-picked to serve as the reformatory's steward), maintaining that "one pair of serious-minded work horses" were "Calvinists in disposition," named them John Calvin and John Knox. The pigs, "originally installed as an economy" since they "disposed of the garbage, during the year, and were eaten at Thanksgiving," also acquired names, all beginning with the letter P. "There were Pansy, Penelope, Palinurus and Phrixos," one account explained, until "the 'P's' gave out at last and another naming system had to be evolved."[49]

Finally, there were horses and donkeys to draw the cart that transported both inmates and staff to and from the reformatory. In 1910, when Davis's sister-in-law, Lillian, died after an extended battle with cancer, her three-year-old daughter, named Frances after her grandmother, came to Bedford to stay with Davis for several months. Young

Katharine Bement Davis adored children. As a girl, she dreamed of having six—three girls and three boys. Although she never became a biological mother, she cared for "other people's children" throughout her life. At Bedford Reformatory, this included the many children born to inmates. Davis also was a committed caregiver to the daughter of her brother Frank, named Frances for their mother, after Frank's wife, Lillian, died in 1910. Young Frances, shown here on the reformatory's donkey-drawn cart, remained a frequent visitor to Bedford throughout the rest of Davis's time there. Courtesy Helen Garber and John Pepper.

Frances remained a frequent visitor to Bedford until her father, Frank, remarried in fall 1913; a photo taken during one of her visits shows her proudly driving the donkey-drawn cart.[50]

Little Frances was by no means the only child at Bedford. So many inmates arrived at the reformatory pregnant that Davis constructed a cottage especially for new mothers and their children, and "the babies in the nursery proved a source of great delight to Dr. Davis." Davis also was extremely fond of "Little Arthur Shortell," the son of two of the original reformatory staff members. She told many stories about him; in one of them, having offered to put him to bed, the Protestant Davis found herself stymied during evening prayers with the Catholic child. She led him in the Lord's Prayer easily enough, but when it came time for the "Hail Mary," Davis, who had not yet memorized the Catholic prayer, sighed, "I guess we will have to stop here, Arthur." To her amusement, "The next morning he said to his mother, 'Isn't it queer, mother, that Miss Davis wasn't taught her prayers when she was a little girl?'"[51]

Davis was better prepared to lead the reformatory's music and drama programs. Given her musical background, it is not surprising that Davis herself initially taught music at the reformatory, although she soon expanded the offerings by hiring a regular music teacher. She opined, "The disciplinary as well as the cultural value of concerted work in music is great when properly used and we cannot afford to overlook this important aid to our efforts in developing stunted lives." Interested inmates could further indulge their musical tastes by joining musical groups, such as the Bedford Glee Club. Inspired by a visit from the Hampton Institute Quartette in 1906, Black inmates formed their own "Plantation Singers" group, which specialized in spirituals.[52]

Amateur theatricals, which had always been important to Davis, were another staple of entertainment at Bedford. Both the Glee Club and the Dramatic Club produced a variety of entertainments, ranging from classic plays by William Shakespeare to popular musicals by Gilbert and Sullivan. In addition, inmates wrote and produced their own original work. On special occasions, such as Christmas Day and Independence Day, Bedford players put on public performances for visiting dignitaries and family members, winning praise not only for their acting skills but also for their ability to construct elaborate costumes and build stage sets.[53]

While Davis encouraged inmates to assume responsibility for all elements of producing dramatic productions, she could not resist joining in the fun. According to one account, when the Bedford players put on *The Mikado*, in addition to coaching the players, "as usual, Miss Davis played nearly as many parts as the versatile Poo-Bah," leading the orchestra (which consisted of reformatory staff), directing the chorus, handling the props, prompting the actors, and welcoming the guests.[54]

As a drama aficionado, Davis was "deeply interested in motion pictures," which she declared she liked "very much" as a source of both entertainment and education. In a profile for *Moving Picture World*, she explained that movies worked "wonderfully well" at Bedford, where she had screened a set of five films, each highlighting a different subject. While Davis approved of inmates' "enthusiasm" for learning about biology, geography, history, and literature through the new medium of film, she acknowledged that it was the humorous sketches featuring comic actor John Bunny that elicited "untold delight." "My girls at Bedford are very fond of Bunny," she explained. "He is always funny and gets from them many a shriek of unrestrained laughter." Indeed, Davis used her "screenic repertoire" to encourage good behavior by reserving permission to attend for those with good weekly records; so popular was the film program, she added, that "the weekly audience increases all the time."[55]

While Davis was an enthusiastic advocate for motion pictures, she held live theater in still higher regard. For Davis, participation in amateur theatricals—which required actors to attend rehearsals regularly and the entire cast to work together toward a common aim—was not just good clean fun but also a form of moral and mental training. (She likely regarded the team building inherent in such activities as especially important for a group she described as "anti-social" and "individualistic in the extreme.") Thus, she praised Bedford's theatrical productions for the "discipline" they provided. Journalist Ida Tarbell, who visited the reformatory in 1912, concurred, celebrating the "wholesome influence" of semiannual dramatic performances.[56]

In addition to fostering discipline and rewarding dedication, plays often conveyed moral messages. In 1914, the reformatory hosted a special performance of an original play, "Ourselves," set at "a reform home for girls" reportedly modeled on Bedford Reformatory. Offering an intriguing combination of Victorian moralizing and vintage slang, the play apparently accurately reflected Bedford culture, as those in attendance alternately cheered and cried as they recognized details of their daily life.[57]

"Ourselves" traces the tale of "Molly," initially led astray by an unscrupulous married man, but ultimately turned away from a life of prostitution thanks to the guidance of "Miss Barrington," an outspoken critic of the sexual double standard. Miss Barrington's views were likely based on those held by Davis. The superintendent, who viewed the play with evident enjoyment, especially appreciated its message about "men and morals." So did the inmates in the audience. At one point in the play, "Miss Barrington" demands to know the point of prosecuting victimized women rather than punishing predatory men, pronouncing, "Once we take to locking up men—we'll get somewhere, and never before." The Bedford audience broke into "spontaneous applause." According to one account of the play, this portion of the script reflected an actual conversation between a former prostitute and Bedford's superintendent. When the reformatory inmate demanded to know why she was "any worse than those men," Davis responded with a resounding repudiation of the sexual double standard: "You are not. It is only the way people feel."[58]

The "Double Standard"

At the same time that she supervised the moral reform of wayward women, Davis denounced the sexual double standard in public speeches as well as private conversations. In 1910, she offered a trenchant critique of the "double code of moral laws" that consigned so many women to the reformatory. "The cause of the crimes committed by the great majority of women," she asserted, "is the fact that there is one set of morals for men and an entirely different standard for women." Indeed, she added, among Bedford's inmates, "there are few who are not the victims, primarily or solely, of this double standard." She continued, "Because of it men escape unscathed with the complete tolerance, if not the approval of society, while women go to a ruin from which they can rarely be reclaimed." Tongue in cheek, Davis proposed that "if it is impossible for men to live by standards which civilization requires of its women, then let us establish an open system of polygamy."[59]

Davis's sarcasm was strategic. While taking direct aim at men's sexual misbehavior, she often used humor to remove the sting of her sharp criticism. For instance, in 1913, when questioned about her views on "segregation of vice" (so-called red-light districts), she quipped, "I would be willing to have a segregated district in New York if there was a fence around it and a gate through which every man would have to pass and register."[60]

More seriously, Davis complained that "man-made" laws governing the sex trade were "not equal, nor equally enforced." Her experiences at Bedford demonstrated "the unequal treatment of men and women." For instance, many Bedford inmates ended up at the reformatory after arrests resulting from the enforcement of the tenement laws, which subjected anybody staying at a residence "used for immoral purposes" to arrest, even if they did not themselves exchange sex for money. The law required little evidence for conviction; moreover, authorities applied it unevenly. Davis offered an example in which police burst into an apartment at noon to find four young women—one a "very young girl" on parole from Bedford—and four young men in residence. All four women ended up in prison, while "the four young men were merely shooed into the street." As Davis pointed out, "The young men were breaking the law as well as the young women, but no attempt was made to punish them." She concluded, "We have been looking at these things all through the ages from the men's point of view"; as a result, "the women have paid the price."[61]

"Sexual Offenses"

Notwithstanding Davis's staunch support of a single standard of sexual ethics and her often sarcastic commentary about men's sexual peccadilloes, during her time at Bedford, she devoted far more attention to women's weakness than to men's malfeasance. Convinced that immorality was the cause of both initial commitments and subsequent infractions, she selectively highlighted information gathered for her 1913 study of women confined to Bedford Reformatory. Even though far more inmates came to Bedford on charges of conduct violations than with convictions for sex work, for instance, she classified them all as prostitutes, insisting that they were "leading the lives of prostitutes" at the time of their arrest.[62]

Focusing her attention on inmate' "sexual offenses," Davis highlighted their alleged moral failings. Somewhat surprisingly, given that she held a doctorate in economics, she frequently downplayed the financial factors driving desperate women into sex work. While Davis astutely ascribed the *demand* for the sex trade to the sexual double standard, which assumed a "sex necessity" for men, she refused to acknowledge economic need as an explanation for the *supply* of sex workers.[63]

Bedford inmates reported that they engaged in commercialized sex for a variety of reasons, often related to their lack of resources. Yet Davis consistently attributed her charges' alleged crimes to personal failings rather than to financial pressures. Even as she observed that women's wages as household helpers and factory operatives were well below "the minimum on which a girl can live decently in New York City," she insisted, "There would seem to be no indication of real economic pressure as a reason for entering an immoral life."[64]

Despite her advanced training in the social sciences, Davis's statistical analysis of Bedford's so-called sex offenders displays significant flaws. A reexamination of Davis's data reveals that many of Bedford's inmates entered the sex trade for economic reasons.[65] For instance, Davis classified being "turned out," or being rejected by one's parents, as a family problem rather than a financial one. Yet other sources indicate that what Davis categorized as "family problems" often had financial dimensions. For instance, in a laudatory account of Bedford, journalist Ida Tarbell recorded the tale of "Clare D.," a motherless child who "was never properly fed, clothed, or sheltered." After running away from her abusive stepmother, the homeless teenager accepted the seeming hospitality of some other young women. As it turned out, Clare had unknowingly taken up residence in a brothel, where the madam insisted on payment in kind for room and board, as well as for the "fine clothes" the unsuspecting adolescent had thought were a gift.[66]

Davis also listed as "personal reasons" some rationales that might instead be seen as economic motivations. These included "needed the money," "easy money," "tired of drudgery," "lazy, hated work," "desire for pleasure," and "desire for money."[67] Another way to read these "reasons" is that some young women simply saw sex work as a way to earn good money. As Davis quoted one youthful offender, "Why, Miss Davis, why should I be good? I earn more in a week than you earn in a month."[68]

When it came to explaining entry into the sex trade, in addition to dismissing the importance of financial pressures, Davis also downplayed the role of sexual assault. Yet Davis was well aware of women's sexual vulnerability. In a statistical analysis of her charges' first "sexual offense"—by which she meant the first occasion that a girl or woman had sex outside of marriage—Davis noted that more than one in five reported forced sex as their first sexual encounter.[69]

One of Davis's later speeches offers insight into this sort of "first offense." During World War I, Davis told the story of a fourteen-year-old girl who went to meet her boyfriend for a date. When the boyfriend did not show up, she accepted another man's invitation to go for a walk. Instead of seeing her safely home, "when it got dark, he assaulted her." Afterward, "afraid to go home" and confide in her parents, she exchanged sex with a different man for dinner, a hotel room, and cash before being "nabbed" by the authorities. Yet rather than condemning the men who took advantage of this hapless teenager, Davis criticized the girl for lack of "moral fiber."[70]

Davis viewed immorality as the chief explanation for relapses after release as well as for initial violations. By 1910, when Davis released a study of the first thousand inmates at Bedford, she had come to view parole violations as a major problem. While more than half of Bedford parolees had completed their parole successfully, Davis focused her attention on those who had violated parole. Leaving a job placement, usually in domestic service, "without permission" was the most common form of parole violation. There were many reasons why an individual might leave a job in domestic service. Indeed, employees' desire to exert control over their own lives was a persistent problem for employers, who complained ceaselessly about "the servant problem." But Davis rather simplistically attributed parolees' departure from domestic service to illicit relationships with unsuitable men. She unequivocally asserted, "The largest single cause has been immorality."[71]

The case of Harriet Cohen, a "woman forger lured by love of opera," may have reinforced Davis's conviction that immorality was the root cause of recidivism. A skilled stenographer, Cohen had a good job at the United Hebrew Societies, but she was sentenced to Bedford in 1908 after she was found guilty of forgery. Impressed by Cohen's administrative abilities and by her "strong, assertive, capable personality," so similar to her own, Davis hired her as her personal secretary during her tenure at Bedford. But after her release, Cohen again turned to forgery to finance the fine life. A 1913 account explained, "She has a temperament which is not satisfied with the life of a working woman. She loves music and art and the atmosphere that goes with them." Even a comparatively good job as a pink-collar professional was not enough to support the cultured lifestyle to which Cohen aspired (and which her time at Bedford would have done nothing to reduce). The "rebel against the dul[l]ness of worker's life" turned to crime once again to "satisfy her longings" for a better life. To host friends at the opera and entertain "lavishly" at "expensive restaurants," Cohen falsely endorsed checks to her company, then so cleverly covered up her malfeasance that investigators were unsure of the total quantity missing from company accounts, although they estimated it to be thousands of dollars. While Davis described her former secretary as "a woman of talent and extraordinary ability," she probably would have agreed with the journalist who attributed her crimes to a lack of "moral fibre," even though Cohen's crimes were financial rather than sexual.[72]

"Oh Boy, I Had a Ball"

The personal account of another Bedford inmate, Mabel Hampton, complicates the simple equation that Davis drew between a lack of "moral fiber," arrests on "morals charges," and parole violations resulting from "immorality." Although Hampton's sentence at Bedford in the 1920s postdated Davis's tenure there, her story was a typical—if unusually well-documented—one. Interviewed in the 1980s, Hampton revealed much about working-class women's lives, African American community, and same-sex relationships in early twentieth-century New York and New Jersey as well as about both discrimination in the judicial system and daily life at Bedford Reformatory.[73]

Like most Bedford inmates, Hampton had a difficult childhood. Born in 1902 and orphaned just two years later, she lived with her grandmother in North Carolina until her guardian's death in 1909 led the seven-year-old to relocate to New York to live with relatives. Unfortunately, within a year, Hampton's uncle sexually assaulted her. Fortunately, she found a safe refuge with a New Jersey family, who took her in and cared for her until she was seventeen. Hampton's girlish admiration for the family's

One of Davis's most important innovations at Bedford Reformatory was her insistence on racial integration. During her tenure as superintendent, between one fifth and one quarter of the inmates were African American. One Black inmate whose sentence postdated Davis's superintendency was Mabel Hampton, pictured here around the time that she served a three-year sentence on false charges of sex work. (In fact, Hampton was a lifelong lesbian who never voluntarily had sex with a man, although she did survive sexual assault by her own uncle.) Hampton's story, told in her own words, offers an important corrective to the false assumptions that Davis made about (im)morality. Mabel Hampton Collection, Lesbian Herstory Archives.

eldest daughter, who not only "looked just like an angel" but also always treated her kindly, set the stage for her later same-sex relationships. As a teenager and young adult, Hampton supported herself as a domestic servant and enjoyed sexual relationships with both Black and white women before an arrest for a violation of the tenement laws—in what she described as a set-up—landed her in New York's Women's Court before Judge Jean Norris, the first woman to preside over the courtroom responsible for prosecuting suspected prostitutes.[74]

Although Hampton's arrest and Norris's appointment both postdated Davis's tenure at Bedford, Hampton's story displayed all the hallmarks of the sexual double standard and the flawed judicial system that Davis observed firsthand. Unfortunately for Hampton—and other girls and women who ended up in her courtroom—Judge Norris was notorious for unfair trials and unduly harsh sentences, which ultimately led to an official investigation and her removal from office. Hampton also indicated that the judge received kickbacks for upholding corrupt police officers' arrests and sentencing suspects to lengthy terms in the city's reformatories and prisons on flimsy evidence. "Railroaded" into a three-year sentence for prostitution, the "innocent" Hampton was paroled into domestic service in New Jersey after eighteen months, but she voluntarily returned to Bedford to serve out the rest of her term rather than risk rearrest for parole violations when her aunt reported her for "immoral" after-hours socializing in New York City.[75]

Although she resented her unjust sentence, Hampton enjoyed both delicious food and delightful companionship at Bedford. Aside from mentioning the comfortable accommodations and the excellent fare, Hampton had little to say about any of Davis's cherished programs or notable innovations; she did not even comment on the unusual practice of racial integration (although the reformatory segregated cottages by race after Davis's departure, dining halls remained integrated). Rather, Hampton focused on the rewarding social life that reformatory residents fostered. After a fellow inmate took the frightened teenager under her wing, Hampton quickly became both a universal favorite and a sought-after sexual partner at the female reformatory, where many inmates "paired off" with each other (and some made homemade wine for unsanctioned gatherings). "Oh, boy, I had a ball," she reminisced.[76]

After her release in 1925, Hampton remained in contact with both Black and white Bedford inmates—a common situation that the reformatory psychologist, Dr. Edith Hale, deplored in her study of "psychopathic" prisoners who engaged in sexual relationships across the color line. But Hampton also expanded her network to include such Harlem luminaries as gender-bending entertainer Gladys Bentley and sexually adventurous socialite A'Lelia Walker, the daughter of successful businesswoman Madam C. J. Walker, the nation's first self-made female millionaire.[77]

In the 1930s, after sharing the stage with Harlem's most in-demand entertainers, frequenting both high-society soirees and Harlem "rent parties," and pursuing sexual relationships with both white and Black women (including her own social worker, a white married woman), Hampton returned to domestic service and settled into a committed relationship with another Black woman, Lillian Foster.[78]

After Foster's death in 1978, Hampton became an outspoken lesbian activist, participating in the nation's first march for lesbian and gay rights in Washington, DC, in 1979 and serving as grand marshal of New York City's Gay Pride March in 1985. At the same time, as a charter member of the Lesbian Herstory Archives, she not only donated lesbian pulp fiction to the archives but also recorded numerous oral histories about her own life.[79]

Mabel Hampton's story—meticulously detailed in tape recordings and typed transcripts held at the Lesbian Herstory Archives—offers a firsthand account of the lived experiences of the "wayward women" who ended up at Bedford Reformatory. The orphaned southern migrant survived sexual assault; served a three-year sentence at Bedford on specious charges of sex work; associated with so-called sexual deviants and actual sex workers; supported herself financially as a singer, dancer, and domestic servant; constructed a vibrant social life; contributed to the Harlem Renaissance; engaged in casual affairs with both Black and white women before committing to a decades-long romantic relationship; documented gay and lesbian culture in and around New York; and promoted LGBTIQ+ rights until her death at age eighty-seven in 1989.

Although she concealed the details of her incarceration for decades—while Hampton lived openly as a lesbian, she did not want to be known as a prostitute—this Bedford veteran also remembered her time at the reformatory fondly. When she departed the grounds for the last time, all her fellow inmates gathered to wave goodbye. Her escort remarked, "I never knew a girl who . . . could come in here and turn the place upside down." She added, "These women likes you." Hampton replied, "I like 'em all. They belong to me."[80] While Hampton confidently asserted her claim to Bedford's community, in point of fact, for more than a decade, Davis was in charge of those she also thought of as "her girls." Moreover, while Hampton's life story revealed the moral complexities, the financial constraints, and the legal challenges confronting the "wayward women" in Davis's care, the superintendent's relentless focus on women's morality increasingly inclined her toward hereditary explanations for female delinquency and drew her to the emerging eugenics movement in early twentieth-century America.

As early as 1906, Davis warned that "bad heredity" was responsible for the problem of "moral imbeciles" in the prison system. These young women often had "good minds" and some were "very bright," she explained, but "they can not distinguish between right and wrong . . . so they become a fearful menace to society."[81] Over the next decade, Davis would refine her ideas about the causes of criminality, becoming an enthusiastic advocate of eugenics and an early adopter of the diagnostic tool espoused by its adherents, intelligence testing. But first, she went on vacation—or at least, she tried to.

"Miss Davis's Extraordinary Work"

The Adriatic Sea was clear and calm, with no more ripples than a mill pond. The sky was perfectly blue, and the sun was shining. Although it was November, the weather was so warm that one New York passenger needed no more than a light sweater. In short, as the prison superintendent–turned–steamship passenger explained in a letter written while on board the RMS *Slavonia*, "It is exactly what the Mediterranean ought to be—and what I understand from old travelers often isn't."[82]

Davis was not an "old" traveler. Indeed, her Mediterranean travels in 1908–1909 were the first real vacation she had taken in years, so preoccupied had she been with the construction of New York's first female reformatory—and the reconstruction of the youthful offenders who resided there. After seven years of nearly uninterrupted work, the usually energetic forty-eight-year-old was exhausted. Generally robust, the fatigued official found she had little appetite. But now, at last, she was ready to relax. Armed with an enormous fruit basket, several boxes of candy, two hot water bottles, and more than twenty books about the history and architecture of the places she planned to visit, she intended to make the most of her time aboard ship, at stops along the way, and in her intended final destination, Naples. "I am beginning to feel quite rested & really have quite a little appetite," she reported just three days into her trip.[83]

Unable to fully quell her instincts toward economy, Davis wrote on both sides of the thin sheets of paper she intended to post at each stop, rendering her usually clear penmanship difficult to decipher. "I expect you will scold me for writing on both sides but I am an economical soul," she jested.[84]

Still, she and her fellow first-class passengers enjoyed leisure and luxury on board the ship, dining on lobster, admiring spectacular sunsets, and playing bridge late into the night. Davis was especially pleased to find that her fellow travelers included several other Seven Sisters graduates; the group immediately became fast friends.[85]

Davis and the other first-class passengers had plenty of room, as there were only thirty-five of them, and the ship, recently refitted as part of the Cunard steamship line, accommodated twice that number. She had little to say about the steerage-class passengers, approximately two thousand Hungarian emigrants who crowded into the ship's hull, although she conceded that "these are very decent looking people—some of them in native costume."[86]

Enjoyable as the journey was, even on vacation, Davis's "dear Bedford family," as she called them in letters to her coworkers, was never far from her mind.[87] At her very first stop, at the Straits of Gibraltar, she reported, "You will 'howl with glee' . . . when you learn that the first place that I visited was a prison!" She explained, "The way of it was this—Our party was seven women—We climbed up to the Moorish Castle—a most picturesque place and the oldest thing on 'the rock'—744 AD—We found a permit was necessary to go on top—as it is now used for a civil prison—There I presented my business card—and that did the work! When the warden found I was a fellow official he was very civil—The view was grand & well worth all the stairs we had to climb."[88]

A month later, after disembarking at Palermo, the capital city of Sicily, Davis continued to draw connections between her sightseeing abroad and her work at Bedford Reformatory. While she reveled in the Roman ruins and read about the history, art, and architecture of the region, she also remarked, "The people interest me tremendously—That has its professional side of course—for it is from these [places] & surroundings my Sicilian girls come."[89] After returning from a strenuous hike up a hillside, she reported, "Thanks to my practice on the road to the upper campus at Bedford I skipped up like a goat!"[90] And after a walk in the blazing sun in the Sicilian hilltop city of Girgenti, she confessed, "I was as hot as when I came in from making cement walks [at Bedford] last fall & had to change my underclothes."[91]

Davis intended to spend a few days each in the Sicilian coastal towns of Girgenti and Syracuse before crossing to the Italian mainland and spending several weeks in Naples. But her plans changed when a devastating earthquake struck Messina, a harbor town located at the northernmost tip of Sicily. The rumbling woke Davis from a sound sleep in her hotel room in Girgenti, more than 160 miles away, but due to the scale of the disaster and the slow communications, it was not until two days later that word of the quake reached Davis, then en route to Syracuse. When a priest with a Red Cross badge boarded Davis's train and she asked what had happened, she understood his reply perfectly, even though he spoke only Italian, and she—despite her decade-old language lessons—spoke only English: "Messina is destroyed."[92]

Thousands of refugees poured into Syracuse, a tourist town ill prepared to deal with an influx of "homeless, penniless, [and] clothesless" fugitives. Davis immediately set to work, raising money and running a makeshift sewing factory in the city's municipal building to provide clothing for the refugees. "One couldn't sit down & read novels in one's hotel in the midst of this horrible suffering," she reflected, so she spent her time "helping make things go."[93]

She postponed further travels indefinitely, explaining, "My training has been exactly the sort to make me useful here, and it would be wicked for me not to use it." She elaborated, "I have dealt with unreasonable women for the past eight years. I do not faint at sight of blood and hysterics do not upset me. I am used to 'bossing the situation' and not speaking Italian I can call the most exalted officials 'Blooming idiots' to their face, and if I do it with a sweet smile they don't know the difference and it relieves my feelings."[94]

Davis had plenty of uncomplimentary remarks to make about Sicilians, characterizing them as corrupt, lazy, incompetent, and disorganized. While she occasionally caught herself, writing "it isn't fair of me to judge," more often she castigated the locals at length, opining that "the Sicilian idea of relief is most primitive & I regret to say that they are totally unable to cope with the situation here."[95]

In Davis's opinion, the problem was not the scale of the horrific disaster but the shortcomings of the local residents. "The natives were perfectly wild," she wrote in one letter home. According to Davis, the Sicilian "ladies"—well-to-do women—had no practical skills whatsoever, while the peasant women required supervision by outsiders—American or British tourists. Davis frequently made invidious comparisons between Sicilians and other, ostensibly more civilized, people. Once the German Red Cross arrived, she explained, the hospital was well run, but in the meantime, "much unnecessary suffering and loss of life had resulted from Sicilian inefficiency, ignorance, shiftlessness, incapacity for concerted action, and *dirt*." Indeed, she summed up, "The Sicilians . . . are generations behind the Anglo-Saxon and Teutonic races."[96]

Davis's casual racism during her time in Sicily reinforced—and in turn was reinforced by—her attitudes toward the Sicilian inmates at Bedford. "You never heard so much talk in your life in proportion to the work done," she remarked to her mother. "They are just like my reformatory girls exactly—even the city officials."[97]

In a letter to her colleagues at Bedford, she asserted, "The people behave as much like our girls as circumstances permit & have to be treated in much the same way—men & all." Although again, Davis briefly checked her criticism, she quickly returned to the theme of Sicilian inferiority: "Of course it has all been horrible & much allowance must be made for all they have been through—& of course they are excitable as a race—& have hysterics & shriek on the slightest provocation so it[']s much like the R.H.," she wrote, comparing the scene in Sicily to the Reception House where Bedford's inmates first arrived.[98]

Despite her shortcomings, Davis was, as family friend May Bragdon rather wryly expressed it, "a 'star performer' in Sicily." She not only coordinated relief efforts on the ground but also conducted a massive fundraising campaign—and then, she carefully managed the money she solicited from major agencies, such as the Red Cross; government entities, such as the US Congress; and private donors, including Rochester residents. Small wonder, then, that the pope gave her a personal audience; the Italian government presented her with an engraved certificate honoring her service; and both the American and the Italian Red Cross presented her with medals commemorating her heroic efforts. (In her memoirs, Davis described the medals as "cherished possessions"; her family still treasures them.) When she at last returned home in April 1909, her relieved family and friends had to wait to greet her until after "a delegation of Italian girls . . . presented her with a handsome bouquet." Subsequently, Davis wrote articles and gave lectures about her "relief work," regaling her audience with "thrilling stories" about her experiences overseas.[99]

Given her frequent comments about "Sicilian shiftlessness," however, it is not surprising that soon after her return to Bedford Reformatory, Davis started to espouse eugenics, a then-popular scientific theory of human evolution that divided humanity into "fit" and "unfit" and that discouraged the reproduction of "unfit" people. While repugnant to modern sensibilities, at the time, eugenics was regarded as cutting-edge science, and Davis's adoption of eugenic ideas actually would enhance her professional standing. Thus, after returning to the United States, Davis not only gave numerous public lectures about what family friend Katherine Bragdon called "Miss Davis's extraordinary work" in Sicily but also started to seriously study the subject of eugenics.[100]

"What I Think About Eugenics"

For Davis, science was the key to understanding—and then improving—society. According to her college friend, Caroline Furness, her Vassar classwork in astronomy, chemistry, and mathematics set the stage for the rest of her career: "She always said when questioned that she esteemed very highly the exact training which came from these studies and felt that they were particularly valuable in her social work because she was trained to approach everything from the scientific point of view which prevented her from being visionary and ineffective."[101] Davis always believed in the importance of environment, but as she grappled with the ongoing challenge of reforming "wayward" women—even in the ideal environment she created at Bedford—she also looked to eugenics—which combined the natural sciences and the social sciences—for answers to intractable problems.

In a statement for an undated pamphlet published by the American Eugenics Society, "What I Think About Eugenics," Davis explained,

> As a person whose special interest for years has been the unadjusted individual, it has been impossible not to recognize the importance of the study of eugenics as a great underlying factor in the production of the right kind of humans. The newer psychology and psychiatry is [*sic*]specially stressing the importance of early environment, but no one who knows anything of the wonders of animal and plant breeding can fail to recognize that there is a point beyond which we cannot go in relying upon environment. There can be no more important study at the present time than that of eugenics, if we wish to produce a race with the minimum number of maladjusted individuals.[102]

Today, when many people refer to eugenics as a "pseudoscience," understanding Davis's fascination with what people then regarded as a new field of scientific inquiry requires some historical context. In the opening decades of the twentieth century, when Davis first was attracted to the emerging discipline and its principal tool, intelligence testing, she joined a generation of intellectuals and reformers eager to find scientific solutions to social problems.[103]

For Davis and her contemporaries, the new intelligence tests seemed to validate the notion that mental capacity (or lack thereof) explained why some individuals seemed incapable of becoming law-abiding, self-supporting members of society. Having a scientific explanation suggested that there was a scientific solution. Believing that heredity was destiny, eugenicists sought to improve society by encouraging the "fit" to reproduce and discouraging the "unfit" from doing so.[104]

In the opening decades of the twentieth century, the eugenics movement appealed to a wide range of influential Americans, including President Theodore Roosevelt, philanthropist John Dr. Rockefeller Jr., feminist author Charlotte Perkins Gilman, and birth-control crusader Margaret Sanger. While most Americans today who consider themselves "progressive" find these ideas repugnant, during the Progressive Era, spanning from the 1880s through the 1920s, eugenics was a quintessentially "progressive" approach to social problems. Eugenics brought together scientific study, social engineering, and state power, all hallmarks of American progressivism. Davis's adoption of eugenics was practically a foregone conclusion for an ambitious thinker and reformer in the opening decades of the twentieth century.[105]

Davis's attraction to eugenics also reflected her concerns about escalating problems at Bedford Reformatory. New York's model reformatory and its celebrated superintendent garnered positive attention both throughout the nation and in international circles. One European visitor, in the United States to attend the International Prison Congress, praised Bedford as "the best institution in America." Nonetheless, Davis worried incessantly about some inmates' resistance to reform. She sought an explanation for recalcitrant inmates, parole violations, and repeat offenses that shielded her—and the institution she guided—from blame.[106]

Just a few years into her tenure at the reformatory, Davis confronted a set of interlocking challenges. One of these was overcrowding resulting from an ever-increasing number of commitments. Bedford's ambitious building program, focused as it was on the cottage system, could not keep pace with its growing population. Davis converted single rooms in the Reception House into triples, then lined corridors with additional beds, and finally placed overflow cots in the hospital and other buildings in order to accommodate an ever-growing number of inmates. By 1913, the overcrowding was so severe that Davis pleaded with the governor for an appropriation for new buildings, explaining that the institution had only 320 beds but 505 inmates, 185 of whom were sleeping in makeshift quarters "in linen closets, hallways, and even washrooms." The housing crisis at Bedford prompted Davis to parole inmates early, which then led to an increased proportion of parole violations and a growing population of "return girls." It was a vicious cycle.[107]

Davis was concerned not only with the growing population of Bedford but also with what she regarded as its changing character. According to Davis, the widespread adoption of probation for first offenses, an increased proportion of parole violations, and judges' decisions to send repeat offenders to Bedford all meant that the reformatory housed an increasingly high proportion of "difficult" inmates. Davis believed that many of these challenging cases involved what she called "moral imbeciles." Because they were unable to resist temptation, she theorized, these individuals required constant supervision. While they were sometimes "exemplary" inmates, she explained, they were unable to adjust to life outside of the institution. Indeed, she warned, such individuals were destined to become "rounders" who served numerous sentences in New York's correctional facilities.[108]

By the time Davis shared her thoughts about "moral imbeciles," in 1906, the phrase was on its way out, along with the vague diagnosis it represented. Popularized in the aftermath of the 1881 trial of President John Garfield's assassin, the catch-all diagnosis of moral imbecility was easy to invoke, but difficult to substantiate. Therefore, when American eugenicist Henry Goddard translated French psychologist Alfred Binet's intelligence tests into English and began to publish studies of the population of the Training School for Feeble-Minded Boys and Girls in Vineland, New Jersey, in 1910, Davis—and others—took note.[109]

Both theoretically and practically, Goddard was responsible for the merger of hereditarian thinking and intelligence testing in the United States. Binet originally had designed his tests to identify learning difficulties among French schoolchildren; to that end, he wished to evaluate students' "mental level" in conjunction with their educational level. Goddard, however, applied the tests without reference to grade level. Moreover, he insisted that intelligence was determined by heredity and was unresponsive to environment. For Goddard and his followers, then, "mental age" became a marker of inherent intelligence rather than a measure of acquired knowledge.[110]

For American eugenicists, the new English-language intelligence tests seemed to provide an objective and reliable measurement of mental ability. Moreover—and of particular interest to Davis—Goddard's version of intelligence tests promised to measure moral capacity as well as innate intelligence. Goddard both popularized and expanded the preexisting classification of "feebleminded" to include a new category, which he dubbed the "moron" (derived from the Greek word for "fool"), to describe individuals whose intelligence tests indicated a "mental age" between eight and twelve. Such "borderline" individuals—people who did not exhibit obvious mental impairment but who nonetheless engaged in antisocial or immoral behavior—were of special concern to Davis, who believed that they were responsible for the majority of disciplinary problems at Bedford Reformatory. She found Goddard's explanation of the connection between mental age and immoral behavior compelling. According to him, since intelligence was fixed, so-called morons were stuck in an atavistic stage of both mental and moral development. In other words, a "moron" could never attain a mental age that made it possible to make moral decisions. Goddard's version of intelligence testing seemed, to Davis and others, to offer an incontrovertible basis for assessing an individual's mental ability and, therefore, their moral capacity.[111]

Davis enthusiastically embraced the new category of "moron," hoping to convince magistrates that some of her inmates were incapable of reform and should be sent to custodial institutions rather than to Bedford Reformatory. But she soon found that New York's judges did not share her views; moreover, they did not accept or understand the new category of "moron" as applied to "borderline" cases of "feeble-mindedness."[112]

In her autobiography, Davis presented the case of a Bedford inmate known as "Fanny." At age twenty, Fanny was the mother of three children by three different fathers. Davis believed that both Fanny and her children were feeble-minded. After having Fanny examined by physicians who confirmed her assessment, Davis presented her in court to request her transfer to the state's asylum for feebleminded women. But the judge, apparently impressed by blonde-haired, blue-eyed Fanny's appearance as well as by her ability to correctly identify the day of the week, rejected the request. "A wrathful cloud overshadowed the judge's face" as he "boomed," "You are trying to railroad this child into an asylum for a lifetime. She is no maroon. . . . Case dismissed." The judge's refusal to apply the new term of "moron" to Fanny—or even to pronounce it correctly—convinced Davis that she needed to adopt new tactics.[113]

"A Rational Plan"

Davis had long believed that treatment—not punishment—should "fit the criminal," not "fit the crime." Initially, this meant that she tailored her program to individual needs and desires. As one admiring account explained, "She believed in treating girls as girls rather than as prisoners." Moreover, because she understood "that no two persons are exactly alike," she treated the young women in her charge "as individuals," rather than as statistics, and she "planned their life at Bedford in accordance with their especial needs." But as Davis increasingly equated moral failings with mental incapacity, she advocated that certain offenders should be confined for life, rather than serving a set sentence for a specific offense. Since she regarded intelligence as a fixed characteristic, Davis asserted that the only "rational" solution to the problem of female immorality was the permanent confinement of what she called "feeble-minded delinquents."[114]

After her return to Bedford from her ill-fated Mediterranean vacation, Davis began to formulate what she called "a rational plan" for sentencing and treating criminal women based on their mental ability. Throughout her tenure at Bedford, Davis frequently hosted visitors interested in learning about female offenders and reformatory methods. In spring 1910, while hosting one such group, Davis—seemingly spontaneously—shared her idea of creating a "clearing house" staffed by physicians and psychologists to study female offenders, determine appropriate "treatment," and assign them to a suitable facility. In this scheme, only individuals deemed capable of moral reform would be sent to Bedford; girls and women judged "feeble-minded" and therefore unable to benefit from reformatory methods would be assigned to long-term custodial care elsewhere. So impressed was one visitor, a member of the Charity Organization Society, that the group invited her to write up her thoughts, which the agency had privately printed and circulated.[115]

Davis's proposal was very much of its time. The widespread adoption of intelligence testing led to a proliferation of both public and private diagnostic centers in America's major cities in the early twentieth century.[116] However, while her proposal found favor among Gotham's charity workers and court officials, Davis knew that she would face an uphill battle in securing legislation to make it policy. Instead of implementing her "rational plan" in the public sector, she sought private funding for a pilot program based at Bedford Reformatory. An initial small-scale study conducted in 1910 convinced Davis of what she had long suspected: that the reformatory had become a dumping ground for "women of much lower mental and moral grade than formerly."[117]

Armed with seemingly incontrovertible evidence that a significant proportion of Bedford's inmates were "feeble-minded" and thus incapable of reform, Davis sent a copy of her plan to wealthy philanthropist and antivice crusader John D. Rockefeller Jr. In many ways, Rockefeller was the ideal benefactor. The scion of one of America's wealthiest families, he had recently served on a grand jury to investigate prostitution in New York City. Moreover, when Davis initiated contact with him in fall 1911, he was in the process of putting together what would come to be known as the Bureau of Social Hygiene, an antivice think tank dedicated to the eradication of sex work.[118]

Impressed both by Davis's proposal and by Davis herself—he later described her as "the cleverest woman he ever met"—Rockefeller underwrote the construction of the Laboratory of Social Hygiene and authorized Davis to hire a staff to study Bedford's inmates there beginning in 1912—the same year that New York's legislature adopted a statute permitting the involuntary sterilization of "feeble-minded" people residing in institutions.[119]

"This Was Our Chance"

To staff the lab and study the inmates, Davis hired a cohort of highly educated women—many of them fellow graduates of the University of Chicago—to collect case histories and conduct intelligence testing. At the time, the emerging disciplines of psychology, sociology, and social work were relatively female friendly—at least when compared to the traditional fields of medicine, law, and the ministry—and many women, like Davis, made their mark in these fields even though they obtained degrees in other specialties. (For instance, many pioneering psychologists earned doctorates in philosophy.) By contrast, the medical profession remained quite hostile to female practitioners; most women physicians were shunted into private practice caring for mothers and children. Virtually all women with doctorates, no matter what their field of study, struggled to establish themselves in rewarding (and remunerative) careers.[120]

Often described as social workers regardless of their academic specialties, pioneering professional women frequently circumvented gender discrimination by working with marginalized populations, such as young, poor, female, immigrant, and nonwhite groups. In particular, many found their niche working with "dependent and delinquent" youth sentenced to specialized institutions or sent to orphan asylums.[121]

In the Progressive Era, privileged women often built their professional careers at the expense of less privileged women; simultaneously, they participated in the construction of the carceral state, which disproportionately targeted working-class, African American, and immigrant women. While Davis and her highly educated, reform-minded colleagues no doubt genuinely believed they acted with "good will to woman," they also built their careers by confining and controlling women categorized as mentally and morally inferior and institutionalized against their will.[122]

For Davis's all-female staff—which included University of Chicago PhD Mabel Ruth Fernald, physician Alberta S. B. Guibord, social worker Virginia P. Robinson, Radcliffe (Harvard) psychology PhD Eleanor Harris Rowland, University of Chicago philosophy PhD Julia Jessie Taft, Tufts Medical School graduate Edith R. Spaulding, and University of Chicago psychology PhD Clara Jean Weidensall—working at Bedford offered unprecedented opportunities for professional advancement.[123]

Jessie Taft, who earned her PhD in philosophy before conducting intelligence testing at Bedford Reformatory, credited Davis with shaping her professional trajectory. "No part of my life seems so colorful in retrospect as those years of association with Miss Davis and the interesting people she attracted," she reflected. "What more thrilling introduction to the world of reality could have come to me just out of the academic influence than to be drawn into the circle of Miss Davis' interests and manifold activities in those years of the vice investigations in New York City, the founding of the Laboratory of Social Hygiene [at Bedford Reformatory] and brilliant work of the Mitchell administration [in New York City]. I have never ceased to be grateful that some happy chance or fate if you will brought me into contact with Katharine Bement Davis during that eventful period of her eventful life."[124]

Those years were eventful for Taft, too. While pursuing her PhD at the University of Chicago, Taft met schoolteacher-turned-summer student Virginia Robinson. The two became colleagues at Bedford Reformatory; they also became life partners, adopting and raising two children together. In her loving biography of Taft, Robinson paid homage to their time together at Bedford, which solidified their relationship. The two had gone different ways, but remained in touch, after meeting in Chicago. When Davis invited them to help her to study female offenders, it meant both "the chance for real experience outside of books" and "the chance to work together." "That we brought no qualifications for working with criminal women except interest did not disturb Miss Davis, nor did it disturb us," Robinson recalled. "This was our chance for vital gripping experience, and we plunged into it without a qualm and with no regrets."[125]

Davis forged close personal and professional relationships with her Bedford colleagues, especially those at the Laboratory of Social Hygiene, nicknamed "the Hilltop" for its location on the hilly campus. Unable to attend her retirement gala in 1928, Dr. Alberta Guibord sent her regrets at her inability to join the gathering in honor of "our dear great leader": "How I should love to join the Hilltop folks at the dinner for Miss Davis!" she exclaimed. "I'd like to squeeze Miss K.B.D. and all the old Laboratory friends a real love squeeze but this time it must be a mental squeeze—hug I mean."[126]

"Puzzling Problems" and "Psychopathic" Prisoners

Bedford's Laboratory of Social Hygiene offered a different kind of "mental squeeze." Davis's staff quickly became conversant with prevailing theories of hereditary traits and the new procedures of intelligence testing. They studied with Henry Goddard, who adapted and popularized French psychologist Alfred Binet's intelligence tests; Charles Davenport, an advocate of selective breeding and founder of the Genetic Research Office; and William Healey, director of Chicago's Juvenile Psychopathic Institute.[127]

With the guidance of these prominent eugenicists, Davis's staff undertook a series of studies of Bedford's residents. Disregarding inmates' low levels of formal education—most had not completed sixth grade—and conducting a battery of tests that included reading comprehension, cursive handwriting, and telling time, they swiftly concluded that the vast majority of inmates had a "mental age" of twelve or lower, meaning they met the then-accepted medical diagnosis of "moron."[128]

Early results convinced Davis not only that a significant proportion of Bedford's inmates were "decidedly mentally defective" but also that a troublesome minority were actually "psychopathic delinquent women." To confine and treat especially recalcitrant residents, the former superintendent—who by then had moved to New York City but who still visited "the Hilltop" regularly—advocated the creation of a Psychopathic Hospital on Bedford's campus. The new clinic—featuring an elaborate intake procedure, extensive intelligence testing, and innovative treatments, such as hydrotherapy—opened in 1916.[129]

Today's readers, familiar with the flaws inherent in intelligence testing and having learned from history the dangers of eugenic thinking, may be horrified by these developments. But at the time, Davis's endorsement of eugenic theories and her implementation of intelligence testing attracted national attention and international acclaim. In particular, feminist publications enthusiastically endorsed the work of Davis and her all-female staff. *The Suffragist* dubbed the research institute "the best laboratory for dealing with prostitution in the world," while the *Woman's Journal and Suffrage News* celebrated the addition of the "special hospital" for "psychopathic" offenders. A detailed profile of the Laboratory of Social Hygiene in the *Bulletin* produced by the General Federation of Women's Clubs declared, "This is the only institution of its kind in the world, and it is believed that many solutions to the puzzling problems of crime will come about through this work."[130]

While the *Bulletin* also asserted that "the girls themselves like the tests to which they are submitted, really obtaining a good deal of enjoyment from them," other records suggest that inmates resented—and resisted—the constant intelligence testing. Dr. Edith Spaulding described an incident in which one patient, known as "Mary," assigned to clean the bathroom, was discovered "hurling full pails of water over the bathroom floor." Mary told the inexperienced staff member who questioned her that "she was supposed to do it this way," apparently delighting in putting one over on the new nurse. "Later, when asked why she took advantage of the nurse's inexperience Mary remarked, 'I was just giving her a test to see if she was feeble-minded. You test us, why shouldn't I test her?'"[131]

When Bedford's staff completed their studies, their publications would challenge the reliability of intelligence testing and offer complex explanations for criminal behavior. But these results came too late to change Davis's mind.[132] Rather, in response to early findings at Bedford and in accordance with then-cutting-edge theories in both the carceral state and the medical profession, Davis confidently conflated the categories of morally compromised and mentally incompetent.[133]

By 1913, an initial battery of intelligence tests applied to alleged sex workers—most of whom had not made it beyond sixth grade—had convinced Davis that nearly one third of them were "decidedly mentally defective." Davis moved quickly from correlation to causality, adopting the eugenic viewpoint that "feeble-minded" girls and women were especially prone to "immorality." Most importantly of all, she asserted that custodial care—long-term institutionalization—was necessary to "safeguard" society from the "dangers" of such women's unrestrained sexuality and its inevitable results: illegitimate births of feebleminded children, or, as Davis put it, "free propagation of defective offspring."[134]

"Too Hasty Generalization from Insufficient Data"

Davis's adoption of eugenic theories and intelligence testing left a damaging legacy. Although Davis was an active member of the Eugenics Research Association, she also became increasingly cautious about pronouncements about both innate intelligence and eugenic theories. Nonetheless, psychologists and policymakers alike used the questionable data she and her colleagues collected at Bedford to assert a link between illicit sexuality and intellectual deficiency—and to disregard evidence that economic need drove sex work.[135]

Despite her disavowal of problematic policies based on eugenic principles—such as involuntary sterilization—Davis remained an enthusiastic promoter of intelligence testing and classifying inmates. In 1920, thanks in large part to Davis's advocacy, the privately funded Laboratory of Social Hygiene was transformed into the publicly funded Division for Mentally Defective Delinquent Women, which housed—one might say warehoused—women who had not committed any serious crime but who performed poorly on flawed intelligence tests.[136]

Davis would never officially withdraw her support for the eugenics movement. Rather, just two years before her death, in 1933, she would renew her membership in the Eugenics Research Association.[137] Because of the lack of either personal or professional correspondence thereafter, there is no way of knowing if she was aware of the news, just beginning to trickle into the United States in the early 1930s, of atrocities committed in German concentration camps in the name of eugenics. In the aftermath of World War II, the mass extermination of those the Nazi regime deemed "unfit"—Jews, homosexuals, Gypsies, and individuals with both physical and intellectual disabilities—would discredit eugenics among mainstream Americans. Davis's death in 1935, well before most Americans were aware of the horrors perpetrated in Nazi Germany, makes it impossible to know how she might have modified her views in response to these developments.

It is clear from Davis's memoirs, which she wrote in the 1930s, that she never denounced eugenics, although she always allied herself more with the movement's research than its policies. She had both political and personal reasons for maintaining her affiliation with eugenicists. As the saying goes, politics makes strange bedfellows, and during Davis's lifetime, the birth-control movement and the eugenics movement represented one of these strategic alliances. In 1933, the same year that Nazi Germany adopted its sterilization program for so-called defectives—a category that included both individuals with disabilities and those suspected of homosexuality—the American Eugenics Society endorsed birth control. But it seems that Davis also remained personally intrigued by the problem of heredity. When she was "chasing ancestors," as she called tracing her family tree, and drafting her memoirs, she reflected, "More than ever, I am glad to believe in heredity, and to find that—so far as I have been able to follow it up, I have a respectable one."[138]

But if Davis never formally repudiated eugenics, she also did not support the draconian measures advocated by some hardline eugenicists, such as the involuntary sterilization of "feeble-minded" women. Throughout her career in corrections, Davis advocated long-term institutionalization of those she deemed incapable of reform. However, she did not play an active role in the shift from custodial care to involuntary sterilization—a policy sanctioned by the US Supreme Court decision in *Buck v. Bell* in 1927, in which Chief Justice Oliver Wendell Holmes, ruling on the constitutionality of sterilizing a "feeble-minded" teenager, declared, "Three generations of imbeciles are enough!"[139]

Rather, Davis became increasingly cautious about her comments about eugenics. For instance, when she assumed her post as New York City's chief corrections official in 1914, she responded to questions about eugenics: "There we must go slowly. Much interesting material has been gathered, but there is a danger of too hasty generalization from insufficient data. We cannot yet lay down a code of general laws."[140] Prior to the first world war, many eugenic thinkers combined hereditarian and environmentalist approaches. Davis, like many of her contemporaries, believed that heredity and environment were intertwined. She always insisted that while some offenders were genetically predisposed to crime, most criminal behavior resulted from a poor environment.[141]

Moreover, while Davis supported eugenics, she repudiated racism. For Davis, the hereditary categories of "fit" and "unfit" did not map easily onto racial categories such as "white" and "nonwhite." While readers today may view Davis's steadfast support for eugenics as running counter to her stated support for racial equality, Davis—and her contemporaries—had a different viewpoint. Even as she implemented intelligence testing at Bedford Reformatory, Davis also insisted on racial integration there, despite encountering significant criticism for her stance. Davis subsequently burnished her credentials as a racial liberal by becoming a board member of two homes for African American women, the Sojourner Truth House for youthful delinquents and the Katy Ferguson Home for unwed mothers. The *New York Age*—an African American newspaper—praised her commitment to all women's welfare. Describing her as "utterly without prejudice," the paper emphasized that "her labors in this work for the relief and rehabilitation of womanhood have known no limits of race and color."[142] In short, despite her enthusiastic embrace of eugenics, Davis regarded herself—and was regarded by others—as an advocate of racial equality.

"Morality Is Not a Question of Color"

Indeed, when it came to contemporary evaluations of her tenure as superintendent of Bedford Reformatory, Davis encountered far more criticism for her commitment to racial integration than she did for her support of eugenics. Shortly after Davis left Bedford in 1914, a special investigation of conditions at Bedford Reformatory, initiated in response to complaints of physical cruelty, instead found evidence of a very different issue: interracial same-sex relationships. Both James Wood, the president of Bedford's Board of Managers, and Jessie Taft, Davis's second-in-command at Bedford, testified that "harmful intimacy," "immoral friendships," and "unfortunate attachments" had posed disciplinary difficulties, or "sex trouble," throughout Bedford's history, although overcrowding had exacerbated the situation. Subsequently, head physician Edith Spaulding published a study of "emotional episodes" among reformatory inmates that indicated both the frequency and the intensity of lesbian relationships across the color line both during and after Davis's tenure as superintendent.[143]

The special committee's investigation of same-sex relationships at Bedford Reformatory highlighted a moment of profound change in Americans' attitudes toward women's relationships. With some notable exceptions, by and large, nineteenth-century Americans had regarded well-to-do, white women as "passionless." Popular culture celebrated such women's "romantic friendships" as ideal relationships, presumably free of the corrupting influences of sexual passion. At the turn of the century, however, the emergence of a new field of study—sexology—led to increased scrutiny of and stigma surrounding same-sex relationships, including women's relationships. Pioneered in Europe at the end of the nineteenth century, these new ideas became widespread in America in the opening decades of the twentieth century.[144]

The timing was significant. New theories about women's sexuality gained traction at the same time that growing numbers of "new women" laid claim to previously male prerogatives, such as higher education, professional careers, and voting rights. Often conflating same-sex desire with a reversal of gender roles—known as "sexual inversion"—new theories about lesbianism simultaneously marked women's relationships as sexual and condemned women's quest for equality. In doing so, they stigmatized both same-sex relationships and feminist goals as "abnormal."[145]

Single-sex institutions would become a focal point for these concerns, so much so that by the mid-twentieth century, women's prisons would become synonymous with lesbianism. But in the opening decades of the twentieth century, most experts on both sex and crime ignored the issue, discussing criminal women's sexual deviance largely in terms of commercialized heterosexual sex. At the time of the Bedford sex scandal, most public discussions of criminal women's sexual behavior overlooked lesbianism.[146]

Interracial same-sex relationships were the exception to this rule, however. Shortly before Davis left Bedford, the *Journal of Abnormal Psychology* ran an article suggesting that "intensely sexual" relationships were common in mixed-race reform schools, where, one researcher posited, "the difference in color . . . takes the place of difference in sex."[147]

Similarly, the special committee's investigation of Bedford Reformatory evinced special concern, not with same-sex relationships per se but with interracial same-sex relationships. The new superintendent, Jessie Taft—herself involved in a romantic relationship with fellow staffer Virginia Robinson—insisted that Bedford's inmates engaged in "a romantic attachment rather than any immoral relation." Yet, while she acknowledged that "there is as much of this romantic attachment between white girls as there is between white and colored girls," she also asserted, "There is no denying that the colored girls are extremely attractive to certain white girls and the feeling is apt to be more intense than between white girls alone." While Taft rather self-servingly dismissed the sexual nature of such relationships, James Wood perhaps inadvertently emphasized them by vaguely referring to "vile practices." Ultimately, stating that most disciplinary problems were a result of "unfortunate attachments" across the color line, the investigating committee recommended imposing racial segregation at Bedford Reformatory.[148]

The investigation posed both a professional and a personal quandary for the former superintendent. While the original charges of cruelty were quickly dropped, Davis still desired both to protect her professional reputation and to shield her private life.[149]

Accordingly, the former superintendent responded to the sex scandal by avoiding discussing same-sex relationships at Bedford while vigorously defending racial integration there. In her testimony, Davis claimed full "responsibility" for the reformatory's race mixing. She explained, "I contended that it was proper in a public institution of this kind, and in accordance with the best reformatory methods, to classify the colored like the white girls, in groups according to age, character, and mental and educational qualifications." Defending her record, Davis continued, "This rule has accomplished reforms, and has been followed successfully since I was connected with the institution, thirteen years ago." Moreover, she concluded, "It is the only fair rule to follow."[150]

In public statements, Davis insisted, "Morality is not a question of color." She added, "When large groups of abnormal individuals of one sex are congregated together, a certain amount of vice is unavoidable." Avoiding commenting on "immoral friendships" at the female reformatory, Davis instead asserted that racial segregation itself was "immoral." Davis's comments reflected both her unusual commitment to racial integration and conventional wisdom about women's sexuality. In this older paradigm, lesbianism per se did not necessitate special attention, because all of women's sexual behavior outside of marriage was equally problematic. Women sentenced to Bedford for prostitution and related offenses were, by definition, "abnormal" and addicted to "vice"; engaging in lesbian sex was to be expected. In response to reporters' questions, then, Davis simultaneously defended her record on racial integration and deflected attention from lesbian sexuality.[151]

Indeed, throughout her tenure at Bedford—and beyond, until the 1929 publication of her monumental study on "normal" women featuring two chapters on female "homosexuality"—Davis consistently avoided the subject of lesbianism. In her detailed statistical studies of Bedford's inmates, one category that Davis did not include in her analysis was lesbians. Given the predominance of people we would now categorize as queer in women's prisons, both past and present, this is a curious omission. The overrepresentation of LGBTIQ+ people in prisons is especially notable since the disproportionate prosecution and incarceration of queer women was—and remains—a feature, not a bug, of New York's criminal justice system. Like other major cities, Gotham has long policed gender as well as crime by targeting gender-nonconforming individuals, including women who engaged in same-sex relationships and adopted men's dress. Since Davis carefully analyzed arrest records, she would have been well aware of this pattern; she simply chose not to discuss it.[152]

While Davis persistently—and often shortsightedly—called attention to the moral failings of reformatory residents, her moral judgments were confined to illicit heterosexual activity. At the same time that she sounded the klaxon of alarm about "moral imbeciles," Davis downplayed the prevalence of same-sex relationships among Bedford's inmates. Given that "emotional episodes" and disciplinary difficulties resulting from "sex temptation" and "aggressive eroticism" during her tenure at Bedford prompted her to propose the creation of the psychopathic clinic, this was certainly not because Davis was unaware of either the frequency or the intensity of lesbian relationships at the female reformatory. Official testimony, case studies, and Davis's own policy of assigning inmates to either single or triple—but not double!—rooms all indicate that Davis was well aware of lesbian relationships at Bedford Reformatory.[153]

At a time when both psychologists and the public considered lesbianism a form of sexual deviance, Davis's silence on same-sex relationships was not a simple oversight but a deliberate decision. Moreover, it was a decision that not only reflected Davis's personal situation but also shaped her professional trajectory.

Davis had good reasons for avoiding the subject of lesbianism among Bedford's inmates, for doing so might have brought attention to her own intimate relationship with another woman. Davis had a long-term—if mostly long-distance—relationship with Fredonia resident Ella Lapham, initiated when Davis taught school in nearby Dunkirk. The two remained fast friends—and likely lovers. Certainly, Davis regarded Lapham as one of the most important people in her life. In the winter of 1908–1909, when her intended holiday was interrupted by a devastating earthquake, Davis wrote regularly to what she called her "three families": her parents and siblings in Rochester, her "Bedford family," and Ella Lapham. The family metaphor was a familiar shorthand for intimacy and importance, and Davis's inclusion of Lapham in her round-robin correspondence (in which each member of a group shared letters with the rest), even though her letters to Lapham do not survive, is a powerful testament to the close relationship Davis fostered with Lapham. Attenuated by distance and cut short by Lapham's premature death in 1917, Davis's relationship with her "particular chum" was among her most significant attachments.[154]

However, like other professional women of her generation, Davis well understood the importance of concealing her own intimate relationships, especially while dealing with a scandal about same-sex relationships. Increased scrutiny of women's relationships, particularly when paired with skepticism about female independence, had important implications for Davis and her contemporaries. While attention to lesbian relationships initially focused on interracial liaisons in institutional settings, well-to-do, white women pursuing higher education, professional careers, and political rights would soon become the target of these new views of women's sexuality. Davis and other new women had to tread carefully to avoid becoming identified with the new woman's "evil twin": the "mannish lesbian."[155]

Thus, Davis downplayed same-sex relationships among inmates to avoid bringing attention to her own. Indeed, throughout her life, Davis was cautious about sharing details of her personal life. Twenty years later, when she penned her never-published autobiography, she took care to assure her potential audience that there were no "'glamorous' affairs" in her past, although she also reassured would-be readers that "I have always been friendly with boys and men" and remarked that she had received proposals of marriage. Well after the contretemps at Bedford, Davis understood the importance of presenting the appearance of propriety—and heterosexuality.[156]

Decades later, another prison reformer—and personal friend—would adopt a similar strategy. Davis was well acquainted with progressive penologist Miriam Van Waters, whose career spanned the country, from California to Massachusetts. Several decades after the scandal at Bedford, Van Waters, like Davis, would weather a sex scandal about lesbian relationships among her charges while also engaged in a secret same-sex relationship. In 1928, when Van Waters left her position as head of El Retiro, an experimental school for female juvenile delinquents in California, Davis recommended her for an academic post. Instead of pursuing a career in academia, however, Pennsylvania-born Van Waters returned to the East Coast and dedicated the rest of her life to prison reform. With the steadfast support of her wealthy partner, Geraldine Thompson, she served as superintendent of a Massachusetts women's reformatory from 1932 to 1957. Although dismissed in 1949 for running a "doll racket"—that is, permitting lesbian relationships among inmates—she later was reinstated. Keenly aware that her professional standing required personal secrecy, Van Waters burned letters to and from her "Dearest Dearest Love," with whom she shared her life for forty years.[157]

Davis was less fortunate in her personal life. At the time of the sex scandal at Bedford Reformatory, Ella Lapham already may have been suffering from the lengthy illness that would result in her premature death in 1917. But in her professional life, Davis's strategy worked. The former superintendent emerged from the Bedford investigation with her professional reputation intact and her personal life private. By characterizing interracial, same-sex liaisons as just one more example of Bedford inmates' immorality, Davis managed to avoid discussing lesbianism in the midst of a sex scandal. Just a few years later, however, she would change course to produce a remarkably candid and nonjudgmental study of women's sexuality in which she revealed—and did not revile—

the pervasiveness of same-sex relationships among "normal" white, well-educated, well-to-do women like herself.[158]

Surely Davis's own life experiences predisposed her to undertake this nonjudgmental treatment of lesbianism. In her 1929 study of women's same-sex relationships, while she did not mention her own relationship history, Davis remarked on her familiarity with female-to-female relationships both at Vassar College and at Bedford Reformatory, writing, "My own observation in both educational and penological institutions leads me to believe that the phenomena described in this study are much more widespread than is generally suspected, or than most administrators are willing to admit."[159] The prevalence of same-sex relationships among both inmates and staff during Davis's tenure at Bedford Reformatory prefigured her sympathetic study of lesbianism a decade later.

"To Make the Punishment Fit the Criminal, Not the Crime"

In her thirteen years at Bedford Reformatory, Davis quite literally built an ideal institution. Bedford attracted widespread acclaim for its attractive campus and innovative policies, and Davis gained an international reputation as a prison reformer. At the same time, Davis's experimentation with intelligence testing solidified her reputation as a social scientist as well as a progressive penologist. Among the many laudatory articles devoted to Davis's work at Bedford, one lengthy profile in the *New York Times* published shortly after the establishment of the Laboratory of Social Hygiene praised her determination "to make punishment fit the criminal, not the crime." This mantra would appear frequently in future assessments of Davis's work as a prison reformer.[160]

While adopting modern methods of reformatory management, Davis also upheld Victorian standards of female virtue. She created an ideal environment for "moral regeneration" and established a comprehensive program intended to transform "moral weaklings" into moral women. As one admiring account averred, her "faith in people" meant that "neither a task nor a person does she deem impossible." One seemingly "impossible" inmate attested, "You can say anything and she doesn't get mad," adding, "I broke her eyeglasses one day and she invited me to tea for the next afternoon."[161]

Yet even Davis's "constructive faith" had its limits. When she encountered apparently intractable inmates and struggled with seemingly insurmountable difficulties at the reformatory, Davis blamed both "immorality" and "heredity" for the rising tide of commitments, the troubling rate of parole violations, and the persistent problem of repeat offenses. To validate her views, she successfully sought the support of wealthy philanthropist John D. Rockefeller Jr., initiating a long and productive relationship with his sex research think tank, the Bureau of Social Hygiene, which subsidized her 1913 study of sex workers and, many years later, would sponsor her pathbreaking study of "normal" women's sexuality. She also turned to the emerging field of eugenics, which sought scientific explanations for social problems. While later generations would justly criticize both the eugenics movement and the problematic policies it spawned, at the time, Davis's use of eugenic theories and intelligence testing enhanced the reformatory's reputation as "the most scientific institution of its kind in the world."[162]

Davis's stellar reputation as a social scientist as well as a social reformer helped her to weather the storm of an investigation into allegations of cruelty at Bedford that quickly morphed into a scandal about interracial lesbian relationships there. Simultaneously defending her record and deflecting attention from same-sex relationships, Davis emerged from the scandal unscathed and ready to confront a new set of challenges as New York City's first female commissioner of correction.

4

Doing a "Man's Job" and Demanding a Woman's Vote

Clad in a tailored blue skirt suit, a small but sturdy figure strode into the offices of the New York City Department of Correction. Removing her jacket to reveal a blue-and-white-striped blouse, she quickly patted her graying hair into place in its practical chignon before taking a seat at her oak rolltop desk. Flanked by a congratulatory bouquet of pink roses and a utilitarian black candlestick phone, she turned to greet her employees and visitors with a ready smile and a twinkle in her blue eyes, impressing them with both her pleasant expression and her professional demeanor. Then, against the backdrop of a blackboard covered with statistical information about the city's correctional facilities, Katharine Bement Davis proceeded to take questions from the reporters who had flocked to her office to interview the nation's first female commissioner of correction.[1]

When Davis took the oath of office on January 1, 1914, she not only became New York City's first female public official; as a woman doing what many regarded as "a man's job," she became an instant celebrity.[2] Newspapers around the country ran articles about Davis's appointment, complete with photographs of the new commissioner in decorative floral frames. Highlighting the novelty of a woman in office, journalists lavished attention on Davis's appearance, and women's pages featured profiles of Davis alongside embroidery designs.[3]

Well aware of potential criticism—at the time (as today), antifeminists often cast aspersions on feminist activists, calling them "masculine creatures" and "mistakes of nature"—the media-savvy Davis cultivated an image as "a perfectly womanly woman."[4] As one journalist approvingly noted, while "Miss Davis," as "an expert in prison reform," was not likely to "allow her kindly human sentiment to degenerate into maudlin sentimentality," she also was "a human being as well as a public official," and she demonstrated genuine concern for the offenders in her care, extending a helping hand and operating on the theory that "the germs

When Davis took office as New York City's first female commissioner of correction in 1914, journalists flocked to her office to quiz her about how a woman would tackle what many called "a man's job." The media-savvy public official consciously cultivated an image as "a perfectly womanly woman," impressing visitors with both her "business-like manner" and her pleasant appearance. George Grantham Bain Collection, Prints and Photographs Division, Library of Congress.

of goodness cannot die." The article applauded her attitude: "This is just what should be expected from a woman."[5]

Davis also impressed visitors and journalists with both her "business-like manner" and her pleasing appearance.[6] Short and solidly built, Davis looked the part of a middle-aged matron, which she played to the hilt by referring to those in her charge as "her girls" and "her boys."[7] As one observer put it, "One knows perfectly well on seeing her that if Dr. Davis had not taken up public work she would have been the best housekeeper in the United States."[8]

Of course, Davis had taken up public work. Indeed, she had enjoyed a meteoric rise to prominence, from country schoolteacher in western New York to public official in the nation's largest city, thanks to her successful leadership of Bedford Reformatory, a two-hour train ride north of the city, where she had implemented cutting-edge practices and established herself as a leader in juvenile justice. Davis owed her new position not only to her national reputation as a successful penal reformer but also to the support of Gotham's reform-minded "boy mayor," John P. Mitchel. The youthful Mitchel, who had wrested control from Tammany Hall with campaign promises to clean up city hall, hoped to win favor with the city's suffragists and demonstrate his commitment to good government by appointing Davis as both a symbol of women's rights and an exemplar of efficient administration.[9] For her part, asked why she accepted the post, Davis—a longtime advocate of women's rights—promptly replied, "Because I think woman has a place in municipal government and I decided to try to demonstrate it."[10]

Speculation about the significance of Davis's appointment ran rampant. "Was her appointment a victory for the suffragists, and did it presage a petticoat government for New York?" demanded one reporter.[11] While expressing her support for women's rights, Davis dismissed suggestions that she owed her appointment to the suffrage movement. Announcing that she had no intention of running her office as "a woman's administration," she insisted that the office was about professional qualifications rather than gender politics.[12] As one reporter quoted an anonymous source, "Her new position is not a woman's job, nor a man's job; it is a job for someone who knows how. Miss Davis knows how."[13]

Nonetheless, nobody doubted that the new public official supported woman suffrage. Shortly before beginning her new position, in fall 1913, Davis participated in a three-week "suffrage school" in New York City, sharing the speaker's podium with such local luminaries as International Woman Suffrage Alliance president Carrie Chapman Catt, National Women's Trade Union League president Margaret Dreier Robins, Hull House head resident Jane Addams, and National American Woman Suffrage Association president Anna Howard Shaw. As superintendent of Bedford Reformatory, Davis spoke on "Women of the Underworld"; she likely also joined the tours of the Night Court and the Women's House of Detention, over which she would soon wield new authority.[14]

Suffrage supporters thus especially welcomed Davis's appointment. Mary Garrett Hay, a member of the Board of Directors at Bedford Reformatory, noted that Davis was "a good suffragist" whose ancestors had long supported "the cause of women." In a fulsome press release, Hay reviewed Davis's illustrious career to date, highlighting her energy and vigor both at Bedford and during her relief work in Italy. Hay regarded Davis as the ideal exemplar of women's rights: "She is a firm believer in her sex as well as a splendid monument herself of feminine achievement."[15]

Beyond Davis's own support for suffrage, both supporters and opponents of the women's rights movement were keenly aware of the symbolic significance of Davis's appointment. Suffrage supporters regarded Davis's appointment as "a happy omen for the new year," as movement leader Anna Howard Shaw put it.[16] Other voting-rights advocates pointed to her achievements as an example of "the awakening of woman."[17] Antisuffrage activists also weighed in, pointing to Davis's appointment as evidence that women did not need voting rights to hold important positions in local government. Even opponents of women's rights had to concede that her position was praiseworthy. One prominent antisuffragist, Congregationalist theologian and *Outlook* editor Lyman Abbott, declared that Davis's accomplishment "marked an epoch in civilization."[18]

Regardless of their stance on suffrage, everyone understood that Davis's performance in office would serve as a referendum on women's ability to participate in public affairs. And Davis's post was an especially important one, for as the statistics on the chalkboard indicated, the new commissioner had her work cut out for her in taking charge of the city's long-neglected and justly maligned jails and prisons. As one reporter waspishly pointed out, "A triumph here where failures by men have been numerous cannot fail to establish new standards for the sex."[19]

"Pitiably Inadequate for Any Proper Correctional Purpose"

Davis's new role was "a revolutionary appointment" not only because she was the first woman in the nation to hold such an important public position but also because her task was "to revolutionize the methods of dealing with crime."[20] Davis's work at Bedford Reformatory had established her reputation as a leader in penal reform, and the expectation was that she would bring this experience to bear on New York City's extensive—and outdated—system of jails, prisons, workhouses, and reformatories. Davis demurred when reporters asked her to discuss her plans in detail, explaining that she needed to acquaint herself with the facilities under her charge and review the budget before announcing any definite plans. (A would-be wit declared, "Here's a Woman Who Holds Her Tongue.")[21] But from the start, Davis made it clear that she hoped to apply the principles and policies she had developed at Bedford Reformatory to New York's City's criminal justice system.

Davis faced a daunting task. As commissioner of correction, she oversaw seven district prisons and three city prisons distributed throughout the city's five boroughs. In addition, on Blackwell's Island, Riker's Island, and Hart's Island, all located in the East River, three additional workhouses, the city penitentiary, and a male reformatory fell under her purview. Moreover, the new commissioner was responsible for the welfare of thousands of people. At the beginning of Davis's first year in office, the total prison population hovered around 4,600; by the end of that year, there were more than 6,400 people in custody. But since so many individuals served short sentences or were transferred between institutions, the prison population on any given day was only a part of the picture; in a single year, the city's penal institutions received more than 80,000 people (approximately 65,500 men and 12,500 women) and transferred more than 45,000 prisoners (nearly 38,000 men and approximately 7,600 women), meaning that the city handled more than 130,000 prisoner interactions (nearly 110,000 men and more than 20,000 women) in a single year. (Because this figure does not take into account the many "repeaters" or "rounders," it is a count of interactions rather than individuals.) This was a monumental task compared to Davis's work at Bedford, where the population of youthful female offenders, while steadily increasing, barely topped 500 during her tenure there.[22]

Even setting aside the sheer scale of the city's penal system, the challenges confronting the new commissioner were enormous. Gotham's dreary and dilapidated correctional facilities offered a dramatic contrast to the bucolic Bedford campus, which featured rolling hills, lush grounds, productive gardens, and charming "cottages" in a rural setting. Indeed, New York's entire penal system fell far short of Davis's cherished ideals for corrections, both in design and in daily life. As she dryly noted in the 1914 annual report, "The institutional buildings, almost without exception, were of antiquated construction, faulty in design for their purpose, unsanitary and overcrowded."[23]

On Blackwell's Island, both the penitentiary and the workhouse had been built prior to the Civil War. Constructed of locally quarried gray stone to resemble medieval fortresses, the austere and imposing buildings offered few comforts. Prisoners crowded into stone-floored cells, slept on vermin-infested blankets, and relieved themselves in slop buckets. Davis condemned the penitentiary as "wet, slimy, dark, [and] foul smelling" and judged the cells there "unfit for pigs to wallow in." The superintendent of the women's wing of the workhouse described the building as "a depressingly grim place" that fostered a sense of "utter desolation."[24]

Conditions in the City Prison, known colloquially as the Tombs, were no better. The Tombs initially may have acquired its nickname because of the original building's Egyptian Revival design, but the moniker also referred to the history of hangings conducted there and the ongoing health risks posed by the prison's dampness, resulting from its location atop the city's former water source: the condemned and abandoned, but never adequately drained, Collect Pond. The construction of a new building in 1902 had done little to improve the City Prison's comfort or reputation. Davis was highly critical of the windowless cells, inadequate sanitation, and crowded conditions there. She remarked, "It is all that a prison ought not to be and nothing which a prison ought to be."[25]

The city's other facilities were equally dismal. Moreover, due to severe overcrowding, except for housing men and women in different parts of each building, there was no way to separate different types of offenders. Young and old, first offenders and habitual criminals, healthy and diseased—all ate, worked, and slept together in institutional mess halls, poorly lit workshops, and cramped stone-floored cells. This situation offered a sharp contrast to the Bedford campus, where careful classification of inmates and assignment to comfortable "cottages," complete with well-appointed common areas and individual bedrooms, had been central to Davis's approach to corrections. Davis described Gotham's dilapidated jails and overcrowded prisons as "pitiably inadequate for any proper correctional purpose."[26]

Davis was equally critical of the treatment of the unfortunate people who found themselves in these squalid conditions. Davis had built her reputation on the principle of tailoring treatment to the criminal, not the crime; rather than completing a fixed sentence based on the offense committed, inmates at Bedford completed a lengthy, but indeterminate, sentence of up to three years for all offenses, ranging from disorderly conduct to deliberate homicide. Davis believed that indeterminate sentencing, combined with personal supervision, psychological testing, and a parole system, offered the ideal circumstances for the rehabilitation of youthful offenders.

By contrast, the crude classification created by New York City courts' criminal convictions and definite sentences offered few opportunities to tailor treatment to the individual. Generally speaking, workhouse inmates convicted of minor offenses, such as disorderly conduct, public intoxication, vagrancy, and prostitution, served shorter sentences, counted in days rather than months. Penitentiary inmates convicted of more serious offenses, such as assault or larceny, served longer sentences, counted in months or years. Davis regarded all these sentences as far too short to implement the educational programs and industrial training she had established at Bedford, and that she saw as necessary for true "correction and reformation."[27]

When Davis had taken charge at Bedford Reformatory in 1901, the institution was not yet operational, providing the new superintendent with an ideal setting for penal reform. By contrast, New York City's decaying buildings and outdated practices presented numerous obstacles to meaningful rehabilitation. Summing up the situation at a suffrage soiree, Davis quipped, "In New York we have penitentiaries in which no one is penitent, reformatories which do not reform, and houses of correction which do not correct."[28]

Davis rose to the challenge. Indeed, she welcomed it. As she once declared, she could not abide "routine work." "I can't stay in a rut," she explained. "If the direction of a perfect institution were offered me, I should refuse it."[29] New York's correctional system was far from perfect, but Davis intended to rectify that situation. Building on her experiences at Bedford Reformatory, she was determined "to make the city's correctional institutions truly reformatory . . . institutions that correct rather than confirm habits of crime."[30]

"Bad Boys"

Perhaps not surprisingly for a former reformatory official, the new commissioner of correction began with the youngest offenders in her charge, the inmates of what was officially known as the City Reformatory for Male Misdemeanants, located on Hart's Island in the East River. "I turned to the boys first," Davis explained, because young people offered "greater possibilities." Moreover, both by inclination and experience, Davis preferred the reformatory model, based on the premise that with proper supervision and training during an indeterminate sentence, wayward youth could be transformed into responsible citizens. "Most prisons are futile," Davis opined, "but you can do something with a reformatory."[31]

Like Bedford Reformatory, the City Reformatory received offenders between the ages of sixteen and thirty. But the dilapidated facilities at Hart's Island were not up to Davis's standards; just as importantly, overcrowding meant that the juvenile offenders could not be kept apart from the adult men who inhabited a branch of the city workhouse on Hart's Island. Thus, much as she had developed Bedford Reformatory for "wayward women," Davis intended to establish a new institution, what she called a "male Bedford," for the city's "bad boys."[32]

Confronted by the challenges of the city's correctional system, Davis looked to youth for hope and inspiration. "Given the right surroundings and treated with the right understanding," she told one journalist, "I believe that the young in crime can be taught to develop a moral strength which will make the first offense the last offense."[33] The proper setting, of course, was a rural one. Learning that the city owned a six-hundred-acre farm in Orange County, Davis "begged and borrowed" to acquire horses and harnesses, acquired philanthropic funding to hire a project supervisor, and secured the volunteer services of "several college boys" to assist in building bunkhouses.[34]

Davis launched her "experiment" with twelve "boys" in March 1914.[35] After meeting with the hand-picked group to impress upon them the great responsibility of "the success of the whole experiment" and securing each participant's "word of honor to do his very best," the animal-loving Davis presented the young men with a puppy as a mascot and personally escorted them to their new home, known as New Hampton

Farm.[36] There, without armed guards or security fences, a select group of "city boys" learned "scientific farming methods" and cultivated food crops, which added variety to the diets of prisoners throughout the city at the same time that it served as an early experiment in "agriculture as rehab in the carceral state." While inmates devoted most of their time to working on the farm, they had daily breaks for swimming and played baseball on weekends.[37]

Even more than Bedford Reformatory, New Hampton Farm emphasized outdoor living. "An active out-of-door life is a fine thing," Davis asserted, "and air and sunlight are great moral, mental, and physical medicines."[38] By May 1915, 150 inmates cultivated one hundred acres. Ultimately, Davis intended to transfer all 370 "city boys" from Hart's Island to the new facility. She planned a campus similar to Bedford's, complete with a reception building for inmates to be studied and classified and individual cottages to house different groups of inmates.[39] But first, she had to deal with an entirely different issue: drug abuse.

The "Drug Evil"

Building on her early success with the city's "bad boys," Davis hoped to institute similar reforms throughout New York City's correctional facilities. She planned to abandon the dilapidated facilities at Blackwell's Island entirely. In their place, she envisioned creating new farm-based facilities for both men and women. Men would be assigned to a "modern municipal farm" at Riker's Island, while women would inhabit "an Adamless Eden" outside the city. In the city itself, in place of the Tombs, Davis proposed building a new facility for male offenders as well as what newspapers dubbed a "detention home de luxe" for women awaiting trial.[40]

In these new facilities, Davis hoped to apply her "rational plan for female offenders" to all lawbreakers by establishing "a graded system of reformatories" that would include separate facilities for first offenders, "inebriates and vagrants," and "hardened criminals." Naturally, she also favored using intelligence testing to identify "feeble-minded" individuals—and their children. While some of these might become "permanent wards" of the state, she hoped that most could eventually be released from "custodial care."[41]

Modifying her earlier stance on eugenics, Davis explained that "statistics affirms" that "criminality itself . . . is not hereditary." Nonetheless, Davis believed that some individuals were predisposed, if not predestined, to criminal behavior. Whereas earlier Davis had applied eugenic theories and policies to suspected sex workers, now she reserved them for violent offenders. She offered Boston's "boy murderer," Jesse Pomeroy—who began brutally torturing younger children when he was just thirteen years old and ultimately, at age fifteen, was convicted of kidnapping and killing a ten-year-old girl—as an example of "the type of hopeless degenerate and defective that she believed should be confined for life."[42]

Finally, while Davis recommended that "murderous impulses should be analyzed as the symptoms of an invalid would be analyzed and diagnosed by physician," she opposed capital punishment. "It seems to me illogical to kill legally when we are teaching people not to kill," she pronounced.[43]

Before Davis could raise funds to implement her ambitious plans, however, she had to turn her attention to a more pressing matter in the city's prisons: drugs. In some ways, Davis's concerns about drugs were a logical extension of her longstanding reservations about liquor. Davis traced her lifelong advocacy of temperance to her grandmother, Rhoda Bement, who so strongly opposed alcohol that she refused even to take communion wine.[44]

Davis's feminist commitments reinforced her opposition to what many activists called "Demon Rum." Like many of her colleagues in the suffrage movement, she regarded alcohol abuse as a contributing factor to poverty and violence and therefore supported temperance: the voluntary choice to renounce alcohol. During her career in corrections, Davis also became a proponent of prohibition—the criminalization of the production and sale of alcohol—in large part because alcohol played such a prominent role in the unhappy fates of the people who ended up in her care both at Bedford Reformatory and in New York City. One incident in particular—in which a drunken man raped a young woman while he and another fellow were supposed to be safely escorting her home from work, then defended himself with the argument that he and his friends were "perfect gentlemen when sober" but "did not know what they were doing" when "in their cups"—convinced Davis that alcohol contributed to both criminal behavior and sexual assault.[45]

Always open to changing her mind on the basis of new information, however, Davis would later recant her support for the Eighteenth Amendment, because she determined that prohibition increased crime rather than deterring it. As a result, she decided that "the Constitution of the United States is not the place for prohibitions of this kind." Instead, Davis declared, proper education, rather than law enforcement, was the key to moral reform. This insight ultimately would inform her approach to sex as well as to liquor.[46]

In the meantime, however, Davis was responsible for enforcing existing laws, and she assumed her responsibilities as New York City's chief correctional official at a time when new legislation criminalized previously legal substances. While Davis had always been concerned about mind-altering substances, drug abuse attracted increased attention during her tenure as commissioner of correction. New laws at both the state and the national level went into effect soon after Davis took office. At the federal level, the Harrison Narcotics Act placed new restrictions on products derived from opium and cocaine. At the state level, the Boylan Law required a physician's prescription to dispense opium and morphine, which previously had been readily available without a prescription. Indeed, opiates were common ingredients in patent medicines touted as a cure for a wide variety of ailments and marketed to women and children. By criminalizing the sale and purchase of these substances, the new laws practically guaranteed an increased prison population. Moreover, the state law mandated addiction treatment for offenders, thereby placing an increased burden of responsibility on the Department of Correction. Davis, who estimated that between one third and one half of New York's prisoners were addicted to drugs, was determined to crack down on the "drug evil" in Gotham's jails and prisons. She swiftly enacted a three-pronged approach to the problem, which included preventing smuggling, providing treatment, and firing prison personnel involved in the drug trade.[47]

Early in her administration, Davis employed undercover agents to conduct inside investigations of the city's correctional facilities. At the Tombs, her agents discovered an extensive drug trade. Prisoners and suppliers employed a variety of creative methods to smuggle drugs into the jail. Fashionable lady visitors smuggled drugs in beads in their hatpins. A shoemaker hollowed out the heels of shoes to contain contraband. Magazines enjoyed a period of unprecedented popularity after clever readers found a way to layer drugs over illustrations and then cover the contraband with a similar picture, carefully pasted over the original and the drugs. To address these issues, Davis instituted mail inspections and visitor screening. In addition, to curb the importation of illegal drugs along with special meals, she banned food deliveries and established a commissary in the Tombs, complete with menu cards printed in English, German, Italian, and Yiddish. Using insights gained from her time at the Philadelphia settlement house, Davis made sure to supply "a Kosher cook, with her own stove and cooking appliances for orthodox Jews."[48]

Most dramatically, Davis hired a "woman sleuth" to go undercover in the women's wing of the Blackwell's Island Workhouse to discover the source of drugs there. The investigation resulted in the arrest, trial, and conviction of the prison physician for providing inmates with illegal drugs; Davis used the resulting publicity to advance her aim of hiring a woman physician to replace the drug-dealing doctor.[49]

Meanwhile, Davis requested additional funds to establish "drug wards" to provide medical treatment for opium addicts in the city's prisons. Mayor Mitchel touted his commissioner's success at combating the drug problem, telling one reporter that she had achieved "amazing things—unbelievable things" in reducing drug use and providing effective treatment in the city's prisons. Davis herself told reporters, "The habit has been reduced a great deal."[50]

"Feminine Efficiency"

Davis took advantage of the media attention garnered by her early months in office to promote women's political rights. Although Davis initially had distanced herself from the suffrage struggle, once she had established herself in office, New York's famous woman official used her celebrity to advance the cause. She often linked her work in corrections to the suffrage movement, arguing that if women had voting rights, they would help her to set things right in Gotham's jails. More generally, she saw women as having a meaningful role to play in promoting what she called "humane, just and efficient management of our public affairs."[51]

Like many other suffrage advocates at the time, Davis drew connections between household management and city governance to promote women's rights. Pointing out that city departments existed to establish and maintain decent homes in which to bring up children, she also emphasized that housewives, as the managers of household budgets, had an excellent understanding of finances and extensive background in administration. In short, then, both women's experiences and their interests made them ideal voters. As she put it, "A woman's interest in her home makes her feel most keenly and see most clearly . . . the ways in which efficient government protects the home and makes the training of children possible on the highest plane, and because she has this insight into the needs of the home, she can best represent it in government."[52]

What family friend Katherine Bragdon called "Kate's wonderful work" as head of corrections was an excellent example of "woman's efficiency in office," as one laudatory account put it. In addition to praising her "feminine efficiency" in dealing with the drug problem, Mayor Mitchel highlighted his commissioner's "domestic efficiency and good housekeeping" in improving the prison diet on a limited budget.[53]

During Davis's first year in office, the city cut the prison food budget, allocating only sixteen cents per capita per diem for inmates' food. (This was a considerable reduction from the previous year, which allowed just under eighteen cents per capita per diem; it also was only one cent more than the budget allowed at the model home Davis had supervised at the World's Fair more than twenty years earlier.) Even under the previous budget, the meals served prisoners were monotonous in the extreme; dinner (the main meal of the day) was unvaryingly meat and potatoes (except for Fridays, when fish replaced beef), while breakfast and supper consisted, equally unvaryingly, of bread, coffee, and tea. When Davis took office, the wardens of the city's institutions sounded the alarm, warning that if the current conditions continued, there were likely to be food riots.[54]

Given her experience in feeding a family on a budget at the World's Fair, Davis was the perfect person to find ways to cut costs, improve nutrition, and increase variety. She promptly devised an entirely new menu, implemented throughout the prison system, that provided much greater variety within the prescribed budget. The new plan provided different

When Davis accepted a position as New York City's chief corrections official, she assumed responsibility for dilapidated jails and dismal prisons that she described as "pitiably inadequate for any proper correctional purpose." Davis was especially critical of the prison and workhouse at Blackwell's Island, where inmates crowded into stone-floored cells, slept on vermin-infested blankets, and relieved themselves in slop buckets. In July 1914, when male prisoners rioted to protest unsanitary conditions and cruel treatment, the "plucky" public official subdued the riot, instituted reforms, and gained public acclaim. George Grantham Bain Collection, Prints and Photographs Division, Library of Congress.

menus for each meal of the day and each day of the week. For instance, breakfast might now include oatmeal, beef hash, or hominy as well as bread and coffee; dinner offerings included a variety of soups and fresh vegetables as well as meat and potatoes, and supper options included baked beans, apple sauce, and macaroni and cheese as well as bread and coffee.[55]

Suffrage leaders were quick to capitalize on Davis's accomplishments and claim them as evidence of women's capacity for citizenship. One suffrage periodical celebrated the woman commissioner's "splendid report" after her first six months in office, praising her as "a civic housekeeper of the first rank" for her improvements in both the budget and the diet of the city's prisons. Another contended that her example proved that "women are the economical sex" and that "justice saves money."[56]

Not all New Yorkers appreciated Davis's early efforts, however, especially where crackdowns on drug smuggling were involved. Rather, those involved in the illicit drug trade sent her threats, prompting the mayor to provide her with a bodyguard for several days.[57] Moreover, at least according to some accounts, the disruptions to the drug supply were a contributing factor to a serious challenge to Davis's authority: a prison riot at Blackwell's Island in July 1914.[58]

"You Fellows Must Behave"

On July 10, Commissioner Davis was attending a women's rights gathering held at the home of socialite suffragist Alva Belmont in the exclusive vacation enclave of Newport, Rhode Island. There, she argued that she needed women's votes to help her make her department "one of correction and not merely of jails." Complaining about crowding, corruption, and cocaine, she concluded, "My department is one hundred years behind the times, and it is for this reason that I want New York women to get the vote in 1915 so as to help me out. Women may make mistakes, but they always get somewhere."[59]

As Davis returned to Manhattan via boat, she could hear "catcalls and shrieking" from Blackwell's Island. She quickly made her way to the Twenty-Sixth Street dock to take the ferry to the island, still wearing her finery, leading some papers to report that she had donned her best clothing for the occasion and that she subdued the prisoners at the point of her parasol! (Davis denied carrying a parasol.) There, she found that approximately seven hundred male prisoners—half the prison population—had staged a violent revolt.[60]

Although some accounts initially attributed the uprising to frustrated drug users, most ultimately described the unrest as a protest against the horrific conditions at the prison and the sadistic warden who held sway there. Mainstream newspapers, such as *The New York Times*, and socialist outlets, such as *The Masses*, not surprisingly offered different versions of events, but all agreed that the penitentiary at Blackwell's Island was a disgrace. Not only were the facilities severely overcrowded and disgustingly unsanitary, but the warden, Patrick Hayes, was an "old school" disciplinarian who sanctioned severe punishments for minor infractions. In addition to authorizing the guards to beat prisoners with clubs to maintain order, Hayes subjected so-called troublemakers to long sentences in the "coolers," as the solitary confinement cells with double-walled refrigerator doors were called. The nickname became even more apt when, after subduing fractious inmates with a high-powered water hose, Hayes left cell windows open so that the cool night air added to the discomfort of sleeping on stone floors in several inches of water. But according to Frank Tanenbaum, a radical labor organizer who wrote for *The Masses*, even worse than the physical conditions was the psychological abuse. Tanenbaum, who served a year-long sentence after staging a protest at a Catholic church, complained bitterly about the warden's cruel jokes at the prisoners' expense, asserting that Warden Hayes seemed determined "to break the spirits of the prisoners."[61]

After days of murmuring, on July 8, 1914, violence erupted after the warden sent a group of restive inmates to the coolers, leading to still more complaints. Ordered to return to their cells, prisoners dining in the mess hall instead attacked the guards, known as "keepers," with heavy ceramic bowls.[62] Although the trouble began with only a handful of prisoners, the harsh treatment of the so-called ringleaders, who were placed in solitary confinement and restricted to a diet of bread and water, inspired sympathizers to join the uprising. In the prison's workshops, Tanenbaum gave fiery speeches and launched a strike in solidarity with inmates being held in the prison's disciplinary cells. Imprisoned workers sabotaged machinery and started fires before joining their colleagues in solitary confinement, leading to still more unrest among the prison population. Within three days, half of the fourteen hundred prisoners had joined the rebellion, protesting poor treatment and demanding the warden's resignation. They attacked the keepers who attempted to restore order with stones from the exercise yards, tools from the workshops, and slop buckets from the cells before being forced into the coolers at gunpoint. Even then, their curses and complaints were so loud that they could be heard on the mainland. The situation did not improve until the arrival of the new commissioner of correction.[63]

"Short of stature, but with a will of iron and nerves of steel," Davis took charge at once. Holding a hastily packed suitcase aloft, she announced her intention to remain on the island until order was restored. Davis established her authority with a combination of benevolence and sternness. While she continued the bread and water diet for the ringleaders, she increased the rations. She threatened to call out the militia if necessary, but she also promised to listen to the inmates' concerns. She methodically walked through every tier of the penitentiary, requesting suggestions for delegates to represent the prisoners' concerns in private meetings with her. In all, she spoke to nearly one hundred prisoners that first day. She remained at the penitentiary, sleeping on site, for three nights, meeting one on one with prisoners as well as delivering speeches at meals.[64]

Davis's matter-of-fact, no-nonsense manner, as well as her willingness to listen to prisoners' concerns, quickly won the inmates' confidence and respect. Addressing the prisoners—ranging from teenage pickpockets to seasoned criminals—as "boys," she established herself as a stern but fair maternal figure. She treated the refractory inmates as if they were wayward children, pronouncing, "You fellows must behave. I'll have it no other way."[65]

National newspapers reported, with apparent astonishment, that the "plucky" public official showed no fear.[66] *The Washington Post* noted that the petite woman had "quell[ed] mobs that would have taken the heart and courage out of many stalwart men," adding, "She shows no sign of hysterical strain."[67] At mealtimes, Davis mounted a soapbox to address the "orderly prisoners" who were permitted out of their cells to assemble in the dining hall. She was well received. The inmates laughed at her funny stories and cheered her speeches. According to *The New York Times*, "It was impressive to see a woman handling such a mob of men, and she did it well. Her auditors were as orderly as Sunday school children and more quiet."[68]

The comparison to Sunday school was apt. That weekend, building on her experience at Bedford, Davis conducted religious services for the inmates—Protestant, Catholic, and Jewish—reading scriptures, telling homely anecdotes, and adjuring adherence to prison rules. While each service was tailored to the audience, the take-home message was the same: Prisoners should use their time in confinement to better themselves. "If you can learn two things while you are here, obedience to the law and self-control, you will not regret having been here," she promised. "You can go out and become useful members of society again." Capitalizing on her musical background, Davis even led the inmates in song, and "camp-meeting tunes" replaced the curses and catcalls that had greeted her when she first arrived.[69]

Within three days, Davis had restored order and established her own authority. Before leaving the island, she received a note composed by several prisoners, who wrote, "We believe you have spoken from a sister's and a mother's heart of affection to erring and unfortunate brothers and sons, and also as our beloved and trusted commissioner."[70] Davis expressed great satisfaction with her signal success on the island. "The riots in the penitentiary were perhaps a good thing after all," she later reflected. "They cleared the air like a thunderstorm. They convinced everybody in the beginning that to have a woman commissioner didn't mean that discipline was going to be lax."[71]

In addition to disproving critics who believed that directing New York City's Department of Corrections was "a man's job," Davis's actions at Blackwell's Island brought her popular acclaim. In the aftermath of the riot, while a grand jury conducted an investigation of the abysmal conditions of Gotham's prisons, its members commended Davis for her "energy, justice, and ability" in coping with the recent uprising.[72]

"The Coming Great Force in Government"

Davis's victory at Blackwell's Island increased her visibility as a suffrage advocate. Shortly before the mutiny at Blackwell's Island, Davis had joined the Congressional Union, an offshoot of the National American Woman Suffrage Association that focused its efforts on the federal suffrage amendment. While Davis's affiliation with the Congressional Union indicated her support for a federal suffrage amendment, she also was enthusiastic about both state and local activism.[73]

To advance women's rights at the local level, Davis had cultivated relationships with the city's suffragists ever since taking office. She especially targeted "society women," who had both leisure time and financial resources to devote to the cause. Indeed, at the time of the mutiny, she had been one of the featured speakers at a stylish suffrage soiree in

After peacefully subduing a prison riot, Commissioner Davis used her high-profile position as a public official to advocate for women's suffrage, declaring, "The methods of wise motherhood are what government most needs." In 1915, she participated in one of the nation's largest suffrage parades as part of a delegation of city workers. George Grantham Bain Collection, Prints and Photographs Division, Library of Congress.

Newport, Rhode Island, at the opulent vacation home of high-society doyenne Alva Belmont.[74]

After quelling the mutiny, Davis sought to use her success at Blackwell's Island to build support for voting rights at a pivotal moment in the suffrage movement. The public official's term coincided with a major push for women's suffrage in the Empire State and throughout the nation. Suffrage supporters hoped that a victory in the populous state would ensure the success of the Susan B. Anthony Amendment.[75]

At this critical juncture, the childless Davis, like many of her colleagues, adopted the language of "maternalism," arguing that women needed the right to vote in order to fulfill their duties as mothers—either as mothers of their own children or as "mothers of all children." Like many of her ostensibly childless contemporaries, even though she had no children of her own, Davis both practiced "othermothering"—by helping to bring up her motherless niece—and cast her professional work as a form of public motherhood—by "looking after other people's . . . children." Moreover, she used examples of what she called "the maternal instinct" in public life as evidence that all of American society would benefit from woman suffrage.[76]

Interviewed after the uprising, Davis pronounced, "Criminals . . . are not merely 'like bad boys.' They are bad boys, and they must be treated as such." Her success in quelling the uprising, she explained, was "only what must be expected and demanded in the government of the future by injecting the maternal instinct into municipal affairs." Both capitalizing on the publicity and forestalling potential criticism, she added, "I would not welcome a new matriarchate. But I would see women working shoulder to shoulder with men for the city's good."[77]

Davis reinforced this message in a lengthy op-ed in which she predicted that "maternalism" was "the coming great force for government." Again comparing prisoners to "bad boys," she explained that, while not a mother herself, she used what she characterized as a maternal "combination of kindness and firmness" to subdue the rebellion. She concluded, "The methods of wise motherhood are what government most needs."[78]

The timing of the fracas at Blackwell's Island was fortuitous for the suffragist commissioner, putting her in the perfect position to play an important role in state politics. Fall 1914 was an exciting time for suffrage advocates, as both the old-guard Republican Party and the upstart third-party Progressive Party endorsed woman suffrage. Meanwhile, New York launched a constitutional convention and chose a total of six women—five district delegates and one delegate-at-large—to rewrite the state's constitution. When the New York Progressive Party nominated Davis as a delegate-at-large to the constitutional convention, "there was a strong outburst of applause."[79]

Davis's ecumenical politics made her the perfect choice for the position. A lifelong Republican, Davis also was a longtime admirer of Progressive Party candidate Teddy Roosevelt. In 1899, while she had been in Europe, homesick and longing for letters from home, she had teased, "I do think father or Chat [Charlotte] might have sent me the account of 'Teddy's' visit to R. [Rochester] since they know how much interest I take in him."[80]

As delegate-at-large, Davis was expected to represent a variety of political perspectives but, ultimately, to represent reform. "Who knows better than Dr. Davis the special needs of reform?" demanded one supporter. "Primarily reform is what a Constitutional Convention is for, to correct the errors in the Constitution, effect changes, and remedy conditions." Davis—who as commissioner of correction knew how to correct and change—had "proved herself worthy of the great responsibilities of her position."[81]

The constitutional convention became the focal point for both pro- and antisuffrage activism. It also solidified Davis's leadership in the state suffrage movement. In April 1914, Frances Davis invited May Bragdon to accompany her to Buffalo to hear her daughter speak; later that year, the entire Bragdon family went "to a fine suffrage meeting" to watch Davis share the speaker's platform with Carrie Chapman Catt—then the leader of the Empire State Campaign Committee and shortly to resume the presidency of the National American Woman Suffrage Association. While the new constitution ultimately did not extend voting rights to women, the convention showcased the suffrage issue and intensified the state suffrage movement, which adopted as its new motto, "Victory in 1917."[82]

Accordingly, a year into her tenure as commissioner of correction, Davis stepped up her suffrage activities. Proudly proclaiming that she was "born a suffragist," she won election to office in the National American Woman Suffrage Association in 1915. That same year, she co-founded the Woman's City Club of New York, a civic reform organization formed with the goal of preparing women for full citizenship. She also participated in one of the nation's largest suffrage parades as part of a delegation of city workers, using her public position to advance women's rights.[83]

A "Winning Plan"

Davis's suffrage activities showcased her strategic approach to social reform. At the time that Davis joined the voting rights struggle, the suffrage movement itself struggled with internal divisions. At the national level, trouble was brewing between the mainstream leaders of the National American Woman Suffrage Association (NAWSA) and the militant adherents of the Congressional Union, soon to become its own organization, the National Woman's Party (NWP). While NAWSA focused on state action and followed a conservative policy of ladylike lobbying, the NWP, dedicated to the federal amendment, would adopt the flamboyant policy of picketing the White House.[84]

Meanwhile, at the state level, two New Yorkers vied for dominance. Harriot Stanton Blatch, daughter of Seneca Falls organizer Elizabeth Cady Stanton, had reinvigorated the suffrage movement in New York by bringing it out of private parlors and into public streets with open-air tactics such as streetcorner speeches and suffrage parades. Building on the work of the Women's Trade Union League, Blatch also forged alliances with working women, founding the Equality League for Self-Supporting Women in 1907 (later renamed the Women's Political Union, or WPU).[85]

Blatch's organization was known for its militant direct-action tactics, which it borrowed from British suffrage leader Emmeline Pankhurst, whose motto was "deeds, not words." The WPU's colors—green, purple, and white—echoed those of the British suffrage movement, while its members' penchant for spectacle reflected its founders' acquaintance with the United Kingdom's militant "suffragettes," the term adopted by radical women's rights activists in the United Kingdom and used as a disparaging term for suffrage advocates in the United States. Pankhurst and her followers garnered attention for the cause by engaging in civil disobedience, such as smashing the windows of Parliament in London beginning in 1912—much as Davis and her fellow settlement house workers had done in Philadelphia in the 1890s.[86]

Given Blatch's connection to Seneca Falls, where Davis's own grandmother had participated in the historic suffrage gathering in 1848, it is no surprise that Davis became an enthusiastic member of the Women's Political Union. However, Davis also trumpeted her support for Carrie Chapman Catt, who would emerge as Blatch's chief competitor for leadership in the state suffrage movement—and with whom Davis also had a close connection.

In Davis's high school home town, Rochester's suffrage pioneer, Susan B. Anthony, had personally selected Catt to lead a new national suffrage organization. In the aftermath of the Civil War, two competing suffrage organizations emerged: the American Woman Suffrage Association and the National Woman Suffrage Association. The rivalry was the result of irreconcilable differences over whether to accept or reject the nation's decision—in the form of the Fourteenth Amendment—to enshrine Black men's citizenship in the Constitution while excluding all women from the franchise in the aftermath of the Civil War. For the next twenty years, the two organizations would run parallel campaigns for woman suffrage, with AWSA conducting state-level campaigns and NWSA focused on a federal amendment. Finally, in 1890, the same year that Davis matriculated at Vassar College, they joined to form the National American Woman Suffrage Association (NAWSA), with Catt at its helm.[87]

Catt stepped down after just four years in office, but she remained active in suffrage circles, founding the New York City Woman Suffrage Party (WSP), in part as an alternative to the militant tactics of British suffrage advocate Emmeline Pankhurst, then on the brink of her first visit to the United States. Resuming her post at the helm of the national organization in 1915, Catt would soon implement her so-called winning plan of fusing state-by-state suffrage struggles with the final push to ratify the federal suffrage amendment.[88]

In 1914, however, when Davis took office as commissioner of correction, Catt and Blatch were competing for leadership of the state suffrage movement and running two parallel state suffrage movements: the WSP's Empire State Campaign Committee, led by Catt, and the Women's Political Union, led by Blatch. In New York City, the WSP coopted the movement among immigrants and workers, previously associated with the Equality League and the WPU, while the WPU shifted its attention to wealthy women whose funding was essential to organizing. Upstate, however, the class dynamic was reversed. While the organizations engaged in "jurisdictional battles" north of the city, within the city, the two organizations cooperated relatively well.[89]

Davis threaded the needle by allying herself with both organizations, a decision probably made easier by socialist women's decision to withdraw from organizations of "bourgeois suffragists." Davis not only joined the WPU but also, in 1915, marched under the organization's banner as part of a special division of municipal employees in a suffrage parade, at which official estimates placed the total number of participants at twenty-five thousand. In advance of the event, Davis even hosted a special "suffragist tea" at her office in the municipal building, in which she urged all female city employees to pledge to participate in the parade; she also told reporters that the male voters in her department would support women's rights: "All men under her will vote 'right,'" she asserted.[90]

But that same year, Davis—by then an officer in NAWSA—lauded Catt's selection as president of the national organization, opining that while there were "other women" capable of directing the state campaign (perhaps she had Blatch in mind?), "there was no one else who was fully equal to the great responsibilities of directing the national work."[91]

Just as Catt's "winning plan" involved working simultaneously on state and federal suffrage campaigns, Davis's own "winning plan" included participating in multiple organizations at both national and state levels. At the federal level, Davis displayed her characteristic combination of caution and commitment by allying herself with what would become rival national suffrage organizations. In 1914, she had joined the Congressional Union, an offshoot of NAWSA dedicated to the federal amendment that would ultimately become a rival national organization, the National Woman's Party. But in 1915 and 1916, she would hold office in NAWSA, which would vigorously oppose the militant actions of the NWP's members, who during World War I would picket the White House, be imprisoned for civil disobedience, and earn the moniker "iron-jawed angels" for engaging a hunger strike.

Meanwhile, in New York, while Davis's election as third vice-president of NAWSA increasingly allied her with Catt rather than with Blatch, she continued to work with both state organizations. Although her own self-supporting status allied her with the WPU, she also was attracted by Catt's more moderate (as opposed to militant) tactics. In addition—and of vital importance to both state suffrage societies—despite her own modest origins, Davis proved to be especially adept at wooing wealthy women to support the cause. But, in keeping with her almost uncanny ability to walk a tightrope when the situation demanded it, and foreshadowing her interest in "average" women, Davis also reached out to ordinary housewives.

Both on the platform and in the press, Davis appealed to women of all backgrounds, from working wives to society matrons, by pointing out that "every working mother" paid taxes on the goods she purchased to feed her family, and that "any woman who can learn to play auction bridge can learn to understand the tariff." Over and over again, Davis argued that all women had both the ability to be good citizens and the

As commissioner of correction, Katharine Bement Davis used her public position to advocate for women's suffrage. But at the same time that she promoted voting rights, Davis also policed women's speech—and their bodies. The self-supporting Davis cared about women's rights, but she also cared about keeping her job. When these priorities came into conflict, the choice was clear. Frequently tangling with free-speech advocates, militant labor leaders, and birth-control advocates, Davis upheld the duties of her office and cherished the visible sign of her authority: her official badge, handed down from generation to generation and still in her family's possession. (The badge also correctly displayed her title, Commissioner of Correction, although both at the time and since, reporters often mistakenly rendered it as Commissioner of Corrections.) Photo by Wendy Magee, courtesy of John Pepper.

responsibility to do good. She declared, "Another reason I have for believing in equal suffrage is that I want to see some things done."[92] In keeping with her characteristic desire to get things done, Davis used her public position to advocate for women's voting rights, constantly hammering home the message that she needed women's help to reform Gotham's prisons. As she put it, "I see daily in my work in the Department of Corrections reasons why women should have a vote."[93]

"Womanly Patience"

Even as Davis used her public position to promote women's voting rights, she became embroiled in an ugly conflict with the city's most radical women activists. Soon after Davis took up residence at Blackwell's Island to deal with the prison riot and its leaders, including Frank Tanenbaum, a member of the International Workers of the World (IWW), she tangled with another IWW radical, this time at the women's workhouse. Rebecca Edelson (sometimes spelled Edelsohn) was a relative newcomer to the city's anarchist circles, but she quickly made a name for herself as a free-speech radical following her arrest at a protest in April 1914.[94]

After Edelson refused to post bail to ensure her future silence, in July 1914, she was sentenced to ninety days at the Blackwell's Island Workhouse. She immediately announced her intention to stage a hunger strike. While militant suffrage activists in England had attracted both sympathy and condemnation by engaging in hunger striking, this was the first such action by a woman in the United States. Edelson and her anarchist colleagues made the most of this opportunity for publicity. In a letter to fellow IWW member Alexander Berkman, Edelson stated her readiness "to die as a martyr," reflecting that "if the worst comes to the worst I can only die once and it will make glorious propaganda." Meanwhile, radical activists planned—and publicized—a funeral in the event of Edelson's death.[95]

Commissioner Davis was prepared. She promptly announced that she would feed the prisoner by force if necessary. Indeed, both the commissioner and city hall seemed eager to join battle with "Militant Becky" and the anarchist element she represented. Davis may even have seen Edelson's sentence at the women's workhouse as an opportunity for some good public relations, since her presence highlighted some of the changes Davis had made there, including hiring women for senior staff positions. According to *The New York Times*, "At City Hall much satisfaction was expressed because the problem of this country's first woman hunger striker was being met by a woman Commissioner of Correction, with a woman surgeon, a woman trained nurse, and a woman matron to assist her." City authorities seemed confident that with a woman in charge, the representatives of law and order would prevail without either undue cruelty or negative publicity. After making a special trip to the island "to see that Miss Edelson's hunger strike got a start under proper supervision and without the use of forcible means," Davis told reporters that she believed "a policy of 'watchful waiting,' with much womanly patience, will win."[96]

"Womanly patience" did not ensure benevolent treatment, however. While workhouse staff monitored Edelson's health, Davis prepared for the possibility of forcible feeding. Claiming that the process was painless unless the prisoner struggled, she assured readers that struggling could be prevented by wrapping the prisoner in a heavy blanket. In this way, she explained, the "mummified" subject could not resist while a rubber tube was inserted through the nose and into the esophagus. (With inadvertent irony, one newspaper carried this story on the "women's page" beneath an illustrated story on "Easy & Practical Home Dress Making Lessons"!)[97]

It is unclear if Edelson ever was subjected to this inhumane treatment. After an initial flurry of publicity, Davis announced that she would no longer issue regular updates on the situation.[98] Moreover, Davis and her supporters claimed that Edelson's strike was a sham and that the so-called hunger striker secretly acquired food throughout her sentence.[99]

If stonewalling journalists and discrediting the hunger striker were strategies intended to protect Davis's reputation, they backfired. In the absence of solid information, anarchist sympathizers and conservative commentators around the country used the threat of force feeding to support their respective stances. Along the way, they called attention to the conflict between two women—the free-speech radical, Rebecca Edelson, and the law-and-order public official, Katharine Davis—on opposite sides of the issue. A Georgia newspaper praised Davis's firm stance, noting that as a woman, she was not handicapped, as British authorities were, by gentlemanly chivalry.[100] Meanwhile, stirred by a plea from feminist, free lover, and free-speech advocate Emma Goldman, laborers in the mining town of Butte, Montana, sent a telegram to Davis calling her "a disgrace to your sex."[101]

Whether the IWW protester's hunger strike represented true suffering or a publicity stunt, the contretemps ensured that Davis would be persona non grata in radical feminist circles. In the pages of *The Woman Rebel*, free-speech activist and birth-control advocate Margaret Sanger sharply criticized Davis, calling her "a brilliant example of that rapidly growing group of respectable folk who have discovered profitable and highly honorable careers in the exploitation of the victims of our social 'law and order.'"[102]

As a city official, Davis was committed to upholding existing laws, regardless of her personal beliefs. But her announcement that she planned to construct a new disciplinary building on Riker's Island—which journalists dubbed an "Anarchist Prison" and described as a "Special Prison for I.W.W. Orators"—did nothing to endear her to the city's radical element.[103] Nor, for that matter, did her refusal to grant passes to journalists who wished to conduct independent investigations of conditions on Blackwell's Island. When Davis claimed that journalists disrupted prison discipline by circulating "preposterous stories" about prison conditions, she provided free-speech advocates with fresh ammunition.[104]

The escalating conflict between legal authority and free speech put Davis—and the institutions she oversaw—in the crosshairs. After her release, Edelson wasted no time in publishing lengthy statements denouncing conditions in the women's workhouse.[105] Her testimony, combined with an ongoing investigation of conditions at the men's prison, revealed serious problems at Blackwell's Island, including severe overcrowding, filthy conditions, and physical cruelty. A full year after the unrest on the island, a grand jury released a report describing prison administration as "severe, harsh, and repressive." While the grand jury reserved its strongest criticism for Warden Hayes, it also held Davis's department liable for "neglect and indifference."[106]

Initially, Davis attempted to use this evidence to advance her goal of building new facilities elsewhere.[107] However, she became increasingly frustrated with the seemingly unending criticism of the institutions under her charge. In public statements, she defended her brief record, pointing out that she had planned many far-reaching reforms, but had been stymied for lack of funds. It was unfair, she insisted, for her office to become a "scapegoat" for longstanding problems, such as "antiquated buildings," which made it difficult to enact the best practices in progressive penal reform. Mayor Mitchel also defended Davis, arguing that his commissioner should be given a chance to carry out her plans, which included "transfer[ring] the prisoners to new and sanitary quarters, where the modern principles of corrective penology can be applied."[108]

In a group letter published in the periodical of the General Federation of Women's Clubs, some women activists also came to Davis's defense. "We women of New York City are very proud of Dr. Katherine Bement Davis, Commissioner of Charities and Corrections," they wrote, expressing their admiration for Davis, despite getting both the spelling of her name and her proper title wrong. They continued, "When Dr. Davis is maligned we as one woman regret it, and when she is commended, we as one woman rejoice." This strong statement of sisterhood and solidarity highlighted Davis's appeal to middle-class clubwomen, even as she alienated the city's radical women activists.[109]

"Locking Up and Letting Out and Locking Up Again Is Useless"

As Davis became increasingly frustrated with both her position at the helm of the Department of Correction and the criticism it drew, she looked for new ways to achieve her goals of penal reform. Piecemeal reforms in response to public outcry were not her preferred method. Rather, Davis had always sought innovative solutions to social problems. As one colleague explained, she "had a scientific mind, and by natural bent as well as professional training was not satisfied with treating symptoms, but probed deep into the basis of social ills."[110]

One of the social ills that most concerned the city official was the problem of "rounders." At the time Davis assumed her post as commissioner of correction, "rounders" were familiar figures in the city's prisons. Usually arrested for petty offenses such as vagrancy or drunkenness, these repeat offenders served numerous short sentences in the workhouse. Many were rearrested and recommitted just days, or even hours, after release. As the "ardent dry" prohibition advocate explained the problem, after serving a sentence ranging from ten days to six months, workhouse regulars debarked from the ferry that shuttled people between Blackwell's Island and the Twenty-Sixth Street dock with "no money" and "no friends," only "a desire to forget 'the island.'" It was no surprise, then, that many of these newly released people sought comfort in the "nearest saloon," only to be rearrested before nightfall. "Back they go to the workhouse," concluded Davis, "with nothing to fortify them but the anticipation of their next release."[111]

Outlook magazine highlighted the problem of "rounders" shortly after Davis took office by presenting "the story of Sadie," a twenty-five-year-old completing her eighth six-month sentence in six years at the women's workhouse. Sadie ran afoul of the law on a variety of conduct charges, including soliciting, vagrancy, and "drunk and disorderly" conduct. Disfigured by lesions resulting from syphilis, Sadie demanded, "Look at me. D'you think anybody'd give *me* work? What can I do but go back on the streets?" While Davis's reforms at the workhouse provided a separate treatment ward, complete with a female physician, for inmates like Sadie, they did not solve the problem of providing women like her with either job opportunities or ongoing care.[112]

Davis decided to study rounders systematically. She began taking fingerprints for all prisoners, allowing her department to collect reliable information about repeat offenders for the first time. During her first year in office, Davis found that more than half of all prisoners were being committed for the second time, and nearly one third were being committed for a third (or subsequent) offense.[113]

Davis also commissioned a study of repeat offenders in the women's workhouse, which included intelligence testing. Perhaps not surprisingly, given Davis's work along these lines at Bedford Reformatory, the report concluded that there was a strong correlation between lower test scores and higher recidivism rates.[114]

Both individual situations and statistical analysis convinced Davis that the current system, relying as it did on short-term sentences that provided no opportunity for meaningful rehabilitation, was broken beyond repair. Davis pronounced, "Locking up and letting out and locking up again is useless."[115]

"A Great Laboratory for the Study of Social Ills"

In seeking solutions to recidivism, Davis relied on her previous experience. The solution she came up with was an innovative one, but it also was in line with national directions in penal reform, which had laid increased emphasis on indeterminate sentencing, probation, and parole since the late nineteenth century. New York State had adopted indeterminate sentencing and parole in 1889 for state institutions, thus laying the groundwork for the system that Davis had employed at Bedford. However, in New York City, with the exception of juvenile offenders, the Department of Correction continued to rely on definite sentencing, in which judges assigned a fixed sentence at the same time that they delivered a guilty verdict.[116]

During her first year in office as commissioner of correction, Davis decided that parole was the key to reform for adults as well as youth. A system of indeterminate sentencing and parole would allow prison authorities to tailor sentences to individual cases, thereby implementing Davis's cherished vision of making the punishment fit the criminal, rather than the crime.

Ideally, an indeterminate sentence encouraged good behavior and led to early release. As Davis explained, "The prisoner should recognize that her only hope of freedom is in preparing herself to lead an industrious, self-supporting life."[117] But if early release was the carrot, permanent institutionalization was the stick. As Davis explained at the 1915 meeting of the American Prison Association, "a genuinely indeterminate sentence has as its logical outcome the custodial care of all prisoners whom it is not possible to train to good citizenship."[118]

Convinced that she could use the carceral state to promote "good citizenship," Davis worked with a group of city judges and prison reformers to author and advocate a new bill to create a parole system in New York City. The bill established a board responsible for establishing guidelines for granting parole and early release to all prisoners in city institutions, much as Davis had done for youthful female offenders at Bedford Reformatory. Moreover, the new parole law, in effect, extended indeterminate sentencing, previously limited to youthful offenders, to most adult offenders. Penitentiary prisoners now served indefinite sentences of up to three years; while first-time offenders sentenced to the workhouse continued to serve definite sentences (limited to six months), repeat workhouse offenders now served indefinite sentences of up to two years. The new law thus granted the parole board broad authority to determine the length of sentences, up to the maximum penalty. In addition to having the power to release any prisoner serving an indeterminate sentence, the board also could offer early release to those serving definite sentences with the approval of the committing judge.[119]

Although the parole board had to work within the parameters established by sentencing guidelines and by the committing judge, it had wide discretion to determine an individual prisoner's eligibility for parole. Before recommending parole, the board considered an individual's physical health, criminal record, prison conduct, work record, and probability of employment.[120] Davis considered the "composite judgment" of the parole board to be eminently preferable to the often arbitrary judgment of a single sitting magistrate.[121]

In addition to having authority to shorten sentences by granting parole, the board also had the power to deny parole and require prisoners to serve the maximum sentence. Davis, like her fellow advocates of the parole system in the early twentieth century, regarded parole as suitable only for those who were "physically, mentally and morally fit"; all others were not candidates for parole but rather for long-term custodial care.[122]

New York City's new parole system, thus, dovetailed nicely with Davis's interest in both reform and eugenics. For prisoners deemed worthy, parole offered a chance for early release. But for those judged unworthy, the system guaranteed longer sentences. In public lectures, Davis asserted that most offenders were victims of society. "Environment is responsible for most people's downfall," she stated.[123] Those driven to crime by social and economic factors were salvageable; through the intervention of the correctional system, they could be transformed into "decent citizens." However, Davis did not regard all offenders as capable of reform. Some, she insisted, such as the "mentally defective," should be confined as long as the law allowed.[124]

In addition to tailoring prison sentences to personal circumstances, the parole board, much like Bedford's Laboratory of Social Hygiene, was tasked with collecting information about "individual cases."[125] Davis hoped that keeping careful records on each prisoner would be a step toward establishing the sort of "clearing house" she had advocated back in 1910, with her "rational plan" for female offenders. "Through our increasing knowledge of the real underlying causes of the crimes of individuals," she predicted, "we will acquire information invaluable in the work of crime prevention." In doing so, she declared, "we will make New York City a great laboratory for the study of social ills."[126]

When it was enacted in late 1915, the new parole law realized many of Davis's most cherished ideas about penal reform. It also offered Davis new professional opportunities. When the mayor invited Davis to head the new parole board, the beleaguered commissioner eagerly accepted.[127] She had become increasingly dissatisfied with her position as commissioner of correction, which subjected her to constant criticism for conditions over which she had limited control. Moreover, Davis was always happiest when she was in charge of something new. As she once stated, "I like to experiment. Following new trails and developing new solutions for problems interests me."[128]

At the same time that directing the work of the new parole board allowed Davis to extend reformatory methods to adult offenders and advance the "science of correction and reformation," it also maintained her connection with the Department of Correction and built upon her record at Bedford Reformatory.[129] She described the new position as "merely another step along the same road I have been traveling for a long time, and with the same object in view."[130] Davis took to her new role with gusto, making site visits, devising a tally sheet to track inmates' work record, and convening weekly meetings of the parole board.[131]

"Women Need the Ballot"

Davis enjoyed a brief hiatus from her responsibilities on the parole board in October 1916, when she embarked on a cross-country train trip to join an all-female political campaign on behalf of Charles Evan Hughes, the Republican candidate for the president. While Davis was a lifelong Republican—and no fan of the Democratic incumbent, Woodrow Wilson—she stumped for Hughes because he shared her support for women's suffrage.[132]

By 1916, Davis had increased her suffrage activities yet again. In addition to serving a second term as third vice-president of the National American Woman Suffrage Association, she also became the director of the Manhattan branch of New York's Woman Suffrage Party, which united several existing suffrage organizations under one banner. At the annual meeting of the National American Woman Suffrage Association, she shared the podium with NAWSA president Carrie Chapman Catt, National Woman's Trade Union League president Margaret Dreier Robins, US Children's Bureau chief Julia Lathrop, and even US president Woodrow Wilson.[133]

Hughes, unlike Wilson, had publicly declared his support for the federal woman suffrage amendment, inspiring strong support from Davis and other suffrage advocates. Women's rights activists sponsored a cross-country train trip from the East Coast to the West Coast, and back again, making whistle-stop tours along the way. Davis and her fellow "feminine orators"—a group of prominent women that included welfare workers, labor organizers, and well-known writers—kept up a demanding pace for the entire month of October.[134]

Davis expected the tour—"the first thing of its kind ever undertaken by women," as she remarked—to be "a wonderful trip," as well as her first vacation in several years. "I am going to forget for a month that criminals exist—except in politics!" she joked. "We shall be too busy to think of anything except 'Votes for Hughes!'"[135]

The "feminine spellbinders" aboard the train hoped to usher in a new era in women's political activism.[136] Although the "Hughesettes" intentionally steered clear of the suffrage issue on the campaign trail to keep the focus on the candidate, one of Davis's "chief reasons" for supporting Hughes was his strong suffrage stance.[137] On the campaign trail, she spoke principally about Hughes's record as governor of New York, although she also emphasized that he, unlike the states-rights incumbent, represented the "federal ideal" and would support "national legislation" to address "the great economic and social unrests of the day."[138]

Although Wilson prevailed in the presidential election, Davis's enthusiasm for politics was unquenched. After completing the cross-country tour, she returned to her home state and joined forces with both state and national movement leaders to campaign for women's suffrage. According to one fellow suffragist, her demanding work schedule was no obstacle to her suffrage activism. Rather, after concluding long days and weeks at the office, she gave "rousing speeches" for woman suffrage on evenings and weekends.[139]

The Empire State was the only state with woman suffrage on the ballot in fall 1917. Supporters and opponents alike regarded this campaign as important to the national movement, since a victory in the state would garner support for the federal amendment in Congress. Davis continued to capitalize on her position as a public official to promote women's rights. Asserting that women's equality was just plain common sense—"arguing for equal suffrage seems like trying to prove that two and two make four," she once stated—she also insisted that women had a special part to play in social reform. "In any reform work it is impossible not to face the fact that women need the ballot," she declared.[140]

"The Sum of Feminine Achievement"

Meanwhile, Davis continued her own reform work as head of New York City's parole board. Just a year into her new position, Davis could point to significant successes. Although plans to establish a comprehensive "clearing house," complete with facilities for evaluating new inmates, had not yet come to fruition, Davis had developed a system of collecting, recording, and sharing information about newly sentenced individuals; a scheme for determining at what point prisoners became eligible for parole; and a method of maintaining records documenting inmates' conduct and work experience.[141]

The New York Prison Association praised Davis's unique approach to determining eligibility for parole, which combined the parole board's initial evaluation of individuals (which determined when they became eligible to be considered for parole) and individual prisoners' acquisition of points (which determined when, and if, the board actually granted parole). Unlike most parole systems, which relied either on a point system or on the parole board's judgment, the combined system provided both a communal judgment of the individual's readiness for release and strong incentive for inmates to demonstrate their capacity for civilian life. The parole board also required evidence of good health, proper housing, and suitable employment prior to granting parole.[142]

In addition to designing the basic outlines of the city's parole system, Davis worked with multiple charitable societies to organize a cooperative employment agency for paroled prisoners.[143] She also chose women parole officers to work with female offenders.[144] As part of this initiative, she appointed the city's first African American parole officer.[145] Most impressive of all, Davis and her colleagues, by holding prisoners until and unless their record—in the board's judgment—warranted release, dramatically reduced the proportion of recommitments, thereby reducing the problem of "rounders."[146] Small wonder, then, that the author of a series of biographical dictionaries along the lines of *Who's Who* pointed to Davis as an example of "the sum of feminine achievement."[147]

Even some of Davis's former detractors admired her work on the parole board. Radical feminist Rheta Childe Dorr praised the new parole chief for her determination to eliminate the sexual double standard in law enforcement. The case in question involved a "feeble-minded" fourteen-year-old girl who had been tricked into prostitution. Both a man and a woman were tried, found guilty, and imprisoned for their role in this "atrocious crime." But the male offender's lawyer attempted to secure early release for his client, arguing that the girl had "deliberately tempted" him, as well as asserting that "what he did"—presumably, sexually assaulted the teen—"might happen to any man." Davis refused to countenance this backwards argument and the "double standard of morals" that it reflected, asserting, "I shall do everything in my power to see that this man stays in prison at least as long as the woman does." Dorr—who like other radical feminists had not been impressed by Davis's tenure as commissioner of correction—now approvingly noted, "As prison commissioner Miss Davis did nothing to offend the respectable element, but as chairman of the parole board she is overturning customs and theories in a manner bewildering to men accustomed to looking at things from a traditional viewpoint."[148]

"Prison Horrors"

In many ways, Davis's tenure at the helm of New York City's parole board was an unqualified success. Unlike her position as commissioner of correction, which simultaneously demanded that she correct decades-old problems and repeatedly erected stumbling blocks to doing so, her post at the head of the parole board, like her position at Bedford Reformatory, allowed Davis to fashion something entirely new—and to do it well. By 1917, Davis had attained a reputation as "the greatest woman authority on prison reform in the world," frequently invited to speak on prison reform at local, national, and international gatherings.[149] And yet, she continued to deal with public criticism, both of her administration of the city's correctional facilities and of her implementation of the city's new parole law.

Ironically, given Davis's commitment to women's rights, much of this criticism came from fellow feminists. Margaret Sanger, who had criticized Davis for her treatment of anarchist hunger striker Rebecca

Edelson in 1914, resumed her campaign against Davis three years later, when both Sanger and her sister served sentences for violating the state's anti-obscenity laws, known as "little Comstock Laws" because they were modeled on the federal Comstock Law, which made both the dissemination of information about birth control and the distribution of birth-control devices a criminal offense.[150]

After Sanger and her sister, Ethel Byrne, opened a birth-control clinic in Brooklyn, both women served prison terms, Byrne in the Blackwell's Island Workhouse and Sanger in the Queens County Jail. Indignant at what she regarded as a wrongful conviction and horrified at the conditions in the workhouse, Byrne staged a hunger strike. Davis, who sympathized with the prisoner's aims, if not her methods, visited her in her cell in an unsuccessful attempt to convince her to give up the hunger strike. But the "belligerent" birth-control advocate insisted on protesting her imprisonment. Moreover, after her release, Byrne roundly denounced the "prison horrors" she encountered at Blackwell's Island, including inedible food, lice-ridden bedding, and force-feeding. Still more damningly, she insisted that the terrible physical conditions were not the worst part of her experience. Rather, comparing her experience to "a bad fairy tale," she related a hair-raising tale of being kept awake at night by the unearthly shrieks of a fellow prisoner.[151]

Sanger, who began her own sentence at Queens County Jail the day her sister was released from the workhouse, issued her own statement after her release. Like her sister, Sanger insisted that the psychic damage of imprisonment was worse even than the physical conditions. Taking direct aim at the former commissioner of correction, Sanger accused Davis of "studied cruelty and heartlessness in the treatment of the jail's population." According to Sanger, "Every inmate of the jail learns to hate Miss Davis with a bitterness and a depth of resentment that one would scarcely believe possible," and "the girls complain that Miss Davis delights in the exercise of authority that amounts to tyranny." Indeed, Sanger denounced Davis's entire record as a penal reformer: "Her idea of prison management and of reform for prisoners seem to be a discipline so harsh and unfeeling that every decent emotion of her victim is killed by it."[152]

Stung, Davis defended her record and denied allegations of cruelty. Explaining that she had never met Sanger, she attributed the fiery activist's "personal attack" to Davis's well-known opposition to lawbreaking as a tool for changing the law. As the head of the parole board and a prominent advocate of the indeterminate sentence, she especially took exception to Sanger's claim that Davis had scoffed at a prisoner who expressed a preference for a fixed sentence with a definite release date. Conceding that many offenders disliked the indeterminate sentence, Davis reiterated her support for the new system. "Exhaustive investigations," detailed records, and committee decision making, she argued, made for fair decisions about parole, and the emphasis on "earning" early release "by conduct and work in the institution," she insisted, was "one of the most valid arguments in favor of the parole system."[153]

Free-speech advocate, birth-control activist, labor leader, and outspoken anarchist Emma Goldman—who, like Sanger, had denounced Davis during the Edelson debacle—also publicly denounced both Davis and the prison system. A sharp critic of state power in general, and the carceral state in particular, Goldman characterized New York's prisons as "chambers of horrors" and wrote extensively on what she called "the utter futility of prisons as a means of deterrence or reform."[154]

In 1916, Goldman had served a two-week sentence in the women's workhouse at Blackwell's Island for lecturing about birth control in violation of the Comstock Laws. After her release, she took direct aim at Davis, juxtaposing the public official's righteousness and authority with female lawbreakers' desperation and powerlessness. "Oh, the cruelty of the indeterminate sentence!" she exclaimed. "Only a mind parched with the stale virginity of a Katherine B. Davis could have conceived of such a law, which turns the prisoner over, body and soul, to the mercy of the prison and the patrol authorities, and undermines her health and spirits with constant uncertainty and fear." Highlighting the individual stories of the women she met in the workhouse—whether driven to petty theft by sheer hunger or falsely accused of sexual misconduct—Goldman, like Sanger, questioned Davis's true commitment to women's welfare.[155]

These disagreements about indeterminate sentencing were not merely personal disputes. Rather, they represented an early salvo in what would become an ongoing debate among feminist activists about the legitimacy and purpose of what scholars now refer to as the carceral state: the state's power to police citizens through law enforcement, the court system, and the prison industry. Then as now, feminists debated whether (and how) state power could or should be used to shape society by exerting authority over individuals. While some feminists support(ed) the carceral state as a path to social reform, others regard(ed) it as a means of social control—especially over already-disenfranchised groups, including women, immigrants, African Americans, and sex workers.[156]

Such disagreements, of course, were not limited to feminists, nor to the carceral state. As Alice Stone Blackwell pointed out during the 1916 presidential campaign, when Jane Addams supported incumbent Woodrow Wilson, and Davis supported challenger Hughes, "Even the most intelligent women differ in their political views, as the most intelligent men do."[157]

"This Is the Woman's Day"

Despite her public disagreements with radical women, Davis continued to work for women's political rights, even as she anticipated the end of her own position as a public official. For better or for worse, Davis's high-profile position as a member of Mayor Mitchel's cabinet was short-lived. Most likely, Davis had always understood that her position as a public official had an early expiration date. From the beginning, the Republican mayor and his cabinet confronted opposition from the city's powerful Democratic "machine," known as Tammany Hall, which dominated the city's political landscape for decades. While New York reformers had briefly united behind Mitchel's candidacy in 1913 to elect the thirty-four-year-old Irish Catholic on a platform of efficiency and honesty (as opposed to Tammany's legendary corruption and wastefulness), it came as no surprise when the "boy mayor" was defeated by Tammany Hall's preferred candidate in the 1917 election.[158]

If the 1917 election spelled defeat for Mitchel and his cabinet, it also ushered in a major victory for Davis and her fellow suffragists. Although no longer an officer in the national suffrage organization, Davis was eager to see the state suffrage struggle through to a successful conclusion. As election day approached, Davis was confident that the suffrage movement in her state was poised for success. "This is the woman's day," she declared.[159]

On Election Day, 1917, the city's women rose early and headed out before dawn to monitor polling places, determined to ensure an orderly and legitimate process and to secure ratification of the most important initiative on the ballot: a referendum on woman suffrage. Many of these advocates of women's voting rights gathered at Davis's home in midtown Manhattan, which functioned as "a supply depot for food and suffrage literature." Davis, an official city poll inspector, sallied forth with a flashlight to locate polling places in the early morning darkness. Throughout the day and into the night, fellow suffragists delivered sandwiches and coffee to a veritable "army of workers at the polls." By the time darkness enveloped the city, it was clear that the Empire State had become the first state east of the Mississippi River to fully enfranchise women, extending the right to vote in local, state, and federal elections.[160]

Davis was poised to make the most of women's newfound political power. As she stumped for suffrage, Davis strengthened her commitment to sexual equality as well as political equality. Davis had dedicated much of her professional career to enforcing laws that criminalized women's—but not men's—sexuality. But enforcing discriminatory legislation ultimately reinforced Davis's opposition to the sexual double standard. At the same time that she upheld laws that supported the sexual double standard, Davis also critiqued what she called "the fallacy that a man must sow his wild oats," which was often invoked to defend men's sexual misbehavior. "For as men sow, so women reap," she soberly warned. While at Bedford, Davis had bemoaned women's lack of "moral fiber"; now, she insisted that men needed to bulk up their own "moral fiber."[161]

During the successful campaign for women's suffrage in the Empire State, Davis frequently called for the adoption of a single sexual standard, even titling one suffrage lecture "A Necessary Safeguard for Public Morals." Invoking numerous examples from her extensive experience in law enforcement and prison reform, she observed, "The laws are not equal, nor equally enforced." Davis insisted that women's political equality would advance sexual equality. "Public morals are corrupted because woman's point of view has no representation," she asserted. With voting rights, however, Davis was confident that women voters would usher in a new era. She predicted, "Women will take an unusual interest in the effort to clean up vicious conditions, because all down the ages women have paid the price of vice and crime."[162]

Although Davis expressed tremendous faith in women voters to establish a new moral code, the federal suffrage amendment remained stalled in Congress, and the nation's politicians were preoccupied with US entry into World War I. Moreover, as Davis herself frequently reminded her listeners, one could not expect women's suffrage to be a panacea. Women and men would need to work together, she argued, to bring about a single sexual standard. "While I do not anticipate that woman suffrage will bring the millennium," she pronounced, "I believe that the fact that women are men's comrades in every avenue of our common life will make it possible to do much toward breaking down the notion that things which are reprehensible if done by women may be winked at if they can be done without discovery by men."[163]

Davis would soon have an exciting new opportunity to work with like-minded reformers—both women and men—to promote a single standard of sexual morality in wartime America. Well before the election results made it clear that Davis would not continue as a member of Mayor Mitchel's cabinet, Davis's longtime supporter, John D. Rockefeller Jr., offered her a position as general secretary of the Bureau of Social Hygiene.

Davis's new job description closely aligned with her interest in reforming public morals. As Rockefeller put it, "The important duties of the position will be for the next few years at least an effort to bring into harmonious, effective and economic relationship the various organizations in this city dealing with prostitution and vice." Moreover, given the ongoing war effort, the philanthropist expressed his willingness to "lend" his new employee to the various private and public agencies then framing what would come to be known as the "American Plan," designed to keep American military men "fit to fight" by combating both commercialized sex and sexually transmitted infections. Davis eagerly accepted Rockefeller's offer, although she postponed an official announcement until after the election. She was, she confided, eager to find a position where she could be useful, and in particular, in wartime, where she might be "of special service to the country."[164] For the duration of the war effort, Davis would collaborate with military men and women reformers to promote a single standard of sexual morality. In the process, she became convinced that the way forward was scientifically sound sex education—a position that ultimately would lead her to initiate a pathbreaking study of women's sexuality.

5

“Sex Ethics”

Two roads there are in Life.
One reaches upward toward
The Land of Perfect Love.
The other reaches down into
The Dark Valley of Despair
Where the sun never shines.
—Title Card, *The End of the Road* (1919)

Soon after the conclusion of World War I, newspapers around the nation advertised a new feature film, *The End of the Road*. Originally intended as a companion piece to the wartime film *Fit to Fight*, produced for military men, *The End of the Road* was aimed at civilian women. Both films were part of the wartime campaign for “social hygiene,” a euphemism for early efforts at sexual education and the prevention of sexually transmitted infections. But *The End of the Road*, a romantic melodrama that dramatized the dangers of illicit sexuality, was unique in that it was the first such film to be aimed at a female audience and written by a woman. It also was notable for its stalwart insistence on providing women with accurate sexual information and for its forthright condemnation of the sexual double standard.[1]

“A picture with a purpose,” *The End of the Road* attracted both praise and criticism for its candid treatment of illicit sex and its deadly consequences. Although it was far more graphic in its depiction of the symptoms of sexually transmitted infections—weeping sores, crusty chancres, and raised lesions—than in its representation of actual sexual activity, *Photoplay* exclaimed that the film was “the most daring picture of sex relations ever told!”[2]

Alternately condemned and celebrated by moralists, the silent film soon gained a reputation as “The Most Talked About Picture in America.” Threats of censorship may well have increased interest in the com-

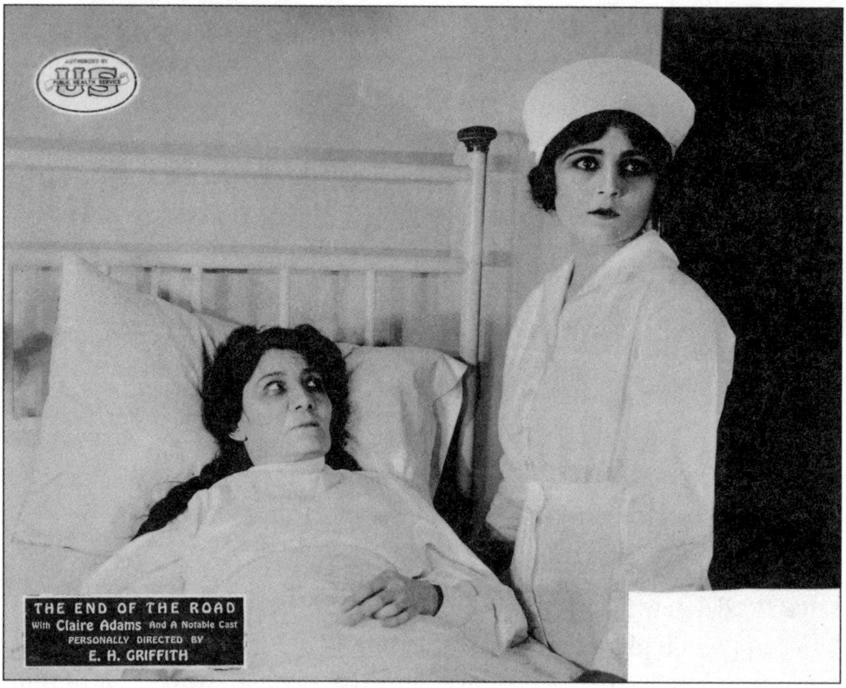

In the wartime "social hygiene" film, *The End of the Road*, Nurse Mary sees the terrible cost of men's sexual peccadilloes and women's sexual ignorance, spotlighted by the example of Mrs. Elbridge, who voluntarily undergoes a hysterectomy after giving birth to a son with congenital blindness caused by gonorrhea, which she contracted from her straying husband. Katharine Bement Davis, who wrote the screenplay for the film, departed from conventional scripts by placing the blame for such situations squarely upon men, reflecting her distaste for the sexual double standard. Davis's wartime experiences marked a significant turning point in her career. Instead of enforcing sexual standards, as she had done during her career in corrections, she henceforth devoted herself to sexual education. Claire Adams Photographs. MS.P.008. Special Collections and Archives, UC Irvine Libraries.

munities that allowed the film to be shown. (Typically, community leaders hosted a private screening to determine whether to grant permission for a public screening.) At one of the first public screenings, in December 1918, thousands of people jammed the auditorium in St. Paul, Minnesota. Police had to be called in to restore order and escort disappointed would-be viewers away with the promise that another showing would occur the following evening.[3]

Interest in the film remained keen, despite—or perhaps because of—controversy over the film's sexual content. The following year, in New Jersey, Asbury Park's Garden Theatre offered a four-day "Special Engagement" with two showings each day of what advertisers described as "the most fearless motion picture yet produced." Although local authorities limited the audience to those sixteen years of age or older, they also praised the film as "the most forceful lesson ever known for the protection of young men and young women from evils they know not of—it tells what parents should teach but seldom do!"[4]

Although local censors always had the final say, initially, the US government's backing helped pave the way for the film's circulation. However, the US surgeon general withdrew his endorsement in September 1919. Now lacking the official imprimatur of the US government, *The End of the Road* came to the end of its run as both local religious leaders and the National Association of the Moving Picture Industry blocked further commercial distribution of the government-produced film. In the meantime, however, the motion picture's moving message reached tens of thousands of Americans, mostly teenaged girls and young women, who eagerly flocked to movie theaters and community centers to swoon at the romantic plot, enjoy the titillation of suggestions of illicit sexuality, and shiver at the horrific symptoms of syphilis. All in all, the film was a resounding success. It also was a significant turning point in the career of its screenwriter, Katharine Bement Davis.[5]

During World War I, while US troops engaged in trench warfare overseas, Davis—a lifelong pacifist—fought a different kind of war at home. She became a leader of the "American Plan," a federal campaign to combat both commercialized sex and sexually transmitted infections. Crafted by a coalition of public agencies and private organizations, the American Plan criminalized female sexuality and subjected so-called clandestine prostitutes to involuntary confinement and invasive medical procedures on the flimsiest of evidence. In some ways, the wartime "social hygiene" movement—as supporters dubbed early efforts at sex education—must have reminded Davis of her time at Bedford Reformatory. Indeed, during the war, suspected sex workers at Bedford endured—and sometimes violently resisted—painful and ineffective treatments.[6]

Yet, rather than participating in the American Plan's repression of women's sexuality, Davis instead turned to advocating sexual education. In keeping with the official mandate of the American Plan, Davis sought to curb the spread of sexually transmitted infections by educating women about the dangers of venereal disease. But more importantly, she crafted a broader sexual education program that emphasized providing women with sexual knowledge and combating the sexual double standard. Indeed, *The End of the Road* was, for Davis, a significant bend in the road, marking her dramatic turn from policing women's sexual behavior to promoting women's sexual equality. By the end of the war, Davis had become an outspoken advocate of accurate sex education as the key to "a rational sex ethics."[7]

The "American Plan"

A veteran law enforcement official who built a national reputation by policing women's sexuality, Davis lost her position as New York City's commissioner of correction in the elections of 1917—in which the longtime suffragist also helped usher in full voting rights for the Empire State's women. But Davis's longtime supporter, philanthropist John D. Rockefeller Jr., promptly appointed her general secretary of the Bureau of Social Hygiene, a privately funded think tank dedicated to combating prostitution and venereal disease, which had funded Davis's experiments in intelligence testing at Bedford Reformatory. Davis assumed her new position at a key moment, for the US entry into the war then raging in Europe ushered in new policies governing women's sexuality. With Rockefeller's hearty endorsement, Davis spearheaded a partnership with the US government to make the Bureau of Social Hygiene—and Davis herself—a key player in the wartime social hygiene program.

During World War I, the military recruitment process revealed shockingly high rates of infection with venereal disease, or VD (now commonly referred to as sexually transmitted infections, or STIs). The Wasserman test, a new blood test for syphilis, revealed infection rates of more than one in three new recruits. The federal government, anxious to keep men "fit to fight," implemented new policies to combat commercialized sex and curb the spread of venereal diseases. Unlike some European nations, such as France—which accepted extramarital sex as inevitable and attempted to slow the spread of venereal disease by registering and testing sex workers and by providing soldiers with prophylactics and medical treatment—the US program, known as the American Plan, took direct aim at military men's morals. The War Department created the Commission on Training Camp Activities (CTCA), initially to provide wholesome recreational opportunities at military training encampments and ultimately as the umbrella organization for a wide range of activities associated with the American Plan.[8]

Bureau of Social Hygiene researcher Raymond Fosdick, who had spent several weeks observing (and criticizing) rampant alcoholism and open prostitution in the vicinity of Texas military encampments during the recent conflict with Mexico, chaired the new commission. In addition to arranging entertainment for military men, the CTCA had the power to ban both alcohol and prostitution near military camps. The commission also encouraged men to engage in approved "moral" behavior and avoid risky sexual behavior by requiring them to attend lectures on social hygiene that dramatized the dangers of sexually transmitted infections and emphasized the importance of male sexual continence. Perhaps recognizing that this approach flew in the face of commonly held ideas about men's uncontrollable sexual urges, however, the military did not punish enlisted men who were exposed to venereal disease, except for requiring them to undergo a painful treatment regimen involving flushing the penis with mercury.[9]

Instead of punishing military men for illicit sexual behavior, the CTCA—through its Law Enforcement Division—prosecuted civilian women suspected of carrying venereal disease. Officials targeted not only professional prostitutes but all girls and women simply suspected of being sexually active: "clandestine" or part-time prostitutes; "charity girls" who engaged in nonmarital sex without financial compensation; and completely innocent young women who ventured out at night without a chaperone. Historians estimate that up to thirty thousand women were incarcerated in federal facilities and subjected to invasive medical exams and painful medical treatments under the American Plan. Countless others were detained in local jails and state reformatories, including Bedford Reformatory. Moreover, the wartime program put in place an extensive system of surveillance, control, and incarceration that endured for decades.[10]

"What a Foul Place"

Bedford Reformatory quickly became a key part of the American Plan. While girls and women always had been sent to Bedford on vaguely defined and often unproven "morals" charges, wartime concerns about keeping military men "fit to fight" led to increased scrutiny of female sexuality. One group of young women, for instance, were arrested after spending an evening flirting with sailors at Coney Island. One member of the party was sentenced to Bedford because she had offered to help obtain alcohol for her male companions, in violation of military restrictions on alcohol in or near military encampments. Coney Island also featured prominently in the case history of another wartime Bedford inmate, who literally ran away from home and joined the circus there, where she met—and allegedly had sexual intercourse with—the sailors who also frequented the beachfront park. Coney Island also cropped up in the case histories of Bedford inmates who resisted the American Plan. One young woman sentenced to Bedford pushed back, demanding, "Can't I enjoy myself when I go to Coney Island? . . . Can't a person have a good time?"[11]

As a popular and affordable entertainment venue, Coney Island was a common place for young women—including former Bedford inmate Mabel Hampton and her family and friends—to seek excitement and companionship, but it also was rife with danger. In addition to running the risk of arrest and imprisonment, young women at Coney Island were vulnerable to exploitation and assault. One young woman who ended up at Bedford recounted a terrifying tale to the staff there. After she and another young woman enjoyed several shows at Coney Island, they agreed to walk along the boardwalk with two sailors. An evening's entertainment ended in violence when the sailors ordered the young women to go beneath the boardwalk and then raped them. Although the reformatory staff believed the victim's claim that she had been a virgin prior to the assault and that she had been an unwilling participant, her family was less understanding. Because their daughter preferred to spend time seeking pleasure rather than staying home with her parents, they committed her to Bedford for "associating with disorderly persons."[12]

Unfortunately, under the American Plan, women's vulnerability to sexual assault continued during detention. Indeed, by expanding the

Mabel Hampton, formerly incarcerated at Bedford Reformatory on false charges of prostitution, later cherished a forty-year relationship with Lillian Foster. The committed couple enjoyed spending time with female friends and their chosen family at Coney Island, the affordable playground for working-class New Yorkers. During World War I, the beachfront park featured prominently in the case histories of girls and women arrested and imprisoned under the American Plan. One young woman sentenced to Bedford Reformatory resisted state surveillance, demanding, "Can't I enjoy myself when I go to Coney Island?" Mabel Hampton Papers, Lesbian Herstory Archives.

power of both medical and military authorities, the American Plan subjected girls and women to what amounted to physical assault in the name of public health, including blood tests, pelvic exams, and mercury injections. These violations of women's bodies magnified the civil rights violations authorized under the American Plan—and revealed in a major study later conducted under the auspices of the Bureau of Social Hygiene.[13]

At Davis's instigation, Bedford had pioneered using the Wasserman blood test to screen for venereal diseases at Bedford. Then the gold standard, the test was later revealed to be flawed, resulting in a high proportion of false positives, which helps to explain why, in 1914, Davis found infection rates of up to 85 percent.[14] Davis also introduced the Wasserman test at the Women's Workhouse during her tenure as commissioner of correction, leading one disgruntled "rounder" to complain, "Kate Davis has just about ruined the place."[15]

As bad as blood tests were, physical examinations were worse. During World War I, Bedford, like other women's detention homes, also practiced far more invasive tests, conducted by male physicians, that included the manual examination of an inmate's genitals and cervix.[16] Journalist Ben Reitman (Emma Goldman's lover) created a composite character, "Boxcar Bertha," to represent the experiences of sex workers he encountered in the early twentieth century. Describing women's attitude toward mandatory medical treatment, the ostensible author of the fictionalized autobiography explained that women arrested on suspicion of prostitution were subject to physical examinations prior to arraignment. If a woman was free of infection, she was permitted to post bail, but if she was deemed infected, she was sent to a "lock hospital," where six weeks of "treatment" functioned as punishment for individuals never found guilty in court. "The pinch did not seem to mean anything to the girls," she observed. "The thing that bothered most of them was the fear that they might be diseased. That would mean a month or six weeks in the hospital, and they all dreaded this."[17]

Small wonder! Although ostensibly intended to protect public health, these facilities functioned as prisons; quarantine and treatment, which could last anywhere from two weeks to two months, substituted for either a fine or jail time. A Bureau of Social Hygiene publication included the case study of "Millicent," a twenty-eight-year-old sex worker who had entered the sex trade at age sixteen. Arrested numerous times for soliciting, she was less concerned about "the 'pinch'" than about public health policies that resulted in her testing "positive on a smear" and being sent to a lock hospital, even though she insisted she did not have an active infection. "Oh, how I hate that place," she expostulated. "They poke at you . . . and they call themselves doctors. God what a foul place."[18]

Physicians did indeed "poke at" alleged prostitutes. Treatment for venereal disease was both invasive and uncomfortable. At Bedford's psychopathic hospital, where the vast majority of inmates were confined for "sex offenses of various kinds," and where a whopping 45 percent of patients were diagnosed—possibly misdiagnosed—with syphilis and a shocking 85 percent with gonorrhea, some patients resisted the biweekly treatments. As Dr. Edith Spaulding pointed out with notable understatement, mercury injections caused "temporary discomfort," and some patients resisted this treatment. Dr. Spaulding summarized some of the responses heard: "I tell you I am not going to have any treatment this morning—I am sick of this damn joint. All you get is treatments, treatments, treatments. Can't you let me alone?"[19]

Resisting treatment, however, could lead to further problems. Indeed, Dr. Spaulding noted that one of her patients, "a good-natured, fun-loving colored girl of 18," originally was committed to a reform home at her father's behest, evidently on charges of incorrigibility, as he complained of her "going out at night and associating with undesirable people." Like many women caught up in the American Plan, however, "Martha S." was transferred to the city hospital for treatment for gonorrhea. However, she "refused treatment, because it was painful, and was consequently given a three years' indeterminate sentence at Bedford."[20]

Despite all the problems with the American Plan, which exacerbated preexisting patterns of prosecuting—and in some cases, persecuting—sexually active (or simply socially active) women, Davis likely would not have objected to the way that the plan played out at the reformatory she had once headed. For all her commitment to a single sexual standard and her prediction that women voters would bring about a more even-handed judicial system, Davis accepted the shortcomings of discriminatory laws and practices. Unlike some of her colleagues in the social hygiene movement—including Dr. Mary Gordon, a British physician and prison reformer who would participate in an international conference Davis would organize at the end of the war—Davis believed that it was important to aggressively prosecute suspected sex workers. "I do not agree that if one innocent girl is arrested on the street it discredits our whole system," she declared. Indeed, she insisted, "as a matter of fact, in 20 years' experience I have never seen one innocent girl sent to prison or sent to a reformatory institution." Even in cases of obvious entrapment, in which an undercover police officer approached a woman hoping to entice her into solicitation, Davis argued that a lone woman in a public place was likely to be a sex worker. "When you get right down to it," she reasoned, "they were out looking for an opportunity to practice their profession." She concluded with the shocking statement, "There is no more danger of an innocent girl being arrested and taken to court than a thunderbolt striking this room at the present moment."[21]

Davis's attitudes aligned well with the American Plan—or, at least, with some versions of it. While the American Plan ultimately pursued a course of policing women's sexual behavior, like many Progressive Era programs, it also sought to protect women from sexual exploitation. Initially, the Commission on Training Camp Activities (CTCA) sponsored a Committee on Protective Work for Girls (CPWG), headed by New York social reformer Maude Miner. As the name of the agency indicated, the assumption was that "girls" needed "protection" from bad influences. Miner hoped that sympathetic social workers, by providing innocent but vulnerable young women with proper guidance, would protect them from bad influences. However, male authorities soon became convinced that it was military men, not vulnerable women, who needed protection. Instead of providing young women with guidance and protection, the American Plan subjected them to surveillance and quarantine.[22]

Both in the interest of public health and in the name of law enforcement, Davis had a history of endorsing repressive methods of suppressing the sex trade and curbing the spread of sexually transmitted infections. However, during World War I, even as the American Plan sanctioned increased control over women's sexuality, Davis became more interested in promoting women's sexual agency by increasing women's sexual knowledge. Her participation in the American Plan highlighted the power struggle within the movement, which often pitted female and male reformers against each other. Within this context, Davis—as she had so often done before—utilized her superb interpersonal skills to successfully navigate a complex set of circumstances, both to advance her own career and to promote women's equality.

"Genuine Service"

Even before she officially started her new job as general secretary of the Bureau of Social Hygiene, Davis began to investigate how she might work hand in hand with the new government program. Davis hoped that by partnering with the federal government during a national crisis, she—and the social hygiene movement—would be able to achieve much more, much more quickly, than by working in voluntary organizations in peacetime. With the imprimatur of the national government, Davis believed that she would have greater influence than ever before. "The sanction carried by the stationery and approval of the War Department is great at this time," she reflected, adding, "It opens up avenues and secures an entrance which it would take long to secure through ordinary means."[23]

At the time that Davis was contemplating how best to participate in the American Plan, Maude Miner and Raymond Fosdick were engaged in a contest over how to allocate funds for detention and treatment centers for women. Miner envisioned providing individualized social work in newly constructed community centers—built, like Bedford Reformatory, on the "cottage plan." In her plan, the Committee on Protective Work for Girls would maintain control over both the funding and the operation of these centers. But Fosdick chose instead to create a new Committee on Reformatories and Detention Homes to administer federal funding for local and state institutions, such as Bedford, that participated in the American Plan. By placing this committee under the purview of the Law Enforcement Division, he demonstrated the shift from protecting girls to imprisoning them.[24]

Fosdick appointed Martha Falconer, then head of a girls' reformatory in Pennsylvania, to head the new agency. (Originally, he invited Davis to fill this post, but she declined.) Although Falconer, like Davis, was a former settlement house worker and an advocate of progressive penal reform, she also believed that delinquent girls posed a medical and moral menace to the nation and advocated lengthy sentences to ensure sufficient treatment and training. Davis might well have approved of Falconer's approach, which involved classifying female offenders and assigning them to appropriate facilities, much as Davis had suggested in her "rational plan for female offenders" back in 1910. In Falconer's scheme, merely "silly" girls could be sent back home; "feeble-minded" women would be consigned to permanent custodial facilities; and those in danger of "drifting into a life of prostitution" would serve sentences at reformatories.[25]

These views mostly aligned with those Davis expressed during the war. At "a delightful informal tea" held in South Carolina for members of a local CTCA committee, Davis, drawing on her classical education, addressed the "girl problem" in wartime: "Girls, like all Gaul, may be divided into three parts. First, the good girl, the girl with proper bringing up, the girl who can be counted upon in helping the less fortunate girls. Then there is the girl who needs protection, the girl who has less will power than some and with less training. Lastly, there is the girl beyond the pale. The girl whose presence is a menace to the soldiers. These girls, happily, are in the minority everywhere."[26]

Davis's classification of the three types of young women in need of guidance, protection, or detention reflected divergent approaches to the "girl problem" more generally. It also suggested her own movement away from the more punitive approaches to the "problem." While the American Plan, as a whole, shifted away from protecting girls and toward protecting soldiers, Davis suggested that approaches should be tailored to different groups of girls—some of whom needed to be protected from soldiers.

Even though Davis continued to insist that some girls, "beyond the pale," posed a "menace" to society and should be confined and controlled, she moved decisively in the direction of educating and supporting both "good girls" and "less fortunate girls"—who, she now believed, constituted the majority. Davis's evolving views led her to reject Fosdick's offer to affiliate herself with the enforcement division of the CTCA and instead to ally herself with the educational department of the government agency. This move not only represented Davis's shift away from the carceral state but also her growing distance from the eugenics movement—which was beginning to face legal challenges. In the very same issue, the *Eugenical News* announced Davis's appointment and decried a court decision declaring New York's sterilization statute unconstitutional. However, Davis's participation in the American Plan also meant that she continued to collaborate with eugenicists, including Dr. William F. Snow, who would direct the CTCA's Social Hygiene Division, which—after lengthy discussions—would appoint Davis as the head of the Section on Women's Work.[27]

"One Standard of Morality"

Davis believed she could be of "genuine service" in this role, which gave her considerably more authority than other women involved in the American Plan, including the embattled Maude Miner, who struggled to maintain a protective—as opposed to a prosecutorial—program for young women. As Davis explained in a private letter to Rockefeller, the coalition that created and enacted the American Plan was rife with divisions both between and among female reformers and male policymakers, and there was considerable shuffling of responsibility and vying for authority as new committees were created and old ones were discontinued.[28]

While Miner was "anxious that the educational work along social hygiene lines be done by a sub-committee under her Committee on the Protection of Girls," other organizations, including the YWCA, objected to being "identified with work for delinquent girls." Meanwhile, Fosdick believed it was "wise to confine the work of Miss Miner's Protective Committee exclusively to the definite work with delinquent and borderline girls" and "make the [other] committees . . . subcommittees, [and] coordinate committees directly under Mr. Fosdick."[29]

Typically of the misogynistic Fosdick, the CTCA leader also favored having "a man member of his Commission act as General Chairman, attempting to link up together the work done by the Protective Committee, the Committee on Reformatories, the Committee on Social Work in Venereal Clinics and the Committee on Education." Indicating the challenge of coordinating such disparate committees with sometimes divergent aims, Davis added, parenthetically, "I wish him joy of his job!" But Fosdick and other male leaders conceded that "all the work for women will have to be correlated somehow."[30]

Meanwhile, other men involved in the American Plan, more committed to public health than to policing prostitution, supported both the creation of an educational committee and Davis's appointment as its leader. William F. Snow, a physician affiliated with the American Social Hygiene Association, a private antivice group with strong ties to the Bureau of Social Hygiene, supported appointing Davis to a leadership role on an educational committee that might fall under the purview of a proposed "Medical Board." Davis explained, "It is understood that I am not a medical woman, but I am asked to serve on this Board to head up and report work being done along educational lines in social hygiene throughout the country, not only in camp centers, but in industrial centers as well, and to make recommendations and suggestions for the prosecution of this work to be carried out with the government's approval."[31]

As part of these lengthy negotiations, Davis also conferred with Dr. Robert Latou Dickinson, a progressive gynecologist married to social reformer Sarah Kidder Truslow, who served, with Davis, on the YWCA Social Morality Committee. Dickinson supported Davis's appointment as a sort of social hygiene czar, in part because he saw that she—because of her experience working with Protestants, Jews, and Catholics at Bedford—could extend the reach of the YWCA to non-Protestants with the "official recognition" of a new government agency. Swayed by the authority of these medical men, Dr. Abraham Flexner, Davis's colleague at the Bureau of Social Hygiene, cautiously supported this plan. Eventually—possibly at Rockefeller's behest—so did Fosdick.[32]

Ultimately, Miner's "protective" committee was replaced by a new Section on Women and Girls. Under the leadership of Jane Deeter Rippin—a former probation officer from Philadelphia—the new section, working in conjunction with the Law Enforcement Division, emphasized preventing venereal disease more than protecting young women. At the same time, however, Fosdick also created a new Division of Social Hygiene, under the leadership of Dr. Snow. Fosdick offered Davis a position in this new division, as the head of the Section on Women's Work, with a focus on promoting sex education for women and girls. While Davis had rejected Fosdick's earlier invitation to head up the Committee on Reformatories and Detention Homes, which so closely aligned with her work at Bedford, she eagerly accepted the opportunity to return to her roots as an educator, telling Rockefeller that "under war conditions . . . we can do ten years' ordinary work in one."[33]

The "work" Davis had in mind was very different from what she had done in her previous positions in prison administration and law enforcement. For Davis, the American Plan offered an opportunity to explore a new approach to reforming sexual morality: sex education. Somewhat surprisingly given Davis's earlier emphasis on punishing women suspected of engaging in illicit sex, Davis's sex education agenda would emphasize sexual equality and female agency. By providing accurate information about sex, Davis hoped to empower women to take control of their own bodies and their own destinies. Of course, she hoped that they would choose the "right" path: abstinence prior to marriage and monogamy within marriage. But she wanted them to do so based on information, not ignorance. Both in *The End of the Road* and in more specialized publications, she insisted that ignorance was the cause of both illness and unhappiness. The film filled a frame with the message that "ignorance is the cause of so much unhappiness," while Davis wrote in the academic journal *Social Hygiene* that the misguided practice of preventing women from knowing "the real truth in regard to sexual relationships" was responsible for the rampant spread of sexually transmitted infections. In keeping with the goals of the American Plan, Davis's sex education program would, of course, prioritize the prevention of venereal disease. But underneath the dominant messages about avoiding disease ran a steady drumbeat of a different message: Women both needed and deserved to have accurate information about sex.[34]

Initially, for Davis, the most appealing part of the American Plan was the emphasis on promoting a new standard of sexual behavior for all Americans. Davis was a longstanding critic of the sexual double standard, including what she called "the fallacy that a man must sow his wild oats." These ideas, she explained, always worked to women's disadvantage: "For as men sow, so women reap."[35] Davis had long advocated that "men must be taught that there is only one standard of morality, the one commonly reserved for our women, and that they must live up to it."[36] Now, at last, Davis had governmental support for her longstanding campaign. As she explained, the federal government "has assumed as its basic principle the possibility of a single standard for men and women, based on chastity outside of the marriage relation."[37]

Davis was excited about the prospect of tackling moral reform from a new angle—and with government support. For more than fifteen years, Davis, first as the supervisor of Bedford Reformatory and then as a corrections official in New York City, had played a leading role in addressing sexual behavior by repressing women's sexuality. What Davis called "the suppression of prostitution" clearly was the centerpiece of the American Plan. National policies and federal funding intensified the Progressive Era's campaign to suppress the sex trade by targeting not just sex workers but all women suspected of engaging in sexual activity outside of marriage. Under the American Plan, the surveillance of women's sexuality became ever more intense; new policies to protect public health permitted the detention, examination, and incarceration of tens of thousands of American girls and women.[38]

And yet, when Davis chose to ally herself with the American Plan, she did so under the auspices of an agency that emphasized sex education rather than law enforcement. Instead of capitalizing on her career in corrections, Davis embraced the opportunity to return to her roots as an educator. Indicating her commitment to education rather than incarceration, Davis rejected an offer to head up the CTCA's Committee of Reformatories and Detention Homes, established under the umbrella of the Division of Law Enforcement, which received federal funding to establish facilities for the incarceration of suspected sex workers.[39]

Instead, she accepted a position within the Division of Social Hygiene, which received funding from the Bureau of Social Hygiene to provide sexual education and moral guidance to American citizens. The position, Davis predicted, represented "a genuine field for usefulness" both for herself and for the bureau. In addition to providing the bureau with "a wonderful opportunity for forwarding its fight against prostitution," it offered Davis herself the chance to use wartime patriotism and military necessity "as the entering wedge to drive home the necessity for high moral standards."[40]

"Social Hygiene"

As the head of "women's work" for the CTCA's social hygiene division, Davis was in charge of education and outreach aimed at women and girls. Well before World War I, Davis had advocated education as the best way to shape public opinion. As early as 1913, she declared that education was "the supreme need of the hour."[41] Now with the support of the federal government, Davis believed the moment had come to launch a widespread educational campaign to reshape "public morals."[42] The former schoolteacher regarded sex education, then referred to as "social hygiene," as far more important than the American Plan's primary emphasis on policing women's sexuality. While "the chief means" of the government program involved "the suppression of prostitution," she explained, "its second and equally, if not more, important tool is its educational propaganda."[43]

Obviously, given the government's priorities, Davis's wartime social hygiene campaign sought to slow, if not stop, the spread of sexually transmitted infections. Her section provided a wide range of printed materials warning against the dangers of venereal disease and asserting the importance of sexual continence. Enclosures in pay envelopes warned that infections of both gonorrhea and syphilis were difficult, if not impossible, to cure, and that they led to serious problems, including (but not limited to) chronic illness, infantile blindness, and premature death.[44]

Placards posted in restrooms and restaurants reiterated these frightening warnings. One, headlined "SOME FACTS ABOUT VENEREAL DISEASES," highlighted both the high prevalence and the severe consequences of gonorrhea and syphilis, warned that "one act of sexual intercourse may produce the infection," and cautioned, "The only sure prevention is to avoid promiscuous sexual relations."[45]

But Davis's educational program was not simply fear-mongering. Rather, Davis consistently emphasized two cardinal principles in her sex education program: establishing a single standard of sexual behavior and providing women with accurate information about sex. After the war, the second principle would inform Davis's work on her magnum opus, the first comprehensive study of female sexuality conducted by a female researcher.

"Refuse to Be Ignorant"

While they certainly did not shy away from detailing the dangers of venereal disease, Davis's educational materials and programs were not limited to disease prevention. Rather, they provided accurate scientific information about the mechanics of human reproduction as well as the vectors of disease transmission. Davis deplored women's ignorance about their own bodies. In the past, she averred, women were expected to be not only chaste but also ignorant. "It was believed that a woman should not know anything of vice or disease, much less discuss them," she complained. "Her ignorance, which was confounded with innocence, was her charm." In particular, Davis charged that physicians had participated in a "conspiracy of silence" by dismissing women's suffering as "female weaknesses" rather than frankly attributing "the complaints of women" to sexually transmitted infections. However, the wartime revelations about the high incidence of venereal disease among enlisted men was not only "a rude awakening" but also a salutary wake-up call for Americans, who now had the opportunity—indeed, the responsibility—to inform themselves about the transmission and prevention of sexually transmitted infections.[46]

By providing women with accurate information about sex, Davis hoped to replace ignorance with information. Davis lamented that the "taboo" on discussions of human sexuality had prevented women from knowing "the real truth in regard to sexual relationships and the perils of sexual irregularities." But the war, she believed, had changed everything. Now, with new information about the prevalence of venereal disease among the civilian population, it was imperative for all citizens to join in a concerted effort to establish and enforce "a single standard as to social relationships" as the only sure way to stop the spread of sexually transmitted infections.[47]

Women, Davis declared, had both the ability and the responsibility to redefine the nation's morals and protect the nation's health. To do so, however, they required "accurate knowledge," not only about the hard facts about sexually transmitted infections but also about effective medical treatment and legal regulation of prostitution. Reflecting the importance Davis attached to accurate information, one placard produced by her agency demanded, "WILL *YOU* FACE THE *FACTS*?" Another declared, "WOMEN HAVE NOT KNOWN the truth about venereal diseases and how they occur." The message continued, "We must know now in order to do our share in saving our country from a grave menace."[48]

Davis's sex education campaign went well beyond informing women of the dangers of sexually transmitted diseases and recruiting them in a patriotic effort to curb the spread of venereal disease, however. One pamphlet, titled "Girls—A Home Guard," sought to enlist young women in the moral regeneration of the nation. But in addition to urging young women to insist on moral propriety in their relationships with men, the pamphlet also included a frank explanation of reproductive organs and a candid acknowledgment of sexual attraction. Only after providing these basic facts did the pamphlet proceed to warnings against the dangers of prostitution and venereal disease. Finally, the pamphlet urged young women to "be a real home guard" by exerting "self-control"—and insisting that men do the same. "Although we are not in training camps," the pamphlet concluded, "we should think of ourselves as really in training for the fine new democracy in which men and women will work together to make the world safe for all humanity."[49]

The actual workings of the American Plan—which forcibly detained women, but not men, suspected of sexual activity outside of marriage—often reinforced the sexual double standard. And yet, Davis herself consistently—one might say insistently—emphasized the government's official position in support of a single sexual standard. In particular, Davis challenged the popular wisdom that "sexual indulgence" was necessary for men's welfare. While Americans had long believed that a man should "sow his wild oats" before settling down to marriage, Davis used government physicians' latest findings to contest this "double standard of morals."[50]

One leaflet distributed by Davis's organization highlighted the change in consciousness that she hoped to bring about. Emphasizing both the importance of accurate information and the rejection of a sexual double standard, the leaflet began by pointing out that "women have believed" in the necessity of sexual indulgence for men and the desirability of sexual ignorance for women, beliefs that sanctioned a sexual double standard that condoned men's sexual experimentation while condemning women's sexual experience. But, the leaflet continued, "women know today" that there was "no such necessity for either men or women," and furthermore, that sexual experimentation posed grave dangers to themselves, their communities, and their nation. Therefore, the leaflet concluded, it was "women's duty" to "refuse to be ignorant." Rather than hiding behind a false sense of feminine modesty, patriotic women needed to "face the facts" about venereal disease and vice districts and do their part to eliminate not only sexually transmitted infections but also the sex trade itself.[51]

Printed materials formed only a part of Davis's sex education campaign. Another important aspect of her wartime work was coordinating a series of public lectures on social hygiene. Even more than the printed materials she produced, the lecture bureau she organized highlighted her emphasis on providing women with accurate information and challenging the sexual double standard.

During World War I, female reformers partnered with the federal government to promote a single standard of sexual behavior and combat the spread of sexually transmitted infections. The Young Women's Christian Association established both affordable housing for working women and "hostess houses" to provide servicemen and civilian women with safe spaces for social interaction. Davis not only helped design YWCA housing but also produced pamphlets advising young women on modest attire for social occasions. George Grantham Bain Collection, Prints and Photographs Division, Library of Congress.

Davis had a longstanding relationship with the Young Women's Christian Association. She, her mother, and her sisters were all longtime members of the organization. In addition, by the time the United States entered World War I, her sister Helen had risen in the ranks from being a local gymnastics instructor to holding a national leadership position. Capitalizing on these relationships, during the war, Davis's agency assumed general oversight of the YWCA's Social Morality Committee's preexisting lecture program, which became the official lecture bureau for the Section on Women's Work. (Seeing in the affiliation with the federal program an opportunity for increased influence, the YWCA continued to fund and staff the program.)[52]

In the public lectures she delivered under the auspices of the YWCA's Social Morality Committee, as in the printed materials her section distributed, Davis emphasized the importance of information. "Nothing is sadder," she told one group, "than the girl who says, 'Oh, if I had only known.'" Insisting that the subject of sexual education was "a clean one," Davis optimistically predicted that a day would come when mothers would discuss sex with their daughters as candidly as they dealt with the topic of indigestion.[53]

To overcome prevailing notions of feminine modesty that made honest conversations about sexuality taboo, Davis characterized sex education as a form of patriotism. At the same time that Davis characterized women's morality as a patriotic duty, she also reminded her listeners to reject the sexual double standard. In one talk, "The Nation's Call to Young Women," Davis urged young women to "heed the highest demands of patriotism" and show soldiers "a good time in the right way." While she cautioned young women against being "traitors" by leading men astray, Davis also critiqued "the unfairness of the double standard of morality."[54]

While Davis and other members of the YWCA continued to speak at women's colleges during the war, Davis also launched a new lecture bureau featuring female physicians to reach out to a wider audience that included clubwomen, working women, and high school students. As she explained, reluctant mothers, teachers, and clubwomen were more likely to engage in a discussion of delicate subjects with the guidance of women physicians, who also were qualified to answer questions raised by the audience. Davis and her staff recruited more than one hundred female physicians to participate in this effort. The resulting "whirlwind social hygiene campaign," held in high schools, at workplaces, and in lecture halls, reached nearly one million listeners, many of whom participated in personal conferences with the featured physicians following the official lectures.[55]

"Scientific Information" and the "Single Standard"

The lecture bureau, even more than the printed materials, reiterated Davis's all-important emphasis on accurate information and a single standard. While there was, Davis explained, "no cut-and-dried lecture given on all occasions," each lecturer covered a set list of topics, usually in a series of lectures tailored to the specific audience. (For instance, for women's clubs, one lecture might be sufficient, but for high school and factory audiences, at least three lectures were recommended.) Among the required topics was a discussion of "the importance of the single standard of morals, considered from physical, social, and patriotic points of view." Davis wanted to make sure that the medical lecturers emphasized "the government's position in declaring that continence is compatible with health," as well as that "the only absolute safeguard against venereal disease is self-control."[56]

A set of "Suggestions to Lecturers on Social Morality" repeatedly emphasized the importance of establishing a single sexual standard for women and men. The basic goal, the guidelines began, was to provide "scientific information" to women and girls to enlist them in "the Government's effort to establish a single standard." Davis encouraged speakers to highlight medical experts' position that "continence is compatible with health" and to reinforce the government's effort to promote "the acceptance of the single standard."[57]

Rachelle Yarros, an Illinois-based physician who participated in the lecture bureau, shared Davis's commitment to a single sexual standard. Describing the government program as "at once idealistic and practical," Dr. Yarros praised the War Department for its recognition that "continence is consistent with health" as well as being "the best preventive of venereal disease." As she explained, echoing Davis, "This challenged the oldest, strongest and most common reason heretofore given for promiscuous indulgence."[58]

In an article published in *Social Hygiene*, Dr. Yarros offered a precis of her approach, which she tailored to the audience. For adult women, Dr. Yarros emphasized the government's "strongest backing for a single standard of morals and the possibility of a definite change in the attitude of man toward the problem of promiscuous sex indulgence." She further emphasized the necessity of women obtaining accurate information, saying that "women must learn the scientific facts about venereal diseases and face the situation frankly." After addressing the dangers of venereal diseases not only to the primary sufferers but also to their children, Dr. Yarros urged mothers "to instruct their children early in facts of life and later in matters of sex." She included a follow-up lecture offering specific examples of how mothers might teach their children about "the story of life," offering examples from nature, such as the pollination of flowers by bees and the building of nests by birds. But in addition to this talk about the birds and the bees, Dr. Yarros urged mothers to explain frankly how human babies came into the world, by describing the female reproductive system and explaining the process by which the egg was fertilized by the sperm.[59]

For young women and girls, Dr. Yarros gave a three-part lecture, beginning with "a general patriotic appeal" and framing the adoption of a single standard of sexual behavior as an expression of patriotism. In a second talk, she discussed "the essential facts regarding the prevalence and dangers of venereal diseases and prostitution." In her third talk, Dr. Yarros emphasized the importance of honesty and information. "Our mothers thought that by keeping us ignorant as to sex feelings, they were curbing them. But, as a matter of fact, that sex instinct, which begins to manifest itself early in life, is so strong that it cannot be eliminated or ignored, and should therefore be understood, regulated and directed." To this end, Dr. Yarros provided an overview of the physical and emotional changes associated with adolescence. While acknowledging both girls' and boys' desire for sex and romance, she also warned against both premarital sexual experimentation and sex with prostitutes. Throughout, Dr. Yarros emphasized the importance of "definite ideals" and maintaining both moral standards and physical health—both of which, she cautioned, were jeopardized by nonmarital sex.[60]

Excerpts from letters from community leaders indicated that lecturers like Dr. Yarros were well received. Those who attended the lectures offered by female physicians noted that the programs "vividly depicted" the dangers of venereal disease, but they also expressed appreciation for the speakers' "frank, clear statements of fact." One factory manager, who was pleasantly surprised that the speaker was not "a man-hater," also noted, "The lecturer enlightened the girls and did not frighten them."[61]

Campus authorities also praised the visiting physicians. During the war, Dr. Edith Hale Swift spoke at multiple college campuses, laying the groundwork for her future career as a sex educator. Deans of women lauded her efforts, describing her "splendid lectures" as "the best" ever delivered on the subject of sex on their campuses. Praising Dr. Swift's "personality and presence," administrators also noted that her status as both a physician and a mother lent credence to her thorough and thoughtful treatment of "a very delicate subject." "She won the confidence of our young women in her first lecture," one testified. Another averred, "Her last lecture seemed really inspired, bringing before the girls the beauty and the compensation of high standards in life's relationships in a way which they can never forget." Still other administrators noted that she impressed everybody with whom she came into contact, "men as well as women," and that parents and faculty members, as well as students, enthusiastically attended her lectures, sometimes more than once. In addition to lecturing, Dr. Swift also held informal conversations and private conferences with college coeds. Collectively, the female administrators concurred that Dr. Swift convinced her audience of "the normal quality and the dignity of the entire subject" of sex.[62]

Davis herself would soon undertake a new project aimed at persuading a still larger audience that the "entire subject" of sex was a "normal" part of life. In the meantime, however, she no doubt felt great satisfaction that audience responses suggested that the all-important message about a single sexual standard came through. One YWCA staffer, summarizing a series of thirty-six talks to a combined audience of more than six thousand young women in a variety of settings near a military encampment, reported that "everywhere the girls received Dr. —— with interest and responded heartily to her appeal to them to support the work of the government in attempting to establish a single standard of morals."[63]

In addition to providing print materials and coordinating a lecture bureau, Davis used the power of imagery to promote her goals. Her agency offered exhibitions featuring illustrated posters and slide shows. After Davis wrote and produced an original sex education film, *The End of the Road*, stills and clips from the film also became part of the exhibition, which toured major cities, including San Francisco, Chicago, Cincinnati, Detroit, and Milwaukee. According to the YWCA, more than four million people attended the exhibition.[64]

"To Inform and Educate Women"

The culmination of Davis's wartime sex education program was an original film, *The End of the Road*. The silent film gave Davis the opportunity to bring together her lifelong interest in the theater with her newfound commitment to sex education. Produced with the cooperation of the CTCA's Motion Picture Section, which had previously produced a film directed at military men, *Fit to Fight*, the film featured well-known leads and military extras—and portions of it were filmed at Davis's alma mater, Vassar College! Davis consulted with physicians to ensure "fidelity to medical fact" as well as with educators to achieve "psychological effect." In addition, she explained, "the stories in the film are all taken from life," based on Davis's extensive contact with adolescent girls and young women at Bedford Reformatory. Although Davis did not say so, the film's emphasis on the benefits of close mother-daughter relationships probably reflected her bond with her own mother. Perhaps most importantly, Davis used the film as a vehicle to convey her most important messages. While the film obviously highlighted the deadly results of sexually transmitted diseases, it just as strongly warned against the dangers of sexual ignorance and the destructiveness of the sexual double standard.[65]

The silent film revolves around the divergent roads taken by its principal characters, Mary and Vera—both white, well-to-do women from the same small town in upstate New York. From the start, the film highlights the importance of information, ideally transmitted from mother to daughter. Mary, the film's protagonist, has the advantage of early instruction in the facts of life. When she points out a bird's nest full of eggs to her mother, the attentive and affectionate woman explains that new life comes from eggs. She also informs Mary that she herself came from an egg that grew inside her mother's body. As Mary enters her teens, her mother offers additional information about sex and reproduction—although in keeping with the restrictive Comstock Laws, which made open discussion of such issues a federal crime, the film is short on details. Nonetheless, viewers see Mary and her mother earnestly discussing a suitably vaguely titled book, *Ideals of Social Relationships*, authored by a woman physician, which cautions teenage girls against "cheapening the greatest emotion in life" by engaging in "spooning," or premarital sexual activity.[66]

Over the course of the film, Mary develops into an honorable character who evinces the highest ideals. At her high school graduation, she earnestly implores her classmates to strive for "one truly great ideal—development of oneself for service to Mankind." With her mother's support, she pursues a degree in nursing rather than marrying a childhood sweetheart. Her career takes her to New York City, where she works closely with a distinguished physician, Dr. Philip Bell. Reflecting Davis's own commitment to life as a single professional, Mary repeatedly rejects offers of marriage to focus on service to others. Along the way, she learns about the terrible cost of nonmarital sex and sexually transmitted infections. She nurses a young immigrant who bears a child out of wedlock, offers refuge to a lovestruck teenager who contracts herpes from a military recruit, and assists in the voluntary sterilization of a betrayed wife whose son is born blind after his mother contracts gonorrhea from his unfaithful father.

Mary's values are put to the test when her hometown sweetheart, now a military recruit, implores her to sleep with him before he ships out. In wartime speeches, Davis warned that some "khaki crazy" contemporaries and "charity girls" engaged in "patriotic" sexual experimentation, thereby contributing to a relaxed moral code and the proliferation of disease.[67] But not Mary! Rather, she summarily rejects this suitor's improper advances, recognizing his insistence as a sure sign that he doesn't know "what love means." Mary's high ideals are rewarded, as in the closing scene, she finally finds love with her physician, with whom she serves on the battlefields of France during World War I.

Meanwhile, the film also follows the story of Vera, who lacks Mary's education and her ideals. Vera's mother demonstrates that she is not the "right kind of mother" when she scolds her young daughter for asking "naughty" questions about where babies come from. As Vera enters her teens, her "scheming and unsympathetic" mother continues to lead her astray, dismissing a local suitor and urging her daughter to go to New York City to seek a rich husband. There, on a date with an unscrupulous bounder who plies her with alcohol, Vera narrowly escapes rape thanks to Mary's intervention. But when her mercenary mother pressures her to marry for money, Vera yields to temptation and becomes the man's mistress. After developing a mysterious rash, which turns out to be syphilis, Vera begs her lover to marry her. Instead, he abandons her. To ensure that viewers got the message, an intertitle explains that in the absence of information and ideals, Vera "step by step goes along the road that leads in the end to disease, desertion, and disgrace."[68]

Importantly, however, this is not, despite the film's title, the end of the road for the unfortunate young woman. Prevailing wisdom and public policy, in accordance with the sexual double standard, held women alone responsible for illicit sex and venereal disease. But rather than portraying a woman's sexual missteps as leading inevitably to dire consequences with no hope of redemption, in *The End of the Road*, Davis chose to highlight the possibility of rehabilitation. In the film, although initially resistant to treatment, Vera changes her mind after Mary and the doctor take her on a tour of a hospital for women in advanced stages of syphilis. Horrified by the unfortunate patients' toothless grimaces, nerveless limbs, and suppurating sores, Vera undergoes successful treatment and ultimately finds a respectable and patriotic job in a wartime factory. There, viewers see her "happy in the consciousness of doing her part in the world struggle."

In addition to depicting wayward women as capable of redemption, in a dramatic departure from similar social hygiene films, *The End of the Road* presented men, rather than women, as the primary source of infection. Moreover, while Davis chose to depict the women in the film as amenable to rehabilitation, the male villains of the piece—unrepentant rakes and unfaithful husbands—stubbornly refuse to change their ways. For instance, even after infecting his wife with gonorrhea, leading to her invalidism and their son's blindness, Mr. Elbridge continues to engage in extramarital affairs. Mrs. Elbridge chooses to have a hysterectomy rather than run the risk of giving birth to another child with congenital problems resulting from "the sins of the father." An intertitle displayed during the procedure soberly informs viewers that "some man's criminal folly" is to blame for thousands of such operations each year. Soon thereafter, Mr. Elbridge's newest conquest, finding herself pregnant, hurls herself off a cliff into the crashing waves. The take-home message is that it is men's "sins," not women's, that threaten both public health and private happiness.[69]

The sterilization storyline in *The End of the Road* allowed Davis to return to another topic that had intrigued her for years: eugenics. But whereas Davis's earlier interest in eugenics had sometimes veered toward "negative" eugenics—the type of thinking that ultimately led to involuntary sterilization in the United States and mass genocide in Europe—her treatment of eugenics in *The End of the Road* was more focused on "positive" eugenics: voluntary decisions to promote human betterment. Moreover, the form of eugenics featured in the film rejected the racialized (and racist) tendencies of the movement writ large. Unlike contemporary films such as *The Black Stork*, which dramatized the dangers of reproduction by racial "inferiors," *The End of the Road* warned against reproducing disease itself in the form of congenital defects. Whereas the "unfit" in other eugenic films were "inferior" nonwhites, the "unfit" in *The End of the Road* were infected whites.[70]

Finally, and in contrast to both contemporary and later abuses in the name of eugenics, the only sterilization featured in the film is a voluntary one. Roundly denouncing men's sexual peccadilloes, the film shows the wronged wife choosing sterilization as the only sure way to avoid giving birth to another child destined to pay such a high price "for the sins of his father." While displaying a disdain for disability, consistent with eugenic thinking, the emphasis of this scene is on the wife's actions and the husband's "sins." That is, Davis once again highlighted women's bodily agency and denounced the sexual double standard. At the same time, she insisted on the importance of candid conversations about women's sexuality. Responding to the distressed mother's comments about the father's "sins," Dr. Bell reminds her (and the audience) that "ignorance, prudery, and false standards are more to blame than your husband."[71]

Davis based the film in part on the real stories of young women she encountered at Bedford Reformatory. Arguably, she treated the film characters with more sympathy than the reformatory inmates. One scene depicts a young immigrant who finds a job in domestic service, like so many Bedford inmates. After falling in love with an unscrupulous chauffeur who abandons her after she discovers she is pregnant, the young woman shoots and kills him, leading to a sentence at a reformatory. However, when we encounter her in the film, she has been released to give birth (and then to collapse and, presumably, die) "free." Another character is a former seamstress who, exhausted from hard work and desperate for excitement, strays from the path of virtue before ending up at a YWCA Hostess House. (Maintaining her long record of housing reform, Davis also was involved in wartime efforts to develop safe and sanitary housing for women workers, serving on the YWCA's Housing Committee along with her sister, Helen, and the wife of her employer, Abby Aldrich Rockefeller.) Rather than being sent to a reformatory as a "wayward girl," however, this young woman becomes the beneficiary of Mary's goodwill, as the nurse intervenes and sends her to live with her own mother.[72]

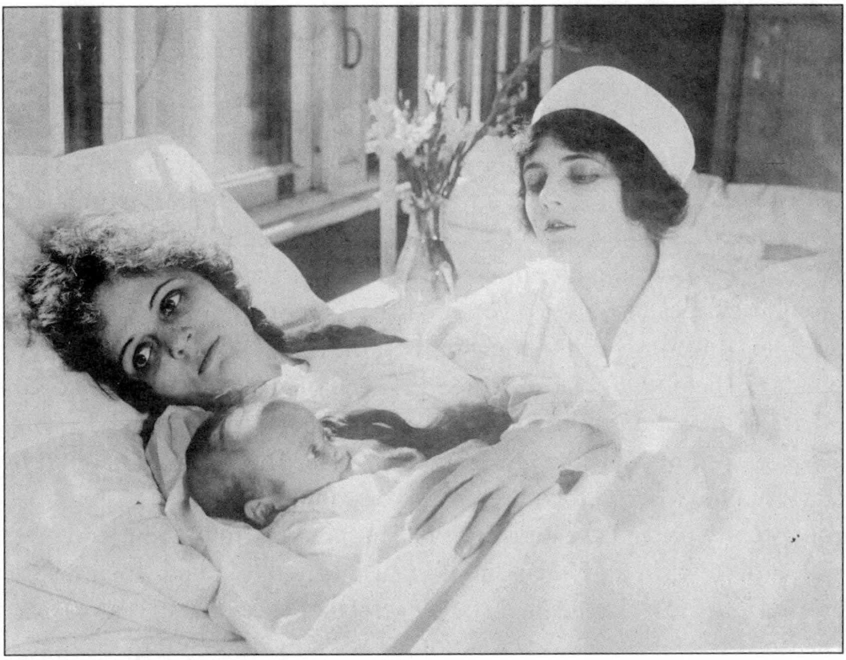

During World War I, Katharine Bement Davis translated her lifelong interest in drama into a feature film, *The End of the Road*, in which she drew upon her experiences at Bedford Reformatory to offer cautionary tales based on true stories. One storyline traced the tragic tale of a young woman, impregnated and abandoned, who shot and killed her faithless lover and was sentenced to a reformatory. While in real life she likely would have lived in the cottage reserved for mothers and babies while serving a three-year sentence, in the film version, the pregnant teen is released to give birth—and then, presumably, die—"free." Claire Adams Photographs. MS.P.008. Special Collections and Archives, UC Irvine Libraries.

Like Davis's other wartime social hygiene materials, *The End of the Road* emphasized the importance of information. Designed to be viewed by single-sex audiences and followed by an informative Q&A with female physicians as part of the wartime social hygiene program, the film was not completed until shortly after the armistice.[73] In peacetime, as planned, women's clubs and reform organizations sponsored screenings in private venues. In Philadelphia, the New Century Club, a women's reform organization, screened the film alongside "an illustrated lecture on social and sex hygiene" presented by a woman physician. The goal of both the lecture and the film, an approving article explained, was "to inform and educate women" about issues that were "vital to the health and needs of the entire country" and "to dispel ignorance and reveal the dangers to which a lack of knowledge invariably leads."[74]

Initially with the endorsement of the US attorney general and the approval of the copyright holder, the American Social Hygiene Association, a private antivice group closely affiliated with the Bureau of Social Hygiene, *The End of the Road* also became available for public distribution. However, a government-sponsored film designed to promote moral messages in wartime became the target of community moral arbiters in peacetime. While some praised the film as moral media, others saw it as sheer smut. Condemned in some quarters and celebrated in others, where the film managed to evade the control of local censors, it was a commercial success. Ironically, while the film was banned in Davis's hometown of Rochester, New York, movie houses in major cities consistently packed theaters until fall 1919, when the US surgeon general withdrew his endorsement of what promoters called "the greatest praised and most abused picture ever screened." Less than a year after its release, *The End of the Road* was at the end of its run.[75]

Davis, however, had only begun her journey. While writing the script for *The End of the Road*, Davis also had launched another major project, one that played a key role in her decision to exchange her planned postwar book on "The Delinquent Girl" for an entirely different study on the sex life of "normal" American women. While Davis had become increasingly interested in sex education during the wartime social hygiene campaign, a significant turning point in her approach to the study of sex seems to have been a conference she organized in the immediate aftermath of World War I: the International Conference of Women Physicians.

"To Rouse Interest in the Subject"

As the war drew to a close, Davis requested—and Rockefeller readily granted—financial support for a lengthy trip to Europe on behalf of the YWCA to organize an international conference of women physicians. Prior to US entry into World War I, the YWCA's War Work Council had contemplated sending delegates to Europe to investigate methods to address the problems posed by "disorderly houses" near overseas military camps. Davis had hoped to visit France during the war, but Fosdick had objected, on the basis that the French policies, which authorized legal sex districts, were so different from the American Plan that "they feel it is rather a slap at their own methods." Davis remarked, "I am a bit disappointed, as I have been very interested to see the situation with my own eyes." After peace was declared, the YWCA decided to pursue the plan with a new focus: an international conference of women physicians interested in social hygiene. Because Davis had organized the physicians' lecture bureau, she was the logical choice to make arrangements for this experiment in international sex education.[76]

Accordingly, instead of enjoying Christmas in New York, Davis, accompanied by her secretary, Ruth Topping, and by Boston physician and wartime speakers' bureau participant Edith Hale Swift, sailed for Europe in camouflaged vessels on December 14, 1918. Navigating freezing temperatures and dangerous border crossings in war-ravaged surroundings, the three women visited forty cities in eleven countries: Scotland, England, Norway, Sweden, Denmark, Holland, Belgium, France, Italy, Switzerland, and Germany. Along the way, they no doubt benefited from the women's prior visits to Europe and their fluency in languages. (The Brooklyn-born Topping had made two previous visits to Germany; Swift had studied in Germany; and Davis, thanks to her extensive European travels as well as her studies, was fluent in German and proficient in French and Italian.) Davis's "influential connections" also proved useful, as when British prime minister Lloyd George came aboard the vessel to allow the party to cross the English Channel via the diplomatic route. Because of these advantages, Davis and her companions had a relatively trouble-free journey; although they were "searched for gold" at one border crossing, and Davis "became an unwitting smuggler of the justly famed Swiss chocolate" at another, they were never detained for long. Nonetheless, the laborious process of arriving in a city, studying the directory to identify "the most prominent women physicians of the place," then visiting them at their listed address (which occasionally proved to be erroneous), and discussing the project over an obligatory meal and drinks, proved to be quite time-consuming. All in all, the trip took six months.[77]

Writing to Rockefeller from Geneva in March 1919, Davis explained that the trip had taken much longer than anticipated. "There are practically no express trains and sleepers are not to be had," she wrote, detailing the difficulties of travel. Moreover, "At every city we report to the police when we arrive and before we leave." Furthermore, "Passing from one country to another, about two days are required to visit the Consulates and secure permissions" for border crossings. Finally, "There are for the most part no telephones," meaning that repeated personal visits were necessary in order to make inquiries.[78]

Nonetheless, Davis was optimistic about the project. "Despite the difficulties of travel &c. we have enjoyed our trip and particularly the opportunity it has given of meeting so many people interested in our work," she assured Rockefeller. "Everywhere we have found great interest in our subject," although Davis and her colleagues also had found that European physicians were behind their American counterparts in spearheading social hygiene policies. But for Davis, this was only more evidence of the significance of the planned gathering. "We believe the Conference is going to do much to rouse interest in the subject and inspire the women physicians with the desire of active participation."[79]

"Full Equality"

Davis's lengthy stay in Europe allowed her to reunite with some of her Vassar classmates, who were volunteering with the Red Cross in France.[80] It also gave her the opportunity to play an important role in the founding of the League of Nations. Like many suffragists, Davis also was a pacifist. As she explained in her memoirs, "I am a thorough-going believer in peace, [and] in the settlement of disputes by arbitration." In the aftermath of the horrific destruction of the first world war, women activists in the United States and Europe saw an opportunity to advance both women's rights and world peace.[81]

The National American Woman Suffrage Association chose Davis as an official delegate to an International Congress of Women. Held in Zurich at the same time that male leaders of the "Big Four"—the United States, France, the UK, and Italy—gathered at the Paris Peace Conference in Versailles, the gathering adopted a Women's Charter that demanded not only world peace but also "full equality of women with men politically, socially and economically."[82]

The International Congress of Women also discussed proposals for women's role in the League of Nations, which they transmitted to the

Big Four by way of President Woodrow Wilson. As it happened, there was no typewriter available in the hotel where the women met, so Davis used her own portable typewriter to record the women's resolution, insisting that all positions in the league "shall be open equally to men and women." Davis's memoirs made special mention of these events: "It has always been a matter of pride to Dr. Davis that the one little paragraph in the Covenant of the League of Nations, which directly concerns women, was first written on her Corona."[83]

"High Moral Standards"

Davis would advocate for the League of Nations and world peace for the remainder of her life. In the immediate aftermath of the war, however, she focused on promoting international cooperation in the interest of public health. After an eventful six months in Europe, Davis returned to New York to finalize plans for the International Conference of Women Physicians. The month-long gathering in fall 1919, with more than six thousand registrants representing fifteen countries, was the starting point for the Medical Women's International Association, still functioning today. It also provided Davis with a platform for what would prove to be her last published writing on prostitution.[84]

At the conference, Davis's musings on "The Problem of Prostitution" reaffirmed her distaste for the sexual double standard, which she regarded as the root of the problem. She advocated the widespread adoption of "the so-called woman's standard, imposing chastity and continence outside of the marriage relation on both men and women" alongside "a fight for the complete abolition of prostitution," which would include both vigorous law enforcement and a major sex education initiative. For Davis, the American Plan's adoption of a "single standard" suggested the great possibilities of this approach, even as the wartime relaxation of moral codes served as a cautionary tale about the "permanent evil consequences" that could result if these "temporary modifications" became the basis for "a changed social order."[85]

Davis's staunch support for a single sexual standard—one that insisted upon sexual continence for both women and men—led her to join the new League of Women Voters' Social Hygiene Committee, which met in conjunction with the physicians' conference. This group's proposed tripartite program advocated the elimination of red-light districts and the aggressive prosecution of both prostitutes and their patrons; laws allowing local health authorities to detain and examine those suspected of carrying STIs; and establishing additional detention facilities for delinquent and defective persons. The proposed language was intentionally gender neutral, "thus equalizing the law," the league explained. It thus accorded with the measures that Davis advocated at the physicians' conference. However, because the proposed legislation left implementation to local authorities, it ended up reinforcing, rather than challenging, discriminatory treatment.[86]

In addition, Davis co-convened the International Council of Women's Equal Moral Standards Committee, waging an ongoing campaign to change the name to "Equal High Moral Standards." As one acquaintance put it, "She is not in favor of lowering the standards of women to those which have prevailed for men, although she is fully aware of the fact that today there are not a few women who believe that in certain matters of sex relationship women should have much greater freedom than they have had in the past."[87] And yet, within a year, Davis would chart a new path forward, one that set aside sexual morality and instead emphasized social science.

"Health and Morality"

The International Conference of Women Physicians played a key role in Davis's evolving attitude toward the study of sex. Davis dedicated nearly a year to organizing and orchestrating the conference, which took place in New York City in October 1919. While there are no detailed records of Davis's time in Europe, it seems likely that she may have met with several prominent sexologists during her time there. In Berlin, where she spent time "looking up old friends," she may have consulted with Magnus Hirschfeld and Albert Moll, whose work she would cite in her magnum opus, and who offered nuanced understandings of homosexuality, gender nonconformity, and transgender identity.[88]

She could have made a side trip to Vienna in order to meet with Sigmund Freud, the father of psychoanalysis. By that time, Freud—a latecomer to sexology—had published extensively on women's sexuality, but Davis was not impressed with his theories about sexual "complexes," which were hardly complimentary to either women or homosexuals. In her memoirs, she explained that she was "glad" to have been brought up before Freud's ideas gained currency. "In those far off days," she explained, "no one thought of the Narcissus or Oedipus complexes that might be lying around loose,—or the terrible inferiority complexes that might develop if a child were spanked."[89]

Davis would of course acknowledge Freud's theories when she wrote *Factors*, but while she gave Havelock Ellis pride of place, citing his positive assessment of lesbianism first, she saved "the Freudian explanation of homosexuality"—which posited that while all people are born bisexual, only queer people fail to mature into heterosexuals—for last.[90] Thus, it seems unlikely that Davis felt it worth her while to seek Freud out during this European sojourn. She was more interested in speaking with Freud's former acolyte, Carl Jung, whose growing interest in the subconscious had alienated him from his former mentor in 1912. According to her memoirs, "At Zurich, an afternoon spent with Professor Jung stands out prominently in recollections of this trip. Dr. Davis was anxious to get him to come to the conference, but he would not consider it, for he thought that Psycho-analysis was a science that could not be promoted by discussions in large groups."[91]

In London, she may have met with renowned sexologist Havelock Ellis and encountered birth-control advocate Marie Stopes—both of whom wrote extensively about "sexual periodicity," a subject she would address in her 1929 sex study—as well as convincing physician Constance Long, who translated Jung's writings into English, to participate in the international conference.[92]

Davis met with many other European physicians who participated in the conference, which explored a wide range of topics. Indicating the initial emphasis of the social hygiene movement on sexually transmitted infections and commercialized sex, the entire contingent of Norwegian physicians addressed the topic of venereal disease, including "prevention of venereal disease by education." Sex work and sexually transmitted infections also attracted attention from other European participants, including British physician Mary Gordon, who discussed "objections to prophylaxis." ("Prophylaxis" referred to using condoms or applying chemicals to the penis to prevent infection; unlike their French counterparts, most American and British authorities regarded prophylaxis as an invitation to promiscuity rather than a public health measure.) But other European participants widened the scope of the social hygiene movement to address a broader range of human sexuality. For instance, Dutch physician Ada Potter addressed "voluntary parenthood," and Italian physician Clelia Lollini spoke about "a new sexual morality."[93]

The conference also featured a full slate of American participants, including pioneering physicians, physiologists, and psychologists. Among these were Boston-based physician and physical education advocate Anna L. Brown, Pennsylvania gynecologist and social worker Ellen C. Potter, and Texas pediatrician Augusta Rucker, later the author of *Ten Talks to Girls on Health*. The inclusion of several gymnastics instructors and dress reformers likely reflected the interests of Davis's sister Helen, a former gymnastics instructor, as well as Davis herself, who had donned bloomers in the 1880s. But her memoirs indicated that the emphasis on psychoanalysis originated not with Davis but with other members of the planning committee, who "had become greatly interested" in the subject. (Despite her admiration for Jung, Davis believed "that phase of the question was over-emphasized on the conference program.")[94]

Although Davis was less than enthusiastic about the emphasis on psychoanalysis, a pathbreaking group of feminist psychologists—Beatrice Hinkle, Estelle Bertine, Kristine Mann, and Constance Long, who attended the conference, plus Mary Harding, who joined forces with them in the 1920s—would be responsible for popularizing Jungian psychoanalysis, establishing the field of feminist psychology, and promoting positive views of same-sex relationships.[95]

The "little group of five" developed a close personal relationship, spending holidays together; the US-based members (all but Long) also forged strong professional ties as Jungian analysts in Manhattan in the 1920s. The destruction of the group's personal papers makes it difficult to decipher the exact nature of their relationship. However, local records strongly suggest that Bertine and Harding were life partners, while Mann (never married) and Hinkle (married, widowed, remarried, and finally divorced) had romantic relationships with women outside of the immediate group. Certainly the "very congenial" group valued women's relationships highly; they also challenged conventional wisdom about (homo)sexuality, offering an alternative to Freud's unflattering (psycho) analysis of lesbianism as immaturity.[96]

At the 1919 conference, Bertine delivered a paper in which she critiqued "conventional morality" as potentially causing "serious distortions of personality" if not in line with "the best that we know about human development." During the discussion that followed, she asserted, "I can conceive of circumstances under which a so-called immoral act might be a real step in the forward development of an individual."[97]

Similarly, Hinkle—who had introduced Jung at a Heterodoxy gathering during his 1912 visit to New York—challenged both Freud's "rigid sexual hypotheses" and women's "psychic bondage." By the 1920s, Hinkle would issue a clarion call for "a new morality" defined by and for women. Castigating men for casting sex as "something shameful and unclean" because of "the inferior and inadequate nature of masculine sexuality," she argued that women must lead the way in promoting all forms of "self-creation," including (but not limited to) sexual expression.[98]

"The Broader Kind of Feminism"

The Jungian group was only one of several overlapping groups represented at the conference. As one might expect, given Davis's role as organizer, many of them were linked to Davis in some way. Many participants, like Davis, had graduated from Vassar or other women's colleges. Also like Davis, some of them had an association with Bedford; both Jessie Taft, Davis's second-in-command and successor at Bedford, and Dr. Edith Spaulding, head of the psychopathic division there, participated in the conference. Again like Davis, most participants were longtime feminist activists, many of them leaders in the suffrage movement. Finally, like Davis, several participants had longstanding associations with the YWCA; some, like Dr. Edith Hale Swift, were veterans of the wartime speakers' bureau.[99]

Unlike Davis, however, many US participants were members of Heterodoxy. In addition to Beatrice Hinkle, Heterodoxy speakers included Columbia faculty member and author Helen R. Hull, who kept her relationship with fellow faculty member Mabel Louise Robinson secret but whose novels discussed lesbian love; New York City physician and public health inspector Sara Josephine "Jo" Baker, known for her androgynous self-presentation and her openly lesbian relationships; and feminist economist and author Charlotte Perkins Gilman, whose short story about a woman's descent into madness as a result of her physician-husband's "prescription" of the "rest cure," *The Yellow Wallpaper*, attracted little attention at the time of its publication in 1892 but became a feminist classic when it was rediscovered in the 1970s.[100]

Davis had avoided associating with Heterodoxy and its iconoclastic—and sometimes lawbreaking—members during her tenure as a corrections official. During the war, many Heterodites had joined the National Women's Party (NWP), picketed the White House, served prison terms, and staged hunger strikes, earning them the moniker "Iron-Jawed Angels." Their attention-grabbing tactics—in conjunction with careful lobbying by the National American Woman Suffrage Association (NAWSA)—would help ensure the adoption of the Nineteenth Amendment, extending voting rights to many American women (mostly white and native born) soon after the war's conclusion, in 1920.

There is no record of what Davis thought of the NWP's militant tactics, although there is no doubt that she was more closely aligned with mainstream feminists of the NAWSA. (While she had been a member of the Congressional Union, the NWP's predecessor, Davis was more closely affiliated with NAWSA, in which she held office.) However, by the end of the war, she clearly was acquainted with—and supportive of—several of Heterodoxy's most influential members, since she invited them to participate in the conference. Indeed, it is conceivable that Davis's denunciations of the "taboo" on open discussions of sexuality can be traced to her acquaintance with the anthropologically minded Heterodites, who eagerly discussed such ideas and even spoofed them in a faux research paper on "Marriage Customs and Taboo Among the Early Heterodites."[101]

Apparently, this association helped change Davis's perspective on both conventional morality and feminist goals. Soon after the conference—and the achievement of the federal suffrage amendment—she would turn her attention away from voting rights to sexual equality. As Heterodite Katherine Anthony expressed it, "Now that suffrage is out of the way, there is a great need for the broader kind of feminism"—one that addressed personal freedom as well as political equality.[102]

"Woman's Physical Freedom"

One advocate of "the broader kind of feminism" who attended the conference was another woman who would later gain acclaim as a trailblazing sex researcher: Clelia Mosher. Just three years younger than Davis and born just three hundred miles away from Davis's birthplace, Mosher was a biologist with a mission: to promote what she called "woman's physical freedom." After graduating from Stanford University in 1893, she spent years researching women's health, seeking to demonstrate that menstruation did not pose insurmountable barriers to women's pursuit of higher education or their participation in the workforce. In her social hygiene classes at Stanford University, she recommended less restrictive clothing, regular exercise, deep breathing, and better posture. As a colleague recalled, instead of sending students to bed, she prescribed gentle exercises, showed them pictures of Greek women's statues, and recommended "clippings and articles on modern women's achievements and books on feminism."[103]

It would be more than three decades after Mosher's death in 1940 that a historian discovered her unpublished "Study of the Physiology and Hygiene of Marriage," which she began in 1892 and continued to collect data for through 1920. Mosher's study was small—the sample included just forty-seven married women—but her questions were daring. Her survey posed candid questions about women's attitudes about the purpose and pleasure of sex, the frequency with which they engaged in sexual intercourse, their use of contraception and other forms of birth control (such as periodic abstinence or coitus interruptus), and how often they experienced orgasms. Davis, who would pose similar questions in her own sex survey just a few years after the two women met at the conference, surely discussed Mosher's study with her; indeed, their conversations may have inspired Mosher to collect the final five surveys in her study, which were completed in 1920.[104]

Despite its name, the International Conference of Women Physicians also included a handful of men, not all of them physicians. Some of them were not only medical men but also civil rights pioneers. For instance, Jewish physician Joel Goldthwait, an orthopedic specialist, was an advocate for disabled patients. Others, like Freudian psychologist Horace Frink, were more conventional in their outlook. Frink lectured on masturbation, which he offered as an example of "morbid fears and compulsions." (Frink perhaps spoke from experience; he would suspend his practice as a psychoanalyst due to a manic-depressive diagnosis and die in a mental institution.) The military men were especially rigid in their views. For example, US Navy Major Bascom Johnson, director of the CTCA Division of Law Enforcement, advocated what he called "eternal vigilance"![105]

There must have been some heated discussions among the psychologists in attendance. While G. Stanley Hall, who introduced Freud to American audiences in 1909, spoke on "Points of Difference Between Men and Women," Beatrice Hinkle addressed "Arbitrary Use of the Terms 'Masculine' and 'Feminine.'" Fellow Heterodite Elizabeth Irwin, after hearing her speak, reported to her partner, Katherine Anthony, that Hinkle was "one of the best on the program," and that her paper was "very interesting indeed." Opining that "the psychological aspect of the sex impulse has been all too little handled," Anthony vowed, "We must manage to get hold of the manuscript and read it."[106]

While Freud and his followers cast homosexuality as a form of delayed development, Hinkle regarded sexual diversity in a much more positive light. Agreeing with Freud that bisexuality was "latent in everyone," she followed Jung in interpreting human sexuality in light of psychological types rather than psychological development. Thus, she argued that one's personality type might transcend gender identity and defy sexual categorization "as far as objective conditions allow."[107]

While Davis no doubt learned from the refreshing perspectives offered by the Jungian psychologists and the instructive example provided by Clelia Mosher, the most well-documented connection she forged at the conference was with Max J. Exner, a physician affiliated with the YMCA. While Exner had a strong moralistic streak—he denounced both masturbation and "morbid curiosities" about sex—he also was the author of a pioneering statistical study of college men's sex education, published in 1915. His interest in the subject grew during the war, which he saw as having unfortunate "sensualizing" effects on young men in military camps. Despite his own moralizing tendencies, Exner played a key role in prompting Davis to abandon her efforts at moral reform and instead take up the mantle of what she would come to call "the scientific study of sex."[108]

At the conference, Exner spoke on "Sex Education in Colleges," a subject close to Davis's heart in the immediate aftermath of her wartime sex education campaign. It was likely at the conference that Exner first suggested to her that she conduct a similar study of college women. Davis responded enthusiastically to his suggestion. Indeed, she would go much further than Exner probably intended by conducting the world's first large-scale statistical study of "normal" women's sexuality. In addition, soon after the conference—after hiring as a research assistant a psychology graduate student named Earl F. Zinn, whose growing interest in studying sexuality had alienated him from his former advisor, Freudian follower G. Stanley Hall—Exner would come to Davis with another proposal: to establish an agency responsible for coordinating sex research. Again, Davis would seize upon this suggestion to establish what would become the nation's first entity dedicated to the study of human sexuality.[109]

"An Opportunity for Social Progress"

Shortly before the armistice, Davis penned a lengthy and laudatory account of women's wartime social hygiene work. "Never before in the history of any country has there been such an opportunity for social progress, for social justice, for individual ideas as that which faces our country at this time," she proclaimed. In particular, she averred, women had an unprecedented opportunity to play a central role in social reform. "The responsibility is peculiarly upon women in this matter," she insisted, and it was incumbent upon them to make the most of the present moment. "Never before have the women and girls of any country had such an opportunity to make their convictions so felt and their ideals count for so much," she declared, urging her peers to play their part in "the development of a clean and true democracy."[110]

For her part, Davis believed that the key to "civic progress and a true democracy" was educating the "rising generation." Although originally drawn to this work by wartime exigencies, Davis was adamant that "educational work . . . can by no means end with the war." For the next decade, she would commit herself wholeheartedly to "educational work"—with a difference. While combating the sexual double standard remained important to Davis, after the physicians' conference, she was more strongly committed to promoting women's sexual knowledge. Instead of advocating "social hygiene," she advanced sex education; instead of warning against sexually transmitted infections, she investigated women's sexual experiences; and instead of cautioning against moral decay, she campaigned for "the scientific study of sex."[111]

Ultimately, this concerted campaign would lead to her summary ejection from the Bureau of Social Hygiene. However, Davis managed to maintain the generous support of her wealthy sponsor, John D. Rockefeller Jr., long enough to conduct a remarkably comprehensive and candid study of women's sexual behavior. When it was published in 1929, Davis's study would become the first study of women's sexuality authored by a woman. Just as importantly, it would fundamentally reshape Americans' understandings of "normal" female sexuality.

6

"The Scientific Study of Sex"

On February 2, 1928, New York's Waldorf-Astoria Hotel hosted a grand event in honor of sixty-eight-year-old Katharine Bement Davis, who had recently announced her retirement from the Bureau of Social Hygiene, a think tank dedicated to combating commercialized sex and curbing the spread of venereal disease. Organized by the National Council of Women, the "testimonial dinner" was intended, as the official invitation put it, "to pay some public tribute to her untiring efforts and her constructive contributions in behalf of social betterment." Featuring a total of nineteen speakers representing every stage of Davis's career—from her high school years through her ten-year term at the Bureau of Social Hygiene—the evening's entertainment was sponsored by such luminaries as settlement house pioneer Jane Addams and suffragist Carrie Chapman Catt, as well as Davis's longtime benefactor, philanthropist John D. Rockefeller Jr., and a host of other well-known public figures.[1]

During an "unforgettable evening," hundreds of friends, colleagues, and admirers gathered to honor the public service veteran. Throughout her long and varied career, Davis had applied what one admirer called "her wealth of knowledge and her wise judgment" to a wide range of issues, including settlement work, prison reform, social hygiene, and, finally, sex research. It seemed impossible to Davis's many professional colleagues and personal friends that such an energetic, engaged, and enthusiastic individual—what one admirer called "the greatest of our generation"—could possibly retire. Accordingly, while her acquaintances wrote to Davis to wish her well in her retirement, they also expressed the hope, as one put it, that official retirement from "an active life so rich in achievement" not only would grant Davis some well-earned rest but also permit her to "give us in fuller measure the fruits of her long and unique experience."[2]

Neither the press coverage of Davis's retirement gala nor the plaudits of her friends gave any hint that Davis had announced her retirement under duress. As a matter of fact, Davis had hoped to continue her work at the bureau for at least another two years, until she reached her seventieth birthday. She intended to use that time both to complete a pathbreaking study of women's sexuality and to cement the organization's commitment to research in human sexuality. Instead, Davis's enthusiasm for what she called "the scientific study of sex" torpedoed her career and led to her forced retirement. Despite this setback—as well as significant health challenges—Davis succeeded in establishing a new Rockefeller-funded agency dedicated to research on sexuality, with profound ramifications for future scholarship. She also continued work on her magnum opus, the first comprehensive study of women's sexuality conducted by a female researcher, as well as the first such study to focus on "normal women."[3]

"Sex o'Clock in America"

Davis's commitment to the science of sex—also known as sexology—was timely. In early twentieth-century America, sex seemed to be everywhere. Radical feminists in New York City's Greenwich Village formed an organization known as Heterodoxy, whose members openly advocated "free love" and enthusiastically engaged in extramarital affairs and same-sex relationships. Reformers like Margaret Sanger and Mary Ware Dennett distributed birth control and disseminated sexual information in defiance of the law, insisting that women should be able to enjoy sexual pleasure without running the risk of unplanned pregnancy. During World War I, social reformers partnered with the federal government to promote "social hygiene" to prevent the spread of sexually transmitted infections, protect public health, and keep the nation's military men "fit to fight." In the aftermath of the war, a growing proportion of high schools across the country offered at least rudimentary sex education classes, initiating a "century-long battle between truth and doctrine."[4]

Meanwhile, popular culture became suffused with sex. Contestants in beauty pageants displayed their charms in skimpy bathing costumes and short skirts. On stage and screen, actresses openly flaunted their sex appeal. Young women throughout the nation imitated the brash style—short skirts, silk stockings, bobbed hair, and bold lipstick—associated with the sexy "flapper" depicted on magazine covers and in contempo-

In the 1920s, a "revolution in manners and morals" was underway. Feminist activists promoted sex education and birth control, "flaming youth" enjoyed unprecedented sexual freedom, and popular culture celebrated "sex appeal." During the nation's "first sexual revolution," young women like Miss Yonkers competed in America's earliest beauty contests, displaying their charms in short skirts and skimpy swimsuits. Beauty Contests, Prints and Photographs Division, Library of Congress.

rary novels. If not all young people participated in "petting parties" or indulged in "bathtub gin," most were familiar with these iconic symbols of liberated lifestyles. Even in small towns, the newly ubiquitous automobile—which one juvenile court judge dubbed "a house of prostitution on wheels"—rendered adult chaperonage obsolete. As dating replaced courtship, a shift "from front porch to back seat" granted young people unprecedented sexual freedom in both word and deed.[5]

In the first two decades of the twentieth century, it seemed that the Victorian value of sexual self-restraint was yielding to a modern ethos of sexual self-fulfillment. As early as 1913, one concerned social commentator declared that it was "Sex o'Clock in America." "A wave of sex hysteria and sex discussion seems to have invaded this country," he warned.

"Our former reticence on matters of sex is giving way to a frankness that would startle even Paris." Over the next decade, a growing number of Americans—with a mixture of alarm and admiration—agreed that attitudes toward sex had changed profoundly. Indeed, some observers regarded the "revolution in manners and morals" that characterized the 1920s as the nation's first sexual revolution.[6]

"Salient Facts with Regard to Sex"

At this pivotal moment, Davis adopted an innovative research program focusing on "normal experiences of sex." Explaining that "except on the pathological side, sex is scientifically an unexplored country," Davis advocated serious research into average Americans' sexuality as the basis for both sound "educational programs" and "a rational sex ethics." As one of her colleagues explained, a research program focused on human sexuality would demystify the "repressed" subject, encourage open discussion, and advance future research. "A knowledge of the salient facts with regard to sex life as it actually exists among normal and average people today, will constitute a necessary point of departure" for all future studies, Dr. Helen Thompson asserted.[7]

Davis's proposal was not only timely but also prescient. Studies of "normal" behavior among "average" Americans would become the gold standard for social scientists over the coming decades. The study of sex also would gain both scientific credence and social acceptance over the next twenty years. These developments would converge with the highly publicized release of Dr. Alfred Kinsey's studies of human sexuality—the first, *Sexual Behavior in the Human Male*, in 1948, and the second, *Sexual Behavior in the Human Female*, in 1953. Together, the so-called Kinsey Reports would revolutionize Americans' understandings of normal sexuality. In the 1920s, when Davis launched her own study of women's sexuality and lobbied for the bureau to dedicate its resources to the study of sex, she paved the way for these developments, but she also lost her job.[8]

Decades before Dr. Alfred Kinsey began his controversial studies of human sexuality, Davis conducted her own revelatory studies of female sexuality. Moreover, she campaigned to establish the National Research Council's Committee for Research on the Problems of Sex, which ultimately funded Kinsey's work. Unfortunately for Davis, her benefactor at the Bureau of Social Hygiene, John D. Rockefeller Jr., did not share her enthusiasm for sexological research. Instead, the straitlaced philanthropist preferred to dictate social standards. Meanwhile, her male coworkers used her most innovative ideas against her, convincing Rockefeller to terminate her employment. While gender discrimination and professional rivalries limited her success, Davis deserves recognition as a pathbreaking scholar of human sexuality. Her 1929 volume, *Factors in the Sex Life of Twenty-Two Hundred Women*, profoundly reshaped Americans' understanding of women's sexuality, challenging both patriarchal views of female sexuality and the pathological model of homosexuality. Moreover, Davis's approach to the subject profoundly influenced Kinsey's now better-known studies. Finally, the Committee for Research on the Problems of Sex that Davis founded continued its work, not only funding Kinsey's work but also sponsoring research that ultimately led to the development of oral contraceptives, better known simply as "the pill." For all these reasons, Davis deserves recognition both for her work as a trailblazing sex researcher and for her role in ushering in a sexual revolution.[9]

"This New Opportunity"

Although Davis's commitment to sexology remains one of her most important legacies, it also led to her unceremonious ejection from the Bureau of Social Hygiene after a long and fruitful collaboration with the agency's founder, John D. Rockefeller Jr. At the time that Davis and Rockefeller initiated their collaboration in 1911, their aims were in alignment. Rockefeller, having recently completed his tenure as foreman of a grand jury to investigate prostitution in New York City, had just begun the Bureau of Social Hygiene to study social problems related to sex work. As the celebrated superintendent of Bedford Reformatory, where nearly half of inmates had been confined for prostitution, Davis shared the movie-star-handsome philanthropist's concern about "social hygiene," the Progressive Era euphemism for curbing the spread of sexually transmitted diseases. When the Bureau of Social Hygiene incorporated in 1913, Davis and Rockefeller were united in strong support of its mission, defined as "the study, amelioration and prevention of those social conditions, crimes and diseases which adversely affect the well-being of society, with special reference to prostitution and the evils associated therewith."[10]

In addition to funding Davis's Laboratory of Social Hygiene at Bedford, the Bureau of Social Hygiene (BSH) hired two researchers, Raymond B. Fosdick and Abraham Flexner. Fosdick, a clean-shaven lawyer with piercing eyes, and Flexner, a bespectacled, balding physician, almost immediately began an extended campaign to undermine Davis. Motivated by a toxic combination of professional jealousy and profound misogyny, they argued that Davis lacked the scholarly credentials to undertake serious research—although, of the three, she was the only one to hold a PhD. Flexner, who had established himself as an influential gatekeeper in the medical profession and shored up his own status by asserting that the female-dominated field of social work was not a profession, was not impressed by Davis's achievements in either settlement work or law enforcement. Fosdick, despite being a fellow native New Yorker, also had no interest in developing a collegial relationship with Davis. Instead, he campaigned to be named director of the BSH—a campaign that backfired when, in 1917, Rockefeller hand-picked Davis to direct the bureau.[11]

Flexner and Fosdick were furious at having to report to a female supervisor, but Rockefeller was enthusiastic about Davis's appointment. "Long before I first met you at Bedford," he confided, "I had formed the highest opinion of your ability and your splendid consecration, an opinion which my association during the past years has constantly strengthened. You will see, therefore, with what genuine pleasure I am looking forward to this new opportunity for work with you." Rockefeller's word choice, associating Davis's "new opportunity" to lead the bureau with the "consecrated" task of purifying the nation's morals, was telling. So long as she shared his views about the need to suppress extramarital sex, he enthusiastically backed her up. But when she began to promote the scientific study of sex, he backed away.[12]

Rockefeller's support remained steadfast during World War I, when Davis dedicated most of her time to "war activities": combating illicit sexuality and controlling venereal disease. At the end of the war, all the signs seemed to suggest that Davis was poised to return to her original mission at the helm of the Bureau of Social Hygiene: coordinating the efforts of a range of organizations dedicated to promoting "social hygiene" and combating sex work. In 1919, Rockefeller described her as "at work on a plan for federating the various organizations in New York City which have to do with prostitution in its different phases."[13]

But after organizing the International Conference of Women Physicians—and with a new year and a new decade dawning—Davis was ready to redirect her energies toward research. Accordingly, in early 1920, she requested and received funding from Rockefeller to increase the salary for her longtime secretary, Ruth Topping, and appoint her as the official liaison officer to facilitate collaboration among city agencies concerned with vice, crime, and delinquency.[14]

"Normal Sex Life"

Meanwhile—with profound consequences both for her own career and for Americans' understandings of sexuality—Davis undertook two major new initiatives that reflected an entirely new approach to the subject of sexuality. First, she turned her planned study into "The Delinquent Girl" into a very different project: the study of "normal" female sexuality. Second, instead of coordinating citywide efforts to combat vice, Davis founded a new committee dedicated to the scientific study of sex. Davis launched both of these projects in 1920; the new decade, for Davis, represented a new departure.

Davis's new approach clearly grew out of her wartime work. Davis's staunch opposition to the sexual double standard ran counter to the workings of the American Plan, which targeted women—but not men—suspected of engaging in nonmarital sex. Instead of imprisoning suspected sex workers, Davis increasingly was drawn to the possibilities of offering reliable information about sex to young women. By the war's conclusion, Davis was less interested in studying "delinquent" sexuality and more interested in contributing to a scientifically informed sex education agenda.

While her wartime social hygiene campaign had laid the groundwork for Davis's new orientation to the study of sexuality, the true turning point seems to have been the 1919 International Conference of Women Physicians. After that conference, Davis replaced her planned study on women's sexual delinquency with a very different project: the study of "normal" female sexuality—that is, the study of "the woman who was not pathological mentally or physically and who was capable of adjusting herself satisfactorily to her social group."[15]

Davis's original idea was very much in keeping with Progressive Era concerns and scholarship about "precocious" adolescent sexuality, especially among poor, immigrant, and African American girls. Indeed, sociologists and social workers issued a steady stream of studies about "wayward women" in the 1910s—most, like Davis's charges at Bedford, young working-class women who, willingly or not, engaged in premarital sex. While some writers wrung their hands over "women adrift," who left home to live on their own, most were concerned about so-called charity girls: working-class women who used their sexuality to barter for "city pleasures" while still contributing the bulk of their earnings to their families. For many observers, women's increased sexual independence in wartime—or, at least, the increased visibility of their sexual activity—increased their interest in (and their anxiety about) young women's sexual behavior as growing numbers of "respectable," middle-class, white women expected their dates to engage in the practice of "treating" (and sometimes themselves engaged in "tricking").[16]

However, Davis's participation in the wartime social hygiene program, coupled with the ideas she was exposed to at the physicians' conference and the connections she made there, shifted Davis's approach toward the study of sexuality. According to extant records, most importantly, Dr. Max Exner, who had conducted his own study of the sexual experiences of collegiate men, urged her to collect information on college-educated women "in connection with framing a sound education programme."[17]

Davis eagerly embraced this plan, making a seemingly seamless shift from social hygiene to sex education. After World War I, many social hygiene reformers, previously focused on STI prevention, became sex education advocates intent on scientific information. While many of these educators and advocates continued to combine medical and moral approaches, all were eager to use the federal funds originally allocated to the American Plan to establish a national sex education system, through either state hygiene boards or the public school system. But to do this well, they needed better information. Davis stepped into the breach. As she explained to her benefactor and boss, a study of "the normal sex life of women" would "determine the facts on the basis of normal experience which could be used as a guide for sex education in schools and colleges."[18]

Offering an indication of just how much more acceptable the war years had made open discussions of sex, the moralistic philanthropist promptly granted Davis's request for financial support for a study of the sex lives of married women in spring 1920. Despite the stark contrast between the planned study of delinquent adolescents and the new proposal to study married women, Rockefeller evidently was convinced that, as his assistant put it, Davis's new project was "entirely in line with the objects of the Bureau."[19]

Davis herself never fully explained the dramatic shift in her approach to the study of sex away from a focus on supposedly deviant behavior among so-called abnormal populations to presumably ordinary behavior among normal women. Her unfinished, unpublished autobiography did not cover this stage of her career. Both in bureau correspondence and in public statements, Davis justified the study as necessary for an accurate sexual education program. Yet, as the furor aroused by the study indicated, her determination to study—and share—accurate information about women's actual sexual desires and behavior required tremendous courage and commitment. Although Davis never explicitly said so, surely both her faith in social science and her feminist principles led her to undertake—and sustain—a controversial study that took many years to complete, and that had such profound consequences for her professional career.

From childhood, Davis had been determined to understand the world around her. In college, Davis learned to look to science for explanations. In graduate school, she discovered social science, a then-new field that applied scientific methods to social issues. Like many reformers in the Progressive Era, Davis soon turned to statistical analysis to analyze social problems. As she confided to a fellow Vassar student and lifelong friend, she regarded her scientific training as "particularly valuable in her social work because she was trained to approach everything from the scientific point of view."[20]

In the opening decades of the twentieth century, while working in corrections, Davis applied social-scientific methods to studies of criminal behavior, including sex work. In the 1920s, while working at the Bureau of Social Hygiene, she turned her attention away from explaining abnormal or deviant behavior to probing normal or average behavior. As usual, she was at the cutting edge of scientific endeavor.

It was in the 1920s that social scientists first redirected their attention away from the abnormal and toward the normal, producing studies such as *Middletown*, a study of middle America written by a husband-and-wife sociological team, Helen and Robert Lynd. Studies like *Middletown* spoke to a postwar generation eager to know more about the daily lives of ordinary Americans in modern America; Davis shared her fellow social scientists' interest in probing the intimate details of everyday life.[21]

Davis's zeal for her new research project about women's sexuality combined a progressive's characteristic faith in scientific data with a feminist's quest to improve women's lives. As a girl, Davis spent countless hours listening to her grandmother, who attended the nation's first women's rights convention at Seneca Falls, New York, in 1848, describe her role in "the struggle for rights for women."[22] As an adult, Davis described herself as "born a suffragist."[23] In addition to supporting women's suffrage, Davis was committed to women's welfare. She saw it as her life work to do "woman's work for women," as one newspaper account put it in the 1920s.[24]

After the Nineteenth Amendment granted many—but not all—American women voting rights, in 1920, Davis turned her attention from women's political rights to their personal lives. In the course of her outreach work during World War I, Davis had become intimately familiar with women's profound ignorance in sexual matters. Discussions of sexuality were "taboo," she complained, and as a result, women knew very little about their own bodies.[25]

While Davis attributed this sad situation in large part to the sexual double standard, she also recognized that it resulted from a lack of sex education based in scientific study. In the absence of reliable data, Davis noted, most women received "meager information," at best, about sex and reproduction, leading to a mix of shame and fear. Many had no idea how pregnancy occurred, instead believing that they might unwittingly fall pregnant as a result of eating certain foods or sitting beside someone on public transportation. Some were unprepared even for menstruation; one study participant reported that when she began to menstruate at age fourteen, "I naturally thought I was bleeding to death." In short, Davis found that inadequate sex instruction led to "distorted views, baffled speculation, or unfortunate experiences." Davis would have agreed with a study subject who opined, "Our present secrecy, fear, and repression are responsible for most of our sex ills." As a first step toward correcting this unfortunate situation, then, Davis turned to the collection of accurate information to serve as the basis for better sex education. By providing women with scientifically verifiable information, she hoped to better women's (sex) lives.[26]

"An Amazing Piece of Work"

To launch her study of women's sexuality, Davis recruited an all-female advisory board with impeccable credentials—clubwomen, professors, and physicians—who designed a detailed questionnaire and distributed it to a list provided from the membership of the YWCA, the General Federation of Women's Clubs, and collegiate alumnae registers. Although the original survey has not been preserved, the cover letter suggested it would ask explicit questions and solicit honest answers about "the sex experiences in girlhood, womanhood, and marriage." To encourage participation, the initial query emphasized that the questionnaire had been composed by "a committee of well-known women of scientific training." Davis also promised absolute anonymity (using a double-envelope system) and assured participants that their cooperation would "be of great social value."[27]

The trouble began the following year. In 1921, when Davis requested authorization to extend her study to include unmarried women, her male coworkers intensified their campaign against her. When Rockefeller asked him to review the sex questionnaire, Fosdick responded, "The questionnaire is an amazing piece of work, and I confess its frankness quite takes my breath away." It was not a compliment. Flexner joined Fosdick in opposition to Davis, asserting that her study "would not be of sufficient scientific value to be worthwhile."[28]

But Rockefeller, perhaps flattered by Davis's explanation that "such a study can be best made by an organization like the Bureau of Social Hygiene which is known to have already made unbiased and impartial investigations," endorsed her plan.[29] Responding to Fosdick's criticisms, he remarked, "While the investigation may be hardly a scientific one, it is resulting in the securing of a considerable amount of information that is highly suggestive and valuable."[30]

In the 1920s, Katharine Davis recruited "average" American women—white, well-educated, and well-to-do—from lists of clubwomen and college graduates for a pioneering study of "normal" female sexuality. Detailed questionnaires completed by women "of good standing in the community" provided her with statistical data to challenge pervasive stereotypes about female "passionlessness." Petworth Women's Club, October 5, 1922, National Photo Company Collection, Prints and Photographs Division, Library of Congress.

"A Sane Outlook on All Matters Pertaining to Sex"

Rockefeller based his opinion not only on early responses to the questionnaire but also on the strong support of the male leadership of both the American Social Hygiene Association and the Young Men's Christian Association. A letter from Dr. Max Exner—who spoke for both organizations—was especially decisive. Exner, perhaps at Davis's request, wrote directly to Rockefeller to express his support for Davis's research, declaring, "I look upon it as one of the most important and the most fundamental things to be done in the interest of sane and effective development of social hygiene. Our greatest need is a much more adequate body of scientifically derived data upon which to build a sound educational movement," Exner opined, concluding, "We greatly need research which will help us in arriving at a rational sex ethics." While Rockefeller, as it turned out, would not be a supporter of "a rational sex ethics," he could not help but be impressed by Exner's comments on the "effective development of social hygiene," which was, after all, the purpose of the Bureau of Social Hygiene.[31]

With Rockefeller's support, Davis carried on with her study. After spending a relaxing month in Italy with her sister Helen, in July 1922 Davis returned to New York "much refreshed" and ready to analyze the "10000 written pages of material" she had accumulated on the sex lives of married women.[32]

Davis released some of her early findings in a three-part article, "A Study of the Sex Life of the Normal Married Woman," in the *Journal of Social Hygiene*, published by the American Social Hygiene Association, a private antivice organization with close ties to the Bureau of Social Hygiene. After sending a total of ten thousand query letters to clubwomen and college graduates, Davis and her colleagues assembled a sample of one thousand responses to an eight-page questionnaire that covered childhood, adolescence, marriage, and menopause and posed pointed questions about sexual attitudes and experiences. Reflecting both her interest in sex education and her commitment to social science, Davis began, "In no part of the field of education is there greater difference of opinion than in that which deals with sex. This is largely because, except on the pathological side, sex is scientifically an unexplored country."[33]

Davis kicked off the series in April 1922 with a provocative piece on contraceptive use among married women. For half a century, the Comstock Laws had defined information about birth control as obscene and prohibited the distribution of contraception. By the 1920s, however, some fortunate women were able to acquire contraceptives with the assistance of sympathetic (or simply well-paid) physicians, who in some states—including New York—were legally permitted to prescribe birth-control devices (such as diaphragms) to protect patients' health. Despite the controversial status of contraceptives, Davis's analysis indicated a high level of support for birth control among married women. Nearly three fourths of the sample indicated general support for "voluntary parenthood," and the same proportion reported using contraceptive methods themselves. Available methods, including condoms, diaphragms, and cervical caps, were far from foolproof; nearly one in ten women revealed that they had undergone at least one abortion, even though the procedure was entirely illegal.[34]

The second article in the series, published in January 1923, tackled the question of marital satisfaction. Davis's questionnaires attempted to correlate marital happiness (or lack thereof) with several factors, including quality of previous "sex instruction," degree of premarital sexual experience, age differences between spouses, initial sexual contact, and general health. Davis's study revealed a surprisingly high incidence of premarital sexual activity. Nearly one fourth of respondents indicated that they masturbated as children, and the same proportion indicated engaging in "sex play" prior to age fourteen.[35]

Turning her attention to the years between adolescence and marriage, Davis found even more evidence of premarital sexual experience. Nearly a third (30 percent) of respondents acknowledged that they had masturbated, and more than a third (37 percent) reported "spooning," although only a small minority (7 percent) indicated that they had engaged in sexual intercourse. As a separate category, Davis addressed "emotional relations with other women," including "with physical expression" and "without physical expression." She found that nearly one third (30 percent) of the sample reported strong emotional ties to other women, with slightly more than half of these acknowledging that their relationships included "physical expression" beyond kissing and hugging.[36]

Davis's data on same-sex relationships would arguably become her most important intervention in the nascent field of sexology. The portion of Davis's discussion of sexual behavior that attracted the most attention at the time, however, was her discussion of "spooning" and marital happiness. Davis reported that well over one third of married women—nearly 40 percent in all—engaged in premarital "spooning," a catch-all term that included "hugging, kissing and fondling," "intimate fondling," and in a few instances, "intimate fondling including sex intercourse." Because only 38 percent of those who engaged in these activities reported that they were happy, and 44 percent of those who spooned reported that they were unhappy, Davis concluded that spooning and sex before marriage "militat[ed] against the happiness of married life," although she also cautioned that the sample was too small, and the group too selective, to use as a basis for "general deductions."[37]

However, newspapers immediately pounced upon Davis's discussion of spooning, running sensational headlines such as "If You Spoon Before You Meet Your Husband Chances Are Against Being Happily Married."[38] While some newspapers commented favorably on the study overall—the *Atlanta Constitution* remarked that Davis had produced "the first exhaustive scientific investigation that has been made of the sex life of the moral, educated women" of the nation—others were less positive.[39]

Raymond Fosdick's worst fears were realized in May 1923 when the *Boston Paragraph* ran an article condemning "Rockefeller's 'Scientists,'" using scare quotes in the title to cast additional doubt on Davis's project. Avoiding offering any details about the "nauseating statistics" or "gruesome facts" revealed by the study, the article asserted that "the treason of the Rockefellers is an unpardonable insult to decency." Without mentioning her by name, the article criticized Davis especially harshly, declaring, "The fact that the pseudo-scientist bears the name of a female does not make the treason the less unprofessional." While Fosdick described the article as "scurrilous and perhaps libelous," the BSH lawyer did not take legal action against the publication. Instead, he intensified his campaign to oust Davis.[40]

Fosdick, like the anonymous author of the article, was shocked by Davis's frank discussion of sexual behavior. Davis did not call attention to the fact that her study revealed that approximately three fourths of her sample engaged in some form of premarital intimacy, when "spooning," "ordinary endearments of courtship," and "physical expression" of "emotional relations with other women" are combined. Nonetheless, Davis's revelations about women's sexual desire and behavior—both heterosexual and homosexual—posed a profound challenge to prevailing wisdom about female sexuality, which held that respectable, "passionless" women neither experienced sexual desire nor engaged in sexual activity—except to please their husbands or for the purpose of reproduction.[41]

The media showed less interest in the third part of Davis's initial series of articles, although—in terms of revealing Davis's feelings, as opposed to her findings—it was in some ways the most radical of the three. In March 1923, Davis published a follow-up article on marital happiness, this one focused on the relationship between "sex instruction for the young" and marital satisfaction.[42]

Davis's early findings intensified her commitment to sex education. Among her sample of married women, she reported that a scant plurality (just under 56 percent) of her respondents believed that they had been "adequately prepared by instruction for the sex side of marriage." She also reported a significant difference between "happy" and "unhappy" wives where "general sex instruction" was concerned; while 57 percent of self-declared happy wives received some sex education, only 44 percent of self-described unhappy wives had.[43]

However, the level of instruction Davis's respondents categorized as sufficient was shockingly low—an impression Davis heightened with the liberal use of exclamation points in her discussion. For most, sex instruction meant the bare minimum of information about the mechanics of coitus; only about 10 percent of those who reported receiving sex education indicated that this included information about birth control.[44]

Turning to the group who reported insufficient or no instruction, the majority (nearly 60 percent) stated that they believed that premarital sex education would have improved their marriages.[45] Davis also addressed whether the women were "attracted or repelled" by their initial sexual experience, finding that most of those who had favorable first experiences also reported themselves as happy in their marriages.[46] Finally, Davis offered a series of tabulations indicating "a very positive trend in the direction of adequate preparation, the attractiveness of the sex relationship, and happiness of marriage."[47]

Concluding that "proper preparation is a factor for happiness," Davis offered her most ringing endorsement yet of scientifically informed sex education, as opposed to fearmongering about the risk of sexually transmitted infections. Contending that "the mere warning against possible undesirable practices is useless, if not positively dangerous," she called for "a sane outlook on all matters pertaining to sex."[48]

"The B.C. Movement"

Davis's musings on both sex education and contraceptive use paved the way for a rapprochement with birth-control crusader Margaret Sanger, with whom Davis had tangled when she was New York City's commissioner of correction over the alleged mistreatment of hunger striker Rebecca Edelson. After stepping down from that post to head Gotham's new parole board, Davis next supervised Sanger's thirty-day incarceration for violating a state law prohibiting the distribution of contraceptives when the fiery free-speech advocate and former public health nurse opened a free birth-control clinic in Brooklyn. Sanger, whose affiliation with socialists, anarchists, and freethinkers as well as her lawlessness had pitted her against the law-and-order prison official, had sharply criticized conditions in New York's prisons. In addition, Sanger's *Woman Rebel* had run excoriating editorials about "good, respectable Miss Davis."[49]

But by the 1920s, Sanger had distanced herself from her radical past. Courting respectability, she sought financial support for a new project: legitimizing and legalizing birth control. At the same time, she became an advocate of eugenics, arguing that birth control would enable the restriction of reproduction by the "unfit" and allow the "fit" to plan healthy families. Davis shared Sanger's interest in both eugenic theories and family planning; moreover, as head of the Bureau of Social Hygiene, she was well positioned to provide Sanger with the financial backing that she desperately needed. Thus, in the 1920s, the two former antagonists moved cautiously toward a professional alliance.[50]

Starting in 1923, Davis directed funds toward Sanger's new Clinical Research Bureau, her second, if sub-rosa, birth-control clinic. As Davis explained, the new clinic aimed to make "a scientific study of methods of contraception" and to prescribe birth control in accordance with a recent decision in a New York appellate court authorizing licensed physicians to prescribe birth control to married women. (In her memo requesting funds, Davis conveniently omitted mentioning that the case in question was *People v. Sanger*, which upheld Sanger's conviction but also expanded physicians' authority to prescribe contraceptives.) Davis, who hoped that accurate record keeping at the clinic would provide the basis for statistical analysis, urged Rockefeller to support the project. She persuaded him to do so, on one condition: the donor would remain anonymous. Grateful for her support—and hoping it would continue—Sanger begged Davis to "reserve a little time" in her busy schedule "for the B.C. movement."[51]

Although Davis proudly described herself as "born a suffragist," she frequently came into conflict with fellow feminists. Her position in law enforcement initially pitted her against Margaret Sanger, who served jail time in 1917 for operating a birth-control clinic in defiance of the law. By the 1920s, however, Davis used her position in the Bureau of Social Hygiene to support Sanger's work. George Grantham Bain Collection, Prints and Photographs Division, Library of Congress.

Having established a cordial relationship with Davis, Sanger continued to appeal to her for financial support. By the mid-1920s, Davis regularly sent Sanger ten thousand dollars each year, always with the proviso that Sanger keep Rockefeller's name secret. Davis's ongoing support inspired Sanger's "deepest appreciation." "I can not tell you what this means to the Whole Birth Control Movement," she gushed in one handwritten letter. The two women deepened their friendship, lunching together, exchanging holiday cards, and sharing health updates as well as corresponding about the birth-control movement. Even as Davis prepared for retirement in 1927, she continued to advocate for Sanger's projects, although she was able to persuade Rockefeller to give only five thousand dollars that year, and she could only hope that her imminent departure from the bureau would "not in any way effect [*sic*] the interest in your work."[52]

"Scientific Examination" of "Sex Behavior"

Davis's impending retirement was a product of her intensified commitment to the scientific study of sex. At the same time that Davis studied women's sexual behavior and supported the birth-control movement, she also sought to shift the direction of the BSH toward scientific studies of human sexuality. Working with Earl F. Zinn, a psychology student affiliated with Dr. Max Exner, who had initially encouraged Davis to undertake her study of female sexuality, she proposed a large-scale study of human sexuality conducted by a team of natural and social scientists to "increase our body of scientifically derived data" as the basis for "a rational sex ethics." Perhaps predictably, Davis's so-called colleague, Abraham Flexner, balked at the proposal, describing the ambitious plan as "too comprehensive and general."[53]

With Rockefeller's support, however, Davis convened a group of physicians, professors, and other professionals to discuss the proposal in fall 1921. At the conclusion of the meeting, the group adopted a resolution expressing concerns about the current state of sexual knowledge and recommending the formation of a new agency dedicated to "scientific examination" of "sex behavior."[54]

The group's resolution mirrored Davis's rationale for undertaking her own sex study. It condemned the "fog of mystery, reticence, and shame" that surrounded sex and impeded both scientific inquiry and open discussion, with the unfortunate result that "attitudes toward the subject have been fixed by moral teaching, medical instruction and social propaganda, all based on only a slight foundation of established fact." While recognizing the difficulties posed by "secrecy and prejudice," participants argued that scholars could and should subject sexual behavior to "scientific examination." To mark a definite departure from existing agencies and to avoid "any suggestion that such inquiry is undertaken for purposes of propaganda," they recommended that the new agency "should be sponsored by a body of investigators whose disinterested devotion to science is well recognized."[55]

With Davis's enthusiastic advocacy and Rockefeller's financial support, the group established a Committee for Research on the Problems of Sex, located within the Division of Medical Sciences of the National Research Council—an organization established in 1916 under the auspices of the National Academy of Science, which received funding from Rockefeller. Although not a founding member of the committee, which originally included only male researchers, Davis was thrilled both at the group's creation and at Rockefeller's support. "Those of us who have been interested in this plan were very greatly pleased that it seemed wise to you to endorse it," she confided to Rockefeller.[56]

The committee's aims aligned with Davis's priorities. Indeed, although not (yet) an official member of the committee, she may well have helped draft the committee's preliminary report, issued in March 1922, which echoed her own complaints in its damning statement, "Our knowledge of sex is in a chaotic state." After conducting a survey of professionals in the field—including psychologists and gynecologists—the committee concluded that there was "a lack of consensus of opinion on fundamental questions" among "those best qualified to speak." As a result, both "popular education" efforts and legal campaigns were being carried out on the basis of "inadequate scientifically derived data." Committee members expressed "considerable uneasiness" about their belief that "widely disseminated information on sex questions is running somewhat ahead of established fact." This situation convinced them of "the need for a concerted, systematic effort to secure data."[57] Davis fully supported these goals. When she submitted the first annual report to Rockefeller, she included a cover letter expressing her enthusiasm for the group's "plan for the systematic study of research in sex."[58]

Given Davis's success in lobbying for financial backing and her support of the committee's goals, it is not surprising that she quickly moved from being a liaison to being a full-fledged committee member. Initially, the group included "a committee of four medical men," representing the disciplines of physiology, biology, psychiatry, and psychology. The committee's preliminary report, issued in 1922, explained that the group wished to appoint a woman for the fifth slot, "preferably one who is married, whose training has been in sociology or anthropology, and who stands high in her professional field, by virtue of work done."[59]

Davis met some—but by no means all—of these criteria. While she had gained acclaim as a sociologist, her graduate degree was not in sociology but in economics. Most significantly, she was not married—a preference intended to lend respectability to a position dedicated to the study of sex. But the committee evidently was swayed by the points made by "Mrs. P. G. Woolley," whose married name obscured her identity as Dr. Helen B. Thompson, a fellow University of Chicago PhD and a member of the cooperating committee for Davis's sex study. At the 1921 Conference on Sex Problems, she declared, "The best attempt of which I know to gather such facts, is that made by Miss Catherine [*sic*] Davis of the Bureau of Social Hygiene." Davis's advanced age—at the time, she was sixty-one years old—probably functioned as a proxy for marital status in terms of making her an acceptable committee member.[60] Her physical appearance—contemporaries often described the petite but plump Davis, with her round face, old-fashioned bun, ready smile, and sparkling blue eyes, as projecting a matronly persona—also may have helped dispel skepticism.[61]

By the time the committee had completed its first year, its members had decided to formally invite Davis to join their ranks. She explained to Rockefeller that she was supposed to represent the sociological perspective. "This is one of the most difficult sciences in which to outline a scientific sex program," she explained, because studying human sexuality was "extremely delicate and difficult."[62]

Although the committee's work initially focused on biological topics, such as research on sex hormones, Davis persistently pushed for a greater focus on social-scientific studies like her own. For instance, in 1922, Rockefeller increased funding from ten thousand to twenty-five thousand dollars, with the additional funds supporting a variety of proj-

Throughout her adult life, Davis cultivated a genteel appearance and projected a matronly persona, which helped her establish a reputation as a pioneering sexologist and lent respectability to her revelatory study of women's sexuality. May Bragdon Papers, University of Rochester.

ects, including a study of university students' sex lives and a study of male homosexuality. Reflecting her growing interest both in the work of sexologists overseas and in the study of homosexuality, Davis also maintained a cordial correspondence with European sexologists, including Havelock Ellis, known for his sympathetic perspective on homosexuality. Over the next several years, Davis kept Rockefeller apprised of the committee's work, assuring him, "We are delving into fundamental problems which underlie the whole question of sex."[63]

"New Vistas"

At the same time that she was publishing her initial findings on women's sexuality and organizing the committee for the study of sex, Davis joined forces with a progressive gynecologist, Dr. Robert Latou Dickinson, to promote birth control and combat the Comstock Laws. Thanks to the outcome of *People v. Sanger*, physicians were uniquely positioned not only to prescribe birth control but also to discuss it openly. Nonetheless, most medical men steered well clear of the rocky shoals of birth-control politics. For the most part, those who did venture into these dangerous waters did so either in the name of eugenics or to enhance their own authority.[64]

Dr. Dickinson was different. While he was undoubtedly part of the "positive" eugenics movement—he believed he could promote "better babies" by providing (certain) couples with marital counseling and sex therapy—and while his methods—including (apparently consensually) manually stimulating female patients with both a dildo and his fingers—certainly raise red flags, he also took both women's pain and their pleasure seriously. Although he initially warned that self-stimulation might injure women's health, he ultimately came to see women's sexual satisfaction as an essential aspect of their health. Moreover, he understood that women could not enjoy sexual activity unless they could do so without running the risk of unwanted, unaffordable, and unsafe pregnancies. Thus, in 1923, just as he wrapped up his career as a clinical practitioner to focus on the sex research that he would publish, with Lura Beam, as *A Thousand Marriages* (1931) and *The Single Woman* (1934), he founded the Committee for Maternal Health. The coyly named committee was dedicated to researching effective contraceptive methods and challenging the restrictive Comstock Laws.[65]

Davis is omnipresent in the committee's correspondence from its founding in 1923 through her retirement in 1928. Indeed, the Rockefeller Archives Center's records for the committee consist almost entirely of exchanges between Dr. Dickinson and Dr. Davis—as he, unlike so many other male colleagues, respectfully addressed her.[66]

A genial, bearded man with twinkling blue eyes, Dr. Dickinson was just a year younger than Dr. Davis. While they eventually would become personal friends, their initial relationship was as professional colleagues. They may have met through Dickinson's wife, Sarah Kidder Truslow, who was active in several service organizations, including the YWCA; by 1918, Dickinson already was on Davis's team, advocating for her leadership role in the American Plan. By the 1920s, he was clearly familiar with her scholarship on women's sexuality. Moreover, he was eager to work with her on both the study of sexuality and the promotion of legal birth control.

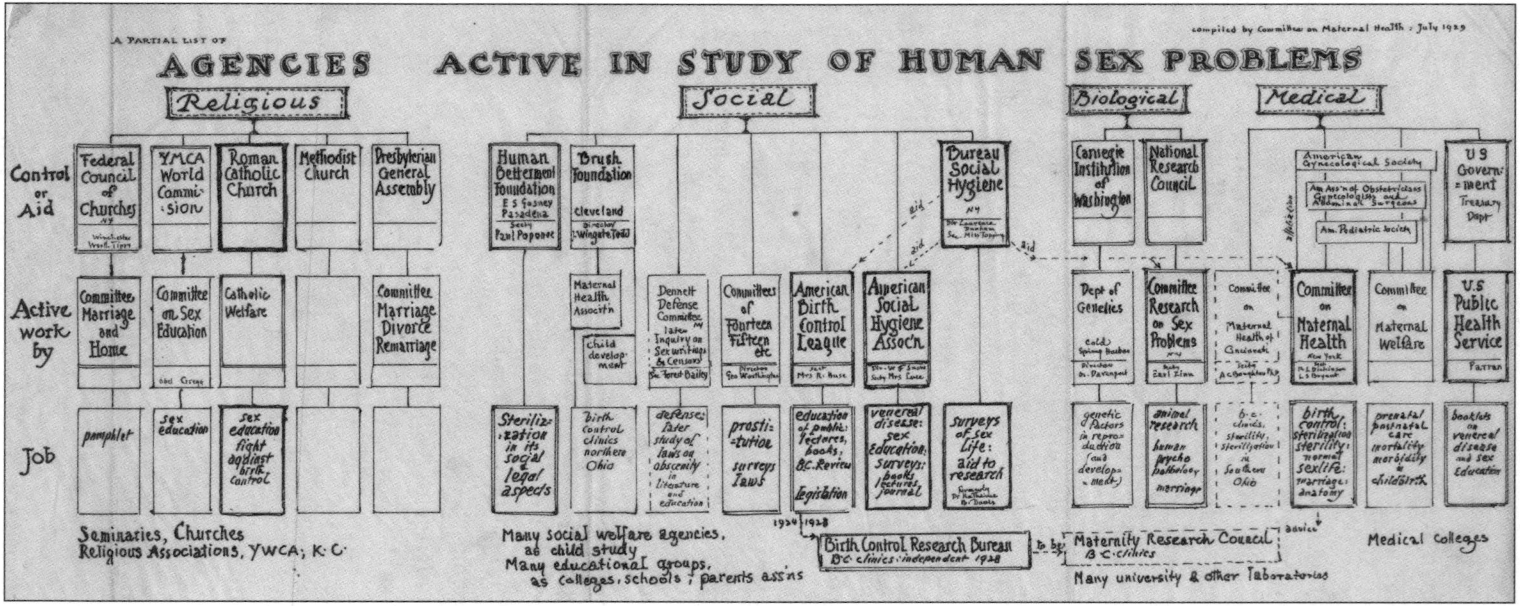

During the 1920s, Davis was a member of multiple "agencies active in study of human sex problems," as detailed in this 1929 chart by progressive gynecologist and birth-control advocate Robert Latou Dickinson. These included the Bureau of Social Hygiene, Davis's employer; the Birth Control Research Bureau, Margaret Sanger's birth-control clinic, which conducted studies of the effectiveness of contraceptives; Dennett's Defense Committee, which successfully defended Mary Ware Dennett against obscenity charges for her sex education pamphlet, *The Sex Side of Life*; the Committee on Research on Sex Problems, which Davis founded under the auspices of the National Research Council; and the National Committee on Maternal Health, which advocated the legalization of birth control. Dr. Dickinson highlighted Davis's "Surveys of Sex Life" in his chart of interrelated organizations in the 1920s. Image courtesy the Harvard Medical Library collection, Center for the History of Medicine in the Countway Library of Medicine, Harvard University.

In their first preserved correspondence, a letter dated July 26, 1923, Dickinson referred to their previous conversations about the lack of scholarly literature on contraception and to Davis's recently published article on married women's use of birth control. "Dear Doctor," he began, "You will be interested to know that you were right in thinking that a careful review of the literature would show that there was almost no clinical data on the subject of contraceptive measures."[67]

Sure that Davis would share his outrage, he continued, "The literature is a literature of opinion and prejudice, and not of clinical cases, hence the high esteem in which we hold your report from one thousand intelligent married women." With Davis's input, Dickinson was eager to summarize the scant scientific scholarship on birth control, conduct a clinical study of contraceptive devices (condoms, contraceptive jellies, and pessaries, the forerunner of diaphragms), and—most importantly—help women. As he put it, "Our main purpose is social service, namely: the safeguarding of the health of women."[68]

Over the next five years, the two doctors remained in close contact as they collaborated on research on contraceptive methods and strategized about how best to challenge legal restrictions on birth control. Drawn together by their shared commitment to women's welfare, Davis and Dickinson also shared a pragmatic outlook on political activism. Understanding that the ignorance and prejudices bred by Anthony Comstock and his supporters long outlived him, they sought effective ways to promote birth control in the Comstock era by appealing to the only people with the legal authority to circumvent the Comstock Laws: family physicians. As Dickinson put it in that same letter, "We have had to go cautiously, step by step, in order to keep the good will of many leaders in our profession who are conservative, but who are important friends to have because they are in charge of major clinics in which our studies should be conducted."[69]

Those cautious steps included supporting existing clinics that legally distributed contraceptives and collected data on their effectiveness; establishing a new "demonstration clinic" run by Margaret Sanger in strict accordance with state laws permitting physicians to prescribe birth control; corresponding with donors and supporters (including hardline eugenicists like Marie Stopes in the UK and Charles Davenport in the United States); collecting data on medical school coursework; surveying medical practitioners on their (abysmally lacking) knowledge about birth control; and disseminating information about contraceptive methods, safety, and efficacy to physicians. The latter task included encouraging the American Gynecological Society to push back against the Comstock Laws by endorsing a statement that "medical and scientific" journals and texts should be permitted to circulate through the US mail.[70]

All of these activities required money. An important part of Davis's work for the Committee on Maternal Health was fundraising, which included not only approaching individual donors but also guaranteeing up to ten thousand dollars annually in matching funds from the Bureau of Social Hygiene and up to twenty thousand dollars annually as direct donations. As she did for Sanger's work, Davis secured this funding with Rockefeller's approval but on condition of anonymity. As she wrote from her vacation home in the Georgian Bay in 1924, "Personally I should have no objections to mentioning the Bureau. I fancy some of our Board, however, might prefer that this not be done."[71]

Albeit anonymously, the Bureau of Social Hygiene thus effectively subsidized the birth-control movement throughout the 1920s. Perhaps because of Rockefeller's support, even Davis's antagonist, Raymond Fosdick, was willing to venture into what he called "the controversial field of birth control."[72]

In addition to fundraising for the committee, Davis also contributed substantially to its research. As Dickinson put it, "Our Committee early established relations with the Bureau of Social Hygiene and Dr. Davis has been very cordial in putting some of her unpublished material at our disposal."[73]

Throughout, Dickinson expressed the utmost respect for Davis and her "epoch-making study" by citing her in his professional presentations and inviting her to be a coauthor on an article. (Davis was "flattered" but declined to be a coauthor, although she read several drafts and made suggestions for improvement; when Dickinson published this article in the *Journal of the American Medical Association*, he noted, "Its data were mainly milked out of your investigation. If you had skimmed your own cream it would have whipped into better shape.")[74]

At one point, Dickinson apologized for being unable to invite Davis to speak at a meeting of the New York Obstetrical Society, since it met at the Yale Club "in which sacrosanct precincts no woman may enter." Davis, "amused," responded that she actually had visited the "sacred" bastion of male privilege before—as commissioner of correction. While freely giving Dickinson permission to cite her figures on women's contraceptive use, she also consulted with him on how they could do so without running afoul of the Comstock Laws. "Although I am entirely familiar with the insides of prisons," she quipped, "I do not want to go to one!"[75]

Davis's collaboration with Dickinson only reinforced her conviction that the Comstock Laws had to go. At the same time, her correspondence indicated how carefully she had to proceed with her own controversial research. For instance, in 1923, Dickinson asked Davis for more data about her study participants' knowledge and use of contraception—information she had not included in the published article. Davis responded with detailed case studies showing that her survey respondents had used many methods—condoms, douches, withdrawal, sponges, and "capsules"—and had acquired information about contraceptives anywhere they could. One claimed that "her information was obtained from '100 sources, among them Margaret Sanger's pamphlet.'" Survey respondents also indicated how important birth control was. One reported that she was "happily married; has only had one pregnancy and one child. She believes in the use of contraceptives and gives as a reason: 'I believe no child should be an accident. Also, the sex relation is so valuable in itself that it should be freed from fear of pregnancy.'" For another woman, "no method has proved successful"; in fifteen years, she had given birth to twelve children, including three who died within hours of birth, despite utilizing every available method of birth control. "Her marriage has not been entirely happy," explained Davis, because of the couple's inability to control their fertility.[76]

Meanwhile, the two doctors continued their research on women's sexuality. Deeply impressed by Davis's use of questionnaires, Dickinson incorporated this method into his own research. "You always open up new vistas," he praised her. They also forged close ties with the American Birth Control League, Sanger's organization, then working to persuade medical schools to educate future doctors about contraceptive methods, physicians to prescribe birth control, and lawmakers to adopt a "doctors only" exception to the Comstock Law's prohibition on providing information about birth control.[77]

"To Put Sex on the Scientific Map"

At the same time that she furthered her study of women's sexuality, supported the birth-control movement, and challenged the Comstock Laws, Davis also pressured Rockefeller to reorganize the BSH to put more emphasis on the study of human sexuality. In 1927, Davis advocated that the bureau adopt a broader definition of "social hygiene."[78] Quoting from the original mission statement and underlining for emphasis, she wrote, "The purposes of the Bureau of Social Hygiene as set forth in its charter are 'for the study, amelioration and prevention of those social conditions, crimes and diseases which, adversely, affect the wellbeing of society, with special reference to prostitution and the evils associated therewith.'" She explained that while the organization initially had focused on commercialized sex, "the situation has greatly changed within the past ten years," and "the Bureau has increasingly concerned itself with the promoting and subsidizing of research in the broader field indicated in the underscored phrases."[79]

While Davis approved of this general trend, she also observed that the agency had "followed an opportunistic policy" and that "it would be wise to define more definitely its purposes." Specifically, she believed that the bureau should focus on the study of sex:

> There are two fundamental aspects of life, nutrition and sex. The former has been and is receiving adequate attention from the biological sciences and is promulgated through the great variety of health agencies. Sex, on the other hand, has not received the same attention though it is the fundamental on which the life of the race depends. It is the most important and basic fact of human society. Its abuses have led to the social evils the Bureau was organized to combat. The study of sex in a scientific way has received scant attention until very recently. Opinion and education in this field cannot be sound unless it is based on accurate scientific study.[80]

As her ten-year contract drew to a close, Davis peppered Rockefeller with lengthy memoranda and detailed letters, hoping to secure his ongoing support for sex research. Characterizing the sex research committee as the bureau's "most outstanding and important piece of work," she urged him to make "the scientific study of sex" the bureau's top priority. Opining that the committee's work thus far had dispelled the "ill-repute" associated with the study of sex and had "helped enormously to put sex on the scientific map," she asserted, "I believe the time has come when the subject can stand on its own feet. I believe the time has come when the cause of Social Hygiene will be furthest advanced by frankly making Sex Research the pivotal point of the Bureau's activities."[81] Significantly—if perhaps unwisely—Davis proposed that the BSH should eschew "propaganda" and become "purely a research organization."[82]

Unfortunately for Davis, Rockefeller was not prepared to countenance his longtime collaborator's new interest in studying sexual behavior "in vacuo," rather than as a social problem. When he solicited feedback from BSH staffer Leonard Harrison, the criminologist criticized Davis's "promotion of scientific research in sex per se," opining that it was a mistake "to lift sex research from its customary setting"—that is, as a social problem in need of social reform. "The subject of the whole range of sex life . . . does not readily lend itself to research, except in the cases of abnormally constituted persons," Harrison declared. Since other entities were already engaged in the study of abnormal sexuality, Harrison advised against committing more bureau resources to this effort. Instead, he self-servingly urged Rockefeller to consider that "the Bureau has before it a most inviting field of opportunity much wider than sex research": the study of crime.[83]

While Harrison's critiques were a product of his own research interests, Davis's detractors quickly seized the opportunity to oust her from the BSH. In 1927, Fosdick urged Rockefeller to terminate Davis's employment, asserting, "She is fast losing her grip," and was unsuited even to "an advisory position."[84]

Fosdick's opinion of Davis's mental state clearly was linked to his distaste for her advocacy of sex research. The following year, when the sex study committee submitted a new five-year plan and request for funding, he denounced the entire project in a letter to Lawrence B. Dunham, a lawyer, former police commissioner, and criminologist for the Laura Spelman Rockefeller Memorial who would become Davis's successor as head of the BSH. "I frankly think the Committee on Sex Research has gone stark mad," Fosdick expostulated. "The project as developed is far too scopey and comprehensive for serious consideration. . . . This proposition sounds like the work of a lot of college professors who have assumed that millions are at their disposal. . . . Altogether the thing sounds phony to me."[85]

Rockefeller acceded to his male advisors' suggestions. He informed Davis that he intended to reorganize the bureau—although not along the lines she had suggested. Echoing her statement that "the situation is entirely different than when the Bureau was organized," he indicated that her services would not be needed in the revamped agency. Although he praised Davis's career "of extraordinary usefulness," he also described that career as coming to an end, although he softened the blow by offering a generous severance package and ongoing funding for her study of women's sexuality. Davis—who had hoped to postpone her departure until she reached her self-appointed retirement age of seventy—must have been cut to the quick by her abrupt dismissal by a man she considered a personal friend as well as a professional colleague. Perhaps mindful of maintaining his financial support, however, she expressed gratitude for her one-time supporter's "generous financial provision" and promised, "Naturally I shall submit with I hope good grace to your decision and will not need to be carried off the stage kicking and screaming!" However, she confessed, "It *is* hard to see it all stated in black and white on paper that my working days are so nearly done."[86]

Even after Davis's retirement, her detractors continued their campaign against her. In particular, they suggested that her health problems made her unfit for continued research. From the mid-1920s forward, Davis suffered from declining health, including persistent headaches, eye strain, and dental problems.[87] In 1924, a "bad bronchial cold" prevented her from attending a dinner in honor of her one-time collaborator, African American intellectual and civil rights leader W. E. B. Du Bois.[88]

As she entered her midsixties, Davis's health problems intensified. In 1926, she suffered from an especially severe and lengthy bout of "grippe," or influenza; she then was "laid up with an attack of gall bladder as a sequel," as she humorously expressed it.[89] When Rockefeller dismissed her from the bureau, he excused himself by referring to multiple "distressing physical conditions."[90]

But while Rockefeller was content to allow Davis to continue work on her sex study following her forced retirement in January 1928, his advisors had other ideas. In May 1928, as Davis turned her attention to the publication of the study in book form, her successor, Lawrence

Dunham, wrote confidentially to Rockefeller in an attempt to persuade him that Davis's poor health—both physical and mental—incapacitated her for continued work. On top of high blood pressure and "impaired heart action," he opined, Davis suffered from what he called "a bad nervous condition," which he attributed to "the failure to achieve as yet a complete mental adjustment to her approaching retirement." Indeed, Dunham argued that Davis's continued work on the sex study put her under "great strain." Dunham concluded that it was impossible for Davis to keep up the pace until July 1, the date she was due to deliver the book manuscript and her bureau funding for the project would expire. He opined, "There is grave danger that if Miss Davis endeavors to continue from now until the first of July, she will undergo a complete breakdown which will be either physical, mental or both."[91]

Dunham's scheme backfired, however, when Rockefeller suggested that Davis take a paid vacation of several months and offered to extend her salary and that of her staff as necessary to allow her to complete and publish her study of women's sexuality.[92] Disappointed as she was to leave her post at the head of the Bureau of Social Hygiene, Davis was heartened by Rockefeller's continued support for her research. "I'm glad," she confided, "that I may finish the research I have in hand for I am convinced of its importance."[93]

"Why They Failed to Marry"

The publication of selections from Davis's research on single women in *Harper's Magazine* shortly after her official retirement validated her judgment about the significance of her study of women's sexuality. Davis's choice of outlet—a popular magazine rather than an academic journal—probably was related to her departure from the bureau, given that she no longer was an official representative of the Rockefeller-funded agency. It also was an astute marketing ploy, since the magazine was produced by the publishing house that would publish her book about women's sex lives. In addition to providing some advance publicity for the book, the article also offered some intriguing insights into Davis's own life choices and personal views.

Published under the provocative title, "Why They Failed to Marry," the *Harper's* article was clearly a response to anxiety about "race suicide":

social critics' concern that while white, Anglo-Saxon Protestant women increasingly gave birth to fewer children, immigrant, Black, and Catholic women continued to bear children at higher rates. In particular, conservative commentators warned that college-educated women were less likely to marry, and if married, were likely to have fewer children, than their less-educated counterparts.[94]

Davis simultaneously appealed to and countered these concerns. In a throwback to her earlier fascination with eugenics, she wrote, "From the point of view of eugenics I shall maintain . . . that it would be a good thing for the race if a higher per cent of our college women were to marry and produce children." Yet Davis also contended that the various explanations for college-educated women's low marriage rates—that they had limited contact with men, that they were more concerned with careers than family life, that they were overly critical of men, that they were able to support themselves, that they were unattractive, or that men were intimidated by intelligent women—were inaccurate. "Probably there is a certain amount of truth in each of these contentions," she noted. However, statistically speaking, college-educated women had ample opportunities to meet and marry men, and most of them regarded marriage favorably; they simply had "never met the right man."[95]

Drawn from Davis's larger study, the article relied upon surveys from twelve hundred never-married women who had graduated from college at least five years previously, ranging in age from twenty-two to sixty-eight (Davis's own age at the time). However, the bulk of the *Harper's* article, unlike the earlier pieces in the *Journal of Social Hygiene*, consisted not of statistical analysis but of individual testimonials. This made a great deal of sense, given that the most common reason given for remaining single—never meeting the right man—accounted for less than a third of the total (28 percent). Given the lack of a clear consensus, Davis remarked, "nothing short of careful individual study" could provide a compelling explanation.[96]

Indeed, the *Harper's* piece is more revealing about Davis herself than about the research subjects, given that she herself met the criteria for the sample, as well as that she selected certain themes to highlight out of the four-hundred-plus-page final study. Notably, Davis's questionnaire included candid questions about same-sex intimacy, inviting the research subjects to discuss this topic openly. At the time, many advice givers denounced lesbianism, regarding women's relationships as a dire threat to their marital prospects. Davis found that half of all single women reported intense emotional relationships with other women, and of these, half (or one quarter of the total) indicated that the relationships were sexual in nature. However, very few single women—less than 7 percent overall—attributed their unwed status to same-sex relationships. Instead of commenting on what some cultural critics dubbed a "lesbian threat" to marriage, Davis allowed respondents to speak for themselves by including extensive quotations from survey participants. One explained, "I think I have a strong homo-sexual tendency and that the women I have loved have satisfied my need for affection and companionship."[97]

While this respondent sought an explanation for her lack of interest in men—in this case, "sex antagonism" fostered in childhood by her parents' unhappy marriage—others pushed back against the assumption that same-sex relationships were unnatural. For example, another respondent explained that "she always preferred girls to boys." She added that this preference increased when she attended a women's college. But rather than seeing either her youthful disposition or her college crushes as problematic, she regarded women's relationships as "natural expressions of love for others . . . not sex perversions," even though she understood that prevailing scientific opinion disagreed. She insisted, with remarkable persistence and prescience, "I incline to wager that the future scientist will find some attributes *human*, belonging to both sexes, that are now gummed up with Freudian terms."[98]

Did Davis allow this woman to speak for her, reflecting her ideas about her own never-discussed relationship with Ella Lapham? Was she so nonjudgmental of lesbianism because she recognized the same tendencies in her own life, even if she never admitted acting on them? Frustratingly, by omitting any discussion of same-sex relationships in her own memoirs and leaving behind few personal letters, she ensured that nobody would ever know the answers for sure. Perhaps like her contemporary and colleague, prison reformer Miriam Van Waters, she purposely destroyed evidence of any intimate relationships to protect her professional reputation. Davis, who probed the innermost feelings of her subjects, kept her own emotions a closely guarded secret.[99]

A clearer line may be drawn between Davis's own ideas about marriage and family and those of her research subjects. When commenting on the respondents who regretted their single state, Davis noted that far more women explained that they longed for children or a home and children (more than 25 percent) than that they longed for a husband or a husband, home, and children (less than 10 percent). This statistical data echoes Davis's own comment, in her unfinished autobiography, that while she had no regrets about turning down the marriage proposals she had received, she did lament never having had children.[100]

In addition, when turning her attention to those who did not regret remaining single, Davis pinpointed several satisfactions of single life that may well have applied to herself, such as being "absorbed in their work" or enjoying "freedom and independence." Davis translated one woman's reasons for remaining single into verse:

> I have a good job;
> I earn a good living;
> I am contented and happy;
> Why be encumbered?

By poetically paraphrasing this woman's response, Davis may well have been speaking for herself, for she added approvingly, "It might be an answer to our question!"[101]

Davis had never been "encumbered" by a husband, but her activities had been constrained, as well as supported, by her longtime association with John D. Rockefeller Jr. Now that she had severed ties—however reluctantly—with the moralizing philanthropist and his reform organization, she was ready to translate years of careful research into a groundbreaking study of female sexuality. As her friends and former colleagues hoped, Davis would use her retirement "to continue her great work to the peak of her heart's desire," taking advantage of "freedom from routine" as a golden opportunity "for the attainment of full fruition of many plans and hopes." Just as one well-wisher predicted, Davis would bring together her "expert knowledge" and her "love of humanity" to produce a study of stunning significance, "a wonderful example of what a human mind may achieve!"[102]

7

Redefining "Normal" Women's Sexuality

Imagine yourself as a well-to-do white woman in 1921. You may live in a large city or a small town, in an affluent suburb or in a rural hamlet. You are active in your community as a member of several local women's clubs and a strong advocate of civic reform. Now in your late thirties, you married at twenty-five and have two young children. You held a job before your marriage, but you now dedicate yourself to homemaking, childcare, and community building. Although you received a fine formal education, you knew very little about "the facts of life" on your wedding night. While you and your husband generally enjoy marital relations, you believe that your adjustment to marriage might have been easier had you known what to expect. You think that perhaps youthful experimentation with self-stimulation may have benefited your marriage, even though your mother and your minister both warned you against the dangers of this practice. Although birth control is not really legal—thanks to the Comstock Laws that define information about contraception as "obscenity"—you managed to get your hands on one of Margaret Sanger's pamphlets and learn that it was possible to practice "voluntary motherhood." With the help of a sympathetic family physician, you have used contraceptives to limit the size of your family. While you probably have never had an abortion, it is likely that at least one woman in your social circle has terminated an unwanted pregnancy either by ingesting an abortifacient or by paying an "abortionist" to perform a mysterious operation.[1]

In your experience, the subjects of sex and reproduction are discussed in hushed tones, or not at all, so you have not openly discussed these matters with your friends or family. Thus, you are surprised when you open the mail one day to find a letter addressed to you from the Bureau of Social Hygiene in New York City. You are familiar with the bureau's work, of course. During the recent Great War, the bureau worked closely with women's clubs and local branches of the Young Women's Christian

Association to combat prostitution and prevent the spread of venereal disease. In some communities, the bureau even partnered with parent-teacher associations to sponsor "social hygiene" films to educate young people about proper relationships and warn them against the dangers of premarital sex. But why would the bureau be writing to you?

Checking to be sure you are alone and unlikely to be disturbed, you carefully open the envelope. "Dear Madam," the letter begins. "Will you permit us to take the liberty of asking your intelligent and sympathetic cooperation in a very important sociological study?" The letter goes on to detail the work of the bureau in promoting public health and preventing prostitution. Perhaps, you think, this is yet another fundraising appeal. But then you pause to read the next few sentences more carefully. The letter goes on to state that the bureau is "well on its way to making wise education in matters of sex an integral part of the whole scheme of education." You nod approvingly. You do not want your own children to enter adulthood ignorant about "the sex side of life," as Mary Ware Dennett put it in the informative pamphlet she wrote for her own sons. Even though many schools now offer "social hygiene" courses, you find that they are often short on facts. Indeed, you have found your children secretly reading racy literature and dog-earing dictionaries in a quest for information, much as you did at their age. It is a mother's job to prepare her children for life, but how can you do so when your own preparation was so inadequate? It sounds like the bureau has once again struck on an admirable scheme, you reflect.[2]

But then you tighten your grip on the letter as you read the following sentences: "It is in directing the educational aspects of this movement that we need reliable information of the most personal nature. . . . We have prepared a questionnaire for this purpose. The questions relate to the early sex information in girlhood, its sources and effects, and the sex experiences in girlhood, womanhood, and marriage." Surely this must be a mistake. Everyone knows that sex studies are conducted on "bad" women, on prostitutes or psychopaths. You, on the other hand, have always thought of yourself as a perfectly ordinary woman. You are normal! What information could you possibly provide?[3]

Although you are tempted to crumple up the letter and throw it in the dustbin, you look ahead to the second page to see that it is signed by the bureau's general secretary, Dr. Katharine Bement Davis. You recognize the name of this celebrated social scientist and social reformer. Before taking a position at the bureau, Dr. Davis was the superintendent of New York State's female reformatory and then the first woman commissioner of correction for New York City. Her research on female offenders—mostly sex workers—made national headlines, as did her work promoting both woman suffrage and "social hygiene" during the Great War.

Somewhat reassured, and still curious, you flip back to the first page and look more closely at the masthead. There are many impressive and familiar names there. In addition to Dr. Davis, the "Cooperating Committee on Inquiry"—that sounds very official, doesn't it?—includes Martha Falconer of the American Social Hygiene Association, an organization dedicated to promoting high morals. Surely she would only lend her name to a reputable enterprise. And then there is Mrs. Elmer Blair, who not only has the good sense to use her husband's name but also is the chair of the public health committee of the General Federation of Women's Clubs. You yourself belong to at least one club affiliated with the federation, which publishes a regular newsletter and recently played a leading role in drumming up support for the Nineteenth Amendment. Like many of your peers, you believe that women have the power to clean up politics, and that women voters will represent the interests of families and children, rather than of corrupt special interests. Indeed, you swelled with pride, just this past year, when you cast your ballot for the first time. Oh, look, the committee also includes Dr. Valeria Parker, chair of the National League of Women Voters' Social Hygiene Committee. The league puts out publications educating women voters about their new responsibilities, scrupulously refraining from partisanship. Nothing could be more respectable. Well, then. You might as well see what these important women have to say.[4]

Even though you don't recognize all the names, the letter assures you that they are "well-known women of scientific training." Dr. Davis earned her doctorate at the University of Chicago. So the other MDs and PhDs on the list must be equally qualified. Look at the names of those schools where they teach! Bryn Mawr College and Wellesley College are on the list; these are some of the best women's colleges in the country. Surely this must be a legitimate sociological study. But can you risk sharing the most intimate details of your life with strangers? You read on.[5]

"In order to protect completely the natural reticence which every woman feels with respect to these intimately personal experiences in her development, the questionnaire will be conducted in such a way that the identity of every woman answering it will be completely lost, so that *no one can possibly know from whom the answers came, or even from what towns or sections of the country*," Dr. Davis promises. Really? How could that be? She goes on to explain that a carefully devised, double-envelope system will make it impossible to trace the identity of anyone who responds to the study. She further explains that at this point, all she is asking is that you return a form indicating your willingness to participate in the study. Finally, she closes, "Your cooperation in this matter will be of great social value." You close your eyes for a moment. You take a deep breath. And then, before you can change your mind, you sign the form, place it in the postage-paid, preaddressed envelope, and drop it in the mailbox.[6]

Around the country, twenty thousand women—their names selected from lists of clubwomen and college graduates—received invitations like this one between 1921 and 1923. In all, about one in ten of the women who received the initial query—one thousand married women and twelve hundred unmarried women—responded to the questionnaire. The completed forms and handwritten commentary provided the basis for *Factors in the Sex Life of Twenty-Two Hundred Women*, the world's first large-scale study of women's sexuality written by a woman. That woman was Katharine Bement Davis, and her study profoundly reshaped understandings of female sexuality in modern America.[7]

A "Special Piece of Work"

Davis dedicated nearly a decade to the study of women's sexuality, which she referred to as her own "special piece of work."[8] Davis had long regarded sex as "the most important and the basic fact of human society."[9] And yet, despite its significance, the subject of sex remained shrouded in secrecy and stigma. As Davis explained, "Except on the pathological side, sex to a large extent is scientifically an unexplored country."[10] In the 1920s, Davis blazed a trail into the unknown by studying "normal" women's sexuality.

Davis conducted her study during a decade in which the nation experienced a profound "revolution in manners and morals" that some historians have dubbed the nation's "first sexual revolution." "Flaming youth" flaunted their sexuality in smoky speakeasies, teenagers engaged in eager experimentation in the big back seats of ubiquitous automobiles, actresses showcased their sex appeal on stage and screen, and a "pansy craze" highlighted the rise of queer culture.[11]

Even as sex suffused popular culture, however, Davis complained that a powerful "taboo" on open discussions of sexuality persisted.[12] Cultural beliefs about women's "passionlessness" found support in the Comstock Laws, which defined all information about sexuality and reproduction as obscene and restricted the circulation of printed material about both sex and birth control.[13] In the absence of reliable information, "false information" flourished.[14] The situation convinced Davis that the subject of sex warranted scholarly attention. Indeed, she insisted, "accurate scientific study" was essential to achieving what she called "a sane outlook on all matters pertaining to sex."[15]

To that end, Davis designed and distributed a detailed sex survey to thousands of "average" American women, urging participants to "have no hesitancy in stating the facts."[16] One of Davis's colleagues at the Bureau of Social Hygiene was horrified by the questionnaire, which solicited candid responses to pointed questions about the most intimate details of women's lives. "The questionnaire is an amazing piece of work," Raymond Fosdick commented in a letter to John D. Rockefeller Jr., adding, "I confess its frankness quite takes my breath away."[17]

But women responded eagerly to Davis's appeal. While sex was in the spotlight in the early twentieth century, solid information remained in short supply. Expressing their discontent with what one called the "conspiracy of silence" surrounding women's sexuality, more than two thousand women eagerly shared the most intimate details of their personal lives. In addition to completing lengthy forms—eight pages for married women and twelve pages for single women—many appended additional comments on separate sheets of paper, providing Davis with approximately ten thousand pages of "frank and detailed statements" about women's sexual knowledge, experience, and desire. Survey participants hoped that sharing their own personal stories would improve all women's lives. As one explained, "The more we air the whole subject the less trouble will we have with it. Our present secrecy, fear, and repression are responsible for most of our sex ills."[18]

Davis was thrilled with the responses, which she characterized as "the result of careful and painstaking efforts to present truthfully and accurately the personal experiences of the writers." The completed forms and handwritten commentary provided the basis for Davis's major study of women's sexuality, *Factors in the Sex Life of Twenty-Two Hundred Women*, published by Harper & Brothers in 1929. At the time of its publication, *Factors* was both the first published study focused on women's sexuality, and the first study of sexuality authored by a woman. But the significance of Davis's volume went well beyond being "first." Unlike other sexuality studies, Davis's book centered women's experiences; unlike other works on women, it validated female sexuality. Indeed, *Factors* was the most ambitious study to date of the sexual experiences and desires of "normal" women.[19]

Although Davis sought to understand "average" women, her research methodology—using lists of college graduates and clubwomen—did not result in a representative sample. However, for her purposes—studying well-educated, well-adjusted, well-regarded women capable of expressing themselves in writing—it was ideal. The study also was perfect for reevaluating long-held beliefs about women's "passionlessness": the idea that "proper" women did not experience sexual desire or enjoy sexual activity. Davis's revelations that many women used birth control, engaged in masturbation, and had lesbian relationships shocked a generation of Americans struggling with the prolonged—and contested—shift from Victorian to modern ideas about sexuality. *Factors in the Sex Life of Twenty-Two Hundred Women* fundamentally redefined "normal" women's sexuality. By discussing subjects usually cloaked in secrecy and by documenting behaviors often shrouded in stigma, Davis's revelatory study both documented the full range of women's sexual behavior and defined women's sexuality as entirely normal.[20]

Literally by design, Davis's sex study challenged prevailing notions of female "passionlessness," or the assumption that respectable women lacked sexual desire and engaged in sexual activity only to please their husbands or for purposes of reproduction. By collecting information from thousands of women and providing statistical breakdowns of the

In the 1920s, as young women adopted more revealing fashions, Katharine Bement Davis's pioneering study, *Factors in the Sex Life of Twenty-Two Hundred Women* (1929) revealed that women of all ages, far from being "passionless," engaged in sexual activity purely for pleasure. George Grantham Bain Collection, Prints and Photographs Division, Library of Congress.

results, Davis's research departed from existing studies of sexuality, which tended to rely upon a relatively small number of individual case studies of "abnormal" women: prisoners or patients.

Davis's study was pathbreaking in its choice of subjects as well as in its scope. By focusing on "normal" women and asking questions about their sexual feelings and experiences—including using birth control, indulging in masturbation, and engaging in same-sex relationships—the study assumed that women had sexual desires and engaged in sexual activity beyond the boundaries of matrimony and reproduction.

Davis's findings—detailed in dozens of statistical tables and charts and illustrated with personal testimonials—validated this supposition, demonstrating that both married and unmarried women had active, and often satisfying, sex lives. Ultimately, Davis redefined women's sexuality itself as "normal," offering both participants and readers a new way to regard sexual desire and sexual activity.

"The Normal Sex Life of Women"

From the start, Davis's decision to focus on "normal" women set her study apart. Initially, Davis had planned to write a book about young women's sexual delinquency. Such a project built upon her study of sex workers at Bedford Reformatory; it also was consistent with existing studies of sexuality, which focused on abnormal sexual behavior. But Davis's planned study on "The Delinquent Girl" quickly morphed into a very different project: the study of "normal" female sexuality. As Davis explained, a study of "the normal sex life of women" would "determine the facts on the basis of normal experience which could be used as a guide for sex education in schools and colleges."[21]

Women in modern America desperately needed better sex education. When Davis launched her study in the early 1920s, fewer than half of high school seniors received any sex instruction in school; even those received extremely limited information, often focused on heredity and disease. As one teacher complained, "Sex rarely comes up as an issue in school other than as a problem." In standard sex-segregated sex education classes, girls learned even less than boys. While visiting speakers subjected boys to stern lectures about the dangers of venereal disease, they often were unwilling to discuss any aspect of sex with girls. One state's public health official admitted, "We have never learned just what should be taught to young girls." Even in college, women's sex education was seriously lacking. At Davis's alma mater, Vassar College, one student enrolled in the first-year hygiene course in 1921 was so unimpressed by the annual sex lecture—which consisted of coy warnings to save sex for marriage to "Mr. Right"—that she dedicated her future career to sex education.[22]

Responses to the questionnaires that Davis distributed in the 1920s demonstrated women's abysmal ignorance about sex. Fewer than a third of all respondents received any sex instruction from their parents. Desperate for information, girls turned to friends, neighbors, and servants for insight on everything from menstruation to the mechanics of sex. They scoured the Bible for sexual references, dog-eared sex scenes in novels, and pored through dictionaries for definitions of unfamiliar terms. After leaving home, some young women augmented their knowledge by consulting medical treatises, attending social hygiene lectures, or enrolling in relevant college courses. Still, only a little over a half of all married respondents believed they had been "adequately prepared by instruction for the sex side of marriage." Moreover, the "preparation" they received varied widely. While some gained scientific knowledge of anatomy, intercourse, and reproduction, others primarily received conduct lessons emphasizing "what not to do and how to protect myself from attack," as one woman described her sex instruction.[23]

As a result, there were significant gaps in most women's knowledge. For instance, one recalled wondering why children resembled their fathers; she concluded that perhaps wives drank their husbands' blood to achieve this result! Perhaps even more importantly, many women imbibed extremely negative lessons about sex. Some women, "having acquired the feeling as a small child that any sex pleasure was shameful and a great sin," never overcame these negative associations with sex. One woman regarded all sexual thoughts as "something to be shunned like the devil." Another wrote, "To tell the truth, I have no more personal interest in sex than I have in leprosy." Small wonder, then, that Davis regarded accurate information about sex as essential to women's welfare.[24]

Davis was strongly committed not only to better sex education but also to a better understanding of "normal" female sexuality. This was a new approach to the topic, as most studies of sexual practices—including Davis's own study of sex workers—focused on criminalized practices among marginalized populations. Davis was convinced that "the lack of data as to normal experiences of sex" not only impeded the development of sound "educational programs" but also prevented "more satisfactory adjustments of the sex relationship."[25]

A social scientist to her core, Davis believed that accurate information was the best starting point for any social reform. Moreover, she was well aware that while past studies had focused on people who were "physically or mentally sick," confined to institutions, or receiving medical treatment, the cutting-edge trend was to understand "normality," or the everyday behavior of the "average American."[26] "We have had much investigation and valuable literature on the abnormal woman," she told a reporter, "but we have almost nothing on the normal woman for comparison." Thus, Davis's path forward was clear: "We feel the need of a study of the normal woman to aid scientific investigation."[27]

"Work of Vital Importance"

Davis's interest in understanding "normal" women's sexuality guided the study from start to finish. To gather information about "average" women, Davis decided to conduct a statistical survey with a significant number of participants. Davis's determination to amass a large data set represented a significant departure from previous sex studies, which relied upon a handful of individual case studies. But Davis recognized the authority of numbers in conveying "average" experience. In a cover letter addressed to an initial set of research subjects, she explained that the only way to overcome "ignorance . . . relative to sex" was to conduct a large-scale study. "We can get the normal average condition only through the cooperation of large numbers."[28]

In order to gather information from many women, Davis distributed written questionnaires rather than relying on personal interviews, the method more commonly used by psychologists and psychiatrists. This approach had several advantages. It avoided the somewhat haphazard sampling typical of pioneering studies of sexuality, which often relied heavily upon case studies of personal acquaintances, on the one hand, or troubled patients, on the other. Neither approach offered the scientific rigor that Davis prized; moreover, given Davis's interest in capturing the experiences of "normal," well-adjusted women, it did not make sense to focus on those with sexual problems severe enough to lead them to seek professional advice or force them into institutions. In addition, written questionnaires allowed Davis to gather much more data than she could have done by relying on the time-consuming process of identifying and interviewing individuals, thus enabling her to apply statistical analysis to a significant data set. Accordingly, Davis decided to send a broad-based questionnaire to a large number of participants.[29]

To design the questionnaire, she worked closely with a "cooperating committee" of female professionals and clubwomen. An all-star list of public health professionals, prominent educators, researchers, physicians, and national voluntary organization leaders not only consulted on the survey, she noted, but also "gave status to the inquiry" and helped persuade potential subjects of "the respectability of our study." While women—including several women Davis knew from Bedford Reformatory (Jessie Taft), the wartime social hygiene program (Dr. Edith Hale

Swift), and the 1919 physicians' conference (Dr. Ellen Potter)—directed the study, Davis and her committee also solicited the input of "scientific men," presumably to reassure any skeptics who might question a study conducted entirely by women.[30]

Of the "scientific men" who consulted with Davis, the most important (and the only one Davis named) was Dr. Robert Latou Dickinson, with whom Davis had worked on the Committee for Maternal Health. Dickinson admired Davis's research and kept annotated copies of the articles derived from the study; he also had become a personal friend. Davis and Dickinson's shared commitment to scientific rigor and women's welfare infused the entire study.

Although Davis did not name them in the acknowledgments, her methods also reflected the influence of the German sexologist Magnus Hirschfeld and the British physician Havelock Ellis, both of whom she probably knew personally as well as admiring them professionally. Hirschfeld used a similar questionnaire method, while Ellis relied heavily on individual case studies. Both, however, were interested in cataloging and describing a wide range of sexual behaviors, including autoeroticism and homosexuality, without judging those behaviors. Davis's methods of collecting data, her decision about what subjects to broach, and her forthright presentation of her findings all suggested her familiarity with—and admiration for—the work of these European sexologists. Her approach also differentiated her work from that of most of her American colleagues, who favored patriarchal assumptions about women's sexuality, offered pathological explanations for nonprocreative sexuality, and maintained a conventional emphasis on monogamous marriage.[31]

In keeping with American social scientists' emphasis on marriage, Davis initially focused on married women, for whom she designed an eight-page questionnaire divided into five sections. An introductory section asked for background information on the respondent, such as age, education, health, and occupation. However, Davis did not restrict her questions to married life. The remaining four sections covered different stages of life: childhood, adolescence, marriage, and menopause. During each life stage, Davis solicited details about both marital and nonmarital sexual activity. In requesting information about sex play, sexual experimentation, and sexual desire prior to marriage, as well as by posing questions about birth control, masturbation, and same-sex relationships, Davis severed the supposedly secure link between sex, marriage, and reproduction, studying women's sexuality on its own terms.[32]

Perhaps reflecting her interest in women's sexuality for its own sake, Davis swiftly concluded that it was desirable "to make a similar study of the sex life of unmarried women." Without specifying the reasoning, Davis confided to her longtime benefactor, Bureau of Social Hygiene founder and philanthropist John D. Rockefeller Jr., that both the committee members and outside advisors "deem this work of vital importance."[33]

Davis's own single status may have played a role in her decision to include unmarried women in her study. Regardless of her rationale, the expansion of the original study set her work apart from the emerging field of marital advice books in the 1920s, which sought to promote marriage at a time when women's increased economic independence and sexual freedom offered them other options. Some social commentators expressed anxieties about single women as a threat to the social order, as revealed by the title *Harper's Magazine* gave to Davis's preliminary findings about single women, "Why They Failed to Marry." But Davis did not share these concerns, describing the unwed women in her study as "a highly educated, busy, healthy, happy, and fairly successful group of women." Moreover, her decision to include single as well as married women in her study more than doubled the size of her sample and enhanced her credibility as an expert on the sex lives of "normal" women, regardless of marital status.[34]

Davis and her committee designed a longer and more detailed questionnaire for unmarried women than for married women. The twelve-page survey for single women included definitions of terms, such as "masturbation" and "orgasm," which the committee had concluded were "advisable" because married women's responses to the original survey indicated some confusion as to definitions. The questionnaire for unmarried women also was organized by topic rather than by age. Finally, the survey for single women offered more elaborate justifications of the study and the topics it covered.[35]

"We Must Have More Information"

While the original questionnaires have been lost or destroyed, Davis replicated many of the questions in *Factors*. In addition, she sent a draft copy of the questionnaire for married women to Dr. Dickinson, who carefully preserved and bound the thin onionskin sheets along with annotated copies of Davis's published articles. Thus, it is possible to partially reconstruct the sex surveys.[36]

The questionnaires sent to participants reiterated the importance of understanding the lives of "normal" or "average" women. The "Introductory Statement" in the copy preserved by Dr. Dickinson explained, "We have a good deal of information about the sex life of women who have had serious difficulties of one sort and another. On the other hand the impression has prevailed that most women are without strong sex impulses. These two extremes have largely determined our teaching of the subject for girls. We must have more information about the average woman in order to have any reliable guidance in the training of our girls and boys."[37]

The introductory statement thus reassured informants that completing the survey did not indicate any "serious difficulties," suggested that "average" women might have "strong sex impulses," and solicited assistance with an important goal: collecting accurate information to achieve effective instruction.

To this end, Davis and her collaborators sought candid and detailed responses to the survey. To encourage full and frank replies, the introductory statement continued, "The needed information covers items of personal tendency, personal experiences and personal opinion. To be of real value such information must come out of the life experience of sensible and intelligent women who can be relied upon to furnish thoughtful and frank statements." To elicit such "frank statements," the questionnaire introduction assured participants that the questionnaire was conducted with a double-envelope system that protected the identity of all respondents. Finally, to encourage detailed responses, the survey also included specific directions for completing the questionnaire. In addition to asking respondents to write out their responses on the form (rather than merely checking boxes or answering "yes" or "no," for instance), these directions also encouraged respondents to append additional pages, as needed, to provide longer responses.[38]

The survey for single women went still further in its attempts to reassure respondents and encourage candid responses. Like that for married women, this survey highlighted the scientific and social value of the study as the basis for "sound principles for sex education" and assured participants of anonymity while soliciting honest replies. "Make your replies as complete and accurate as possible," requested a statement at the beginning of the section on "sex feelings and sex experiences." "Whether your experience has been limited or extended, conventional or however unconventional, have no hesitancy in stating the facts. Frank and detailed statements are invaluable."[39]

This language echoed that in the survey for married women as well as the language of the initial letter inviting participation in the study. But the survey for single women made additional efforts to encourage candid responses. For instance, the questionnaire for married women rather bluntly asked them to report if they engaged in any sexual practices prior to marriage before offering a list of possibilities, which included masturbation, intercourse, spooning, and "other forms of sex practice either with your own or the male sex," with the encouragement (in parentheses) to "describe frankly."[40] By contrast, the survey for single women offered a detailed explanation of a variety of "auto-erotic" practices, ranging from simply fantasizing all the way up to self-stimulation to the point of orgasm (which the survey also defined). In addition, the survey for single women devoted significant attention to reassuring respondents that there was no shame in reporting masturbation or other self-stimulating practices. Acknowledging that "there is considerable controversy with regard to auto-eroticism" and that many authorities regarded masturbation as both immoral and unhealthy, the prefatory statement assured study subjects that "harmful physical and mental effects have been greatly exaggerated." Indeed, the statement continued, "some eminent specialists today" maintain that "auto-eroticism, including masturbation, is a normal stage in the development of the sex nature and must be passed through if sexual development is to be complete."[41]

Davis explained, "The purpose of the last statement was to assure the women that whatever their own experiences, they are not isolated, but very common to the human lot; that they are not necessarily signs of degeneracy; and that the phenomena in question are the subject of careful study by many eminent scientists. In this way we hoped to overcome the natural inhibitions of refined women which might stand in the way of honest and full reports."[42]

The surveys also differed in their presentation of material on same-sex relationships. For married women, the treatment was largely limited to questions posed about premarital experience, with brief follow-ups to ascertain whether "intense emotional relations" with another woman (or women) were accompanied by "physical expression" or sex consciousness (awareness of sexual desire, whether acted upon or not). One question in the section on married life asked if the respondent "experienced intense emotional relations with other women" during marriage, and if so, how this affected the marital relationship. It is remarkable that the survey included these questions at all, given prevailing views of homosexuality as a form of sexual deviance. However, Davis regretted not digging deeper into the topic in the first set of surveys. She noted, with evident disappointment, that the questions posed to married women about same-sex relationships were "fewer in number and less definite than in the questionnaire for unmarried women."[43]

By contrast, the survey for single women dedicated an entire section to "emotional experiences with other women." In addition to asking if the subjects had "at any time experienced intense emotional relations with any other girl or woman," the questionnaire posed several follow-up questions about the timing and duration of such relationships, as well as the subjects' opinion of same-sex relationships.[44]

While the survey designed for single women was more detailed, both sets of questionnaires included questions about early sexual awareness and experience, including sex play with either boys or girls (or both!). Both surveys also queried subjects about "sexual periodicity," meaning their level of sexual desire at the onset of menses and before, during, and after subsequent menstrual cycles. In addition, the questionnaire for married women asked them to discuss their attitude toward sexual intercourse, their initial sexual experiences, the frequency of "marriage relations," their interest in sex as compared to that of their husbands, and the degree to which they enjoyed "sex pleasure" or achieved "sexual climax." With respect to the last question, a parenthetical comment explained, "There is much confusion about the facts as they exist among women on this point."[45] Taken together, all of these questions seem intended to dispel the myth of female passionlessness, often used to justify the sexual double standard that Davis so abhorred.

"The Average Woman"

To dispel "confusion about the facts," Davis sought input from "the average woman."[46] In her quest to understand "normal" women's sexuality, Davis recruited study participants not from the ranks of incarcerated or institutionalized women nor from those who sought out treatment for physical or psychological ailments, but rather from the most respectable tier of American society: well-to-do, well-educated, white women. For the study of married women, she contacted a total of ten thousand women using lists drawn from the membership records of national women's organizations and college alumnae registers. She first solicited five thousand names from "a large national organization"—probably the Young Women's Christian Association—specifying that the list should include only "normal married women—that is, women of good standing in the community, with no known physical, mental, or moral handicap, of sufficient intelligence and education to understand and answer in writing a rather exhaustive set of questions as to sex experience." An additional 2,500 names came from the membership lists of clubs affiliated with the General Federation of Women's Clubs, on a "purely arbitrary" basis, but including "the great varieties of types and interests represented in this organization, and with a nationwide distribution." Finally, 2,500 names came from alumnae records of both women's colleges and coeducational universities, with an eye to "age and geographical distribution." Queries sent to 10,000 women yielded 1,073 completed surveys—a response rate of more than 10 percent—although Davis relied only upon the first 1,000 for her study.[47]

For the study of single women, Davis relied entirely upon college and university alumnae records, although she made sure to include both single-sex and coeducational institutions. In addition to ensuring geographical diversity and age distribution, she limited this survey to those who had graduated at least five years previously, so that they would have "sufficient maturity of experience" to offer informed responses. This questionnaire had an even higher response rate than the one for the married women. From the ten thousand single women contacted, Davis received a total of twelve hundred completed surveys; she used all of them in the published study.[48]

The resulting data set of twenty-two hundred questionnaires from college graduates and clubwomen was hardly a representative sample. However, for Davis's purposes—studying well-adjusted, well-educated women who were capable of expressing themselves in writing—it was ideal. The results obtained from the one thousand married respondents, for instance, indicated that they were, as a group, healthy and happy. As Davis pointedly remarked to respond to potential skeptics, they were decidedly not "neurotic and unhappy women."[49]

Where the unmarried group was concerned, as well, Davis insisted that despite some critics' claims that single women who reported on their sexual behavior must be "abnormal," she was convinced that respondents were "sane and sensible" women who "answered our questions carefully and thoughtfully in the hope of making a contribution in a field where such study is greatly needed."[50]

Regardless of their marital status, the survey participants were a literate, articulate, and enthusiastic group, ready and willing to respond to highly personal questions in tremendous detail. As Davis explained, the completed questionnaires "are evidently the result of careful and painstaking effort to present truthfully and accurately the personal experiences of the writers." In addition to completing the lengthy forms, many women inserted supplementary information on separate sheets of paper "in order to give a fuller account of their experience and an expression of their beliefs." Davis took their responses at face value. "On the whole," she concluded, "the answers are as nearly truthful as the writers were able to make them."[51]

Truthfulness was important, for Davis's selection of sensitive topics, such as contraception, masturbation, and lesbianism, was provocative to begin with. Her decision to study "normal" or "average" women—rather than prostitutes or prisoners—made the subject matter still more controversial. The resulting weighty tome, despite its small print, detailed tables, and sometimes stilted prose, was simply breathtaking both in the breadth of topics it covered and in the information it included, even though Davis repeatedly cautioned against drawing broad generalizations from her limited sample.[52]

The four-hundred-plus pages of *Factors* covered a wide array of topics, ranging from sex education to sex play. Running throughout the entire work, however, was one central idea: Women liked sex. Whereas the prevailing idea of "pure" women held that they were "passionless" beings who engaged in sex only for the purpose of procreation or to please their husbands, the data Davis accumulated resoundingly demonstrated that women engaged in sexual activity purely for pleasure. When women reported using birth control, they asserted their interest in sex separate from reproduction. When they discussed masturbation, they showed that women were interested in achieving sexual satisfaction for its own sake. And when they described same-sex relationships, they demonstrated that their interest in sex had nothing to do with pleasing men.

"New Facts in the Field of Birth Control"

Birth control was a contested issue in the 1920s. As Davis acknowledged, her study coincided with a vigorous debate over the Comstock Act, federal legislation dating to the Victorian era that defined both contraception and abortion as obscene and rendered illegal dissemination of either information about or devices for birth control. Following the federal government's lead, most states, including Davis's home state of New York, had adopted "mini–Comstock laws" that criminalized both distributing contraceptives and performing abortions—although by the 1920s, some states provided a legal loophole by permitting physicians to prescribe contraceptives to treat or prevent illness.[53]

Birth-control advocates pushed for increased access, although they disagreed on tactics. While Margaret Sanger partnered with physicians to promote legislation expanding doctors' ability to prescribe contraception, Mary Ware Dennett backed a bill to remove all restrictions on contraception and make it available to all. Meanwhile, physician Robert Latou Dickinson sought to persuade his colleagues to inform themselves and their patients about birth control. Despite their different approaches, all birth-control advocates were eager to obtain reliable information about women's contraceptive use, as well as the safety and efficacy of different methods of preventing pregnancy. Davis's research promised to give them the information they so sorely needed.[54]

Davis supported ongoing efforts to overturn the Comstock Laws and legalize birth control. Behind the scenes, she had directed BSH resources to Margaret Sanger's birth-control clinic and Robert Dickinson's Committee for Maternal Health throughout the 1920s. After her retirement from the Bureau of Social Hygiene, she intensified her commitment to the birth-control movement. In 1929, she wrote to Sanger to congratulate her on the publication of *Motherhood in Bondage*. Deploring the "tragic situation" of the desperate women who wrote to Sanger seeking contraceptive information and hoping Sanger's book might aid in efforts to repeal the Comstock Laws, Davis suggested that she send a copy to newly elected President Herbert Hoover, "who as you know, is deeply interested in the family welfare and in the proper opportunities for the development of children."[55]

That same year, Davis joined the legal defense committee for Mary Ware Dennett, who was fighting a prolonged legal battle after being convicted of sending obscene materials through the US mail in violation of the Comstock Laws.[56] Dennett's pamphlet, *The Sex Side of Life*, designed for young readers, offered simply stated but scientifically accurate information about sex. While she cautioned against sexually transmitted infections and urged her readers to save sex for love relationships, Dennett also defended masturbation and insisted that sex was not a shameful subject. Although Dennett supported legalizing birth control, in an effort to avoid censorship, she refrained from offering information about contraception. However, an all-male jury ruled that her pamphlet, with its illustrations of sex organs and her candid discussion of sexual urges, violated anti-obscenity laws.[57]

In correspondence with Dennett's attorney, civil rights lawyer Morris Ernst, Davis passionately defended Dennett and her work, declaring, "I know of no better pamphlet of its kind." Davis understood that Dennett's case was a test case for sex education writ large; if Dennett's conviction was upheld, parents, educators, and young people would be left with no accurate sources of information, and children would turn to "surreptitious and often truly obscene sources" presenting "generally incorrect" information. Davis wrote, "I do most sincerely hope that this case of Mrs. Dennett's will be decided in such a way that we may go on improving upon and extending our methods in this very important matter of the sex education of children and young people."[58]

Davis collaborated with suffrage veteran, sex education advocate, and birth-control activist Mary Ware Dennett, pictured here stumping for suffrage. When Dennett faced charges of obscenity for circulating her sex education pamphlet, *The Sex Side of Life*, Davis joined her defense committee, assisting with her legal challenge to the restrictive Comstock Act. When the case ended with Dennett's exoneration, her lawyer, Morris Ernst, wrote an editorial for the *Nation* titled "Sex Wins in America." Harris & Ewing Collection, Prints and Photographs Division, Library of Congress.

Davis's support for both Sanger and Dennett represented yet another example of her commitment to women's bodily autonomy—however that might be achieved. Throughout the 1920s, Dennett and Sanger were engaged in a bitter rivalry for leadership of the nation's birth-control movement. Rather than take sides, Davis supported them both—but always behind the scenes.[59]

Throughout the 1920s, Davis had funneled funding both to Sanger's American Birth Control League (ABCL) and to Dr. Dickinson's Committee for Maternal Health—both of which supported clinics that prescribed contraceptives and advocated for the legalization of birth control as well as the free dissemination of sex education materials. (While more closely affiliated with Sanger's birth-control clinic, the committee also supported Dennett by printing and distributing *The Sex Side of Life*.) After her retirement, working through her longtime secretary, Ruth Topping, Davis ensured that the bureau continued to fund both organizations, although Topping—ostensibly on behalf of the bureau—repeatedly remarked that she deplored the deep divisions (which Dickinson referred to as "guerrilla warfare") within the birth-control movement, especially the well-known hostility between Dennett, who favored a "clean repeal" of the Comstock Act, and Sanger, who supported a "doctors only" clause.[60]

While Davis herself—despite her eugenicist leanings—supported birth control as a measure to empower women, support from the now all-male leadership of the bureau depended on economic and eugenicist arguments. These often were intertwined during the Great Depression, when "the financial outlook" was "very black" for both ordinary Americans and fundraising efforts. Highlighting the challenges posed by both economic disaster and legal constraints, Sanger's organization was in dire straits due to business losses suffered by Sanger's estranged husband and financial backer, industrialist James Slee. Worse yet, the Internal Revenue Service denied his claim for income tax exemption for his donations, asserting that the ABCL "violates the Comstock law" and "employs propaganda and lobbying in an effort to change the birth control laws."[61]

To avoid both negative publicity and legal snarls, the BSH now specified that its financial support was only for the strictly scientific work of the Birth Control Clinical Research Bureau, an arm of the ABCL, as opposed to the "propaganda and extension work" of its parent group. As Davis's successor as head of the bureau, Lawrence B. Dunham, put it, "The Rockefeller interests and endeavors are so far flung that we should not enter a controversy of this kind without careful consideration."[62]

Finally, the bureau insisted that such work, especially in the South, should consider the "ethnic make-up of the population" and "its cultural characteristics." While the impetus for the work in the South may have originated from eugenicist interests, Topping also noted that "Negro leaders throughout the South are actively interested in birth control for their race." Topping convinced Fosdick and Dunham to increase their annual appropriation from $10,000 to $17,500 to support the southern campaign, on condition that the bureau "keep absolutely free and clear of any legislative campaigns whether they were conducted by the League or by Mrs. Sanger."[63]

Meanwhile, Davis provided what a half-page advertisement in Sanger's periodical, the *Birth Control Review*, called "new facts in the field of birth control." While she did not discuss actual methods of birth control, which might have led to censorship, Davis included "concrete factual data" on women's use of both contraception and abortion in her massive sex study.[64]

In addition to demonstrating that most women both approved of and practiced birth control, Davis also discussed how women learned about available contraceptive methods, which included diaphragms, condoms, douching, and withdrawal. With a wry nod to US customs rules banning the importation of birth-control information, a review in a biology journal observed, "We note from the table on 'Sources of information as to contraceptive measures' that two women obtained their information from the Bible. This raises the interesting question whether it is not the duty of our customs authorities to exclude the Bible from this country, along with the works of Marie C. Stopes," a British sex education advocate.[65]

Although Davis did not acknowledge her participation in the birth-control movement in *Factors*, the wording of the questionnaire hints at Davis's favorable views on birth control. After inquiring about the subjects' use of contraceptives, the survey posed the question, "What is your opinion as to the use of means to render parenthood voluntary instead of accidental?" Given that advocates of legal contraceptives used similar language—indeed, Mary Ware Dennett's organization was named the Voluntary Parenthood League—this places Davis firmly in the family-planning camp. The contents of the chapter, showing that most respondents both approved of and used contraceptives, also implicitly place Davis on the side of state laws permitting birth control clinics "in which contraceptive information could be given under legitimate, reputable, medical auspices."[66]

In addition to documenting women's favorable attitudes toward contraception and their use of birth control, the chapter correlates the use of contraceptives with education level, family size, and frequency of intercourse. Davis's pro–birth-control leanings are evident in her emphasis on what she called "the important point" that those who reported using contraceptives actually experienced more pregnancies than those who did not. This finding refuted an anti–birth-control argument that contraceptive use caused sterility. Charts relating frequency of intercourse to family size also revealed no correlation between frequent sexual activity and sterility, another shibboleth of the era.[67]

"Natural Sex Feeling"

Davis's attention to birth control revealed her interest not only in women's sexuality in general but also in nonprocreative sexual activity in particular. Her willingness to deal honestly with women's sexual desire, unconnected to reproduction, also informed her discussion of another controversial topic: masturbation. As Davis acknowledged in the survey, both physicians and pastors "vigorously condemned" the practice as immoral and unhealthy. Davis's reassuring statement that "accumulation of facts indicates that the harmful physical and mental effects have been greatly exaggerated" and her comment that "some eminent specialists today" regarded masturbation as "a normal stage" of sexual development were so provocative, in fact, that her secretary later refused to provide even blank copies of the survey to other researchers in an effort to avoid scrutiny and criticism.[68]

Despite the stigma associated with masturbation, Davis's study revealed a high incidence of autoerotic practices among both married and unmarried women. Of those who responded to questions about self-stimulating behaviors, the majority—nearly 65 percent of unmarried women and more than 40 percent of married women—did so positively. Davis assumed that the actual numbers were even higher.[69]

The sheer numbers—suggesting that masturbation was a "normal" practice among "average" women—must have been reassuring to those who indulged in the practice. Attitudes among survey respondents, while mixed, were more positive than one might expect, given the prevailing stigma associated with masturbation. While some women regarded the practice as harmful, leading to "self-disgust," others regarded masturbation as beneficial, reporting that it relieved "nervous tension."[70]

Other survey results were similarly reassuring, suggesting that autoeroticism was not only common but also safe. Among unmarried women, Davis found that those "now practicing" masturbation experienced "better health," thereby confounding prevailing popular opinion that masturbation caused health problems.[71]

Turning her attention to married women, Davis found a "significant" correlation between reports of being unhappily married and reports of masturbating after marriage. However, she refrained from suggesting that masturbation had a negative effect on marriage, which would have accorded with prevailing negative attitudes about what some experts, including Davis's supporter, Dr. Max Exner, still described as "self-abuse." Rather, she whimsically remarked, "As to causal relationship, whether unhappiness in married life leads to masturbation or *vice versa* is a problem for future determination. Perhaps it works both ways!"[72]

While Davis justified her study by saying that its results would help design better sex education programs, the study itself was clearly a sexual education for many of its participants. Davis's detailed descriptions of different "auto-erotic" practices were practically a primer on pleasure. For instance, in the series of definitions, she explained, "Masturbation is an auto-erotic activity carried to the point of orgasm. This may be brought about by manipulation, friction, pressure, and so forth, accompanied or not by sex reveries, or . . . be induced by vivid sex imagery unaided by manipulation. Most frequently, however, manipulation of some sort and sex reveries are involved."[73] Lest survey subjects be unclear on the concept, Davis also supplied a definition of "orgasm": "For the purposes of this study, the term 'orgasm' may be defined as a convulsive contraction of the muscles of the interior sex organs, followed by a definite relaxation."[74]

While some individuals worried about the effects of masturbation, readers of the chapters on autoeroticism may—like some of the respondents to the survey—have found that reading about the subject inspired them to attempt masturbation or achieve climax. Even if some readers came away with a renewed resolve to avoid a practice that some respondents described as degrading, others instead may have felt reassured that the desire to engage in masturbation, at least, was an expression of what one survey participant called "natural sex feeling."[75] The chapters on autoeroticism, like the book as a whole, defined women's sexual desire itself as entirely normal.

"Clear and Courageous"

One of Davis's signal contributions to the study of sex was what British feminist Stella Browne called her "clear and courageous" discussion of same-sex relationships.[76] By the 1920s, homosexuality had become increasingly visible in American cities, especially New York, where gays and lesbians developed a unique subculture that included a vibrant nightlife centered in bars, clubs, and theaters. The "pansy craze" of the decade featured a variety of queer entertainments, including cross-dressing performers and drag balls, centered in hot spots like Greenwich Village and Harlem. Meanwhile, homosexuality was literally in the spotlight on Broadway, where plays such as *The Captive* sympathetically depicted lesbian love. But increased visibility did not mean greater acceptance. Rather, police officers raided gay nightclubs and city officials shut down *The Captive*.[77]

Legal repression reflected prevailing attitudes. Despite sympathetic discussion by some European sexologists, homosexuality remained both stigmatized and criminalized in the United States. Moreover, as women wielded increased political rights and enjoyed greater financial independence, concerned commentators called attention to what they saw as a "lesbian menace" to both heterosexual marriage and social stability. Earlier generations, secure in the assumption of female passionlessness, had celebrated women's presumably asexual relationships. But by the 1920s, modern Americans, conversant with new theories of sexuality, had begun to regard all women's relationships with suspicion. As one of Davis's survey participants reported, "In my city some business women are hesitating to take apartments together for fear of the interpretation that may be put upon it." In this context, including lesbianism in a study of "normal" women was a conscious and courageous choice.[78]

Davis's own experiences probably prompted her to devote attention to the taboo topic of lesbian desire. Her circle of friends in Rochester, New York, included many women who pursued romantic relationships with other women. Family friend, avid diarist, and photography enthusiast May Bragdon, who experienced her fair share of heartbreak as well as what she dubbed "Venus time," documented both her own and her friends' "sentimental moments" and "love affairs."[79]

Combined with other sources, Bragdon's diaries reveal that Davis enjoyed a long-term, if mostly long-distance, relationship with Vassar alumna Ella Lapham, whom she met in the mid-1880s when she was living and teaching in western New York. With common interests in classic literature, outdoor activities, and women's rights, the two immediately became fast friends. Davis lived with Lapham while preparing for her college entrance exams; although they never again shared a residence, the two women remained in regular contact over the following decades. Davis spent time with Lapham on visits home, while Lapham made long visits to both St. Mary's Settlement and Bedford Reformatory. Although the couple's correspondence has not been preserved, in letters to her mother, Davis indicated that she corresponded regularly with Lapham and regarded her as a family member. It must have been a severe blow, then, when Lapham died in 1917. Davis never forgot her "particular chum," as Bragdon referred to her long-distance lover. Rather, in 1924, she donated a brass kettle to Vassar College in her honor.[80]

Davis also had ample opportunities to observe women's intimate relationships both at Vassar College and at Bedford Reformatory. Female friendships flourished at women's colleges in Victorian America. Vassar students filled both their letters home and their cherished scrapbooks with evidence of same-sex "smashes." With the encouragement of sympathetic staff—often themselves involved in long-term domestic partnerships—they even used Valentine's Day as an opportunity to celebrate romantic relationships.[81]

Same-sex relationships also were common at Bedford Reformatory. After Davis's departure, a scandal about interracial lesbian relationships there threatened to damage her legacy. Although Davis downplayed such

Family friend May Bragdon celebrated same-sex relationships—from "sentimental moments" to "love affairs"—in both her diary and her photographs. Some of these were her own, as in this 1902 image of her and an unidentified friend looking out at Lake Ontario in 1902. Bragdon's diaries also documented Davis's long-term relationship with Vassar alumna Ella Lapham. "By the sad 'sea' waves!" July 8–12, 1902, May Bragdon Diaries, Rare Books, Special Collections, and Preservation, University of Rochester River Campus Libraries.

relationships at the time, she was well aware of their existence, which sometimes undermined discipline at the institution. Davis revealed her familiarity with lesbianism at both women's colleges and female reformatories in *Factors*, commenting that in her opinion, same-sex relationships were "much more widespread than is generally suspected, or than most administrators are willing to admit."[82]

Responses to the sex survey confirmed Davis's suspicion that same-sex relationships were commonplace among American women. Of the unmarried group, just over half of the total reported "intense emotional relations" with other women. Of these, approximately half reported "physical expression" or recognized their relationships as sexual.[83] Nearly one third of married respondents reported intense emotional relationships with other women; again, roughly half of these acknowledged that these relationships were accompanied by sexual activity or awareness of sexual attraction. (Davis dryly noted that only a little over half of the group who reported sexual practices—such as mutual masturbation and genital contact—recognized their relationships as sexual in nature at the time. "It seems hardly possible that the others could escape such recognition," she commented wryly, "but so they state.")[84] In short, then, Davis found that many American women engaged in same-sex relationships—including sexual relationships.

Davis's discussion of same-sex relationships among women was nearly sui generis. As she noted in her review of the scholarship on the subject, "much less has been written about the phenomenon among women than among men." Davis discovered only one statistical survey of the subject: a study of female students at the University of Moscow that had been confiscated and destroyed by the Russian government.[85]

Davis knew that her data on women's relationships was not only original but also important. Indeed, at the same time that she was working through the material she had gathered on same-sex relationships, she was discussing the legal implications of her work with civil rights attorneys engaged in defending lesbian plays and books from censorship. In early 1927, she shared information about her research on lesbianism with Arthur Garfield Hays, the free-speech attorney who headed up the legal defense of the lesbian-themed play *The Captive*.[86]

In late 1928, Davis corresponded with civil rights lawyer Morris Ernst, who sought to protect British writer Radclyffe Hall's lesbian-themed novel *The Well of Loneliness*, already banned in the UK, against censorship in the United States. In addition to sharing prepublication data about the high incidence of lesbianism with Ernst, Davis discussed the possibility of testifying in the case. Ultimately, Ernst decided against using either Davis's data or her testimony, choosing instead to downplay the sexual content of the novel. But Davis's willingness to cooperate with Ernst indicates her commitment to challenging the social stigma against same-sex relationships as well as combating the legal restrictions of Comstock-era censorship.[87]

Recognition of the social, as well as the scientific, value of the data she collected on women's same-sex relationships may have motivated Davis to publish her entire study as a scholarly monograph. As she anticipated stepping down from her position at the bureau, Davis was determined "to publish in book form the results of my sex studies"—including two chapters on same-sex relationships, the only pieces of the entire project yet to be completed or published.[88]

Davis doubtless understood that the best, if not the only, way to share her findings about same-sex relationships was in book form. At the time, the very few studies of lesbianism available presented same-sex intimacy as a form of pathology, both in their discussion of the subject and in their choice of venue. For instance, a discussion of lesbian relationships at Bedford Reformatory, authored by one of Davis's colleagues, had appeared as part of a study of "psychopathic delinquent women" in the *Journal of Nervous and Mental Disease*. Presenting a discussion of women's intimacy as part of a larger discussion of "normal" women's sexuality offered a dramatic alternative to the prevailing pathological models.[89]

"'Naturally' Homosexual"

Davis's data on same-sex relationships revealed the astonishing frequency with which "average" American women engaged in "intense emotional relations"—often accompanied by sexual activity—with one another. Her discussion of same-sex relationships also was remarkable for its nonjudgmental stance. At the time, most Americans—laypeople and professionals alike—regarded homosexuality as a form of mental illness, physical abnormality, or both. While some European sexologists were less judgmental, they nonetheless sought explanations for same-sex attraction, indicating that they saw it as unnatural if not also as undesirable. But Davis refrained from making any negative comments about same-sex attraction. Instead, she opened the first chapter on same-sex relationships with statements about the long history of lesbianism, asserting that "homosexual intimacy among women is probably as old as humankind."[90]

After normalizing homosexuality by offering examples of its existence throughout time and across cultures, Davis offered a thorough review of extant literature on homosexuality, citing prominent European sexologists such as Magnus Hirschfeld, Havelock Ellis, and Richard von Krafft-Ebing. While all these sexologists advocated greater acceptance of homosexuals, Davis went much further by classifying same-sex attraction and activity as entirely normal. Davis observed that most studies probed the causes of homosexuality, attributing it to anatomical "abnormalities," arrested psychosexual development, "internal secretions" (hormonal imbalances), "psychopathic degeneration," or, most sympathetically, to the notion that some individuals belong to an "intermediate sex."[91]

Davis departed from such studies by discussing the incidence of same-sex relationships rather than the causes of homosexuality. "In the past, attention has been chiefly centered on the etiology of homosexuality rather than its prevalence," she wrote. But in her study, Davis chose not to pose any questions about "possible physical or anatomical deviations" that might explain homosexuality. Nor did she express any judgment about women's "overt homosexuality." Rather, she simply classified women's relationships as either lacking sexual expression or consciousness (a group she labeled HI) or including sexual activity or awareness (a group she labeled HII). Moreover, she claimed to "make no attempt at interpretation." Noting that "many cases could be selected which would illustrate any one of the theories advanced by the various writers on homosexuality we have quoted," she cautioned, "In advance of further studies of this type it would be a mistake to infer from our data that our results would apply to other groups of women on other social or educational levels, or to the woman population in general."[92]

Although Davis claimed to avoid analysis, her data challenged both the silence and the stigma associated with same-sex relationships. The timing was perfect. One year before Davis published her study, British author Radclyffe Hall published her (in)famous novel, *Well of Loneliness*, in the United Kingdom. The book's central message is a moving plea for the social acceptance of both same-sex love and gender nonconformity. (The main character, Stephen Gordon, born a woman, lives as a man and has love affairs with women.) *Well* garnered praise from European sexologists, including Havelock Ellis, for its sympathetic depiction of "sexual inversion" (what would later be called "gender dysphoria" or "transgender identity") as an inherent and immutable congenital condition.[93]

Despite public outcry and efforts at censorship, the novel eventually overcame legal challenges to distribution in the United States, becoming, for many lesbian readers, literally the only book they ever encountered on the subject. However, the unsuccessful love life of its main character also reinforced the notion that women who loved other women were doomed to live lonely lives. Although one American reader wrote to Hall to laud her championing of the cause of "the poor invert," exclaiming, "No one could finish your book, Miss Hall, without donning a sword and shield forever in the cause of inverts," other readers found the book profoundly depressing. If lesbians could not find happiness even in fiction, what hope was there for them in real life? "Not helpful," another US reader succinctly summarized the situation.[94]

In this context, it is remarkable that Davis's study not only framed same-sex relationships as normal but also debunked associations between homosexuality, unhappiness, and health problems. Given that both dominant medical discourse and prevailing popular opinion defined homosexuality as a mental illness or a sexual perversion, it is somewhat surprising that less than half of those who reported a history of intense emotional relationships with other women described such relationships as "unnatural; abnormal; perversion" and that a substantial minority instead described them as "natural; legitimate." Moreover, when asked about the effects of their own same-sex relationships on their lives, approximately half of respondents regarded them as "helpful," and only a minority described them as "injurious to health."[95]

Even though a higher percentage of the "overt homosexuals" believed in "the unfortunate physical effects of their experiences," in a separate portion of the questionnaire dealing with health questions, the same individuals reported general health in line with that of the entire group. Similarly, in the section of the questionnaire devoted to overall happiness, there were "no significant differences in the answers of the various groups"—meaning that women in homosexual relationships were just as happy as those in heterosexual relationships. Finally, Davis found that most women reporting sexual relationships with other women did not regard these relationships as problematic. She even drew up a table to demonstrate this, commenting that "only 40 of the 312 overt homosexuals regarded their homosexual relationships in the light of a sex problem requiring solution."[96]

In short, then, while Davis ostensibly steered clear of offering interpretations of her data, she strongly suggested that women who loved other women were just as likely to be healthy and happy as women in relationships with men, thereby challenging negative views of lesbianism—including those expressed by some of her subjects!

In addition to providing statistical data and correlation tables, Davis also included a series of case studies in the chapter on single women and same-sex relationships. Both individually and collectively, these case studies reinforced the statistical data by suggesting that same-sex relationships were both natural and beneficial. Davis divided the case studies up into groups, with the largest group being those "who report themselves to be 'naturally' homosexual," thereby suggesting that homosexuality itself was a "natural" state. This group of respondents rated their own same-sex relationships, many of them long-term, highly. One woman, who at the time she completed the survey had been in a relationship with another woman for two years, stated that her lover was "as much a real mate as a husband would be." Another, in a relationship of seventeen years' duration, explained that her life was "perfectly happy because of our mutual love and congeniality in all things." Yet another explained that her relationship with "a woman partner" had "made my life inexpressibly richer and deeper," adding, "I would not have been without the experience for worlds."[97]

Moreover, while recognizing the social stigma attached to such relationships, many also insisted that their same-sex partnerships were not "sex problems." Some offered detailed defenses of homosexuality. One wrote,

> I have come to think that certain women, many, in fact, possibly most of those who are unmarried, are more attracted to women than to men, through no fault of their own, and inherent in their nature; and I am somewhat inclined to think that to mate with one woman is as natural and as healthful and helpful for them as are marital relations between husband and wife . . . I cannot believe that large numbers of women must forego full development because they are attracted to a woman rather than to a man. . . . It seems very prevalent among humans and I feel cannot be wholly bad.[98]

By suggesting that prevalent feelings were "inherent" and that common practices were "natural," this study subject explicitly expressed the approving messages that Davis's scientific charts merely implied: same-sex relationships were normal.

Other "'naturally' homosexual" study subjects reported that they found the social stigma difficult but refused to give up their relationship.

One woman struggled with her "physical attraction" to her live-in lover, expressing the hope that they could "overcome" their sexual impulses without sacrificing "a sincere and genuine love for each other."[99]

Still others used the survey to seek reassurance. One woman in a relationship that "satisfied me entirely" forthrightly stated, "We love to be together, and both get decidedly physical satisfaction from bodily contact." But she went on to query whether these feelings were legitimate: "We have wondered sometimes if this could be harmful, but intellectually and spiritually we are so satisfying that physical contact seems like a symbol of our oneness. . . . We would like to know if there is anything unhealthy in two women loving each other, provided they are able to stimulate each other to do better work."[100] While Davis did not overtly respond to this query, the statistical data she included in *Factors* affirmed the overall health of women in same-sex relationships, while the case studies indicated the happiness of women in lesbian partnerships. If this survey participant and her partner read the published book, they probably would have found its contents quite reassuring.

Books addressing lesbianism were few and far between at the time Davis's book was published. Although there were other literary representations of lesbians—the same year that *The Well of Loneliness* was published, British author Virginia Woolf released *Orlando*, a fictional account of a transgender protagonist inspired by Woolf's lover, novelist Vita Sackville-West, and Greenwich Village author Djuna Barnes authored a roman à clef about a Parisian lesbian community—most readers found literally no examples of themselves in literature other than Stephen Gordon, the cross-dressing central character in Radclyffe Hall's *Well of Loneliness*.[101]

Even reading the most well-circulated book on lesbianism could cause problems. One woman, born in 1920, recalled that when she read *The Well of Loneliness* as a teenager, her father's response was, "Oh, yes, I think I read that in an abnormal psychology class." Decades later, she recalled the sinking feeling that comment inspired. "Well, you can imagine what my stomach did. Errp!"[102]

Locating nonfictional accounts of lesbianism was even more difficult, since most studies of homosexuality focused on men. And when would-be readers did find books about homosexuality, they often had to read them in secret, standing in the shelves of libraries rather than bringing them to the checkout counter, where they might be challenged. A nurse born in 1922 was able to check out a stack of books on homosexuality only because of her profession. Initially, the librarian on staff rejected her request: "Well, you can't check these out without an interview with the [head] librarian." Fortunately, the librarian changed course when she realized the patron was a healthcare provider: "She looked up and said, 'Oh, but you're a registered nurse!' and checked them out."[103]

A lesbian librarian, Jeannette Foster, also gained unusual access to a wide array of books and articles. While Foster was primarily interested in lesbian fiction, she also included "scientific and psychiatric material" as well as publications on "exclusively male studies" in her landmark work, *Sex Variant Women in Literature*, which she published at her own expense in 1956 after spending decades trawling dusty library shelves for literature on gender variance and sexual diversity.[104]

Foster, who discovered Havelock Ellis's six-volume work, *Studies in the Psychology of Sex*, in her college library in the 1910s, was profoundly affected by Davis's study. More than a decade after the release of *Factors*, in 1941, after reading an academic article on endocrinology and homosexuality by biology professor Alfred Kinsey, she would write to him, "Ever since the appearance of Katherine [*sic*] Bement Davis' book on sex factors in the lives of college women I have realized the value of objective case studies. Since, though your present article is limited to male cases, I infer that your total data include women, I am writing to offer my own case as one of the requisite 10,000 if that will help." One wonders if Foster shared Davis's book with "a few of my friends" who she thought also might be willing to participate in Kinsey's study. Highlighting the PhD she shared with Davis (and Kinsey) and their shared scientific mindset, Foster signed off, "Yours in the interests of furthering knowledge, Dr. Jeannette H. Foster."[105]

Like Foster, some of Davis's respondents, despite the difficulties of acquiring books on the subject, were quite conversant with prevailing theories about homosexuality, especially those offered in the second volume in Ellis's series, *Sexual Inversion*, published in the United States in 1900. For instance, a woman who found even the thought of sex with men "repugnant" described herself as a "congenital invert." Evidently intrigued by the European sexologist's theories about "inversion" (which he posited could be either "congenital" or "acquired"), in response to questions about sex problems, she wrote, "I am not bothered by, but am interested in finding the reasons for, sexual inversion."[106]

Davis herself steered clear of seeking explanations for lesbianism. However, her very avoidance of the question seemed to suggest that homosexuality was not a problem that needed to be explained. Indeed, while Davis presented nine case studies of "natural" homosexuality, she included only one instance of "a psychopathic case," noting that this was "one of the very few in our group." Both the statistical data and the case studies suggested that same-sex relationships, including those with a sexual component, were both "normal" and "natural."[107] Davis's sex study thus dispelled the stigma associated with same-sex desire.

"Scientific Truths About Sex"

Beyond its specific findings, Davis's sweeping study was significant for Americans' understanding of women's sexuality writ large, As the *Scientific American* stated in ad copy, "Almost to a certainty this book will upset a number of fondly cherished beliefs."[108] Indeed, both in its overall approach and in its detailed tables, *Factors in the Sex Life of Twenty-Two Hundred Women* challenged prevailing beliefs about "pure" and "passionless" womanhood. By presenting solid sexual information based on social-scientific scholarship, Davis not only avoided censorship but also garnered praise in both academic and popular publications.

Despite the book's controversial claims and the censorship controversies of the era, Harper & Brothers had no reservations about publishing Davis's study. A press representative opined, "We are not in the least disturbed about the idea of publishing it. It is a dignified, scientific piece of work and deserves a place on the list of a good house."[109] However, the publishers did take potential criticism into account in its marketing strategy. As Davis's secretary explained, "The publishers have pushed this book slowly and conservatively in order to avoid undesirable publicity."[110]

Except for an advertisement in *The Nation*—featuring European sexologist Havelock Ellis's description of the book as "the first important study of the sexual life of women made by a competent woman"—the press relied heavily on direct mailing to professionals "particularly interested in the effect of individual sexual experience on adjustment to environment" and on "special promotion" in the *Scientific American*. To bolster the book's standing, the press highlighted the book's sponsorship by the Bureau of Social Hygiene and included an approving blurb from the *Scientific American*, describing the volume as "A THOROUGHLY SCIENTIFIC RECORD OF SCIENTIFIC WORK." The press elaborated, "This pioneer work in its field . . . offers for the first time actual facts and information on a topic which has long been the subject for guesswork." The information contained in the book, the press promised, addressed "some of the most important questions of our day" and provided "conclusive evidence on the whole subject."[111]

Presented as a scientific study aimed at a professional audience, *Factors* not only avoided censorship but also received favorable reviews in a wide range of publications. Prior to the book's publication, the *Scientific American* signaled its support by urging readers to pay attention to "scientific truths about sex." For far too long, the editors argued, real facts had been obscured by false beliefs: "We have thought we knew, yet we did not know." Yet Davis's new study of women's sexuality promised to "revise the very criterion of what actually constitutes average normal sex life," replacing outdated morality with up-to-date science. In an "age of frankness," the journal's editor insisted, "matters of sex are truly matters of science." It was time to set aside "the rather hypocritical standards" of yesteryear in favor of "a more exact, scientific basis." "Now that humanity is coming of age," the editorial concluded, "it is time it stopped deceiving itself."[112]

Taking their cue from the *Scientific American*, both scholarly and popular publications welcomed Davis's study as a valuable contribution to modern knowledge. Medical journals especially welcomed both Davis's scientific approach and her comprehensive coverage. One lauded her for addressing sex "in a proper scientific manner, sex life being regarded just as eating habits or sleeping hours would be regarded," while another described the volume as "perhaps the most remarkable collection of statistics and detailed information upon its subject ever brought together."[113]

Journals representing a wide range of professions joined in praising *Factors*. One religious periodical described Davis's volume as "the best work available as to the influence of sex on a large group of normal women."[114] A representative review in an educators' journal, praising both the book's "scientific tone" and "the frankness of its revelations," described *Factors* as "probably the most authentic and searching study ever made of the sex lives of women."[115]

"Sex and Marriage in a Modern Age"

Beyond calling attention to the scientific accuracy and the sheer quantity of information included in Davis's study, many reviews noted that its publication marked increased openness in discussions of sexuality in both scientific circles and American society. A review of several "respectable volumes" about sexual behavior in the *Journal of the American Medical Association* noted that their appearance augured "the awakening of scientific interest in the subject."[116] A Catholic quarterly likewise included Davis's volume in a list of "books on the scientific side of sex."[117] Meanwhile, the *American Journal of Public Health* suggested that *Factors* not only offered important guidance for public health but also represented "a new fund of knowledge" into the sexual lives of women at the same time that "the trend in modern literature, the stage and the screen is toward the discussion of more and more intimate sex relationship."[118]

Many publications highlighted the timeliness of Davis's study, which coincided with the increased visibility of sexuality—especially women's sexuality—in the opening decades of the twentieth century. Reviewers recognized the importance of Davis's publication as Americans confronted what one periodical called "our changing sex standards."[119] In both specialized and general-interest publications, acute observers seized upon Davis's findings to highlight the ongoing referendum on "sex and marriage in a modern age," as one reviewer put it.[120]

Indeed, *Factors* revolutionized Americans' understandings of "the sex side of life" at a key moment, as Davis's longtime supporter, Dr. Max J. Exner, explained in the pages of *The Survey*, a social work journal. Exner framed his lengthy and positive review in light of the recent decision in the case of Mary Ware Dennett, in which an appeals court determined that Dennett's sexual education pamphlet, previously banned under the Comstock Laws, was not obscene. Exner praised Davis's book not only on its own merits—particularly its "scientific spirit"—but also as evidence of a cultural shift: a move toward considering sex "objectively and calmly" rather than as "inherently 'obscene.'" Highlighting both the originality and the significance of Davis's study, Exner explained that *Factors* paved the way for new "ethical codes" based on accurate information, rather than on outdated morality. In short, in addition to providing "significant and desperately needed data," Davis's work, he concluded, was "illuminating and clarifying in a sector of experience that is vital to human welfare and happiness, and regarding which ignorance and distorting misconceptions largely prevail."[121]

Davis's book challenged fundamental beliefs about female sexuality, especially the stubborn specter of female passionlessness and the sexual double standard that it supported. According to the *Birth Control Review*, in addition to being "the most comprehensive report of the most important investigation of its kind ever conducted," Davis's research resoundingly repudiated "the dogma of the frigid woman," which "cheerfully ignored" any shortcomings in a couple's sex life as a natural consequence of "the double standard of morals" for women and men.[122] Likewise, in the pages of the *Forum*, radical writer Victor Frances Calverton used Davis's data to support his declaration: "The myth of the pure woman is almost at an end."[123]

Released during the nation's first sexual revolution, Davis's research promoted a profound reassessment of women's sexuality in modern America. Countering "false information" with both statistical data and personal stories, Davis boldly redefined women's sexuality by demonstrating that "average" women—not just sex workers or sexual deviants—experienced sexual desire, engaged in sexual activity, and enjoyed sexual satisfaction. Tackling taboo topics such as masturbation, birth control, and lesbianism, Davis not only documented the numerical frequency of such practices among "normal" women but also provided both those who participated in the survey and those who read the book with a primer on pleasure. By redefining women's sexuality as normal, Davis's research both validated the nation's first sexual revolution and paved the way for the second.

Conclusion

"A Revelation to Womankind"

Katharine Bement Davis was many things. She was a schoolteacher, a settlement house worker, and a social scientist. She also was a social reformer and a sex researcher. But above all else, Davis was a feminist, committed to demonstrating women's abilities, advancing women's rights, and expanding women's horizons—professionally, politically, and personally.

Davis expressed her commitment to women's welfare in both words and deeds. In her unfinished autobiography, Davis laid claim to her feminist principles by repeatedly calling attention to times when she was the first woman to fill a position. During her long career in public service, she also gave many speeches in which she highlighted women's accomplishments and demanded women's rights. Finally, Davis demonstrated her feminism in her work, whether that work was promoting prison reform for female lawbreakers or investigating women's sexual desire.

Davis's feminism infused her entire life. Whether teaching high school, reforming prisons, condemning the sexual double standard, demanding voting rights, advocating sex education, challenging censorship, or investigating sexual behavior, Davis championed women's rights.

Well before second-wave feminists adopted the mantra, "The personal is political," Davis lived it. Davis's personal relationships—her admiration for her grandmother Rhoda Bement, an abolitionist and suffragist; the steady support of her family, especially her sisters, Helen and Charlotte; her lasting friendships with fellow students and inspiring faculty at Vassar College; her long-term, long-distance romance with Ella Lapham; her sometimes fraught relationship with birth-control advocate Margaret Sanger; her enduring connection to her financial benefactor, John D. Rockefeller Jr.; her steadfast support for fellow suffragist, pacifist, and sex educator Mary Ware Dennett; and her mutually beneficial relationships with physicians Max J. Exner and Robert Latou Dickinson—both inspired and enabled her lifelong work.

Davis was committed not only to her own professional advancement but to promoting the work of other women. As a high school teacher, she inspired her female students both with her high academic standards and with her daring adoption of split skirts for riding bicycles. As superintendent of Bedford Reformatory and as commissioner of correction for New York City, she hired a cadre of highly educated women, including many of her classmates from both Vassar College and the University of Chicago, helping them to establish successful careers as physicians, psychologists, and prison administrators.

Davis also engaged in political activism. Whether demanding women's voting rights as a suffrage speaker or demonstrating women's capacity as a public official, Davis both espoused and exemplified equal rights for women.

Moreover—and more than many of her contemporaries—Davis advocated on behalf of African American and immigrant women, as well as native-born, white women. Notwithstanding her stigmatizing comments about Sicilians, Davis served immigrants at both the Philadelphia settlement house and Bedford Reformatory—where she learned to respect both ethnic and religious diversity. In addition, Davis consistently advanced African American women's welfare, not only by providing social services for struggling teenagers but also by hiring African American professionals for public positions.

Even Davis's decision to exclude foreign-born and African America women from some of her studies of sex—while she addressed racial and ethnic diversity in her discussion of suspected sex workers, she focused on native-born white women in both the study of "the mentality of the criminal woman" and in her massive study of "normal" women's sex lives—reflected her commitment to racial and ethnic as well as gender equality, since she believed testing nonnative speakers would result in inaccurate results and that calling attention to racial differences would stigmatize, rather than empower, women of color.[1]

Feminists of all time periods often disagree on the details of their agenda. Davis was no exception to feminist diversity. Indeed, some of her sharpest critics throughout her career were fellow feminists, who differed from her both in ideological outlook and in political strategy. Moreover, many of Davis's activities—her participation in the criminalization of women's sexuality, her promotion of the carceral state, her fascination with eugenics, and her endorsement of permanent institutionalization of "feeble-minded" women—would now attract well-deserved criticism in many feminist circles. At the same time, however, Davis's staunch support for a single sexual standard, her persistent advocacy of reproductive rights, her sympathetic attitude toward sexual diversity, and her clarion call for women's control over their sexual destinies all highlight issues that remain central to feminist conversations today.

While contemporary sources devoted more attention to her participation in electoral politics—ranging from delivering suffrage speeches to supporting reform candidates—Davis's most important contribution to American public life dealt with a very personal matter: women's sexuality. By bringing public attention to women's private lives, Davis initiated and informed candid conversations about some of the most controversial topics of her time—and our own.

"The Pioneer Factual Analysis of Sex-Life"

Davis was, as she described herself in her unpublished autobiography, "a busy woman" whose life included many "firsts." After becoming the first woman to earn a PhD in political economy at the University of Chicago, she became the first superintendent of New York State's female reformatory and then the first female commissioner of correction for New York City. But of all her many accomplishments, Davis's most enduring legacy was her pioneering study of female sexuality. *Factors in the Sex Life of Twenty-Two Hundred Women* was the first sex study to focus on women as well as the first sex study published by a woman.[2]

But the importance of Davis's sex study goes well beyond being the first of its kind. It also was the most ambitious in scope—and the most significant in its findings—for decades to come. By focusing on "normal" women and collecting a large sample, Davis set herself apart from other sex researchers of the era. At the same time, her data demonstrated that "average" women were sexual beings. Her key findings—that women used birth control, practiced masturbation, and engaged in same-sex relationships—showed that women neither restricted sexual activity to marriage nor regarded sex solely as a way to please a husband or produce children. Instead, Davis's study indicated that American women engaged in sex purely for pleasure. Davis's study redefined normal women's sexuality, documented the nation's first sexual revolution, and challenged sexual norms in modern America.

Davis's research remained relevant for decades to come. Her study not only remained the landmark work on women's sexuality but also influenced later studies of sexual behavior. As a result, Davis's study not only documented the nation's first sexual revolution but also facilitated the second. Moreover, her attention to what she called "matters of sex"—and her insistence that sex matters—continue to inform contemporary debates over sexuality.

When it was published in the turbulent 1920s, *Factors* not only revealed the realities of women's sexuality but also provided reliable information on the decade's decisive shift in the direction of sexual liberation. It also sold well, despite a lackluster publicity campaign. Harper & Brothers, keen to avoid controversy, avoided mass marketing in favor of direct mailing and limited advertisements in professional journals. Despite the press's cautious approach, the book nearly sold out its initial print run in the first year.[3] With expectations of entirely recouping publication expenses, the press promptly brought out a second printing.[4] By 1932, Davis's secretary optimistically predicted that the book "bids fair to be a best seller"![5] The following year, Davis proudly reported that the book had sold nearly nine thousand copies.[6]

The book sold because its subject mattered. Throughout the 1930s, commentators used Davis's data to demonstrate—and to drive—profound changes in sexual attitudes and sexual behavior. In a 1930 essay on "The Flapper," psychologist Lorine Pruette used Davis's data on sexual experimentation among "yesterday's flappers" to document the rise of "a new conception of womanhood."[7] Journalist Dorothy Dunbar Bromley, who had gained renown for her commentary on flappers and feminism in the 1920s, compared Davis's data on premarital sex to a survey of thirteen hundred college students in her 1938 study,

Youth and Sex, using the significant shift in reported rates of premarital sex to contend that "large numbers of the younger generation have broken with the traditional sex code."[8] Arguing that legal regulation should reflect accepted practice, freelance journalist Helen Buckler contributed an article on "Sex and the Law" to *Scribner's Magazine*, using Davis's data on premarital sex to advocate for reforming laws governing extramarital sex.[9]

Such positive assessments were not limited to women authors. Indicating increased social acceptance of frank conversations about sexual satisfaction, in his 1936 classic, *How to Win Friends and Influence People*, self-help guru Dale Carnegie cited Davis's statistics on marital happiness and sexual satisfaction in his discussion of one of his "Seven Rules for Making Your Home Life Happier," cautioning his readers, "Don't Be a 'Marriage Illiterate.'"[10]

Meanwhile, Davis's book circulated widely, influencing experts in a variety of disciplines. Prominent sex researchers on both sides of the Atlantic recommended her book as an invaluable resource, and many sex education manuals in the 1930s and 1940s cited her study.[11] Davis's "important book," as one pioneering marital advice giver referred to it, also profoundly shaped both the fast-growing field of marriage counseling and scholarly studies of family life from the 1930s forward.[12] Sociologists, psychologists, and even biologists also regarded Davis's book as essential reading.[13]

While it is unclear whether Davis expected this sort of cultural currency, she had anticipated that other researchers might engage in additional analysis of her data. In the introduction to *Factors*, she acknowledged that many other uses might be made of the massive body of material she had collected, although she remarked, "Whether or no any such further use of these histories is made is on the laps of the gods."[14]

The laps of the gods, as it turned out, were not a reliable repository for Davis's data. According to her longtime secretary, Ruth Topping, Davis had intended for the completed questionnaires to be shared with "qualified" researchers. Yet in response to criticism of the survey's candid discussion of masturbation, Topping became increasingly reluctant to share even blank copies of the questionnaire. While "there had been exceptions when the use was for scientific or sociological purposes," she explained, given that "the results of the questionnaire had been published and were available to the public," there was little need for them to be distributed further. Meanwhile, the completed questionnaires mysteriously disappeared, foreclosing the possibility of further analysis of the painstakingly collected data.[15]

Despite the loss of the original data, Davis's study of women's sexuality, unsurpassed for scientific rigor or comprehensive coverage, was a landmark work of scholarship. Nearly two decades after its publication, Davis's colleague and collaborator Dr. Robert Latou Dickinson referred to *Factors* as "the pioneer factual analysis of sex-life."[16] Across the ocean, British sexologist Havelock Ellis recommended Davis's volume as one of three must-read studies.[17] And although foreign-language translation plans never came to fruition, Davis fielded correspondence from as far away as Finland, where one would-be translator, on the basis of advertisements in the *Scientific American*, thrilled, "I know your book—which I have not even seen as yet—must be a revelation to womankind."[18]

"The Ice Should Be Broken Sometime"

Davis's work certainly was a revelation to biology professor Alfred Kinsey, destined to become the nation's first celebrity sex researcher. In 1938, when Kinsey drew up a reading list for his pioneering sex education course at the University of Indiana, Davis's publications literally topped the list. Davis was not only the first author listed but also the only author to have two items featured: her 1926 article on "periodicity of sex desire" and her 1929 book, *Factors in the Sex Life of Twenty-Two Hundred Women*. Even the extremely prolific and internationally famous Havelock Ellis got only one recommendation. Indeed, Davis's publications accounted for more than one fifth of the entire list (which, indicating the sparse offerings, included only nine publications), demonstrating her outsized influence on Kinsey's course.[19]

The students who signed up for the "marriage course"—offered as a non–credit-bearing elective—responded enthusiastically to this material, finding accurate information, clearly conveyed, tremendously useful. One female student, in language that echoed that of some of Davis's survey respondents, wrote, "I believe a thorough understanding of one's own body means less fear of it." Another woman student, defending the controversial course in 1940, commented, "The persons who criticize [the lectures] are those who have not heard them, and still uphold Victorian views of prejudice and ignorance concerning sex and marriage relations. The ice should be broken sometime."[20]

Davis broke the ice. Moreover, Davis's influence on Kinsey was not limited to his teaching. Rather, building upon Davis's pathbreaking research—and with the financial support of the organization she founded—Kinsey published *Sexual Behavior in the Human Male* in 1948 and a follow-up volume, *Sexual Behavior in the Human Female*, in 1953.[21]

Kinsey's "Reports" became instant bestsellers. His book on male sexuality spent six weeks on *The New York Times* bestseller list, and his study of female sexuality appeared on the cover of *Time* magazine.[22] Kinsey was a savvy self-promoter as well as a serious scholar. He fused these talents into a media blitz, carried out in newspapers and magazines as well as on radio broadcasts and television appearances, that brought him celebrity status without undermining his scientific credentials. Indeed, Kinsey consistently emphasized his scientific mindset, scholarly detachment, and statistical methods, suggesting that his scholarly objectivity and scientific rigor made his research distinct from—and superior to—that of all of his predecessors.[23]

For all his claims of scientific objectivity, Kinsey had a clear agenda: to challenge prevailing moral codes. He used scientific evidence to challenge social norms, replacing moral judgments with numerical frequency as the gold standard of "normal" behavior. Even as Kinsey himself strenuously objected to the term "normal," preferring "average" or "typical," he was widely credited with being the first researcher to focus on "normal" sexuality, while simultaneously discrediting social "norms." Thus, for example, Kinsey documented the frequency of nonnormative behavior, such as masturbation, extramarital affairs, and homosexual relationships, thereby demonstrating that numerically "normal" behavior did not align with cultural "norms." As a result, Kinsey gained enormous cultural capital as "the father of the sexual revolution."[24]

But if Kinsey was the father of the sexual revolution, Davis was the founding mother of American sexology. As such, she not only recorded the nation's first sexual revolution but also laid the groundwork for the second by establishing the legitimacy of "the scientific study of sex" and framing the research agenda for decades to come. Davis both anticipated many of Kinsey's methods and conclusions and directly influenced his study. After using Davis's publications in his marriage course at the University of Indiana, Kinsey was so impressed by her quantitative methods, her nonjudgmental attitude, and the way she framed her questionnaire to elicit honest responses that he tried to get a copy of her original survey. (Although he was unable to procure a copy, he nonetheless modeled many of his interview questions on the survey questions she published in *Factors*.) He also found her way of coding same-sex relationships to encompass intense emotional connections, both with and without overt sexual contact, very intriguing—so much so that he built upon her insights to construct his famous "Kinsey Scale." Finally, Kinsey conducted his work with funding from the Committee for Research on the Problems of Sex, which owed both its existence and its funding to Davis.[25]

While Kinsey built upon Davis's work, he hardly advertised the fact. In modern parlance, one might even say that he "mansplained" it. Although Kinsey acknowledged Davis's work in his list of sources, in his many published interviews and public appearances, Kinsey presented his own study as pathbreaking in both approach and findings, emphasizing his large data set, his objective outlook, and his startling revelations about Americans' nonnormative behavior. By presenting himself as a pioneer, he effectively erased Davis from the narrative.[26]

"Too Little Known"

Davis had hoped that publishing her memoirs would ensure her place in history. But when she sought to publish her life story in the mid-1930s, publishing houses turned her down, saying that Davis was "too little known to make it likely to be a profitable undertaking." Adding insult to injury, they defined her simply as a social worker, overlooking her pathbreaking achievements as a sex researcher. "I felt as if I had been hit over the head," Davis despaired. She abandoned the project, never writing the chapters covering her years at the bureau and the sex study she wrote under its auspices.[27]

Nonetheless, *Factors in the Sex Life of Twenty-Two Hundred Women* was—and remains—a landmark achievement. Pathbreaking at the time of its publication and influential for decades afterward, Davis's study garnered increased attention during the second sexual revolution of the 1960s and 1970s. As American women demanded equality in bedrooms as well as boardrooms and as homosexual Americans fought for both visibility and civil rights, Davis's research became just as important as a historical artifact as it was as a sex study. Widely cited in works on women's history and LGBTIQ+ history, *Factors* demonstrated the long history of both women's sexuality and homosexuality in the United States and thereby validated a new generation's demands for sexual equality.[28] Indicating its continued influence, in recent decades, Davis's research has enjoyed a renaissance in both sexuality studies scholarship and sex education textbooks.[29]

Recent events have highlighted the continued relevance of Davis's research. The former schoolmistress launched her ambitious study to provide accurate information about women's actual sexual behavior as the basis for fact-based sexual education. Davis had hoped that the resulting sexual education programs would replace the sexual double standard with scientifically sound information. Such a program, if based on Davis's findings, would include reliable data about the prevalence of a variety of sexual practices that, at the time she conducted her study, were viewed as immoral or criminalized as illegal, including masturbation, contraception, and homosexuality.

And yet, nearly a century after Davis revealed the frequency of these activities and defined them as "normal," sex educators find themselves in the hot seat for broaching these still-controversial topics. One wonders what Davis—a veteran schoolteacher and sex education advocate—might think about the emergence of schools and sex education programs as an epicenter for contemporary culture wars focused on issues of sexuality.

In recent years, many educators have lost their jobs due to parental complaints and political outcry over discussions of sexuality. Much of this furor has focused on LGBTIQ+ material. After Florida adopted its infamous Parental Rights in Education Bill, commonly known as the "Don't Say Gay" bill, in 2022, many other states introduced similar legislation. Such laws—and the attitudes driving them—have had a chilling effect on classrooms throughout the nation. In Georgia, a teacher was fired for reading aloud to fifth graders from a book titled *My Shadow Is Purple*, about a child who cannot relate to the colors blue and pink, conventionally used to indicate masculinity and femininity. An Illinois junior high school English teacher was forced to resign after she recommended *The Book Is Gay*, which centers queer perspectives, to her students.[30] Davis, a former schoolteacher who devoted significant attention to same-sex relationships in the 1920s, likely would be dismayed at the ongoing debate over these subjects in schools a century later.

While the "Don't Say Gay" directive has received the most media attention, similar strictures apply to other topics Davis attempted to normalize in her study, such as masturbation. In 2021, a private school teacher in New York resigned in the aftermath of controversy over showing first-graders a film depicting cartoon characters discussing masturbation. Two years later, a Michigan health department employee encountered public criticism for a sexual education guide advising parents about discussing sexuality with their children. In particular, critics charged that a passage noting that it was normal for young children to experience "genital pleasure" was a directive for parents to teach their toddlers about masturbation.[31] Davis, an educator whose massive study of women's sexuality cast both youthful sexual experimentation and autoerotic activities as normal, probably would be disappointed to see these issues still a matter of political debate rather than the subject of scientific study.

Controversy over gender identity and sexual expression also has become a distinctive feature of contemporary American life. The resulting conflicts have engulfed state legislatures as well as school buildings. Pride flags and personal pronouns alike have become political battlegrounds, with some schools banning the display of the pro–LGBTIQ+ rights flags while others have roused parental ire by honoring students' requests to be referred to by their preferred pronouns. In response, some state lawmakers have proposed legislation limiting the display of the Pride flag; meanwhile, several separate cases involving parental rights and preferred pronouns have moved to federal appeals courts.[32]

Debates over transgender rights, often originating in the public education system, have moved well beyond the schoolhouse. Both youthful athletes and Olympic hopefuls now confront new restrictions on participating in girls' and women's sports as school districts and professional organizations alike enact bans on transgender participants. Many states also have proposed bans on gender-affirming care for transgender minors.[33]

While Davis never commented on either LGBTIQ+ or transgender rights, her admiration for European sexologists Havelock Ellis and Magnus Hirschfield, who were publicly supportive, suggests that she would find these developments disturbing. Moreover, while Davis devoted the first part of her career to upholding conventional morality, for the last decade of her professional life, she had come instead to advocate a "rational sex ethics" based on scientific data rather than on social mores. If she were to undertake her study today, one could imagine her compiling data on state laws regarding LGBTIQ+ rights, the frequency of gender dysphoria, and the typical age at which (and means by which) individuals choose to change their gender.

If schools are one battleground for contemporary culture wars, women's bodies are another. Nearly a century after Davis publicized women's widespread practice of all forms of birth control, including abortion, and advocated for the repeal of the Comstock Laws limiting reproductive rights, these issues have once again come to the forefront of our national consciousness.

Davis's and other activists' successful campaigns to protect free speech and reproductive rights curtailed the reach of the Comstock Laws for more than a century. However, these draconian restrictions still lurk in both federal law and statute books as "zombie" laws, ready to be reanimated by latter-day Comstockians intent on using state power to police sexuality. Nearly a hundred years after the publication of Davis's pathbreaking study of women's sexuality—in the aftermath of the Supreme Court's 2022 decision in *Dobbs v. Jackson Women's Health Organization*, which undermined privacy rights as well as curtailing abortion access, and in light of the explicit intent of Project 2025 to reinvigorate the Comstock Act—Davis's dream of achieving "a rational sex ethics" remains painfully relevant.[34]

Although she did not live to see these decisions, it is clear from her comments on family planning and the Comstock Laws that Davis would have applauded the Supreme Court decisions in *Griswold v. Connecticut* (1965) and *Roe v. Wade* (1973), which affirmed a constitutional right to privacy and ruled that both contraception and abortion fell under this protective umbrella, thereby sidestepping—but not overturning—the Comstock Act of 1873.

However, the Supreme Court ruling in *Dobbs v. Jackson Women's Health Organization* (2022), which returned control over abortion to individual states, also threatens to return the United States to Comstock-like control over women's bodies. In the aftermath of the court's decision, many states quickly enacted so-called trigger laws reinstating restrictions on access to abortion that effectively prohibit abortions under most circumstances, while still more states introduced new legislation to restrict or prohibit abortion.[35]

While pro- and anti-abortion activists fight legal battles in court, individual women find their control over their reproduction, their health, and their lives threatened. By 2020, medication abortions accounted for more than half of the procedures performed in the United States, but—in a neo-Comstockian move—several states have banned mailing abortion pills to patients, while other states have introduced legislation criminalizing medication abortions, banning the use of telehealth appointments to arrange such procedures, and even challenging Food and Drug Administration (FDA) approval of the medication used to induce abortions (as well as for several other purposes). In anticipation of increased restrictions, many Americans have begun to stockpile abortion pills.[36]

In this contentious environment, the legal status of medication abortions is unclear. In Nebraska, a mother-daughter duo faced criminal prosecution in 2023 after the mother provided her daughter with pills to terminate a pregnancy after the ten-week time frame specified by the FDA for the medication's use. Ultimately, the mother was sentenced to two years in prison on charges of providing an abortion after twenty weeks—the time frame then permitted by the state, which has since enacted a twelve-week abortion ban—as well as for disposing of the fetus. The daughter served three months in jail for the latter offense, heightening concerns that obtaining abortions may lead to criminal prosecution for both patients and providers.[37]

While federal legislation to protect women's reproductive rights has stalled, state legislation intended to limit or prohibit abortion has snowballed. In Texas, in addition to a near-total ban on abortion, a 2021 law permits legal actions against anyone who performs, assists, or even intends to aid in an abortion. The shifting status of abortion laws has led to legal jeopardy for medical providers and health risks for female patients.

In one infamous case in 2023, a mother of two carrying a nonviable fetus had to leave the state to terminate her dangerous pregnancy after the state's attorney general threatened legal action if Houston hospitals performed the procedure.[38]

Today, as in Davis's lifetime, poor women and women of color bear the brunt of reproductive restrictions. In early 2024, in Ohio, a Black woman in the midst of a medical emergency was denied medical attention because hospital authorities were concerned about the legal implications of providing her with an abortion beyond the state's permitted time frame, even though the pregnancy was nonviable and its continuation posed a serious risk to her health. After returning home, the woman endured a miscarriage on her own. The fetus became lodged in the plumbing for her toilet, and she was charged with abuse of a corpse. (Several months later, a grand jury declined to issue an indictment.)[39]

The 2024 presidential race brought both reproductive rights and sexual diversity to the forefront of public consciousness. Project 2025, which many regard as a playbook for a second Trump term, aims to enforce the Comstock Act, ban medication abortions, curb access to contraceptives, and defund Planned Parenthood. Although as a candidate, Republican presidential hopeful Donald Trump distanced himself from Project 2025, his running mate, J. D. Vance, made headlines (and inspired memes) for denigrating childless women. On the other hand, Democratic presidential candidate Kamala Harris and her running mate, Tim Walz, made reproductive rights central to their message on the campaign trail. Gender and sexuality also shared the spotlight during the presidential campaign. While Project 2025 proposed rescinding protections for LGBTIQ+ Americans, critics condemned "Tampon Tim" for making menstrual products available in public schools—potentially including boys' bathrooms.[40]

Since Trump took office and issued an immediate flood of executive orders—many of them targeting what he dubs "gender ideology extremism" and taking direct aim at reproductive healthcare and LGBTIQ+ rights—attention to these issues has increased exponentially. While these orders face legal challenges, the Trump administration's hostility to both women and sexual minorities has emboldened self-styled MAGA ("Make American Great Again") supporters to challenge constitutionally protected civil rights.[41]

Indeed, my final revisions were punctuated by the unwelcome news that a new court case has been filed with the intention of overturning the Supreme Court's landmark decision affirming the constitutionality of same-sex marriage. The court upheld the right to such unions in *Obergefell v. Hedges* in 2015; as it happens, I was actually in the nation's capital, conducting research for a biography of another feminist activist and likely lesbian, when the court rendered that verdict. Now, just ten years later, the right to legal marriage for what Davis called "'naturally' homosexual" citizens is once again in jeopardy.[42]

Today's headlines, by highlighting the ongoing importance of the issues that Davis studied, indicate the enduring significance of Davis's life work. In an era in which sex education, reproductive rights, and sexual diversity are all under attack, acknowledging this pioneering sexologist and revisiting her revelatory research is more important than ever.

ACKNOWLEDGMENTS

This is the story of a remarkable woman who dared to speak about sex at a time when the subject was shrouded in secrecy and steeped in stigma. Her frank discussions of sex education, sexual desire, and sexual diversity—as well as her findings on women's fertility control in the Comstock era, when federal and state laws severely curtailed access to both contraception and abortion—remain relevant today, when cultural and legal struggles over these issues are once again in the spotlight—and the Supreme Court.

In telling the story of this extraordinary woman, I have been fortunate beyond measure to have exclusive access to a private collection of Davis materials—including her "autobiographical biography," family correspondence, and personal memorabilia—held by her great-niece, Frances ("Francie") Garber Pepper. After her mother's death, Francie discovered a treasure trove of Davis materials in one of her closets; subsequently, she and her sister, Helen Garber, added copies of personal correspondence, news clippings, and organizational records to the "closet collection." Francie had intended to pen a biography of her estimable ancestor, but a serious illness had made it clear that she would not be able to complete the project. Thus, in early 2021, just as I was beginning to cast about for a new project that I could launch in the COVID-19 era, Francie contacted me to see if I was interested in writing a biography of Davis. I was indeed!

Like most scholars of US women's history, I had long been familiar with Davis's pathbreaking study of women's sexuality. Indeed, not only had I taught about the study, but I had consulted it for my previous book, a biography of yet another pioneering University of Chicago PhD. But, like many other scholars before me, I had been stymied by the lack of a curated collection of Davis's personal papers and by the loss of the original sex surveys, which seemed to render a biography—at least, a feminist biography that combined analysis of the personal, professional, and political dimensions of an individual's life—impossible. Now, though, I had the chance that every historian not-so-secretly dreams about: the opportunity to comb through a previously untapped set of sources. Moreover, I was able to do so from the comfort of my own home at a time when travel was out of the question. Thus, for the next several months, I eagerly welcomed weekly history care packages of photocopied materials from Francie's private collection.

Using the Pepper Papers as a starting point, I tracked clues and augmented family materials with archival collections and oral histories in multiple repositories across the country, including the Arthur and Elizabeth Schlesinger Library on the History of Women in America at the Radcliffe Institute for Advanced Study at Harvard University; the Kinsey Institute for Research in Sex, Gender, and Reproduction at Indiana University; the Lesbian Herstory Archives; the New York Academy of Medicine; the Old Lesbian Oral History Project at Smith College; the Social Welfare History Archives at the University of Minnesota; the Sophia Smith Collection of Women's History at Smith College; the Rockefeller Archive Center; the Department of Rare Books, Special Collections, and Preservation at the River Campus Libraries at the University of Rochester; the Harry Ransom Center at the University of Texas at Austin; the Archives and Special Collections Library at Vassar College; and the Vern and Bonnie Bullough Collection on Sex and Gender at the California State University, Northridge.

I am indebted to research librarians and other staff members at all these locations for their vital assistance in locating, scanning, copying, and photographing research materials during COVID-19-induced shutdowns as well as for their helpful guidance in utilizing digitized materials and their willingness to provide me with camera-ready images for the book.

Special thanks are due to Jennifer Fauxsmith at the Schlesinger Library, Gretchen Lieb at Vassar College, Samuel Edwards at Smith College, Caitlyn Nicholson at the Kinsey Institute, Margaret Purcell at the Old Lesbian Oral History Project at Smith College, Erin Fisher and Andrea G. Reithmayr at the University of Rochester, Michele Reilly at the University of Arkansas, Adrienne Rusinko at Princeton University, Arlene Shaner at the New York Academy of Medicine, and Saskia Scheffer and Desiree Yael Vester at the Lesbian Herstory Archives. Their assistance confirmed for me, yet again, that archivists and librarians are not only truly research superheroes but also genuinely nice people.

To round out my research in archival sources and oral histories, I sought out copies of Davis's many publications as well as the numerous articles written about her and her work during her long and noteworthy career. In this exacting endeavor, I was fortunate to have the financial support of Francie Pepper and her family and the assistance of Andrea G. Reithmayr and Kym MacEwan, who did stellar work in tracking down Davis materials in both national and local publications. The Peppers' support also allowed me to employ several other research assistants to help with late-stage queries; I am grateful to Danielle Brown, Cole Costello, and Cassidy Vander Voort for their timely aid in locating far-flung materials and nailing down last-minute details.

While research and writing can be a lonely business, I count myself fortunate in being part of a community who provide both emotional and practical support. The list of those who have cheered on this project—and cheered me up when I needed it!—is too long to recount here, but I want to extend special recognition to Soazig LeBihan, who has discussed this project—and lots of other things!—with me during countless dog walks and, more broadly, has been the best possible friend, as well as the best hiking buddy, I could wish for.

I am especially grateful to members of the Facebook "Writing Challenge" group. The facilitator, Pamela Toler, extended an invitation to join this group at a critical stage of this project, and I have benefited greatly from this virtual community. In addition to posting daily inspiring GIFs, group members have shared vicariously in the struggle of making headway on creative projects while also completing essential life tasks.

Essential life tasks were challenging for me while working on this book. In the five years I spent working on this book, I also had shoulder surgery and broke my foot; said farewell to one beloved dog and adopted another; survived Legionnaire's Disease and developed celiac disease; bought, sold, and moved houses; adopted two more dogs (puppies!); and helped purchase and renovate a condo for my mother. Throughout all of this, I relied heavily on my family and friends for emotional, practical, and financial support. Special thanks to my family—my partner, Maren Christensen, my mother, Jane Cress Edgar, my stepfather, Ralph Edgar, my uncle, David Cress, and my aunt, Barb McCullough—and my friends Kayla Blackman, Emily Greenwald, Sara Hayden, Soazig LeBihan, Jim Sevaly, Jennifer ("Niffer") Stackpole, and Leanne Young for essential support at various points along the way.

While fortune has not always been on my side during this process, I was fortunate to undertake this project at the same time that several other scholars were writing books on related topics. I'm happy to have shared this journey with Rebecca Davis, Stephanie Gorton, Wendy Kline, Margaret Grace Myers, and Brandy Schillace—whose recently published books have greatly enriched my own.

I also am extremely grateful to many additional scholars who generously shared insights, citations, and sources with me, including Miriam Cohen, Bruce Dorsey, Donna Drucker, Elizabeth Evens, Ellen Fitzpatrick, Lesley Hall, Kimberly Hamlin, Helen Lefkowitz Horowitz, Andy Kirschner, Catherine Prendergast, Helene Quanquin, Einav Rabinovitch-Fox, Wendy Rouse, Hugh Ryan, Sharon Spaulding, Scott W. Stern, Nick Syrett, Lauren MacIvor Thompson, Tiffany Wayne, Nancy Woloch, and Cookie Woolner. (Apologies to anybody I've accidentally omitted from this long list!)

Miriam Cohen at Vassar College went above and beyond by assigning her exceptional research assistant, Louise Ambler, to assist me with research there when first COVID-19 shutdowns and then my own illness prevented me from consulting materials in person.

The University of Montana has been my intellectual home base for thirty years, and I continue to benefit from institutional support and supportive colleagues across campus. I am extremely grateful to the History Department, which granted me both a research leave and a sabbatical in order to produce a first draft of the manuscript. The Humanities Institute not only provided me with a forum for an early exploration of this topic but also supported the publication of this book with a subvention to offset the price of publishing and indexing it. Special thanks also are due to the Women's, Gender, and Sexuality Studies Program, which provided me with a serene setting and congenial company during summer writing retreats at critical stages in the project.

While not an official writers' retreat, my frequent stays at Niffer Stackpole's country home greatly facilitated this project. Niffer shared her house with me, my partner, and our three dogs for several months when a plumbing emergency rendered our residence unlivable; hosted us on her extensive property when illness and injury made it impossible to adequately exercise our dogs in or near town; and generally gave this country-raised but town-based girl many opportunities to enjoy country living complete with all the modern amenities, including reliable Internet service. My self-styled "writing retreats" in the Montana countryside have been invaluable opportunities for recreation, research, writing, and revising in the most beautiful surroundings imaginable.

Every writer benefits from comments from people willing to read early drafts and respond to research presentations, and I am fortunate to have had many "beta readers" for this project. These include attendees at various public talks, ranging from an early presentation at Davis's alma mater, Vassar College, to a recent panel for Missoula Pride in conjunction with Brandy Schillace, whose book on German sex researcher and civil rights advocate Magnus Hirschfeld appeared just in time to help me trace European intellectual influences on Davis's thinking.

Audience members at events at UM's Humanities Institute and the Susan B. Anthony Museum helped me to identify intriguing avenues for further research and important issues for deeper analysis. Participants in the "Archival Kismet" virtual conferences organized by Courtney Thompson also posed thought-provoking questions and encouragement early in the project.

Input from editors of pieces I published along the way—Laura Ansley and others at *Nursing Clio*; Kathryn Cramer Brownell at *The Washington Post*; Laura Crossley, Chelsea Gibson, and Evan Hart at the Society for Historians of the Gilded Age and Progressive Era; Michan Connor at *History News Network*; Joshua Greenberg at *Commonplace*; Nick Lehr at *The Conversation–US*; Alexandra Rutherford at the *Journal of the History of the Behavioral Sciences*; and April White at *Atlas Obscura*—also helped me to clarify both my thinking and my writing.

Speaking of clarifying my thinking and my writing, I am indebted to my agent, Deirdre Mullane at Mullane Literary Associates, for helping me to conceptualize and realize this project. From the moment she responded favorably to my initial query in April 2022—I still have her email with the subject line "Ok! Let's get started!"—she has been a keen reader, a careful editor, and a tireless advocate—and she even brought me home-baked scones when I was in the neighborhood! Likewise, I am grateful to my editor, Clara Platter at NYU Press, for taking on this project and responding promptly and patiently to my many queries throughout the process. Many other people at the press—as well as the anonymous readers for the draft manuscript—also made essential contributions to the final product.

From start to finish, I've had the benefit of the very best beta reader: my partner, Maren Christensen. With unstinting support and keen insights, she has helped me think through challenging intellectual issues, rework tricky passages in the manuscript, and navigate the twists and turns of the publishing process—while also making sure I take breaks to take care of myself and enjoy the outdoors with our three doodles, Cosmo, Maisie, and Otis.

Finally, I extend my deepest gratitude to Davis family members—especially Francie Pepper, John Pepper, and Helen Garber—who not only supplied original sources, subsidized research costs, and shared family photos and memorabilia but also were insightful interlocutors and steadfast supporters throughout the lengthy process of researching and writing this book.

ABBREVIATIONS

AAVC Vassar College Alumnae/i Biographical Files, VCSC

A/B Autobiographical Biography, PP

ACK Alfred C. Kinsey

AF Abraham Flexner

ANCESTRY www.ancestry.com

BSH Bureau of Social Hygiene

COPELAND COLLECTION A Member of the Class of '91, "Letters Home," Student Materials, Box 67 VCSC

CSA College Settlement Association

DENNETT PAPERS Women's Studies Manuscript Collections from Schlesinger Library, Radcliffe College, Series 3: Sexuality, Sex Education, and Reproductive Rights, Part B: The Papers of Mary Ware Dennett and the Voluntary Parenthood League

ERNST PAPERS Morris Leopold Ernst Papers, 359.5, Harry Ransom Center, University of Texas, Austin, Texas

HAD Helen Alling Davis

HERSTORIES Lesbian Elders Oral Herstory Project, LHA

JDR John D. Rockefeller Jr.

JGAPE *Journal of the Gilded Age and Progressive Era*

JPE *Journal of Political Economy*

KBD Katharine Bement Davis

KEB DIARIES Katherine E. Bragdon Diaries, UR

KINSEY INSTITUTE Kinsey Institute, Indiana University, Bloomington, Indiana

LAIDLAW PAPERS Harriet Wright Burton Laidlaw Papers, Schlesinger

LBD Lawrence B. Dunham

LC Library of Congress, Washington, DC

LHA Lesbian Herstory Archives, New York, New York

MB DIARIES May Bragdon Diaries, UR

MHOH Mabel Hampton Oral History Collection, LHA

MS Margaret Sanger

NYAM New York Academy of Medicine, New York, New York

NYT New York Times

NY TRIBUNE New York Tribune

OLOHP Old Lesbian Oral History Project, Smith

OMR Office of the Messrs. Rockefeller

OWENS PAPERS Helen Brewster Owens Papers, Schlesinger

PP Pepper Papers, a private collection used by permission of Frances Garber Pepper, Cincinnati, Ohio

PROCEEDINGS Proceedings of the International Conference of Women Physicians, 6 vols. (Woman's Press, 1920)

RAC Rockefeller Archives Center, Sleepy Hollow, New York

RB Rockefeller Boards

RBF Raymond B. Fosdick

RLD Robert Latou Dickinson

RT Ruth Topping

SCHLESINGER Schlesinger Library, Harvard University, Cambridge, Massachusetts

SMITH Sophia Smith Collection, Smith College, Northampton, Massachusetts

SWHA Social Welfare History Archives, University of Minnesota, Minneapolis, Minnesota

UR Rare Books, Special Collections & Preservation, University of Rochester River Campus Libraries, Rochester, New York

VCSC Vassar College Special Collections, Poughkeepsie, New York

VLBP Vern L. Bullough Papers, Vern and Bonnie Bullough Collection on Sex and Gender, Special Collections and Archives, California State University, Northridge

YWCA YWCA of the USA Records, Record Group 11 (Microfilmed Headquarters Files), Smith College

NOTES

INTRODUCTION

1 "A Distinguished Woman," Rochester *Times-Union*, December 12, 1935, clipping; and "Funeral Service of Noted Woman Held Yesterday," clipping, December 12, 1935, PP.

2 Ellen Fitzpatrick, *Endless Crusade: Women Social Scientists and Progressive Reform* (Oxford University Press, 1990).

3 KBD, *Factors in the Sex Life of Twenty-Two Hundred Women* (Harper & Brothers, 1929).

4 KBD, A/B.

5 KBD, "A Study of the Sex Life of the Normal Married Woman, III: The Happiness of Married Life—Continued," *Journal of Social Hygiene* 9, no. 3 (March 1923): 129–46, quotation on 130 ("matters of sex"); KBD, *Factors*, xi ("normal"); KBD to JDR, April 27, 1927, OMR, RB, FA324, Series O, Box 7, Folder 7, RAC; and Brett Gary, *Dirty Works: Obscenity on Trial in America's First Sexual Revolution* (Stanford University Press, 2021).

6 "Mrs. Catt Selects 12 Greatest Women," New York *Herald*, June 12, 1922, 20.

7 Fitzpatrick, *Endless Crusade*.

8 "Mrs. Catt Selects 12 Greatest Women."

9 KBD, *Factors*, xi.

10 Gary, *Dirty Works*, chaps. 2 and 7.

11 Kimberly A. Hamlin et al., "The History and Legacy of Anthony Comstock and the Comstock Laws," *JGAPE* 23, no. 4 (October 2024): 431–37 (and entire special issue).

12 Amy Sohn, *The Man Who Hated Women: Sex, Censorship, and Civil Liberties in the Gilded Age* (Farrar, Straus and Giroux, 2021).

13 Reva B. Siegel and Mary Ziegler, "Comstockery: How Government Censorship Gave Birth to the Law of Sexual and Reproductive Freedom, and May Again Threaten It," *Yale Law Journal* 134, no. 4 (February 2025): 1068–1181.

14 KBD, "Women's Education in Social Hygiene," *Annals of the American Academy of Political and Social Science* 79 (September 1918): 167–77, quotation 167–68 ("conspiracy of silence"); and KBD, "A Study of the Sex Life of the Normal Married Woman, III," 130 ("sane outlook").

15 KBD, "A Plan of Rational Treatment for Women Offenders," *Journal of the American Institute of Criminal Law and Criminology* 4 (September 1913): 403.

16 KBD, "Social Hygiene and the War: Woman's Part in Social Hygiene," *Journal of Social Hygiene* 4, no. 4 (October 1918): 526 ("taboo"); KBD, *Factors*, 394 ("distorted views").

17 KBD, "Sex Life of the Normal Married Woman, III," 130 ("matters pertaining to sex"); and KBD to JDR ("scientific study of sex"), April 27, 1927, OMR, RB, FA324, Series O, Box 7, Folder 7, RAC.

18 KBD to JDR, January 24, 1928, OMR, RB, FA324, Series O, Box 7, Folder 44, RAC.

19 KBD, *Factors*, xi; see also Nancy F. Cott, "Passionlessness: An Interpretation of Victorian Sexual Ideology, 1790–1850," *Signs* 4, no. 2 (Winter 1978): 219–36.

20 Richard Rhodes, "Father of the Sexual Revolution," *NYT*, November 2, 1997, BR10.

21 KBD, "Sex Life of the Normal Married Women, III," 130.

22 Harriet B. Laidlaw [to Valeria Parker], n.d. [ca. February 2, 1928], PP.

23 KBD to Paul Kellogg, June 14, 1933, Survey Records, Folder 468, SWHA.

24 KBD to Paul Kellogg, June 14, 1933, Survey Records, Folder 468, SWHA; and KBD, A/B.

25 Internal Memo, Paul Kellogg, June 19, 1933, Survey Records, Folder 468, SWHA; and KBD, A/B.

26 KBD to Paul Kellogg, June 14, 1933, Survey Records, Folder 468, SWHA.

27 Paul Kellogg to KBD, June 30, 1933, Survey Records, Folder 468, SWHA.

28 Manuscript Description and Table of Contents, enclosed in KBD to Paul Kellogg, June 14, 1933, Survey Records, Folder 468, SWHA.

29 KBD to JDR, January 24, 1928, OMR, RB, FA324, Series O, Box 7, Folder 44, RAC.

30 Caroline Furness to Miss Barden, January 15, 1936; and HAD to Caroline E. Furness, February 7, 1936, AAVC Biographical File, VCSC.

31 Manuscript Description, June 14, 1933, Survey Records, Folder 468, SWHA; and KBD, A/B.

32 Susan Ware, "The Book I Couldn't Write: Alice Paul and the Challenge of Feminist Biography," *Journal of Women's History* 24, no. 2 (2012): 13–36.

33 KBD, A/B; and Thomas C. McCarthy, "New York City's Suffragist Commissioner" (NYC Department of Correction, 1997), www.correctionhistory.org, retrieved January 15, 2020.

34 KBD, A/B.

35 KBD, A/B; and New York Census, 1865, 1870, 1875, Ancestry.

36 Manuscript Description and Table of Contents, enclosed in KBD to Paul Kellogg, June 14, 1933, Survey Records, Folder 468, SWHA.

37 KBD, A/B.

38 Manuscript Description, June 14, 1933, Survey Records, Folder 468, SWHA.

39 KBD, A/B; and MB Diaries and KEB Diaries.

40 KBD, A/B.

41 Manuscript Description, June 14, 1933, Survey Records, Folder 468, SWHA.

42 May Bragdon, "Among the Islands of Georgian Bay," *Recreation* 20, no. 1 (January 1904): 413–19 (quotation).

43 "From My Window," KBD, A/B.

44 New York Census, 1915; US Census, 1920, Ancestry; KBD, A/B; and "Weddings of the Week," Rochester *Democrat and Chronicle*, September 2, 1935, 10.

45 Beatrice Oppenheim, "Criminologist Now a 'Kitchen Chemist,'" Brooklyn *Daily Eagle*, September 1927, clipping, PP; and "Dr. Davis Dies," *New York Herald Tribune*, December 11, 1935, 20.

46 Christmas card, 1931, PP.

47 Caroline Furness to Miss Barden, February 7, 1936, AAVC, VCSC; see also "Dr. K. B. Davis Dies Today in Pacific Grove," Monterey *Peninsula*, December 10, 1935, clipping; and JDR to KBD, February 19, 1935, PP.

48 Joyce Antler, "'After College, What?': New Graduates and the Family Claim," *American Quarterly* 32, no. 4 (Fall 1980): 409–34; and Patricia A. Palmieri, "Patterns of Achievement of Single Academic Women at Wellesley College, 1880–1920," *Frontiers* 5, no. 1 (Spring 1980): 62–67, especially 64–65.

49 KBD, A/B.

50 MB Diaries, June 15, 1896.

51 Anya Jabour, "Out of the Closet? Reconstructing the Personal Life of Pioneering Sex Researcher Katharine Bement Davis," *Journal of the History of the Behavioral Sciences* 58, no. 4 (2022): 459–66.

52 KBD, A/B.

53 KBD, A/B; and Mary B. Harris, *I Knew Them in Prison* (Viking Press, 1936).

54 KBD to "My dear Bedford Family," November 21, 1908; and Agnes Crowley to Helen Towey, January 30, 1928, PP.

55 Blanche Snow to KBD, February 2, 1928, PP.

56 On Topping, see Ruth Topping passport application, December 4, 1918, Ancestry; "Society," Washington *Evening Star*, November 3, 1927, 19; RT to KBD, March 30, 1932, BSH, Series 1, Box 1, File 61, RAC. On Kopp, see RT to Frank Lorimer, October 17, 1931, BSH, Projects, Social Hygiene Series 3.2, Folder 179, RAC; and Folder 175: Committee for Maternal Health: Miscellaneous, BSH,

Projects, Social Hygiene Series 3.2, Folder 183: Marie Kopp, 1932–1934, RAC; and Marie E. Kopp, *Birth Control in Practice: Analysis of Ten Thousand Case Histories of the Birth Control Clinical Research Bureau* (1933; rpt. Arno Press, 1972).

57 See Stephanie Gorton, *The Icon and the Idealist: Margaret Sanger, Mary Ware Dennett, and the Rivalry That Brought Birth Control to America* (HarperCollins, 2024).

58 See for instance MS to KBD, January 4, 1923, October 19, 1925, November 12, 1927, and December 12, 1927; and KBD to MS, September 25, 1925, October 7 and 15, 1925, October 6, 1926, December 12, 1927, and January 23, 1929, Sanger Papers, LC, copies in PP; MS to KBD, April 4, 1925, May 2, [1925], May 11, 1925, September 24, 1925, October 11, 1926; and KBD to MS, December 28, 1926, RAC, copies in PP; and KBD to MS, April 14, 1927, Philosophical Society Library, copy in PP. On the Committee on Maternal Health, see letterhead for Norman E. Himes to Mary Ware Dennett, September 4, 1930, Dennett Papers.

59 "Resolution," [1915], Laidlaw Papers: Correspondence, 1917 (A-63, folder 140), Schlesinger; Ruth McCormick to Mary Ware Dennett, February 15, 1915, Dennett Papers.

60 KBD to Morris Ernst, February 1, 1929, Ernst Papers; and Mary Ware Dennett Defense Committee Minutes, June 13, 1929, Dennett Papers.

61 Anya Jabour, "'No Men Need Apply': How a Group of 'Perfect Little Ladies' Challenged Gender Norms in Turn-of-the-Century New York," *Women's History Network*, February 7, 2022; and Anya Jabour, "'Perfect Little Ladies': Female Friendship and New Womanhood in Rochester, New York, 1896–1914," in Slav N. Gratchev, Ida Day, and Larry Sheret, eds., *Female Friendship: Literary and Artistic Explorations* (Lexington Books, 2022), 125–42.

62 KBD, A/B.

63 KBD, A/B; and KBD, *Factors*.

64 JDR to Abraham B. Flexner, October 28, 1913, and KBD to Abraham B. Flexner, November 6, 1913, BSH Papers, Folder 171: Commercialized Prostitution in New York, RAC; see also Joanna Scutts, *Hotbed: Bohemian Greenwich Village and the Secret Club That Sparked Modern Feminism* (Seal Press, 2022); Judith Schwartz, *Radical Feminists of Heterodoxy: Greenwich Village, 1912–1940* (New Victoria Publishers, 1986); Christine Stansell, *American Moderns: Bohemian New York and the Creation of a New Century* (Princeton University Press, 2000); and Kate E. Wittenstein, "The Heterodoxy Club and American Feminism, 1912–1930" (PhD dissertation, Boston University, 1989).

65 New York Census, 1915, US Census, 1920, Ancestry; and George Chauncey, *Gay New York: Gender, Urban Culture, and the Making of a Gay Male World, 1890–1940* (1994; rev. Basic Books, 2019); Schwartz, *Radical Feminists of Heterodoxy*; Scutts, *Hotbed*; and Wittenstein, "Heterodoxy Club."

66 *Proceedings*.

67 See for example "Dr. Davis Dies; 1st Woman to Run City's Jails," New York *Herald-Tribune*, December 11, 1935 (clipping); and "Dr. Davis Dies in California," New York *Sun*, December 11, 1935 (clipping), PP; and "Katharine Davis, Reformer, 75, Dead," *NYT*, December 11, 1935.

68 See for instance Linda Gordon, *The Moral Property of Women: A History of Birth Control Politics in America* (University of Illinois Press, 1974), 390n19; Lillian Faderman, *Odd Girls and Twilight Lovers: A History of Lesbian Life in Twentieth-Century America* (Columbia University Press, 1991), 313n14.

69 Alysha Maree Crossan, "Liberals, Ground Breakers, and Graduate Students: Reinvestigating US Sex Surveys and Research Before Kinsey, 1900–1953" (PhD diss., University of Auckland, 2022), chap. 3; John D'Emilio and Estelle Freedman, *Intimate Matters: A History of Sexuality in America* (Harper & Row, 1988), 171–73, 175–78, 180, 193–94; Margot Francis, "'For This Girl Was My Grand Passion': Re-Interpreting the First Large-Scale Survey of Women's Sexuality in America (1929)," *Canadian Woman Studies* 16, no. 2 (Spring 1996): 36–41; Sarah Stage, "What 'Good Girls' Do: Katharine Bement Davis and the Moral Panic of the First U.S. Sexual Survey," in B. Fahs et al., eds., *The Moral Panics of Sexuality* (Palgrave Macmillan 2013), 151–63; and Leslie A. Taylor, "Veritable Hotbeds: Lesbian Scandals in the United States, 1926–1936" (PhD diss., University of Iowa,

1998), chap. 1; and Jennifer Terry, *An American Obsession: Science, Medicine, and Homosexuality in Modern Society* (Chicago University Press, 1999), 126–35.

70 Esme Louise James, *Kinky History: The Stories of Our Intimate Lives, Past and Present* (Pantera Press, 2023), chap. 1; and Rebecca L. Davis, *Fierce Desires: A New History of Sex and Sexuality in America* (Norton, 2024), 214–15.

71 Rhoda E. McCulloch, "The 'Next Things' of One Woman's Life," 207(quotation)–8, clipping from *Association Monthly*, PP.

72 Mabel Jacques Eichel, "Katharine Bement Davis," *Woman's Journal*, April 1928, 20–21.

73 "Woman's Work for Woman," *New York Age*, February 11, 1928, clipping in PP.

CHAPTER 1. "TO WORK FOR AN IDEAL AS WELL AS FOR A LIVING"

1 Amy L. Reed, "Katharine Bement Davis," *Vassar Quarterly* 21, no. 4 (February 15, 1936): 18.

2 "Katharine B. Davis Was Roommate of Mary Swain Wagner at College," Poughkeepsie *Evening Enterprise*, February 20, 1915, 8.

3 Reed, "Katharine Bement Davis," 18.

4 KBD to JDR, April 27, 1927, OMR, RB, FA324, Series O, Box 7, Folder 7, RAC.

5 Rebecca Deming Moore, *When They Were Girls* (F.A. Owen, 1923), 76–77.

6 Moore, *When They Were Girls*, 78; see also KBD, A/B; Ella Caroline Lapham, "Katharine Bement Davis," *Vassar Miscellany* 43, no. 6 (April 1, 1914): 433–38, especially 433; US Census, 1850, 1860; New York Census, 1855; New York Compiled Marriage Index, Ancestry; and Glenn C. Altschuler and Jan M. Saltzgaber, *Revivalism, Social Conscience, and Community in the Burned-Over District: The Trial of Rhoda Bement* (Cornell University Press), 1983.

7 KBD, A/B.

8 KBD, A/B; US Census, 1860, Ancestry; and Lapham, "Katharine Bement Davis," 434.

9 Davis O. Stowell, *Streets, Railroads, and the Great Strike of 1877* (University of Chicago Press, 1999), especially 96–115; New York Census, 1865, 1870, 1875, Ancestry.

10 KBD, A/B.

11 For quotation, see KBD to JDR, December 21, 1927, OMR, RB, FA324, Series O, Box 8, Folder 44, RAC; see also KBD, A/B; US Census, 1880; New York Census, 1892; and Rochester City Directories, 1878–1909, Ancestry.

12 KBD, A/B.

13 MB Diaries, May 15, 1896.

14 KBD, A/B.

15 KBD, A/B.

16 KBD, A/B.

17 KBD, A/B; and Moore, *When They Were Girls*, 75–76.

18 KBD, A/B; and Jane H. Hunter, *How Young Ladies Became Girls: The Victorian Origins of American Girlhood* (Yale University Press, 2002), chaps. 2 and 3.

19 KBD, A/B.

20 KBD, A/B; and Moore, *When They Were Girls*, 75–76.

21 KBD, A/B; US Census, 1900 ("Harriet Cary"), Ancestry.

22 KBD, A/B; see also Martha Vicinus, *Intimate Friends: Women Who Loved Women, 1778–1928* (University of Chicago Press, 2004), 109.

23 KBD, A/B.

24 KBD, A/B; see also Lucy Maud Montgomery, *Anne of Green Gables* (L.C. Page, 1908), chap. 19.

25 KBD, A/B.

26 KBD, A/B.

27 KBD, A/B.

28 KBD, A/B.

29 KBD, A/B; Cornell University Yearbook, 1878, 76, Ancestry; and "Mrs. Harriet Cary, 84, Dies Friday at Plymouth Hospital," *Sheboygan Press*, January 30, 1943, 2.

30 KBD, A/B.
31 KBD, A/B.
32 KBD, A/B.
33 “Recollections of Mrs. Daniel Hawthorn,” PP.
34 “Recollections of Mrs. Daniel Hawthorn,” PP.
35 “Recollections of Mrs. Daniel Hawthorn,” PP.
36 KBD, A/B.
37 “What Girls Can Do,” Springfield (MA) *Daily Republican*, November 19, 1918,
38 KBD, A/B.
39 “Who’ll Be Husband to K. B. Davis?,” *NY Tribune*, April 8, 1914, 5; see also KBD, A/B.

40 KBD, A/B. See also Miriam Cohen, *Julia Lathrop: Social Service and Progressive Government* (Routledge, 2017); Marjorie N. Feld, *Lillian Wald: A Biography* (University of North Carolina Press, 2012); Estelle B. Freedman, *Maternal Justice: Miriam Van Waters and the Female Reform Tradition* (University of Chicago Press, 1996); Anya Jabour, *Sophonisba Breckinridge: Championing Women’s Activism in Modern America* (University of Illinois Press, 2019); and Louise W. Knight, *Citizen: Jane Addams and the Struggle for Democracy* (University of Chicago Press, 2005).

41 Class of 1892 Letters, VCSC.

42 “Alma Mater, Vale!,” *Rochester Democrat and Chronicle*, June 28, 1879, 6; see also Program, Rochester Free Academy 1879 Graduating Exercises, June 17, 1897, PP.

43 Geraldine Joncich Clifford, *Those Good Gertrudes: A Social History of Women Teachers in America* (Johns Hopkins University Press, 2014).

44 “Western New York News,” *Rochester Democrat and Chronicle*, August 30, 1881, 2; “State and Vicinity News,” *Buffalo Evening News*, December 24, 1887, 2; “Want More Pay,” *Westfield Republican*, February 15, 1888, 1; and Lapham, “Katharine Bement Davis,” 434.

45 Clipping, February 2, 1928, PP; see also Patricia Marks, *Bicycles, Bangs, and Bloomers: The New Woman in the Popular Press* (University Press of Kentucky, 1990).

46 MB Diaries, June 15, 1896; see also Lapham, “Katharine Bement Davis,” 434.

47 KBD, A/B.

48 KBD, A/B; Clipping, February 2, 1928, PP; Lapham, “Katharine Bement Davis”; “Women’s Literary Society,” *Dunkirk Observer-Journal*, April 13, 1889, 4; “In the Vicinity,” *Buffalo Daily Courier*, April 15, 1888, 1; “The Loaded Hand-Bag: Woman’s Work in One or Two Neighboring Towns,” *Buffalo Express*, November 21, 1890, 8; *Dunkirk Women’s Literary Society Calendar* (privately published, 1890); Association for the Advancement of Women, *Historical Account of the Association for the Advancement of Women* (1893); and Ann Dodds Costello, *Smart Women: The Search for America’s Historic All-Women’s Study Clubs* (Lulu, 2015), chap. 6.

49 “Advancement of Women,” *Boston Herald*, October 12, 1882; “Woman’s Congress,” *Woman’s Journal*, October 21, 1882, 332; Ella C. Lapham, “The Woman’s Congress,” *Woman’s Journal*, March 8, 1884, 80; “Woman’s Duty to Woman,” *Forum* 1 (1886): 455–67; “Woman’s Kingdom: Ella C. Lapham on Woman’s Duty to Woman,” *Daily Inter Ocean*, July 3, 1886, 11; “Woman’s Duty to Woman,” *Woman’s Journal*, July 17, 1886, 232; “A.A.W.—The Woman’s Congress,” *Woman’s Journal*, November 24, 1888, 378; “Female Suffrage,” *Rocky Mountain News*, October 11, 1889, 7; “For the Advancement of Women,” *NY Tribune*, October 18, 1890, 7; and Anne Firor Scott, *Natural Allies: Women’s Associations in American History* (University of Chicago Press, 1992).

50 “Want More Pay”; “Women’s Educational and Industrial Union of Dunkirk,” *Silver Creek Local*, November 2, 1888, 2; and “Not a Man Was Present,” *Chicago Daily Tribune*, April 24, 1890, 2.

51 Lapham, “Katharine Bement Davis,” 434; and KBD, A/B.

52 KBD, “Another Jubilee,” *Vassar Quarterly* 1, no. 1 (February 1916): 8(quotation)–12. See also Helen Lefkowitz Horowitz, *Alma Mater: Design and Experience in the Women’s Colleges from Their Nineteenth-Century Beginnings to the 1930s* (Knopf, 1985); and Joan Marie Johnson, *Southern Women at the Seven Sister Colleges: Feminist Values and Social Activism, 1875–1915* (University of Georgia Press, 2008).

53 May Copeland to Kate Copeland, October 1, 1887, Copeland Collection, VCSC.

54 Lapham, "Katharine Bement Davis," 434; and KBD, A/B.

55 KBD, A/B.

56 "Cloudy Night Friend," *Katonah Record*, June 18, 1915, 6; "Miss Wagner Tells History of Inn," *Vassar Miscellany News* 9, no. 21 (December 13, 1924): 3; and Mary Swain Wagner, "Katharine Bement Davis at College," *Life and Labor* 4 (1914): 308–9.

57 Caroline Furness to Mary Furness Baker, October 12, 1889, Caroline Furness Papers, VCSC.

58 Caroline Furness to Mary Furness Baker, November 2, 1890 (quotation); see also January 22, 1890, September 9, 1890, and October 6, 1890, Furness Papers, VCSC; and Patricia Ann Palmieri, *In Adamless Eden: The Community of Women Faculty at Wellesley* (Yale University Press, 1995), chap. 11.

59 Wagner, "Katharine Bement Davis at College," 309; and KBD, A/B.

60 Wagner, "Katharine Bement Davis at College," 309; and KBD, A/B.

61 KBD, A/B.

62 KBD, A/B; Horowitz, *Alma Mater*, chap. 11; Wagner, "Katharine Bement Davis at College," 308–9; and Caroline Vandenburgh to Family, September 28, 1890, Vandenburgh Letters, VCSC.

63 Reed, "Katharine Bement Davis," 18.

64 Wagner, "Katharine Bement Davis at College," 309.

65 Wagner, "Katharine Bement Davis at College," 309. See also Anya Jabour, "In the Victorian Era, Valentine's Day Was a Celebration of Same-Sex Romance," *Atlas Obscura*, February 14, 2023; and Wendy L. Rouse, "'A Very Crushable, Kissable Girl': Queer Love and the Invention of the Abnormal Girl Among College Women in the Gilded Age and Progressive Era," *JGAPE* 21, no. 3 (July 2022): 201–20.

66 KBD, *Factors*, chaps. 10–11.

67 KBD, "Why They Failed to Marry," *Harper's Monthly*, March 1928, 460–69, quotation on 466.

68 Caroline Furness to Mary Furness Baker, November 24, 1889, Furness Papers, VCSC.

69 "Miss Wagner Tells History of Inn."

70 May Copeland to Kate Copeland, October 8, 1887, Copeland Collection (quotation), VCSC; see also Florence (Halliday) Gorham '91 (Album 75), VCSC; Natte Fortier, "Framing Femininity: Opportunities for Gender Non-Conformity at U.S. Women's Colleges at the Turn of the Twentieth Century," *Undergraduate Research Awards*, Hollins University (2024), 15–20; and Vicinus, *Intimate Friends*, chap. 7.

71 KBD, A/B; "Western New York News," *Rochester Democrat and Chronicle*, April 5, 1883; "The Union Festival," *Dunkirk Evening Observer*, February 14, 1890, 4.

72 May Copeland to Mother, March 1, 1890, Copeland Collection, VCSC.

73 "Union Festival."

74 Caroline Vandenburgh to Family, September 28, 1890, Vandenburgh Letters, VCSC; May Copeland to Kate Copeland, October 1, 1887, Copeland Collection, VCSC; Mary (Reed) Earl Diary, March 1892, VCSC; and Mary (Lamson) Lockwood (VC 1890) Album 147, VCSC.

75 Lapham, "Katharine Bement Davis," 434; and Caroline Vandenburgh to Family, Sept. 28, 1890, Vandenburgh Letters, VCSC.

76 May Copeland Diary, April 22, [1888], Copeland Collection, VCSC; and Horowitz, *Alma Mater*, 193–94.

77 Mary Earl Diary, November 1891, VCSC.

78 "The Y.M.C.A.," *Dunkirk Evening Observer*, January 29, 1885, 4; and Mary Earl Diary, November 1891, VCSC.

79 "The Missing Term of the Food Problem," *Vassar Miscellany* 21, no. 9 (June 1892): 470(first quotation)–75(second quotation).

80 KBD, A/B.

81 Megan J. Elias, *Stir It Up: Home Economics in American Culture* (University of Pennsylvania Press, 2008); and Sarah Stage and Virginia B. Vincenti, eds., *Rethinking Home Economics: Women and the History of a Profession* (Cornell University Press, 1997).

82 “Commencement at Vassar,” *NY Tribune*, June 9, 1892, 5.

83 KBD, A/B.

84 “Woman’s Sphere in 1915,” Owens Papers. Suffrage. Empire State Campaign Committee Press Bureau Releases, May–July 1915. A-147, Folder 64, Schlesinger; see also Antler, “‘After College, What?’”

CHAPTER 2. “A SCIENTIFIC REFORMER”

1 Reed, “Katharine Bement Davis,” 18; and Joseph W. Barnes, “Katharine B. Davis and the Workingman’s Model Home of 1893,” *Rochester History* 43, no. 1 (January 1981): 1–20.

2 “A Scientific Reformer,” Rochester *Union and Advertiser*, April 12, 1894, 6.

3 KBD, A/B; “Personal,” Dunkirk *Evening Observer*, July 21, 1892, 1; and Personals, *Vassar Miscellany* 22, no. 1 (October 1, 1892): 33.

4 KBD, A/B; “Scientific Reformer.”

5 KBD, “The Scope of Domestic Science,” *Vassar Miscellany* 23, no. 7 (April 1, 1894): 273–80, quotations 273, 275, 276.

6 KBD, “Scope of Domestic Science,” 279–80.

7 KBD, *Report on the Exhibit of the Workingman’s Model Home as Exhibited by the State of New York at the World’s Columbian Exposition* (James B. Lyon, 1893).

8 “About Women,” *Far and Near* 4, no. 37 (November 1893): 15; KBD, A/B; Light Carruyo, “Gender, Race, and the Status of Household Labour in Lucy Maynard Salmon’s *Domestic Service* (1897),” *Women’s History Review* 31, no. 7 (2022): 1127–48; and Lucy Maynard Salmon Papers, VCSC.

9 KBD, A/B; and Barbara J. Harris, *Beyond Her Sphere: Women and the Professions in American History* (Bloomsbury Academic, 1978).

10 Barbara Miller Solomon, *In the Company of Educated Women: A History of Women and Higher Education in America* (Yale University Press, 1985), chap. 6.

11 Gayle Gullett, “‘Our Great Opportunity’: Organized Women Advance Women’s Work at the World’s Columbian Exposition of 1893,” *Illinois Historical Journal* 87, no. 4 (Winter 1994): 259–76.

12 “Social and Personal,” *Westfield Republican*, December 13, 1893, 6.

13 “Alumnae Department,” *Vassar Miscellany* 23, no. 2 (November 1, 1893): 79–82, quotation on 80.

14 “Editor’s Table,” *Vassar Miscellany* 22, no. 1 (May 1, 1893): 429.

15 KBD, *Report on the Exhibit of the Workingman’s Model Home*, 395.

16 KBD, *Report on the Exhibit of the Workingman’s Model Home*, quotation on 407; see also 411–13.

17 “Model Workingman’s Home,” *Milwaukee Sentinel*, June n.d., 1893, 7.

18 KBD, *Report on the Exhibit of the Workingman’s Model Home*, 398.

19 KBD, *Report on the Exhibit of the Workingman’s Model Home*, 399, 401.

20 KBD, *Report on the Exhibit of the Workingman’s Model Home*, 421–25; and “About Women.”

21 Lapham, “Katharine Bement Davis”; and KBD, *Report on the Exhibit of the Workingman’s Model Home*, 442.

22 “Economical Housekeeping,” Rochester *Union and Advertiser*, April 13, 1894, 9.

23 KBD, *Report on the Exhibit of the Workingman’s Model Home*, 414(quotations)–424; and “Economical Housekeeping.”

24 KBD, *Report on the Exhibit of the Workingman’s Model Home*, 426.

25 KBD, *Report on the Exhibit of the Workingman’s Model Home*, 394.

26 “Scientific Reformer.”

27 KBD, A/B.

28 Lapham, “KBD,” *Vassar Miscellany* 43, no. 6 (April 1914): 435; and Kathryn Kish Sklar, “Hull House in the 1890’s: A Community of Women Reformers,” *Signs* 10 (1985): 658–77.

29 Helen Rand Thayer, “The [25 Year] Anniversary Report of the College Settlements Association,” n.d. [1914 or 1915], 20, CSA Pamphlets, Smith.

30 College Settlement Association pamphlet, n.d., [ca. 1902], CSA Pamphlets, Smith.

31 KBD, "Home Life in a College Settlement," *Vassarian*, 1895, 81–83, quotations on 82; Christine Chaplin Bush, *The Colonel's Opera Cloak* (Roberts Brothers, 1879); and Madeleine B. Stern and Daniel Shealy, "The No Name Series," *Studies in the American Renaissance*, 1991, 375–402.

32 KBD, "Home Life," 81; and *Fifth Annual Report of the College Settlement Association, from September 1, 1893, to September 1, 1894* (Dunlap, 1894), 36.

33 KBD, "Home Life," 82; Thayer, "Anniversary Report," 20; and CSA Pamphlets, Smith.

34 "Social Settlement Work," *Baltimore Sun*, March 24, 1897, 2.

35 "Scientific Reformer."

36 KBD, "Settlement Work as a Preparation for Civic Work," *Vassar Quarterly* 2, no. 1 (November 1916): 46–48, quotation on 46.

37 KBD, "Settlement Work as a Preparation for Civic Work," 46.

38 KBD, A/B; see also "Some Facts About the Fifth Ward," *College Settlement News* 3, no. 3 (July 1897): 1.

39 KBD, "Settlement Work as a Preparation for Civic Work," 46; see also Kathryn Kish Sklar, "Hull-House Maps and Papers: Social Science as Women's Work in the 1890s," in Martin Bulmer, Kevin Bales, and Kathryn Kish Sklar, eds., *The Social Survey in Historical Perspective, 1880–1940* (Cambridge University Press, 2011), chap. 4.

40 Mina Carson, *Settlement Folk: Social Thought and the American Settlement Movement, 1885–1930* (University of Chicago Press, 1990); Allan F. Davis, *Spearheads for Reform: The Social Settlements and the Progressive Movement, 1890–1914* (Oxford University Press, 1967); and Joyce E. Williams and Vicky M. MacLean, *Settlement Sociology in the Progressive Years: Faith, Science, and Reform* (Brill, 2015).

41 KBD, "Settlement Work as a Preparation for Civic Work," 47; see also "College Settlements," *Buffalo Courier*, August 26, 1894, clipping in KBD Trustee Biographical File, VCSC.

42 KBD, A/B; "Scientific Reformer"; and "College Settlements."

43 KBD, A/B; "Scientific Reformer"; and "College Settlements."

44 "Guild House," *Brooklyn Standard Union*, May 22, 1894, 7.

45 KBD, A/B; "Scientific Reformer"; and "College Settlements."

46 "Guild House," 7.

47 KBD, A/B.

48 KBD, A/B.

49 KBD, A/B.

50 Percy Alden, "The Social and College Settlements of America: Their Relation to Municipal Reform," *Outlook*, June 22, 1895, 25, 51.

51 KBD, "City Housekeeping," *Vassar Quarterly* 6, no. 4 (August 1, 1921): 245(quotation)–52; Paula Baker, "The Domestication of Politics: Women and American Political Society, 1780–1920," *American Historical Review* 89, no. 3 (June 1984): 620–47; and Kathryn Kish Sklar, *Florence Kelley and the Nation's Work: The Rise of Women's Political Culture, 1830–1900* (Oxford University Press, 1995).

52 KBD, A/B.

53 KBD, A/B.

54 KBD, A/B.

55 "New York's New Commissioner of Correction," Owens Papers, Empire State Campaign Committee: Press Bureau Releasees, January–April 1915, A-147, Folder 63, Schlesinger.

56 College Settlements Association, *Sixth Annual Report of the College Settlements Association* (Dunlap, 1895), 25; KBD, "Report of Division Work by the College Settlement in the First Election Division, South End of the Seventh Ward," in Mrs. Talcott Williams, ed., "The Story of a Woman's Municipal Campaign," *Publications of the American Academy of Political and Social Sciences*, no. 150 (July 2, 1895): 64–69.

57 W. E. B. Du Bois, *The Philadelphia Negro* (University of Pennsylvania Press, 1899); see also KBD, "Settlement Work as a Preparation for Civic Work," *College Settlements Association Quarterly* 2, no. 1 (October 1916): 6–9.

58 KBD, "Settlement Work as a Preparation for Civic Work," 7, 8, 9.

59 KBD, "Settlement Work as a Preparation for Civic Work," 8.

60 KBD, A/B; "Hail Miss Davis as Commissioner," *NY Tribune*, January 1, 1914, 7.

61 "College Settlements," *Buffalo Courier*, August 26, 1894, clipping in KBD Trustee Bio File, VCSC; and KBD to Mrs. Bull, n.d., Autograph Files, VCSC.

62 "The Housing of the Poor," *College Settlement News* 2, no. 3 (June 1896): 1 ("necessary conveniences")–2; "The Housing of the Poor, II," *College Settlement News* 2, no. 4 (July 1896): 1–2; and "The Housing of the Poor, III," *College Settlement News* 2, no. 5 (August 1896): 1–2 ("proven profitable").

63 KBD, A/B; Mary Jo Deegan, "W. E. B. Du Bois and the Women of Hull House," *American Sociologist* 19, no. 4 (Winter 1998): 301–11; and *College Settlement News* 2, no. 6 (September 1896): 5; CSA Pamphlet, n.d. [ca. 1902], 3, CSA Pamphlets, Smith; and Elisabeth Lasch-Quinn, *Black Neighbors: Race and the Limits of Reform in the American Settlement House Movement, 1890–1945* (University of North Carolina Press, 1993).

64 W. E. B. Du Bois, *The Autobiography of W. E. B. Du Bois* (International Publishers, 1968), 195; and W. E. B. Du Bois, *The Philadelphia Negro* (University of Pennsylvania Press, 1899), 58, 304, 307.

65 KBD, "The Condition of the Negro in Philadelphia," *JPE* 8, no. 2 (March 1900): 248–60 (quotations).

66 KBD, A/B.

67 KBD, A/B; and Fitzpatrick, *Endless Crusade*, chaps. 2 and 3; see also Steven J. Diner, *A City and Its Universities: Public Policy in Chicago, 1892–1919* (University of North Carolina Press, 1980); and Monica Mercado and Katherine Turk, *"On Equal Terms": Educating Women at the University of Chicago* (University of Chicago Library, 2009).

68 Fitzpatrick, *Endless Crusade*; and Jabour, *Sophonisba Breckinridge*.

69 Jabour, "Separatism and Equality: Women at the University of Chicago, 1895–1925," *Chicago History* 44, no. 2 (Fall 2020): 30–44.

70 *Fifth Annual Report of the College Settlement Association, from September 1, 1893, to September 1, 1894* (Dunlap Printing, 1894), 36.

71 MB Diaries, June 15, 1896.

72 MB Diaries, May 15 and June 10, 1896 (on Kate's new wheel, which she purchased with newspaper prize money); August 23 (Pedro) and 29 (cycling, dog pound, and phosphates), 1897. On the "floppy" dress, see June 23, 1895.

73 KBD, A/B.

74 KBD, A/B.

75 KBD, A/B.

76 KBD, A/B. See also "College and Alumnae," *Woman's Journal*, June 11, 1898, 192.

77 KBD Passport Application, July 30, 1898, National Archives and Records Administration, RG 59: General Records of the Department of State, Series: Passport Applications, Volume 875: August 1 to 31, 1898. See also Brian Dolan, *Ladies of the Grand Tour: British Women in Pursuit of Enlightenment and Adventure in Eighteenth-Century Europe* (HarperCollins, 2001).

78 KBD, A/B; and MB Diaries, August 23, 1897. See also Shirley Foster, "American Women Travellers to Europe in the Nineteenth and Early Twentieth Centuries," *British Association for American Studies*, Pamphlet No. 27 (1994).

79 KBD, A/B; Erik Grimmer-Solm, *The Rise of Historical Economics and Social Reform in Germany, 1864–1894* (Oxford University Press, 2003); and Heino Heinrich Nau, "Gustav Schmoller's Historico-Ethical Political Economy: Ethics, Politics, and Economics in the Younger German Historical School, 1860–1917," *European Journal of the History of Economic Thought* 7, no. 4 (2000).

80 KBD, A/B.

81 KBD, A/B.

82 KBD, A/B.

83 KBD, A/B.

84 KBD, A/B.

85 KBD, A/B.

86 KBD, A/B.

87 KBD to Mother, July 10, 1899, PP; Andrea Ginzburg, "Menger, Anton (1841–1906)," *The New Palgrave Dictionary of Economics*, 3rd ed. (Palgrave Macmillan, 2018), 8670–71; Friedrich Achleitner, *Austrian Architecture in the 20th Century*, vol. 3 (Residenz-Verlag, 1990), 265; and Helmut Weihsmann, *Red Vienna: Social Democratic Architecture and Local Politics, 1919–1934* (Promedia, 1985), 335.

88 Pieter M. Judson, *The Habsburg Empire: A New History* (Harvard University Press, 2016), 372–74; and Jakub Benes, *Workers and Nationalism: Czech and German Social Democracy in Habsburg Austria, 1890–1918* (Oxford University Press, 2017), 87–98.

89 "Reform of the Currency in Austria-Hungary," *Journal of the Royal Statistical Society* 55, no. 2 (June 1892): 333–39, especially 335n11; and "F. L. Rieger," *Czechoslovak Review* 1 (1917): 11–15.

90 KBD, A/B.

91 KBD, A/B.

92 KBD, A/B.

93 KBD, A/B; and Claire Morelon, "Social Conflict, National Strife, or Political Battle? Violence and Strikebreaking in Late Habsburg Austria," *European History Quarterly* 49, no. 4 (2019): 650–76, especially 666.

94 KBD to Mother, July 10, 1899, PP; and "Eugen Philippovich von Philippsberg, 1858–1917," *History of Economic Thought*, www.hetwebsite.net, retrieved July 15, 2025.

95 KBD, A/B; KBD to Mother, July 10, 1899, PP; and Morelon, "Social Conflict, National Strife, or Political Battle?"

96 KBD, A/B.

97 KBD to Mother, June 26 and July 10, 1899, PP.

98 KBD to Mother, July 10, 1899, PP.

99 KBD to Mother, June 26 and July 10, 1899, PP.

100 KBD, A/B.

101 Hubert C. Kennedy, "The 'Third Sex' Theory of Karl Heinrich Ulrichs," in Salvatore Licata and Robert P. Petersen, eds., *The Gay Past: A Collection of Historical Essays* (Routledge, 2013), 103–11; and Karl Maria Kertbeny to Karl Heinrich Ulrichs, May 6, 1868, in *Capri: Zeitschrift fur Schwule Geschichte* 1 (1987): 25–35.

102 Robert Beachy, *Gay Berlin: Birthplace of a Modern Identity* (Vintage, 2015).

103 KBD, A/B; Shari Benstock, "Paris Lesbianism and the Politics of Reaction, 1900–1940," in Martin Duberman, Martha Vicinus, and George Chauncey, eds., *Hidden from History: Reclaiming the Gay and Lesbian Past* (New American Library, 1989); and Vicinus, *Intimate Friends*, 180–81.

104 Neil McKenna, *The Secret Life of Oscar Wilde: An Intimate Biography* (Basic Books, 2005).

105 KBD, A/B.

106 Vicinus, *Intimate Friends*, chaps. 2 and 7.

107 KBD, A/B.

108 Douglas Pretsell, *Queer Voices in the Works of Richard von Krafft-Ebing, 1883–1901* (Springer, 2023); Douglas Pretsell, ed., *The Correspondence of Karl Heinrich Ulrichs, 1846–1894* (Springer, 2020); see also Harry Oosterhuis, *Stepchildren of Nature: Psychiatry and the Making of Sexual Identity* (University of Chicago Press, 2000), 139–84; and Laura Doan, *Fashioning Sapphism: The Origins of a Modern English Lesbian Culture* (Columbia University Press, 2001), 126–63.

109 KBD, *Factors*, 239n1, 242n1, 243; and KBD, A/B.

110 Brandy Schillace, *The Intermediaries: A Weimar Story* (Norton, 2025).

111 KBD, *Factors*, 243n10.

112 Ellis later republished *A Problem in Greek Ethics* in *Sexual Inversion*. See Eric O. Clarke, *Virtuous Vice: Homoeroticism and the Public Sphere* (Duke University Press, 2000), 144.

113 KBD, *Factors*, 242n1; and Volkmar Sigusch, "The Sexologist Albert Moll: Between Sigmund Freud and Magnus Hirschfeld," *Medical History* 56, no. 2 (April 2012): 184–200.

114 Havelock Ellis and J. A. Symonds, *Das Kontrare Geschlechtsgefuhl* (Georg H. Wigand's Verlag, 1896); and Havelock Ellis and John Addington Symonds, *Sexual Inversion: A Critical Edition*, ed. Ivan Crozier (Palgrave Macmillan, 2008).

115 Havelock Ellis, *Studies in the Psychology of Sex*. Vol. 1, *The Evolution of Modesty, the Phenomena of Sexual Periodicity, Auto-Erotism* (Wilson & Macmillan, 1897); and KBD, *Factors*, chaps. 6, 7, 8, and 9.

116 Havelock Ellis, Letters to Mrs. William B. D. Field I and II, Havelock Ellis Correspondence, Department of Special Collection, Princeton University Library, Princeton, NJ.

117 Havelock Ellis, *Studies in the Psychology of Sex*. Vol. 2, *Sexual Inversion* (University Press, Limited, 1900). Ellis's early studies were collected and reprinted in the United States as *Studies in the Psychology of Sex* (Random House, 1936).

118 KBD, *Factors*, 287(quotation)–88.

119 KBD, *Factors*, 238n1, cites Havelock Ellis, *Studies in the Psychology of Sex*. Vol. 2, *Sexual Inversion* (F.A. Davis, 1902).

120 *The Nation*, January 27, 1932, 122; and Havelock Ellis, *Psychology of Sex: A Manual for Students* (William Heinemann, 1933), 97, 119, 202, 208, 227, 223, 239.

121 Schillace, *Intermediaries*, 9.

122 Schillace, *Intermediaries*, chap. 1.

123 KBD, A/B.

124 Schillace, *Intermediaries*, chap. 1.

125 Schillace, *Intermediaries*, 19; see also Amy Koerber, *From Hysteria to Hormones: A Rhetorical History* (Pennsylvania State University Press, 2018).

126 Francis Galton, *Inquiries into Human Faculty and Its Development* (Macmillan, 1883), 24.

127 Schillace, *Intermediaries*, chap. 1.

128 KBD, A/B; KBD Transcript, Special Collections Research Center, Regenstein Library, University of Chicago.

129 MB Diaries, August 3 (PhD) and 4, 1903 (PhD and bridge) and November 15, 1906 ("jolly time").

130 KBD, "The Modern Condition of Agricultural Labor in Bohemia," *JPE* 8, no. 4 (September 1900): 491–523.

131 KBD, "An Error in Austrian Wage Statistics," *JPE* 8, no. 1 (December 1899): 102–6 (quotation).

CHAPTER 3. "GOD BLESS MISS DAVIS!"

1 "Taming My Rebel Soul," *American Magazine* 78, no. 4 (October 1914): 18–23.

2 "Taming My Rebel Soul," 18.

3 "Taming My Rebel Soul," 19.

4 "Taming My Rebel Soul," 19.

5 "Taming My Rebel Soul," 19 and 22

6 "Taming My Rebel Soul," 22–23.

7 "Taming My Rebel Soul," 23.

8 "Taming My Rebel Soul," 23.

9 "Taming My Rebel Soul," 18; and "Her Rebel Soul," Wilmington (DE) *Daily Commercial*, October 21, 1914, 9.

10 KBD, A/B.

11 KBD, A/B. On "wayward" girls and women, see especially Ruth Alexander, *The "Girl Problem": Female Sexual Delinquency in New York, 1900–1930* (Cornell University Press, 1995); Saidiya Hartman, *Wayward Lives, Beautiful Experiments: Intimate Histories of Riotous Black Girls, Troublesome Women, and Queer Radicals* (Norton, 2020); and Mary E. Odem, *Delinquent Daugh-*

ters: Protecting and Policing Adolescent Female Sexuality in the United States, 1885–1920 (University of North Carolina Press, 1995).

12 Estelle B. Freedman, *Their Sisters' Keepers: Women's Prison Reform in America, 1830–1930* (University of Michigan Press, 1984); and Fitzpatrick, *Endless Crusade*, chap. 5.

13 KBD, A/B.

14 KBD, A/B.

15 KBD, "The Problem of Prostitution," *Proceedings.*

16 KBD, "A Study of Prostitutes Committed from New York City to the State Reformatory for Women at Bedford Hills," in George J. Kneeland, *Commercialized Prostitution in New York City* (1913; rpt. The Century Company, 1917), 163–272, quotation on 191, statistics on 226.

17 KBD, "Plan of Rational Treatment for Women Offenders," 403.

18 On sex work and social policy in the Progressive Era, see especially Elizabeth Alice Clement, *Love for Sale: Courting, Treating, and Prostitution in New York City, 1900–1945* (University of North Carolina Press, 2006); Mark Thomas Connelly, *The Response to Prostitution in the Progressive Era* (University of North Carolina Press, 1980); Timothy J. Gilfoyle, *City of Eros: New York City, Prostitution, and the Commercialization of Sex, 1790–1920* (Norton, 1992); Barbara Meil Hobson, *Uneasy Virtue: The Politics of Prostitution and the American Reform Tradition* (Basic Books, 1987); Jessica R. Pliley, *Policing Sexuality: The Mann Act and the Making of the FBI* (Harvard University Press, 2014); and Ruth Rosen, *The Lost Sisterhood: Prostitution in America, 1900–1918* (Johns Hopkins University Press, 1982).

19 Ida M. Tarbell, "Good Will to Woman," *American Magazine* 75, no. 2 (December 1912): 45–53, quotations on 45, 46.

20 KBD, A/B (quotation); see also Tarbell, "Good Will to Woman," 50.

21 "Heavy Work for Women," *NY Tribune*, June 4, 1905, A5; *Fifth Annual Report of the New York State Reformatory for Women at Bedford, N.Y. for the Year Ending September 30, 1905* (Brandow Printing, 1906), 24; "A Visit to Bedford Hills," *General Federation of Women's Clubs Bulletin* 14, no. 1 (January 1915): 9–10.

22 KBD, A/B.

23 *Seventh Annual Report of the New York State Reformatory for Women at Bedford, N.Y. for the Year Ending September 30, 1907* (J.B. Lyon, 1908), 23–29; *Tenth Annual Report of the New York State Reformatory for Women at Bedford, N.Y. for the Year Ending September 30, 1910* (J.B. Lyon, 1911), 18–19.

24 "Visit to Bedford Hills," 9–10; "Fate of Runaways," *NY Tribune*, June 1, 1902, B9. For juvenile institutions, see especially LeRoy Ashby, *Endangered Children: Dependency, Neglect, and Abuse in American History* (Twayne, 1997); Barbara M. Brenzel, *Daughters of the State: A Social Portrait of the First Reform School for Girls in North America, 1856–1905* (MIT Press, 1983); Victoria Getis, *The Juvenile Court and the Progressives* (University of Illinois Press, 2000); Linda Gordon, *Heroes of Their Own Lives: The Politics and History of Family Violence* (University of Illinois Press, 1988); Joseph M. Hawes, *Children in Urban Society: Juvenile Delinquency in Nineteenth-Century America* (Oxford University Press, 1971); Anthony M. Platt, *The Child Savers: The Invention of Delinquency* (University of Chicago Press, 1969); and Steven L. Schlossman, *Love and the American Delinquent: The Theory and Practice of "Progressive" Juvenile Justice, 1825–1920* (University of Chicago Press, 1977).

25 Appendix I: "Some Results of Ten Years' Work at Bedford," in *Tenth Annual Report*, 54; KBD, "Study of Prostitutes"; and Anne E. Bowler, Chrysanthi S. Leon, and Terry G. Lilley, "'What Shall We Do with the Young Prostitute? Reform Her or Neglect Her?': Domestication as Reform at the New York State Reformatory for Women at Bedford, 1901–1913," *Journal of Social History* 47, no. 2 (Winter 2013): 458–81.

26 "Dr. Davis Defends Bedford's System," *NYT*, December 18, 1914, 10; and "Dr. Davis Answers Bedford Charges," *NYT*, March 12, 1915, 16. On racial segregation in similar institutions, see for instance Anne Meis Knupfer, *Reform and Resistance: Gender, Delinquency, and America's First Juvenile Court* (Routledge, 2001).

27 KBD, A/B.

28 KBD, "Reformation of Women: Modern Methods of Dealing with Offenders," *Annals of the American Academy of Political and Social Science* 36, no. 1 (1910): 37–42, especially 39–41; see also *Annual Report of the New York State Reformatory for Women at Bedford, N.Y. for the Year Ending September 30, 1902* (Argus, 1903), 19; *Annual Report of the New York State Reformatory for Women at Bedford, N.Y. for the Year Ending September 30, 1903* (Oliver A. Quayle, 1904), 21; and *Seventh Annual Report of the New York State Reformatory for Women at Bedford, N.Y. for the Year Ending September 30, 1907* (J B. Lyon, 1908), 38.

29 "Dr. Davis Defends Bedford's System"; and KBD, A/B.

30 *Annual Report . . . 1902*, 23–24; *Annual Report . . . 1903*, 36; and KBD, A/B. On religion in institutions, see especially Peter C. Holloran, *Boston's Wayward Children: Social Services for Children, 1830–1930* (Fairleigh Dickinson University Press, 1989), 65–66 and 92–93.

31 KBD, A/B.

32 *Annual Report . . . 1902*, 19–21; and KBD, "Study of Prostitutes," 174 and 209.

33 *Ninth Annual Report of the New York State Reformatory for Women at Bedford, N.Y. for the Year Ending September 30, 1910* (J.B. Lyon, 1911), 26.

34 *Fifth Annual Report*, 26–27; and Connie Goddard, *Learning for Work: How Industrial Education Fostered Democratic Opportunity* (University of Illinois Press, 2024).

35 *Fifth Annual Report*, 26–27 (quotation); *Ninth Annual Report*, 26; *Tenth Annual Report*, 24; and KBD, A/B.

36 See for instance *Annual Report . . . 1902*, 21; *Annual Report . . . 1903*, 32; *Sixth Annual Report of the New York State Reformatory for Women at Bedford, N.Y. for the Year Ending September 30, 1906* (J. B. Lyon, 1907), 27; and *Ninth Annual Report*, 27–29. See also Dominick Cavallo, *Muscles and Morals: Organized Playgrounds and Urban Reform, 1880–1920* (University of Pennsylvania Press, 1981).

37 See for instance *Fourth Annual Report of the New York State Reformatory for Women at Bedford, N.Y. for the Year Ending September 30, 1904* (Brandow Printing, 1905), 16–17.

38 KBD, A/B.

39 *Annual Report . . . 1903*, 28; and *Annual Report . . . 1902*, 34–35.

40 *Ninth Annual Report*, 23.

41 *Annual Report . . . 1903*, 23–24, 28.

42 *Annual Report . . . 1903*, 41.

43 "The Tuckerman School," *Christian Register* 91, no. 44 (October 31, 1912): 1059.

44 *Fifth Annual Report*, 31; and *Eleventh Annual Report of the New York State Reformatory for Women at Bedford, N.Y. for the Year Ending September 30, 1911* (Argus, 1912), 27–28; and New York State Woman Suffrage Association, Untitled, n.d., Owens Papers. Suffrage. New York State Woman Suffrage Association, 1913–1916, n.d. A-147, Folder 75, Schlesinger.

45 *Annual Report . . . 1902*, 24; and *Fifth Annual Report*, 32.

46 KBD, A/B.

47 Wagner, "Katharine Bement Davis at College"; and KBD, A/B.

48 KBD, A/B.

49 KBD, A/B.

50 On Lillian's illness and death, see KEB Diaries, August 13 and September 9, 1908; December 23, 1909; January 16, 26, February 19, 22, March 8, 9, 12, 14, 1910. On Frances at Bedford, see KEB Diaries, March 17 and September 8, 1910; August 29, 1912; September 27 and October 1, 1913.

51 KBD, A/B.

52 *Sixth Annual Report*, 24–27.

53 *Sixth Annual Report*, 27; *Seventh Annual Report*, 38; *Eighth Annual Report of the New York State Reformatory for Women at Bedford, N.Y. for the Year Ending September 30, 1908* (J. B. Lyon, 1909), 30–31; *Tenth Annual Report*, 29; and "The Fourth at the Reformatory," *Katonah Times*, July 5, 1907, 1.

54 KBD, A/B; and "New York's New Commissioner of Correction," Owens Papers, Empire State Campaign Committee: Press Bureau Releases, January–April 1915, A-147, Folder 63, Schlesinger.

55 Florence Margolis, "Katharine Bement Davis," *Moving Picture World* 21, no. 11 (July–September 1914): 1489. See also C. S. Voll, "Flora Finch and John Bunny, the Forgotten Pioneers of Film Comedy," *Medium*, April 15, 2023.

56 *Annual Report . . . 1902*, 25; and Tarbell, "Good Will to Women," 50.

57 "Bedford Girls See Their Lives in Play," *NYT*, December 3, 1914, 15.

58 "Bedford Girls See Their Lives in Play."

59 "Urges Polygamy as a Crime Cure," Chicago *Tribune*, October 2, 1910, 4.

60 "In Dire Need at Bedford," *NY Tribune*, April 24, 1913, 5.

61 "Women Pay the Price," *Woman's Journal and Suffrage News* 47, no. 39 (September 23, 1916): 308–9.

62 KBD, "Study of Prostitutes," 190.

63 KBD, "Study of Prostitutes," 224; and KBD, "Problem of Prostitution," frame 1027.

64 KBD, "Study of Prostitutes," 178, 185, 197. See also New York Factory Investigating Commission, *Fourth Report of the Investigating Commission* (1915), 390–91.

65 Bowler, Leon, and Lilley, "'What Shall We Do with the Young Prostitute?'"

66 Tarbell, "Good Will to Women," 47.

67 KBD, "Study of Prostitutes," 225.

68 KBD, YWCA Lecture, September 10, 1917, PP.

69 KBD, "Study of Prostitutes," 224.

70 KBD, YWCA Lecture.

71 *Tenth Annual Report*, 59; see also Davis, "The New York State Reformatory for Women at Bedford," *The Survey* 25 (February 1911): 853; Bowler, Leon, and Lilley, "'What Shall We Do with the Young Prostitute?'"; and Faye E. Dudden, *Serving Women: Household Service in Nineteenth Century America* (Wesleyan University Press, 1983).

72 "Woman Forger Lured by Love of Opera," *NY Tribune*, September 14, 1913, 1.

73 MHOH; Cheryl D. Hicks, "'Bright and Good Looking Colored Girl': Black Women's Sexuality and 'Harmful Intimacy' in Early-Twentieth-Century New York," *Journal of the History of Sexuality* 18, no. 3 (September 2009): 418–56; Hicks, *Talk with You like a Woman: African American Women, Justice, and Reform in New York, 1890–1935* (University of North Carolina Press, 2010); and Emily Reed, "Wayward Women and Lady-Lovers: Same-Sex Intimacies Between Women in Progressive-Era New York City, 1901–1930" (Honors thesis, History Department, Barnard College, May 2019).

74 MHOH; and Joan Nestle, "I Lift My Eyes to the Hill: The Life of Mabel Hampton as Told by a White Woman," in Nestle, *A Fragile Union: New and Selected Writings* (Cleis Press, 1998), 258–75, quotation on 265.

75 MHOH, 50, 124; and Mae C. Quinn, "Fallen Woman (Re)Frame: Judge Jean Hortense Norris, New York City—1912–1955," *University of Kansas Law Review* 451 (2019).

76 MHOH, 56, 59.

77 MHOH; and Edith R. Spaulding, "Emotional Episodes Among Psychopathic Delinquent Women," *Journal of Nervous and Mental Disease* 54, no. 4 (1921): 298–323. See also A'Lelia Bundles, *Joy Goddess: A'Lelia Walker and the Harlem Renaissance* (Scribner, 2025); Bundles, *On Her Own Ground: The Life and Times of Madam C. J. Walker* (Scribner, 2002); and Cookie Woolner, *The Famous Lady Lovers: Black Women and Queer Desire Before Stonewall* (University of North Carolina Press, 2023).

78 MHOH.

79 MHOH.

80 MHOH, 83.

81 KBD, "Moral Imbeciles," *Proceedings of the Annual Congress of the National Prison Association* 1906, 345–50, quotations on 347.

82 KBD to Mother, Nov. 27, 1908, PP.
83 KBD to Mother, Nov. 27, 1908, PP.
84 KBD to Mother, Nov. 27, 1908, PP.
85 KBD to Bedford Reformatory, Nov. 12, 1908, PP.
86 KBD to Mother, December 6, 1908, PP.
87 KBD to Bedford Reformatory, Nov. 21, 1908, PP.
88 KBD to Bedford Reformatory, November 27, 1908, PP.
89 KBD to Charlotte Davis, December 14, 1908, PP.
90 KBD to Mother, Dec. 21, 1908, PP.
91 KBD to "My Dear Family" [Bedford Reformatory], Dec. 27, 1908, PP.
92 KBD to Mother, Dec. 30, 1908, PP.
93 KBD to Family [Bedford Reformatory], Jan. 13, 1909; KBD to Mother, Jan. 9 and 14, 1909, PP.
94 KBD to Mother, January 24, 1909, PP.
95 KBD to Mother, Dec. 30, 1908, and KBD to Mother, January 14, 1909, PP.
96 KBD to Family, Jan. 13 and 17, 1909, PP.
97 KBD to Mother, Jan. 6, 1909, PP.
98 KBD to "My dear family" [Bedford Reformatory], Jan. 24, 1909, PP.

99 For quotations, see MB Diaries, April 15, 1909, KEB Diaries, April 11, 1909; and George C. Bragdon Diaries, April 10, 11, and 17, 1909, UR; and KBD, A/B; see also MB Diaries, January 3, 24, February 28, April 9–10, 11, 18 (pope), and May 1 (including typescripts of letters and news clippings), 1909; and KEB Diaries, January 2, 5 (fundraising), 19, March 2, 24, April 9, 10, 18 (pope), and May 11, 1909.

100 KEB Diaries, March 2, 1909; see also "Miss Davis in Sicily," [March 1909]; "Woman's Effective Relief Work," [March 1909]; and "American Relief in Italy," *New York Evening Post*, March 16, 1909, clippings in KBD Trustee Biographical File, VCSC; and "Mt. Kisco Girl Clothes Italy's Quake Refugees," n.d.; "Katharine Davis, Reformer, 75, Dead," *NYT*, December 11, 1935; and "Famed Leader Known in City, Dies on Coast," *Rochester Democrat and Chronicle*, December 11, 1935, clippings, PP.

101 "Prof. Furness of Vassar Reviews Unique Career of Dr. Katherine B. Davis," clipping, KBD File, VCSC.

102 American Eugenics Society, *What I Think About Eugenics* (n.d.), 2.

103 Wendy Kline, *Building a Better Race: Gender, Sexuality, and Eugenics from the Turn of the Century to the Baby Boom* (University of California Press, 2001); Molly Ladd-Taylor, *Fixing the Poor: Eugenic Sterilization and Child Welfare in the Twentieth Century* (Johns Hopkins University Press, 2017); and Alexandra Minna Stern, *Eugenic Nation: Faults and Frontiers of Better Breeding in Modern America* (University of California Press, 2005).

104 Kline, *Building a Better Race.*

105 Kline, *Building a Better Race*, chap. 1; see also Margaret Grace Myers, *The Fight for Sex Ed: The Century-Long Battle Between Truth and Doctrine* (Beacon Press, 2025), 9–10.

106 McCulloch, "Next Things," 207.

107 KBD, A/B; *Annual Report . . . 1902*, 8; *Eighth Annual Report*, 19; *Tenth Annual Report*, 7; and *Twelfth Annual Report for Women at Bedford, N.Y. for the Year Ending September 30, 1912* (J.B. Lyon, 1913), 6, 32, 51; and "In Dire Need at Bedford," *NY Tribune*, April 24, 1913, 5.

108 *Sixth Annual Report*, 16–19.

109 Chelsea D. Chamberlain, "'Why Wait Until They Commit a Crime?': Moral Imbecility and the Problem of Knowledge in Progressive America, 1880–1920 (MA thesis, University of Montana, 2015); Steven A. Gelb, "'Not Simply Bad and Incorrigible': Science, Morality, and Intellectual Deficiency," *History of Education Quarterly* 29, no. 3 (Autumn 1989): 359–79; and Leila Zenderland, *Measuring Minds: Henry Herbert Goddard and the Origins of American Intelligence Testing* (Cambridge University Press, 1998).

110 Kline, *Building a Better Race*, 20–26.

111 Gelb, "'Not Simply Bad and Incorrigible,'" 373–77; Kline, *Building a Better Race*, 20–26; and KBD, "Study of Prostitutes," 187.

112 KBD, A/B.

113 KBD, A/B; and Nicole Hahn Rafter, *Creating Born Criminals* (University of Illinois Press, 1997), chap. 2.

114 KBD, "Plan of Rational Treatment," 403, 408; and McCulloch, "Next Things," 207.

115 KBD, "Introduction," Clara Jean Weidensall, *Mentality of the Criminal Woman* (Warwick and York, 1916), x–xiv.

116 Chamberlain, "'Why Wait Until They Commit a Crime,'" 101–8; and Michael Willrich, *City of Courts: Socializing Justice in Progressive Era Chicago* (Cambridge University Press, 2011), chap. 8.

117 *Tenth Annual Report*, 13, 19, 21.

118 Vernon L. Bullough, "Katharine Bement Davis, Sex Research, and the Rockefeller Foundation," *Journal of the History of Medicine* 62, no. 1 (Spring 1988): 74–89.

119 "Miss Katherine Bement Davis, Commissioner of Corrections, New York City," Belleville (IL) *News-Democrat*, February 20, 1914; Josephine Lacy Hirsch, "Rethinking Criminal Women: The Laboratory of Social Hygiene, 1912–1918" (Senior thesis, Barnard College, 2018); and Harry W. Laughlin, *Eugenical Sterilization in the United States* (Municipal Court of Chicago, 1922), 25–26, 81–86, 144–45.

120 See especially Penina Migdal Glazer and Miriam Slater, *Unequal Colleagues: The Entrance of Women into the Professions* (Rutgers University Press, 1987); Ann Mari May, *Gender and the Dismal Science: Women in the Early Years of the Economics Profession* (Columbia University Press, 2022), especially chap. 9; and Regina Morantz-Sanchez, *Sympathy and Science: Women Physicians in American Medicine* (University of North Carolina Press, 1985).

121 L. S. Abrams and L. Curran, "Wayward Girls and Virtuous Women: Social Workers and Female Juvenile Delinquency in the Progressive Era," *Affilia* 15 (2000): 49–64; A. C. Kennedy, "Eugenics, 'Degenerate Girls,' and Social Workers During the Progressive Era," *Affilia* 23 (2008): 22–37; Regina G. Kunzel, *Fallen Women, Problem Girls: Unmarried Mothers and the Professionalization of Social Work* (Yale University Press, 1993); Robyn Muncy, *Creating a Female Dominion in American Reform, 1890–1935* (Oxford University Press, 1991); and Karen W. Tice, *Tales of Wayward Girls and Immoral Women: Case Records and the Professionalization of Social Work* (University of Illinois Press, 1998).

122 Tarbell, "Good Will to Woman"; Joanne Belknap, "Offending Women: A Double Entendre," *Journal of Criminal Law and Criminology* 100, no. 3 (Summer 2010): 1061–96; Elizabeth Evens, "Regulating Women: Female Professionals and Gendered Surveillance in the Late Nineteenth- and Early Twentieth-Century United States" (PhD diss., University College London, 2021); and Anne Gray Fischer, "Race, Sexuality, and the Carceral State," in Nicholas Syrett and Jen Manion, eds., *Cambridge History of Sexuality in the United States*, vol. 2 (forthcoming).

123 KBD, "Introduction," in Weidensall, *Mentality of the Criminal Woman*.

124 Jessie Taft to Helen Towey, January 23, 1928, PP.

125 Virginia P. Robinson, *Jessie Taft, Therapist and Social Work Educator: A Professional Biography* (University of Pennsylvania Press, 1962), 32–33; and Jean K. Quam and G. S. Whitford, "Jessie Taft and Virginia Robinson: The Power of Relationship," in Jan Andrews, ed., *From Vision to Action: Social Workers of the Second Generation* (College of St. Catherine, University of St. Thomas,1992).

126 KBD to "My dear Bedford Family," November 21, 1908; Alberta S. Guibord to Helen Towey, January 30, 1928; and Agnes Crowley to Helen Towey, January 30, 1928, PP.

127 Willrich, *City of Courts*, chap. 8.

128 Weidensall, *Mentality of the Criminal Woman*, 161; see also KBD, "Study of Prostitutes," 198.

129 KBD, "Study of Prostitutes," 198; and KBD, "Introduction," in Edith R. Spaulding, *An Experimental Study of Psychopathic Delinquent Women* (Bureau of Social Hygiene, 1923). See also

KBD, "Some Institutional Problems in Dealing with Psychopathic Delinquents," *Journal of Criminal Law and Criminology* 10, no. 3 (May 1919–February 1920): 385–408; and Edith R. Spaulding, "The Problem of a Psychopathic Hospital Connected with a Reformatory Institution," *Medical Record* 99, no. 20 (May 14, 1921): 815–21. Hydrotherapy included "continuous baths, shower baths, and wet packs" ("Problem of a Psychopathic Hospital," 815).

130 *The Suffragist* 1, no. 1 (November 15, 1913): 8; *Woman's Journal and Suffrage News* 47, no. 40 (September 30, 1916): 315; and "A Visit to Bedford Hills," General Federation of Women's Clubs *Bulletin* 14, no. 1 (January 1915): 9(quotation)–10.

131 "Visit to Bedford Hills," 10; and Spaulding, "Problem of a Psychopathic Hospital," 817.

132 In addition to Weidensall, *Mentality of the Criminal Woman*, see Mabel Ruth Fernald, *A Study of Delinquent Women in New York State* (Century Company, 1920).

133 Steven Schlossman and Stephanie Wallach, "The Crime of Precocious Sexuality: Female Juvenile Delinquency in the Progressive Era," *Harvard Educational Review* 48, no. 1 (February 1978): 65–94; and Peter Tylor, "'Denied the Power to Choose the Good': Sexuality and Mental Defect in American Medical Practice, 1850–1920," *Journal of Social History* 10, no. 4 (Summer 1997): 472–89.

134 KBD, "Study of Prostitutes," 187–88; and KBD, "Feeble-Minded Women in Reformatory Institutions," *Survey* 27, no. 22 (March 2, 1912): 1851.

135 Lewis Madison Terman, *The Measurement of Intelligence* (Harran, 1916), 8; and New York (State) Factory Investigating Commission, *Fourth Report*, vol. 1, appendix 3, 412–13; and Terry G. Lilley, Chrysanthi S. Leon, and Anne E. Bowler, "The Same Old Arguments: Tropes of Race and Class in the History of Prostitution from the Progressive Era to the Present," *Social Justice* 46, no. 4 (2019): 31–51. See also Leah LaGrone, *Sex Wages: Prostitution and Poverty in Modern America* (Oklahoma University Press, forthcoming).

136 Charles D. Heydt to JDR, March 1, 1920, OMR, RB, FA 324, Series O, Box 7, Folder 44, RAC; see also Rafter, *Creating Born Criminals*, 154–55.

137 H. H. Laughlin, Eugenics Records Office, to KBD, November 18, 1933, PP.

138 KBD, A/B; and Gorton, *Icon and Idealist*, 222–32, 310–12, 317, 335–36.

139 Paul A. Lombardo, *Three Generations, No Imbeciles: Eugenics, the Supreme Court, and Buck v. Bell* (Johns Hopkins University Press, 2022).

140 "New York's First Woman Commissioner of Correction," *NYT*, January 11, 1914, M6.

141 Kathy J. Cooke, "The Limits of Heredity: Nature and Nurture in American Eugenics Before 1915," *Journal of the History of Biology* 31, no. 2 (Summer 1998): 263–78.

142 "Woman's Work for Women," *New York Age*, [February 11, 1928], clipping, PP.

143 "Report of the Special Committee . . . Appointed to Investigate Charges Made Against the New York State Reformatory for Women at Bedford Hills, N.Y.," in *Annual Report of the State Board of Charities of the State of New York* (Weed, Parsons, 1915), 847–74, quotations on 853 and 865; Spaulding, "Emotional Episodes," 319; and KBD, A/B. The original charges of cruelty were dropped, and Davis was fully exonerated. See "Finds Girls' Prison Place of 'Horrors,'" *NYT*, November 14, 1914, 9; and "A Third of Bedford Women Defective," *NYT*, December 15, 1914, 6.

144 George Chauncey, "From Sexual Inversion to Homosexuality: Medicine and the Changing Conceptualization of Female Deviance," *Salmagundi*, no. 58/59 (Fall 1982–Winter 1983): 114–46; and Terry, *American Obsession*, chap. 3.

145 Carroll Smith-Rosenberg, "The New Woman as Androgyne: Social Disorder and Gender Crisis, 1870–1936," in *Disorderly Conduct: Visions of Gender in Victorian America* (Oxford University Press, 1985), 245–96.

146 Estelle B. Freedman, "The Prison Lesbian: Race, Class, and the Construction of the Aggressive Female Homosexual, 1915–1965," *Feminist Studies* 22, no. 2 (Summer 1996): 397–423, especially 397 and 399; and Sarah Potter, "'Undesirable Relations': Same-Sex Relationships and the Meaning of Sexual Desire at a Women's Reformatory During the Progressive Era," *Feminist Studies* 30, no. 2 (Summer 2004): 394–415, especially 400; see also Regina Kunzel, *Criminal Intimacy: Prison and the Uneven History of Modern American Sexuality* (University of Chicago Press, 2008).

147 Margaret Otis, "A Perversion Not Commonly Noted," *Journal of Abnormal Psychology* 13 (June–July 1913): 113–16, quotations on 113 and 114; see also Cookie Woolner, "'Unfortunate Attachments': Interracial Sapphism in Progressive Era Reformatories and Prisons," in *The Nursing Clio Reader* (Rutgers University Press, 2025), 12–16.

148 "Report of the Special Committee," 853, 865.

149 See "Finds Girls' Prison Place of 'Horrors,'" *NYT*, November 14, 1914, 9; and "A Third of Bedford Women Defective," *NYT*, December 15, 1914, 6.

150 "Dr. Davis Defends Bedford's System," *NYT*, December 18, 1914, 10.

151 "Dr. Davis Answers Bedford Charges," *NYT*, March 12, 1915, 16. See also "Dr. Katharine Davis Stands by Bedford," *NYT*, December 24, 1914, 10; and "Miss Davis's Mixing of Races Criticised," *NYT*, March 11, 1915, 6.

152 Elizabeth Evens, "Plainclothes Policewomen on the Trail: NYPD Undercover Investigations of Abortionists and Queer Women, 1913–1926," *Modern American History* 4, no. 1 (March 2021): 49–66, especially 63–66; Anastasia Jones, "'She's That Way': Female Same-Sex Intimacy and the Growth of Modern Sexual Categories in the U.S., 1920–1940" (PhD diss., Yale University, 2013), chap. 4; Hugh Ryan, *The Women's House of Detention: A Queer History of a Forgotten Prison* (Bold Type Books, 2022), 3; and Woolner, *Famous Lady Lovers*, chap. 3.

153 KBD, A/B; and Spaulding, "Emotional Episodes," 319–20.

154 KBD to Family, January 17, 1909, PP; and Jabour, "Out of the Closet?" See also Jabour, "Female Families: Same-Sex Love in the Victorian South," in Jabour and Craig Thompson Friend, eds., *Family Values in the Old South* (University Press of Florida, 2010), 86–108; Sharon Marcus, *Between Women: Friendship, Desire, and Marriage in Victorian England* (Princeton University Press, 2007), 196–204; and Vicinus, *Intimate Friends*, especially xxv.

155 Terry, *American Obsession*, 97–100.

156 KBD, A/B.

157 KBD to Mrs. Jack Macfarland, November 1, 1928, Miriam Van Waters Papers, Series IV: El Retiro and Related Work, Box 19, Schlesinger; Estelle B. Freedman, "'The Burning of Letters Continues': Elusive Identities and the Historical Construction of Sexuality," *Journal of Women's History* 9, no. 4 (Winter 1998): 181–200, quotations on 181 and 188.

158 "Miss Ella C. Lapham Died in Buffalo," Dunkirk *Evening Observer*, January 25, 1917, 11.

159 KBD, *Factors*, 245.

160 "To Make Punishment Fit the Criminal, Not the Crime," *NYT*, September 1, 1912, M1.

161 McCulloch, "Next Things," 208.

162 Fitzpatrick, *Endless Crusade*, 92; and McCulloch, "Next Things," 208.

CHAPTER 4. DOING A "MAN'S JOB" AND DEMANDING A WOMAN'S VOTE

1 "Woman Official Familiar with Job on Her First Day," *Evening World*, January 2, 1914, 2; see also "First Woman in That Office," *Boston Daily Globe*, January 11, 1914, 144; and McCarthy, "New York City's Suffragist Commissioner."

2 Jean Henry Large, "A Man's Job," *University of Chicago Magazine* 26, no. 3 (January 1934): 105–8; and KBD, A/B.

3 "Woman Heads New York's Prison System," Plainfield (NJ) *Courier-News*, January 18, 1914, 14; Tampa *Morning Tribune*, January 11, 1914, 2; "Miss Katherine B. Davis in Charge of New York City's 5,500 Prisoners," San Jose (CA) *Evening News*, January 24, 1914, 1; "First Woman in That Office."

4 Dora Marsden, *Bondwomen* (NAWSA, n.d.), n.p., Owens Papers: Pamphlets, 1912–1915. A-147, folder 105, Schlesinger; and "First Woman in That Office."

5 "The Human Touch," Jackson (MI) *Citizen Press*, December 18, 1914, 4.

6 "Business-like Manner," Tampa *Morning Tribune*, January 11, 1914, 2; "Woman Commissioner at Work," Plainfield (NJ) *Courier-News*, January 21, 1914, 19.

7 Gregory Mason, "A Woman on Guard," *Outlook*, April 11, 1914, 812.

8 "First Woman in That Office."

9 Edwin R. Lewinson, *John Purroy Mitchel: The Boy Mayor of New York* (Astra Books, 1965).

10 KBD, A/B.

11 Mason, "Woman on Guard," 809.

12 "Miss Davis Takes Hold of Her Work," *NYT*, January 13, 1914, 3.

13 "New York's First Woman Commissioner of Correction," *NYT*, January 11, 1914, M6.

14 "Suffrage School a Great Success," *Woman's Journal* 44, no. 39 (September 27, 1913): 310.

15 [Mary Garrett Hay], "New York's New Commissioner of Correction," Owens Papers, Empire State Campaign Committee: Press Bureau Releases, January–April 1915, A-147, Folder 63, Schlesinger.

16 "Hail Miss Davis as Commissioner," *NY Tribune*, January 1, 1914, 7.

17 Josephine Schain, *Women and the Franchise* (McClurg, 1918), 33.

18 Maud Nathan, "One Year's Progress of Equal Suffrage," Margaret Foley Papers, Suffrage Scrapbook, Schlesinger; see also "Antis Like Miss Davis," *NYT*, January 1, 1914, 4.

19 "New York's Woman Commissioner," *Evening World*, January 2, 1914, 2.

20 "A Revolutionary Appointment," *Outlook*, January 17, 1914, 118.

21 "Here's a Woman Who Holds Her Tongue," Trenton (NJ) *Evening Times*, January 11, 1914, 32.

22 City of New York, *Report of the Department of Correction for the Year 1914* (M.B. Brown, [1915]), 120.

23 City of New York, *Report of the Department of Correction for the Year 1914*, 14; and Stacy Horn, *Damnation Island: Poor, Sick, Mad, and Criminal in 19th-Century New York* (Algonquin Books, 2018).

24 "Blackwell's Island a Prison Terrible," *NYT*, March 27, 1914, 20; and Mary B. Harris, *I Knew Them in Prison* (Viking Press, 1936), 7.

25 "New York's First Woman Commissioner of Correction."

26 City of New York, *Report of the Department of Correction for the Year 1914*, 95.

27 City of New York, *Report of the Department of Correction for the Year 1914*, 14.

28 KBD, A/B.

29 KBD, A/B.

30 "Woman's Efficiency in Office Proved, Says Mayor," *The Sun*, May 2, 1915, 39.

31 Mason, "Woman on Guard," 811; see also Heather Veneziano, "Politics, Poverty, and Preservation: A Case Study of the Preservation of Hart Island" (MA thesis, Tulane University, 2014).

32 "College Professor's Unique Vacation," *Evening Post*, October 2, 1915, 27; and Mason, "Woman on Guard," 811.

33 "To Save Delinquent City Boys," Rochester *Democrat and Chronicle*, June 10, 1915, 8.

34 KBD, A/B.

35 "The Experiment of Miss Davis," Springfield *Daily Republican*, March 26, 1914, 8.

36 "Reforming Boys," Springfield *Daily Republican*, May 17, 1914, 15; and KBD, A/B.

37 "Try-Out of Honor System," Richmond *Times Dispatch*, March 19, 1914, 4; and Elizabeth Zoe Alexander, "Imaginaries and Contradictions of Agriculture as Rehab in the Carceral State: A Critical Evaluation" (MA thesis, Rutgers University, 2019).

38 Mason, "Woman on Guard," 812

39 "Woman's Efficiency in Office Proved, Says Mayor," 39; "To Save Delinquent City Boys," Rochester *Democrat and Chronicle*, June 10, 1915, 8; and "Miss Davis Opens Door of Hope to Fallen," *NY Tribune*, July 19, 1914, D1. See also City of New York, *Report of the Department of Correction for the Year 1914*, appendix 2, 192–95.

40 "Miss Davis Opens Door of Hope to Fallen"; "Wants for Women Farm, Not Prison," *NY Tribune*, February 4, 1915, 16; "Court and Detention Home De Luxe Planned for Women," *NYT*, March 22, 1914, 6; City of New York, *Report of the Department of Correction for the Year 1914*, 93–108; and Ryan, *Women's House of Detention.*

41 KBD, A/B.

42 KBD, A/B.

43 KBD, A/B; and Dawn Keetley, *Making a Monster: Jesse Pomeroy, the Boy Murderer of 1870s Boston* (University of Massachusetts Press, 2017).

44 KBD, A/B.

45 KBD, A/B; see also Ruth Borden, *Women and Temperance: The Quest for Power and Liberty, 1873–1900* (Temple University Press, 1981); Barbara Epstein, *The Politics of Domesticity: Women, Evangelicalism, and Temperance in Nineteenth-Century America* (Wesleyan University Press, 1981); Lisa McGirr, *The War on Alcohol: Prohibition and the Rise of the American State* (National Geographic Books, 2015); and Catherine Gilbert Murdock, *Domesticating Drink: Women, Men, and Alcohol in America, 1870–1940* (Johns Hopkins University Press, 1998).

46 KBD, A/B; see also "Her Study Shows Dry Law Fails," New York *Herald Tribune*, May 26, 1930, 7; and "Katherine B. Davis Converted to Wets," *NYT*, May 26, 1930, 2.

47 City of New York, *Report of the Department of Correction for the Year 1914*, 14, 24–25; see also David F. Musto, *The American Disease: Origins of Narcotics Control*, 3rd ed. (Oxford University Press, 1999), chap. 3.

48 KBD, A/B (quotation); Harris, *I Knew Them in Prison*, 24; and "Cafe Des Tombs Menu Good, but There'll Be No Cabaret," *NYT*, May 3, 1914, A3.

49 "Convict Dr. Baxter of Selling Drugs," *NYT*, June 30, 1914, 7.

50 "Island Curing Drug Victims," *NY Tribune*, February 19, 1915, 5; and "Woman's Efficiency in Office Proved."

51 "Why I Am a Suffragist," *NY Tribune*, November 3, 1917, 12.; see also "Need for Suffrage Seen by Dr. Davis," *NY Tribune*, April 9, 1914, 7; "Why Successful Women Want to Vote," *NY Tribune*, May 31, 1914, B10; and "Duchess Makes Plea to Newport Throng," *NYT*, July 9, 1914, 7.

52 "War Has Shown Value of Women in Service," *Binghamton Press*, November 5, 1917, 4; and Baker, "Domestication of Politics."

53 KEB Diaries, June 28, 1914; and "Woman's Efficiency in Office Proved."

54 City of New York, *Report of the Department of Correction for the Year 1914*, 53.

55 City of New York, *Report of the Department of Correction for the Year 1914*, 53–55.

56 "Splendid Report of Woman Commissioner," *The Suffragist* 2, no. 29 (July 18, 1914): 2; and "Justice Saves Money," *Woman's Journal* 45, no. 43 (October 24, 1914): 282.

57 "Bodyguard for Miss Davis," New York *Evening Post*, May 14, 1914, 1; "Varied Activities of Women," *Chicago Daily Tribune*, May 31, 1914, E2; and "Feminine Facts," *Pittsburgh Press*, August 4, 1914, 14.

58 "Quells Riot in Prison," *Washington Post*, July 16, 1914, 12.

59 "Little Money to Aid Women," *Woman's Journal* 45, no. 30 (July 25, 1914): 222; and Johanna Neuman, *Gilded Suffragists: The New York Socialites Who Fought for Women's Right to Vote* (NYU Press, 2017).

60 KBD, A/B.

61 "Warden Hayes Quits Blackwell's Island," *NYT*, July 23, 1915, 18 ("old school" quotation); Frank Tanenbaum, "The Blackwell's Island Hell," *The Masses* 6, no. 9 (June 1915): 16–17 ("break the spirits"); see also Frank Tanenbaum, "What I Saw in Prison," *The Masses* 6, no. 8 (May 1915): 8–9; "State Investigates Blackwell's Prison," *NYT*, July 15, 1915, 7; and "Prisoners Clubbed by Hayes's Helpers," *NYT*, July 24, 1915, 6.

62 Frank Tanenbaum, "A Strike in Prison," *The Masses* 6, no. 10 (July 1915): 16–19.

63 "700 Join Mutiny," *NYT*, July 10, 1914, 1; and Tanenbaum, "Strike in Prison."

64 "Quiet on Island," *NYT*, July 11, 1914, 1; "Woman Calms Blackwell's Mutiny Gang," *NY Tribune*, July 11, 1914, 1; and "Quells Riot in Prison" (quotations).

65 "Quiet on Island."

66 "Miss Davis Takes Rooms in Prison," *Philadelphia Inquirer*, July 12, 1914, 4.

67 "Quells Riot in Prison."

68 "Quiet on Island."

69 "Miss Davis Leads Island Service," *NY Tribune*, July 12, 1914, 1; "Island Voices Are Raised in Song," *NYT*, July 13, 1914, 16; and "Miss Davis's Prison Sermon Quiets Jail," *NYT*, July 12, 1914, 1.

70 "Island Voices Are Raised in Song."

71 "Wants for Women Farm, Not Prison."

72 KBD, A/B; and "Better Prisons for City Urged," *NYT*, September 6, 1914, 9.

73 "Distinguished Members," *The Suffragist* 2, no. 29 (July 18, 1914): 6.

74 "Need for Suffrage Seen by Dr. Davis," *NY Tribune*, April 9, 1914, 7; KBD, A/B.

75 Susan Goodier and Karen Pastorello, *Women Will Vote: Winning Suffrage in New York State* (Cornell University Press, 2017); and Lauren C. Santangelo, *Suffrage and the City: New York Women Battle for the Ballot* (Oxford University Press, 2019)

76 Class of 1892 Letters, VCSC; "Says Prisoners Are 'Bad Boys,'" *Woman's Journal* 45, no. 31 (August 1, 1914): 1; Elizabeth J. Clapp, *Mothers of All Children: Women Reformers and the Rise of Juvenile Courts in Progressive Era America* (Pennsylvania State University Press, 1998); and Molly Ladd-Taylor, "Toward Defining Maternalism in U.S. History," *Journal of Women's History* 5, no. 2 (Fall 1993): 110–13; Kaila Adia Story, ed., *Patricia Hill Collins: Reconceiving Motherhood* (Demeter Press, 2014); and Andrea O'Reilly, *Rocking the Cradle: Thoughts on Motherhood, Feminism, and the Possibility of Empowered Mothering* (Demeter Press, 2006).

77 "Says Prisoners Are 'Bad Boys.'"

78 KBD, "Maternalism the Coming Great Force for Government," *Minneapolis Tribune*, August 2, 1914, Magazine Section.

79 "Parties Endorse Suffrage," *Woman's Journal*, September 5, 1914, 252.

80 KBD to Mother, June 26, 1899, PP; Voter Registration, Manhattan, NY, 1918 and 1926, Ancestry.

81 "New York Women in Politics," September 21, 1914, Owens Papers, Empire State Campaign Committee: Press Bureau Releases, 1914. A-147, Folder 62, Schlesinger.

82 MB Diaries, April 19 and October 15, 1914; see also KEB Diaries, October 15, 1914; and Antonia Petrash, "Victory in 1917," *New York Archives* 16, no. 4 (Spring 2017).

83 "Government Easy, Says Prison Head," New York *Post Standard*, March 27, 1915, 3; *The Hand Book of the National American Woman Suffrage Association and Proceedings of the Forty-Seventh Annual Convention* (NAWSA, 1915), 5, 30–33; "Suffragists to Form City Club in New York," Boston *Herald*, August 1, 1915, 4; "Metropolis Expects 30,000 in Line Today," *Woman's Journal* 46, no. 43, October 23, 1915, 1.

84 Nancy F. Cott, *The Grounding of Modern Feminism* (Yale University Press, 1987), chap. 2.

85 Ellen Carol DuBois, *Harriot Stanton Blatch and the Winning of Woman Suffrage* (Yale University Press, 1997).

86 Jennifer Godfrey, *Secret Missions of the Suffragettes: Glassbreakers and Safe Houses* (Pen & Sword, 2024); and June Purvis, *Emmeline Pankhurst: A Biography* (Routledge, 2002).

87 Ellen Carol DuBois, *Feminism and Suffrage: The Emergence of an Independent Women's Movement in America, 1848–1869* (Cornell University Press, 1980); and Aileen S. Kraditor, *The Ideas of the Woman Suffrage Movement, 1890–1920* (Norton, 1981).

88 DuBois, *Harriot Stanton Blatch*, 156–75.

89 DuBois, *Harriot Stanton Blatch*, 156–75, quotation on 163.

90 DuBois, *Harriot Stanton Blatch*, 163 (bourgeois) and 174–75 (parade); and "Suffragist Tea in Municipal Building," *NYT*, October 9, 1915.

91 "A Joyful Christmas," *Woman's Journal*, December 25, 1915, 1.

92 "Government Easy, Says Prison Head," New York *Post Standard*, March 27, 1915, 3; "Dr. Davis on Suffrage" and "A Lesson in Democracy," *Woman's Journal* 46, no. 3 (January 16, 1915): 20.

93 Untitled, *Woman's Journal and Suffrage News* 46, no. 32 (August 7, 1915): 1.

94 "An I.W.W. Heroine, Although She Ate," *NYT*, April 28, 1914, 6.

95 "Becky Finds It So Hard to Die," *NY Tribune*, August 4, 1914, 14.

96 "Becky Edelson Begins Her Strike," *NYT*, July 22, 1914, 18; "Hunger Strike Will Not Avail Militant Becky," Elmira *Star-Gazette*, July 23, 1914, 1.

97 "New York Commissioner of Correction Faces a Puzzle," Plainfield (NJ) *Courier-News*, July 23, 1914, 14.

98 "No More Publicity for Becky," Philadelphia *Inquirer*, July 31, 1914, 16.

99 "Becky Edelson Fakes on Her Hunger Strike," Ithaca *Journal*, July 24, 1914, 1; "Becky Edelson's Bluff," Rochester *Democrat and Chronicle*, July 26, 1914, 16; see also Harris, *I Knew Them in Prison*, 10–13.

100 "The Conquering of Becky," Macon (GA) *Daily Telegraph*, July 28, 1914.

101 "Becky Makes Record in a Hunger Strike," Anaconda (MT) *Standard*, August 19, 1914.

102 "Another Woman," *Woman Rebel* 1, no. 6 (August 1914): 42.

103 "Anarchist Prison on Riker's Island," *NYT*, November 29, 1914, 14; "Special Prison for I.W.W. Orators," Boston *Sunday Herald*, November 29, 1914, A7.

104 "Abuses at Blackwell's Island as Seen by a Convict," *NY Tribune*, February 17, 1915, 1, 6.

105 "Anarchist Released," *Advertiser-Journal*, August 22, 1914, 3. See also Adam Hochschild, *American Midnight: The Great War, a Violent Peace, and Democracy's Forgotten Crisis* (HarperCollins, 2021); and William Preston, *Aliens and Dissenters: Federal Suppression of Radicals, 1903–1933* (University of Illinois Press, 1963).

106 "Assails Davis Rule at Island Prison," *NYT*, August 7, 1915, 1.

107 "Grand Jurors View Island Institutions," *NYT*, August 22, 1915, 11.

108 "From Dr. Davis: Commissioners Not Responsible When They Lack Power to Act," *NY Tribune*, March 18, 1915, 8; "Warden Hayes Saved by Age, Dr. Davis Says," *NY Tribune*, August 9, 1915, 1; "Mitchel Praises, Court Criticises Dr. Davis's Acts," *NY Tribune*, August 10, 1915, 4.

109 Harriet Bishop Waters, "Intimate Talks by the Editor," *General Federation of Women's Clubs Magazine*, September 1915, 3.

110 Harris, *I Knew Them in Prison*, 74.

111 "Urges Leisure and Rum Instead of Work House," *NY Tribune*, February 2, 1915, 4; and "Katherine Davis, Ardent Dry, Now Convert to Wet Cause," New York *World*, May 26, 1930 (clipping), PP.

112 "How a Woman Commissioner Deals with Prison Problems," *Outlook*, July 25, 1914, 695.

113 City of New York, *Report of the Department of Correction for the Year 1914*, 94; see also 165–66.

114 City of New York, *Report of the Department of Correction for the Year 1914*, appendix I, 187–91.

115 "What the New Parole Board Hopes to Do," *NYT*, January 9, 1916, Magazine Section, 18.

116 John Philip Bramer, *A Treatise Giving the History, Organization, and Administration of Parole* (Irving Press, 1926), 5–36.

117 KBD, "Plan of Rational Treatment," 407.

118 "Report of Committee on Probation and Parole," American Prison Association, [1915], PP.

119 "What the New Parole Board Hopes to Do"; see also *Laws of New York, Chapter 287*, in *Rules and Procedures Adopted by the Parole Commission of the City of New York* (1916), 1–7.

120 "What the New Parole Board Hopes to Do."

121 "Repeaters Fewer with Parole System," *NYT*, December 9, 1917, D80.

122 Bramer, *Treatise*, 19.

123 "Urges Leisure and Rum Instead of Workhouse."

124 "Noted Sociologist Advises Study of Individual Cases," Ithaca *Journal*, April 3, 1916, 2.

125 "Noted Sociologist Advises Study of Individual Cases."

126 "What the New Parole Board Hopes to Do."

127 "Dr. Davis Quits Correction Post," *NY Tribune*, December 29, 1915, 2; "Dr Davis Resigns for New Position," *Woman's Journal* 47, no. 1 (January 1, 1916): 1–2.

128 KBD, A/B.

129 Bramer, *Treatise*, 10.

130 "What the New Parole Board Hopes to Do," Magazine Section, 18.

131 KBD, A/B.

132 KBD, A/B; Voter Registration, Manhattan, NY, 1918 and 1926, Ancestry.

133 Program, 48th Annual Convention, September 8, 1916, Laidlaw Papers, Correspondence (1916), A-63, Folder 121, Schlesinger.

134 "Women Begin Cross Country Campaign Tour," Boston *Herald*, October 3, 1916, 1; and J. Leonard Bates and Vanette M. Schwartz, "Golden Special Campaign Train: Republican Women Campaign for President in 1916," *Montana: The Magazine of Western History* 37, no. 3 (Summer 1987): 26–35.

135 KBD to JDR, September 30, 1916, OMR, RB, FA324, Series O, Box 6, Folder 36, RAC.

136 "Women Tour in Support of Hughes," Binghamton *Press and Leader*, October 4, 1916, 1.

137 "Why I Am for Hughes," San Jose *Mercury Herald*, October 25, 1916.

138 "Noted Women on Campaign Special Tell Why They Are for Mr. Hughes So Strongly," Colorado Springs *Gazette*, October 25, 1916.

139 Clipping, n.d. [ca. February 2, 1928], PP.

140 "Predicts Victory for Suffragists," *NY Tribune*, August 27, 1916, 11.

141 KBD, A/B.

142 *Prison Progress in 1916* (J.B. Lyon, 1917), 139–45; see also *Rules and Procedures Adopted by the Parole Commission of the City of New York*.

143 "Ex-Prisoners Are Obtaining Work," New Rochelle *Pioneer*, October 28, 1916, 3.

144 Harris, *I Knew Them in Prison*, 76.

145 "Colored Women's Clubs in Session," Plainfield (NJ) *Courier-News*, July 27, 1917, 13.

146 At the workhouse, fewer than three thousand repeaters were committed in 1916 and 1917, as compared to an average of four thousand for several preceding years. See "Repeaters Fewer with Parole System."

147 William A. N. Dorland, *The Sum of Feminine Achievement* (Stratford, 1917), 122.

148 Rheta Childe Dorr, "As a Woman Sees It," Harrisburg (PA) *Patriot*, September 22, 1916, 6.

149 See for example "Prison Worker to Lecture Here," Trenton (NJ) *Times-Advertiser*, March 25, 1917, 5.

150 Jean H. Baker, *Margaret Sanger: A Life of Passion* (Farrar, Straus and Giroux, 2012), 115–25.

151 "Mrs. Bryne [*sic*], Birth Control Advocate, Still in Belligerent Mood: Swallows Food Tube," San Diego *Union*, January 30, 1917, 1; and "Mrs. Byrne Tells of Prison Horrors," *NYT*, February 7, 1917, 5.

152 "Mrs. Sanger Flays Miss Davis's Plans," *NYT*, March 7, 1917, 13.

153 "Miss Davis Denies She Was Heartless," *NYT*, March 8, 1917, 13.

154 Emma Goldman, *Anarchism and Other Essays* (1910; 3rd edition, Middle Earth Publishing Association, 1917), 124, 126.

155 Emma Goldman, "To My Friends, Old and New," *Mother Earth* 11 (June 1916): 516–21, quotation on 517.

156 Aya Gruber, *The Feminist War on Crime: The Unexpected Role of Women's Liberation in Mass Incarceration* (University of California Press, 2021); Loretta LeMaster, "Against Carceral Feminisms, Toward Abolitionist Futures," *Women's Studies in Communication* 47, no. 2 (Spring 2024): 97–100; Lilley, Leon, and Bowler, "Same Old Arguments"; and Jennifer Musto, "Domestic Minor Sex Trafficking and the Detention-to-Protection Pipeline," *Dialectical Anthropology* 37, no. 2 (2013): 257–76.

157 "One Scarecrow Gone," *Woman's Journal* 47, no. 45 (November 4, 1916): 356.

158 Kenneth Finegold, "Traditional Reform, Municipal Populism, and Progressivism: Challenges to Machine Politics in Early-Twentieth-Century New York City," *Urban Affairs Review* 31, no. 1 (September 1995): 20–42.

159 "Predicts Victory for Suffragists," *NY Tribune*, August 27, 1916, 11.

160 "Women Lack Votes but Not Courtesy," New York *Press*, November 3, 1917, Clipping, National Woman's Party Papers, Part I, 1913–1974, Series 3: Printed Materials, 1850–1972, Women's Studies Manuscript Collections (microfilm), Schlesinger.

161 "Moral Fiber in Men Necessary to Save Girls," Rochester *Democrat and Chronicle*, December 28, 1914, 13.

162 "Women Pay the Price," *Woman's Journal*, September 23, 1916, 308.

163 "War Has Shown Value of Women in Service," *Binghamton Press*, November 5, 1917, 4.

164 JDR to KBD, July 2, 1917; and KBD to JDR, July 5, 1917, OMR, RB, FA324, Series O, Box 7, Folder 48, RAC.

CHAPTER 5. "SEX ETHICS"

1 Stacie Colwell, "*The End of the Road*: Gender, the Dissemination of Knowledge, and the American Campaign Against Venereal Disease During World War I," *Camera Obscura* 10, no. 2 (1992): 91–129; Jessica Lee Mathiason, "From Sentimentality to Science: Social Utility, Feminist Eugenics, and *The End of the Road* in Progressive Era America," *Gender & History* 33, no. 1 (March 2021): 149–68; Christie Milliken, "Generation Sex: Reconfiguring Sexual Citizenship in Educational Film and Video" (PhD diss., University of Southern California, 2003), chap. 1; and Miriam Posner, "Prostitutes, Charity Girls, and *The End of the Road*," in Christian Bonah et al., eds., *Health Education Films in the Twentieth Century* (University of Rochester Press, 2018), 173–87. The film may be viewed at www.filmpreservation.org.

2 "Business Women's Noonday Meeting," *Atlanta Constitution*, April 2, 1919; and Janet Priest, "That Sly, Dishonest Sign," *Photoplay* 16 (1919): 57–58, quoted in Mathiason, "From Sentimentality to Science," 149 and 164.

3 "Thousands Flock to See Hygiene Film," *Moving Picture World* 39, no. 1 (January 4, 1919): 100; Mathiason, "From Sentimentality to Science," 149–50; see also "To Determine If Health Film Shall Be Shown," Ithaca *Journal*, April 15, 1919, 3.

4 Asbury Park (NJ) *Evening Press*, August 27, 1919, 7; see also Margaret I. MacDonald, "Film on Social Hygiene to Have Wide Distribution—Is Method of Presenting Subject Right or Wrong?," *Motion Picture Educator* 38, no. 10 (December 7, 1918): 1087.

5 Posner, "Prostitutes, Charity Girls, and *The End of the Road*."

6 Nancy K. Bristow, *Making Men Moral: Social Engineering During the Great War* (NYU Press, 1997); Linda Sharon Janke, "Prisoners of War: Sexuality, Venereal Disease, and Women's Incarceration During World War I" (PhD diss., SUNY Binghamton, 2006); David Pivar, *Purity and Hygiene: Women, Prostitution, and the "American Plan," 1900–1930* (Greenwood Press, 2002); and Scott Stern, *The Trials of Nina McCall: Sex, Surveillance, and the Decades-Long Government Plan to Imprison "Promiscuous" Women* (Beacon Press, 2018).

7 M. J. Exner to JDR, June 7, 1921, OMR, RB, FA 324, Series O, Box 7, Folder 50, RAC.

8 See especially Bristow, *Making Men Moral*.

9 Allan M. Brandt, *No Magic Bullet: A Social History of Venereal Disease Since 1880* (Oxford University Press, 1985), 111.

10 In addition to Janke, "Prisoners of War"; and Stern, *Trials of Nina McCall*; see Clement, *Love for Sale*, chaps. 3 and 4; and Mara L. Keire, "Swearing Allegiance: Street Language, US War Propaganda, and the Declining Status of Women in Northeastern Nightlife, 1900–1920," *Journal of the History of Sexuality* 25, no. 2 (2016): 251.

11 Janke, "Prisoners of War," 238, 256, 262.

12 Janke, "Prisoners of War," 239.

13 George Worthington and Ruth Topping, *Specialized Courts Dealing with Sex Delinquency* (1925; rpt. Patterson Smith, 1969).

14 Recommendations of the Laboratory of Social Hygiene (1914), Folder 31, Box 6, Series O, OMR, RAC.

15 Harris, *I Knew Them in Prison*, 26.

16 Janke, "Prisoners of War," 243.

17 Ben Reitman, *Sister of the Road: The Autobiography of Box Car Bertha* (1937, rpt. AK Press/Nabat, 2002), 132–33.

18 Walter C. Reckless, *Vice in Chicago* (University of Chicago Press, 1933), 147–48.

19 Spaulding, "Problem of a Psychopathic Hospital," 816–17 (quotations).

20 Spaulding, "Emotional Episodes," 301.

21 "Prostitution," ca. 1919, PP; and Deborah Cheney, "Dr Mary Louisa Gordon (1861–1941): A Feminist Approach in Prison," *Feminist Legal Studies* 18, no. 2 (August 2010): 115–36.

22 Kayla Blackman, "Public Power, Private Matters: The American Social Hygiene Association and the Policing of Sexual Health in the Progressive Era" (MA thesis, University of Montana, 2014), chap. 3; see also Odem, *Delinquent Daughters*.

23 KBD to JDR, March 11, 1918, OMR, RB, Series O, Box 7, Folder 7, RAC.

24 Janke, "Prisoners of War," 98–105.

25 Martha Falconer, "Work of the Section on Reformatories and Houses of Detention," *Proceedings of the National Conference of Social Work* (1918), 668–72; and Falconer, "The Segregation of Delinquent Women and Girls as a War Problem," *Annals of the American Academy of Political and Social Science* 79 (September 1918): 160–62.

26 "Women Discuss the Problems of Girls," Charleston (SC) *News and Courier*, January 31, 1918, 8.

27 "Personals," and "New York Sterilization Law," *Eugenical News* 3 (April 1918): 28–29; Laughlin, *Eugenical Sterilization*, 217–34; and Julia B. Haager, "'Sex Education's Many Sides': Eugenics and Sex Education in New York City's Progressive Reform Organizations," *JGAPE* 21, no. 2 (April 2022): 74–92.

28 KBD to JDR, July 30, 1918, OMR, RB, FA324, Series O, Box 7, Folder 44, RAC.

29 KBD to JDR, July 30, 1918, OMR, RB, FA324, Series O, Box 7, Folder 44, RAC.

30 KBD to JDR, July 30, 1918, OMR, RB, FA324, Series O, Box 7, Folder 44, RAC.

31 KBD to JDR, July 30, 1918, OMR, RB, FA324, Series O, Box 7, Folder 44, RAC; and Myers, *Fight for Sex Ed*, 22–23.

32 KBD to JDR, July 30, 1918, OMR, RB, FA324, Series O, Box 7, Folder 44, RAC.

33 KBD to JDR, March 23, 1918, OMR, Series O, Box 7, Folder 44, RAC; and Janke, "Prisoners of War," 70.

34 KBD, "Social Hygiene and the War," 526.

35 "Moral Fiber in Men Necessary to Save Girls," Rochester *Democrat and Chronicle*, December 28, 1914, 13.

36 "New Methods of Grappling with the Social Evil," *New York* 54, no. 4 (April 1913): 308.

37 KBD, "Problem of Prostitution," 61–62.

38 KBD, "Problem of Prostitution," 62.

39 Janke, "Prisoners of War," 328.

40 KBD to JDR, March 23, 1918, OMR, RB FA 324, Series O, Box 7, Folder 44, RAC.

41 "New Methods of Grappling with the Social Evil."

42 "Dr. Katherine Davis at the Old South," Boston *Daily Globe*, February 12, 1917, 4.

43 KBD, "Problem of Prostitution," 62.

44 KBD, "Social Hygiene and the War," 525–60, especially 528.

45 KBD, "Women's Education in Social Hygiene," *Annals of the American Academy of Political and Social Science* 79 (September 1918): 167–77, quotation on 172–73.

46 KBD, "Women's Education in Social Hygiene," 167–68.

47 KBD, "Social Hygiene and the War," 526, 531.

48 KBD, "Women's Education in Social Hygiene," 169, 172–73.

49 "Girls—A Home Guard," WWI Social Morality Committee, YWCA.

50 KBD, "Women's Education in Social Hygiene," 167.

51 KBD, "Women's Education in Social Hygiene," 176–77.

52 "Report of Section of Women's Work," Social Hygiene Division, Commission on Training Camp Activities, 62–65, WWI Social Morality Committee, YWCA.

53 "What Girls Can Do," Springfield (MA) *Daily Republican*, November 19, 1918, 7.

54 "Warns of Disease," Springfield (MA) *Daily Republican*, November 20, 1918, 4.

55 "Campaign of Education Has Women Workers," Duluth *News-Tribune*, July 21, 1918, 7; "Report of Section of Women's Work"; and KBD, "Social Hygiene and the War," 536.

56 KBD, "Social Hygiene and the War," 539.

57 "Suggestions to Lecturers on Social Morality," WWI Social Morality Committee, YWCA.

58 Rachelle S. Yarros, "Experiences of a Lecturer," *Social Hygiene* 5 (1919): 205(quotation)–22.

59 Yarros, "Experiences of a Lecturer," 207–10.

60 Yarros, "Experiences of a Lecturer," 210, 211, 213, and 218.

61 "Excerpts from Letters of Social Morality Lecturers," ca. 1918, PP.

62 Publications: Pamphlets: Swift, Edith Hale, Lecturer, American Social Health Association Records (SW 45), Box 171, Folder 10, 1929, SWHA.

63 KBD, "Social Hygiene and the War," 546.

64 "Report of Section of Women's Work."

65 KBD, "Social Hygiene and the War," 557.

66 "Mrs. Brennan Heads Parent-Teachers Clubs," *Davenport Democrat and Leader*, March 28, 1919, 4.

67 KBD, "Prostitution," PP.

68 KBD, "Social Hygiene and the War," 557.

69 Colwell, "*End of the Road*," 116–17.

70 Colwell, "*End of the Road*," 116–17.

71 Colwell, "*End of the Road*," 116–17.

72 YWCA Housing Committee, *Housing for Women in War Work* (YWCA, 1918).

73 "Government Film Warns Girls," *Chicago Tribune*, December 10, 1918, 18.

74 "New Century Club to Hear Sex Hygiene Talk," Philadelphia *Inquirer*, February 18, 1919, 2.

75 "To Determine If Health Film Shall Be Shown"; and Mathiason, "From Sentimentality to Science," 165.

76 KBD to JDR, July 30, 1918, OMR, RB, FA324, Series O, Box 7, Folder 44, RAC; and Report of the Activities of the Bureau of Social Hygiene, January 1, 1918, OMR, RB, FA324, Series O, Box 7, Folder 7, RAC.

77 KBD, A/B (quotations); Report of the Activities of the Bureau of Social Hygiene, January 1, 1918, OMR, RB, FA324, Series O, Box 7, Folder 7, RAC. See also Certificate of Registration of American Citizen, December 9, 1912; List of United States Citizens, USS Pennsylvania, sailing from Hamburg, February 22, 1913, arriving at New York, March 8, 1913; see also Passport Application, Katharine Bement Davis, December 5, 1918; and Passport Application, Ruth Topping, December 4, 1918, Ancestry; and Publications: Pamphlets: Swift, Edith Hale, Lecturer, American Social Health Association Records (SW 45), Box 171, Folder 10, 1929, SWHA.

78 KBD to JDR, March 18, 1919, OMR, RB, Series O, Box 7, Folder 44 (BSH, 1918–1933), RAC.

79 KBD to JDR, March 18, 1919, OMR, RB, Series O, Box 7, Folder 44 (BSH, 1918–1933), RAC.

80 "From Margaret Lambie," *Vassar College Bulletin* 8, no. 3 (May 1919): 12–14.

81 KBD, A/B; Harriet Hyman Alonso, *Peace as a Woman's Issue: A History of the U.S. Movement for World Peace and Women's Rights* (Syracuse University Press, 1993).

82 *Report of the International Congress of Women, Zurich, May 12 to 17, 1919* (Women's International League for Peace and Freedom, [1919]), 243–46 (quotation); and Erika Kuhlman, *Reconstructing Patriarchy After the Great War: Women, Gender, and Postwar Reconciliation Between Nations* (Palgrave Macmillan, 2008), 111–17.

83 KBD, A/B.

84 "Statistics for the International Conference of Women Physicians," November 11, 1919, WWI: Documents Concerning the International Conference of Women Physicians, YWCA; and

Kimberly Jensen, "War, Transnationalism, and Medical Women's Activism: The Medical Women's International Association and the Women's Foundation for Health in the Aftermath of the First World War," *Women's History Review* 26, no. 2 (March 2017): 213–28.

85 KBD, "Problem of Prostitution."

86 "Trumpet Call to Action from the Social Hygiene Committee of the National League of Women Voters," *Woman Citizen* 4, no. 43 (May 15, 1920): 1260–61.

87 KBD, A/B.

88 KBD, A/B; KBD, *Factors*, 242n1; Harry Oosterhuis, "Sexual Modernity in the Works of Richard von Krafft-Ebing and Albert Moll," *Medical History* 56, no. 2 (April 2012): 133–55; and Schillace, *Intermediaries*.

89 KBD, A/B.

90 KBD, *Factors*, 244; and KBD, A/B.

91 KBD, A/B.

92 Jay Sherry, "Beatrice Hinkle and the Early History of Jungian Psychology in New York," *Behavioral Sciences* 3, no. 3 (August 2013): 492–500; and Laura Doan, "Marie Stopes's Wonderful Rhythm Charts: Normalizing the Natural," *Journal of the History of Ideas* 78, no. 4 (October 2017): 595–620.

93 *Proceedings*; Myers, *Fight for Sex Ed*, 24–25.

94 KBD, A/B; and *Proceedings*.

95 Alma A. Paulsen, "Eleanor Bertine," *Journal of Analytical Psychology*, July 1968, 156–58; Sherry, "Beatrice Hinkle"; and Kate Wittenstein, "The Feminist Uses of Psychoanalysis: Beatrice M. Hinkle and the Foreshadowing of Modern Feminism in the United States," *Journal of Women's History* 10, no. 2 (Summer 1998): 38–62.

96 Sherry, "Beatrice Hinkle," 493 and 497 (quotations); and Paulsen, "Eleanor Bertine," 158.

97 Eleanor Bertine, "Health and Morality in the Light of the New Psychology," *Proceedings* 4, 5–14, quotations on 7, 12–13, and 180.

98 Beatrice M. Hinkle, "Changing Marriage," *Survey* 57 (December 1926): 288; and Hinkle, "Women and the New Morality," in Loren Bartiz, ed., *The Culture of the Twenties* (Bobbs-Merrill, 1970), 281.

99 *Proceedings*.

100 *Proceedings*; Program, "International Conference of Women Physicians and Convention of Delegates from National Women's Organizations," WWI: Documents Concerning the International Conference of Women Physicians, YWCA; and Schwartz, *Radical Feminists of Heterodoxy*, appendix C.

101 *Proceedings*; Schwartz, *Radical Feminists of Heterodoxy*, appendix A.

102 Katherine Anthony, *Margaret Fuller: A Psychological Biography* (Harcourt, Brace, and Howe, 1920), 211.

103 Kathryn Allamong Jacob, "The Mosher Report," *American Heritage Magazine* 32, no. 4 (June/July 1981).

104 "Hygiene and Physiology of Women," Vol. X: Sex Survey, Clelia Mosher Papers, Stanford University; Carl N. Degler, "What Ought to Be and What Was: Women's Sexuality in the Nineteenth Century," *American Historical Review* 79, no. 5 (December 1974): 1467–90; and Untitled Manuscript, VLBP, Box 306, Folder 10, 21–23.

105 Obituary, *Marblehead Messenger*, January 19, 1961; Collection Description, Frink Family Collection, Alan Mason Chesney Medical Archives, Johns Hopkins University, Baltimore, Maryland; and Bascom Johnson, "Next Steps," *Journal of Social Hygiene* 4 (1918): 9(quotation)–23.

106 Katharine Anthony to Ethel Sturges Dummer, October 7, 1919, Ethel Sturges Dummer Papers, Box 26, Folder 433, Schlesinger.

107 Wittenstein, "Feminist Uses of Psychoanalysis," 78–79.

108 Untitled Manuscript, Box 306, Folder 10, 28–29, VLBP.

109 Bullough, "Katharine Bement Davis," 82.

110 KBD, "Social Hygiene and the War," 559.

111 KBD, "Social Hygiene and the War," 559; see also "Concerning Our Friends," *General Federation Magazine* 18, no. 2 (February 1919): 7.

CHAPTER 6. "THE SCIENTIFIC STUDY OF SEX"

1 Estimates of attendance ranged from three hundred to fifteen hundred. See Testimonial Dinner Invitation, February 2, 1928; Testimonial Dinner Program, February 2, 1928, "Men and Women of Distinction Pay High Tribute to Dr. Katherine B. Davis, Retiring Social Hygienist," clipping, n.d.; Untitled news clipping, February 2, 1928; and "Dr. Katherine Davis Hailed at Dinner as One of Great Sociologists of U.S.," *Evening World*, February 3, 1928, clipping, PP.

2 Helen D. Pigeon to Valeria Parker, n.d. [February 1928]; Charles F. Thing [?] to Vera, January 24, 1928; and Adelaide Vetting to Valeria Parker, February 1, 1928, PP

3 KBD to JDR, April 27, 1927, OMR, RB, Series O, Box 7, Folder 7, RAC.

4 Gorton, *Icon and Idealist*; Scutts, *Hotbed*; Alexandra M. Lord, *Condom Nation: The U.S. Government's Sex Education Campaign from World War I to the Internet* (Johns Hopkins University Press, 2010), chaps. 2 and 3; Jeffrey P. Moran, *Teaching Sex: The Shaping of Adolescence in the 20th Century* (Harvard University Press, 2000); Myers, *Fight for Sex Ed*, 38–39; Courtney Q. Shah, *Sex Ed, Segregated: The Quest for Sexual Knowledge in Progressive-Era America* (University of Rochester Press, 2015); Schwartz, *Radical Feminists of Heterodoxy*; and Sharon Spaulding, "The Sex Education Pamphlet That Sparked a Landmark Censorship Case," *Smithsonian Magazine*, September 30, 2021.

5 Robert S. Lynd and Helen Merrell Lynd, *Middletown: A Study in Contemporary American Culture* (Harcourt, Brace, 1929), 114 (quotation), 138–40; see also Beth L. Bailey, *From Front Porch to Back Seat: Courtship in Twentieth-Century America* (Johns Hopkins University Press, 1989); Paula S. Fass, *The Damned and the Beautiful: American Youth in the 1920s* (Oxford University Press, 1979); Christina Simmons, *Making Marriage Modern: Women's Sexuality from the Progressive Era to World War II* (Oxford University Press, 2011); and Joshua Zeitz, *Flapper: A Madcap Story of Sex, Style, Celebrity, and the Women Who Made America Modern* (Three Rivers Press, 2006).

6 "Sex o'Clock in America," *Current Opinion* 40 (August 1913): 113–14; Frederick Lewis Allen, *Only Yesterday: An Informal History of the 1920s* (1931; rpt. Harper Perennial Classics, 2010), chap. 5 ("The Revolution in Manners and Morals"); and Gary, *Dirty Works*.

7 KBD, *Factors*, ix; Max Exner to JDR, June 7, 1921, OMR, RB, FA324, Series O, Box 8, Folder 50, RAC; and Minutes, "Conference on Sex Problems," October 28, 1921, OMR, RB, FA324, Series O, Box 7, Folder 50, RAC.

8 Sarah E. Igo, *The Averaged American: Surveys, Citizens, and the Making of a Mass Public* (Harvard University Press, 2007), chaps. 5 and 6.

9 Vern L. Bullough, *Science in the Bedroom: A History of Sex Research* (Basic Books, 1994); Donna J. Drucker, *The Classification of Sex: Alfred Kinsey and the Organization of Knowledge* (University of Pittsburgh Press, 2014), especially 90–92; Julia A. Ericksen, *Kiss and Tell: Surveying Sex in the Twentieth Century* (Harvard University Press, 1999), 29–35; Janice M. Irvine, *Disorders of Desire: Sexuality and Gender in Modern American Sexology*, rev. ed. (Temple University Press, 2005), chap. 1.

10 Certificate of Incorporation of the Bureau of Social Hygiene, Inc., May 19, 1913, BSH, Series 1, Box 2, Folder 25, RAC.

11 Abraham Flexner, "Is Social Work a Profession?" (National Conference of Charities and Corrections, 1915), https://socialwelfare.library.vcu.edu; and Stage, "What 'Good Girls' Do," 155–56.

12 JDR to KBD, July 2, 1917, OMR, RB, FA324, Series O, Box 7, Folder 48, RAC.

13 Report of the Activities of the Bureau of Social Hygiene, January 1, 1918, OMR, RB, FA324, Series O, Box 7, Folder 7, RAC; and JDR to Starr J. Murphy, July 22, 1919, OMR, RB, FA324, Series O, Box 7, Folder 7, RAC.

14 KBD to JDR, January 15, 1920; and JDR to KBD, January 20, 1920; see also JDR to Starr J. Murphy, July 22, 1919; JDR to KBD, December 1, 1919, OMR, RB, FA324, Series O, Box 7, Folder

44, RAC; Memorandum from Katharine Bement Davis to John D. Rockefeller Jr., "Outline of Plan for Caring for Defective Delinquent Women in New York State Institutions," September 1919, Folder 360, Box 25, Series 3, RAC; and KBD, A/B.

15 KBD, *Factors*, 342.

16 Bailey, *From Front Porch to Back Seat*, chap. 4; Joanne Meyerowitz, *Women Adrift: Independent Wage Earners in Chicago, 1880–1930* (University of Chicago Press, 1988); Kathy Peiss, *Cheap Amusements: Working Women and Leisure in Turn-of-the-Century New York* (Temple University Press, 1986); and Christina Simmons, *Making Marriage Modern: Women's Sexuality from the Progressive Era to World War II* (Oxford University Press, 2011).

17 KBD to JDR, April 23, 1920, OMR, RB, FA324, Series O, Box 7, Folder 49, RAC.

18 Report of the Activities of the Bureau of Social Hygiene, January 1, 1918, OMR, RB, FA324, Series O, Box 7, Folder 7, RAC; and Myers, *Fight for Sex Ed*, 27–39.

19 Charles Heydt to JDR, April 26, 1920; see also JDR to KBD, October 26, 1920, OMR, RB, FA324, Series O, Box 7, Folder 49, RAC.

20 "Prof. Furness of Vassar Reviews Unique Career of Dr. Katherine B. Davis," clipping, Alumnae File, VCSC.

21 Lynd and Lynd, *Middletown*; and Igo, *Averaged American*, chaps. 1 and 2.

22 Moore, *When They Were Girls*, 78.

23 "Government Easy, Says Prison Head," Syracuse (NY) *Post-Standard*, March 27, 1915, 3.

24 "Woman's Work for Women," *New York Age*, [February 11, 1928], PP.

25 KBD, "Social Hygiene and the War," 526.

26 KBD, *Factors*, 341, 344, 390, 394, and 376.

27 KBD to "Dear Madam," January 20, 1921, OMR, RB, FA324, Series O, Box 7, Folder 49, RAC.

28 Raymond B. Fosdick to JDR, January 31, 1921; and JDR to Raymond B. Fosdick, January 26, 1921, OMR, RB, FA324, Series O, Box 7, Folder 49, RAC

29 KBD to JDR, January 18, 1921, OMR, RB, FA324, Series O, Box 7, Folder 49, RAC.

30 JDR to Raymond B. Fosdick, January 26, 1921, OMR, RB, FA324, Series O, Box 7, Folder 49, RAC.

31 Max Exner to JDR, June 7, 1921, OMR, RB, FA324, Series O, Box 7, Folder 50, RAC.

32 KBD to JDR, July 6, 1922, OMR, RB, FA324, Series O, Box 7, Folder 44, RAC.

33 KBD, "A Study of the Sex Life of the Normal Married Woman, I: The Use of Contraceptives," *Journal of Social Hygiene* 8, no. 2 (April 1922): 173(quotation)–89.

34 KBD, "Use of Contraceptives," 176–77, 188.

35 KBD, "A Study of the Sex Life of the Normal Married Woman, II: The Happiness of Married Life," *Journal of Social Hygiene* 9, no. 1 (January 1923): 1–26, quotation on 23.

36 KBD, "Happiness of Married Life," 24

37 KBD, "Happiness of Married Life," 25–26.

38 "If You Spoon Before You Meet Your Husband Chances Are Against Being Happily Married," *Boston Daily Globe*, April 8, 1923, A2.

39 "Married Women Tell of Spooning in Frank Letters," *Atlanta Constitution*, April 4, 1923, 1.

40 RBF to A. L. Boulware, May 31, 1923, and enclosed clipping, "Rockefeller's 'Scientists,'" *Boston Paragraph*, May 1923, 9–10, clipping in OMR, RB, FA 324, Series O, Box 7, Folder 49, RAC.

41 KBD, "Happiness of Married Life." See also Cott, "Passionlessness."

42 KBD, "A Study of the Sex Life of the Normal Married Woman, III: The Happiness of Married Life—Continued," *Journal of Social Hygiene* 9, no. 3 (March 1923): 129(quotation)–46.

43 KBD, "Happiness of Married Life—Continued," 130.

44 KBD, "Happiness of Married Life—Continued," 131.

45 KBD, "Happiness of Married Life—Continued," 133.

46 KBD, "Happiness of Married Life—Continued," 136.

47 KBD, "Happiness of Married Life—Continued," 138.

48 KBD, "Happiness of Married Life—Continued," 130, 135.

49 Robert E. Pratt, "Becky and the Respectables," *Woman Rebel* 1, no. 6 (August 1914).

50 See especially Ellen Chesler, *Woman of Valor: Margaret Sanger and the Birth Control Movement in America* (Simon & Schuster, 2007).

51 For quotations, see MS to KBD, January 4, 1923, PP; and KBD, "Request from Mrs. Margaret Sanger to the Bureau of Social Hygiene or to Mr. John D. Rockefeller, Jr. personally," June 10, 1924, OMR, RB, FA 324, Series K, Box 2, Folder 8, RAC. On the request for anonymity, see JDR to KBD, June 17, 1924, PP. See also Gorton, *Icon and Idealist*, 155.

52 For quotations, see MS to KBD, May 2, [1925], OMR, RB, FA 324, Series K, Box 2, Folder 8, RAC; and KBD to MS, December 12, 1927, PP. See also MS to KBD, April 4, 1925, May 11, 1925, Sept. 24, 1925, and Oct. 11, 1926; Secretary to Mrs. Sanger to KBD, Oct. 8 and Oct. 16, 1925; and KBD to MS, September 25, 1925, Oct. 7, 1925, Oct. 15, 1925, Oct. 6, 1926, Oct. 11, 1926, and December 28, 1926, PP.

53 M. J. Exner to JDR, June 7, 1921; "Request for an Appropriation of $10,000 to the Bureau of Social Hygiene to Be Used in Promoting the Working Out of a Plan for Research in the Field of Sex," n.d., 1921; AF to JDR, June 13, 1921 (two letters), OMR, RB, FA324, Series O, Box 7, Folder 50, RAC; see also KBD to JDR, July 8, 1921, OMR, RB, FA324, Series O, Box 7, Folder 50, RAC. See also Bullough, "Katharine Bement Davis, Sex Research, and the Rockefeller Foundation"; Bullough, "Katharine Bement Davis, the Alumna Who Founded Modern Sex Research," VLBP, Box 258, Folder 20; Bullough, Untitled, VLBP, Box 306, Folder 10; and Adele E. Clark, *Disciplining Reproduction: Modernity, American Life Sciences, and "The Problems of Sex"* (University of California Press, 2022), chap. 4.

54 "Preliminary Report of the Committee for Research on Sex Problems," March 15, 1922, OMR, RB, FA324, Series O, Box 7, Folder 50, RAC.

55 "Preliminary Report," March 15, 1922, OMR, RB, FA324, Series O, Box 7, Folder 50, RAC.

56 "Request for an Appropriation of $10,000 to the Bureau of Social Hygiene to Be Used in Promoting the Working Out of a Plan for Research in the Field of Sex," OMR, RB, FA 324, Series O, Box 7, Folder 50; "Preliminary Report," March 15, 1922; and KBD to JDR, July 8, 1921, OMR, RB, FA324, Series O, Box 7, Folder 50, RAC. See also Bullough, "Katharine Bement Davis, Sex Research, and the Rockefeller Foundation"; and Terry, *American Obsession*, 135–37.

57 "Preliminary Report"

58 KBD to JDR, July 12, 1922, OMR, RB, FA324, Series O, Box 7, Folder 50, RAC.

59 "Preliminary Report," March 15, 1922, OMR, RB, FA324, Series O, Box 7, Folder 50, RAC; see also "Report of the Executive Secretary of the Committee for Research on Sex Problems to the Bureau of Social Hygiene for the Period July 1, 1921 to June 30, 1922," July 11, 1922, OMR, RB, FA324, Series O, Box 7, Folder 50, RAC.

60 Conference on Sex Problems, October 28, 1921, OMR, RB, FA324, Series O, Box 7, Folder 50, RAC.

61 See for instance Eichel, "Katharine Bement Davis"; and Esther A. Coster, "Katherine B. Davis to Devote Time to Book on 'Sex Life of Normal Women' on Retirement," clipping, PP.

62 KBD to JDR, July 12, 1922, OMR, RB, FA324, Series O, Box 7, Folder 50, RAC.

63 KBD to JDR, January 5, 1927, OMR, RB, FA324, Series O, Box 7, Folder 49, RAC; see also KBD to JDR, April 27, 1927, OMR, RB, FA324, Series O, Box 7, Folder 44, RAC; and "Report of the Executive Secretary of the Committee for Research on Sex Problems to the Bureau of Social Hygiene for the Period July 1, 1921 to June 30, 1922," July 11, 1922, OMR, RB, FA 324, Series O, Box 7, Folder 50.

64 Gorton, *Icon and Idealist*, 149, 155.

65 Clark, *Disciplining Reproduction*, 217–20; Wendy Kline, *Exposed: The Hidden History of the Pelvic Exam* (Polity, 2024), chap. 4; and Rachel Willis, "Dear Dr. Dickinson: Eugenics, Sexuality, and Pleasure in Early 20th-Century American Gynecology" (Honors thesis, Yale University, 2023); see also Gorton, *Icon and Idealist*, 148–49.

66 BSH Records, Subseries 3.2 (Social Hygiene), Folder 172: Committee on Maternal Health, 1923–1925; and Folder 173: Committee on Maternal Health, 1926–1928, RAC.

67 RLD to KBD, July 26, 1923, BSH Records, Subseries 3.2 (Social Hygiene), Folder 172: Committee on Maternal Health, 1923–1925, RAC.

68 RLD to KBD, July 26, 1923.

69 RLD to KBD, July 26, 1923.

70 RLD to KBD, July 13, 1925, July 26, 1923, August 7, 1924, September 30, 1924; KBD to RLD, September 27, 1924, January 14, 1925, November 19, 1925; RLD to "Dear Doctor" (form letter), November 10, 1925; BSH Records, Subseries 3.2 (Social Hygiene), Folder 172: Committee on Maternal Health, 1923–1925, RAC.

71 KBD to RLD, September 27, 1924 (quotation); KBD to Charles O. Heydt, June 17, 1925; RBF to KBD, June 24, 1924, May 21, 1925; KBD to RBF, June 25, 1924, May 22, 1925; JDR to RBF, June 17, 1924; JDR to RLD, July 17, 1924; Secretary to JDR to RBF, May 19, 1925; KBD Memo, "An Appeal for $20,000," June 10, 1924; Memo, Committee on Maternal Health, August 1924 (quotation); Proposition for a New Clinic to be run by Maternity Research Council, November 18, 1925; Secretary to JDR to Charles O. Heydt (cc to KBD), June 10, 1925; KBD to Mrs. Daniel O'Day, November 19, 1925, BSH Records, Subseries 3.2 (Social Hygiene), Folder 172: Committee on Maternal Health, 1923–1925, RAC.

72 RBF to LBD, December 22, 1927, BSH Records, Subseries 3.2 (Social Hygiene), Folder 173: Committee on Maternal Health, 1926–1928, RAC.

73 "Researches," March 1924, BSH Records, Subseries 3.2 (Social Hygiene), Folder 175: Committee on Maternal Health, Miscellaneous, RAC.

74 RLD to KBD, August 13, 1923, March 2, 1925, May 20, 1925 and enclosed "Recent Studies in Normal Sex Life, and the Relation of Sex Experiences to Genital Findings" ("epoch-making"), May 27, 1925, October 17, 1925 ("cream"), January 14, 1925; and KBD to RLD, August 21, 1923; March 3, May 20 and 22 ("flattered"), 1925; June 16, 1925, BSH Records, Subseries 3.2 (Social Hygiene), Folder 172: Committee on Maternal Health, 1923–1925, RAC.

75 RLD to KBD, August 13, 1923; and KBD to RLD, August 21, 1923, BSH Records, Subseries 3.2 (Social Hygiene), Folder 172: Committee on Maternal Health, 1923–1925, RAC.

76 RLD to KBD, November 20, 1923; and KBD to RLD, November 19 [*sic*], 1923, BSH Records, Subseries 3.2 (Social Hygiene), Folder 172: Committee on Maternal Health, 1923–1925, RAC.

77 RLD to KBD, January 14, 1925 (quotation) and February 18, 1925; RLD to James F. Cooper, February 18, 1925 (draft copy to KBD), BSH Records, Subseries 3.2 (Social Hygiene), Folder 172: Committee on Maternal Health, 1923–1925, RAC.

78 KBD to Charles C. Heydt, December 3, 1927, OMR, RB, FA324, Series O, Box 7, Folder 7, RAC.

79 KBD to JDR, April 27, 1927, OMR, RB, FA324, Series O, Box 7, Folder 7, RAC.

80 KBD to JDR, April 27, 1927.

81 KBD to JDR, April 27, 1927.

82 KBD to JDR, April 27, 1927.

83 Leonard V. Harrison, "Comment on Proposals Made by Miss Katherine Bement Davis for Reorganization of the Bureau of Social Hygiene," [Dec. 6, 1927], BSH, Series 1, Box 1, Folder 7, RAC.

84 RBF to JDR, March 23, 1927, OMR, RB, FA324, Series O, Box 7, Folder 48, RAC.

85 RBF to LBD, March 26, 1928, BSH, Series 3.2, Box 8, Folder 185, RAC.

86 JDR to KBD, April 2, 1927; and KBD to JDR, April 5, 1927, OMR, RB, FA324, Series O, Box 7, Folder 48, RAC.

87 HAD to Family, November 18, 1926, and December 12, 1926, PP.

88 KBD to WEB DuBois, April 14, 1924, W. E. B. Du Bois Papers, Series 1A (General Correspondence), University of Massachusetts, Amherst, Massachusetts.

89 KBD to MS, April 14, 1926; and KBD to MS, April 14, 1927, PP.

90 JDR to KBD, April 2, 1927, OMR, RB, FA324, Series O, Box 7, Folder 48, RAC.

91 LBD to JDR, May 17, 1928, OMR, RB, FA324, Series O, Box 7, Folder 7, RAC.

92 JDR to KBD, May 19, 1928, OMR, RB, FA324, Series O, Box 7, Folder 7, RAC.

93 KBD to JDR, December 21, 1927, OMR, RB, FA324, Series O, Box 8, Folder 44, RAC.

94 KBD, "Why They Failed to Marry," 460–69; and Kline, *Building a Better Race*, chap. 1.

95 KBD, "Why They Failed to Marry," 460(quotation)–62(quotation).

96 KBD, "Why They Failed to Marry," 463.

97 KBD, "Why They Failed to Marry," 463, 465, 466; and Christina Simmons, "Companionate Marriage and the Lesbian Threat," *Frontiers* 4, no. 3 (Autumn 1979): 54–59.

98 KBD, "Why They Failed to Marry," 466.

99 Freedman, "'The Burning of Letters Continues.'"

100 KBD, "Why They Failed to Marry," 468; KBD, A/B.

101 KBD, "Why They Failed to Marry," 467–68.

102 Alberta Guibord to Miss Towey, January 30, 1928; Buford Johnson to KBD, February 1, 1928; and Harriet B. Laidlaw [to Valeria Parker], n.d. [ca. February 2, 1928], PP.

CHAPTER 7. REDEFINING "NORMAL" WOMEN'S SEXUALITY

1 KBD, *Factors*, chaps. 1 and 2.

2 KBD to "Dear Madam," January 20, 1921, OMR, RB, FA324, Series O, Box 7, Folder 49, RAC.

3 KBD to "Dear Madam."

4 KBD to "Dear Madam."

5 KBD to "Dear Madam."

6 KBD to "Dear Madam."

7 Although Clelia Mosher's smaller-scale study of women's sexual behavior predated Davis's, it was never published. See Ericksen, *Kiss and Tell*, 28–35.

8 KBD to JDR, January 24, 1928, OMR, RB, FA324, Series O, Box 7, Folder 44, RAC.

9 KBD to Charles O. Heydt, December 3, 1927, OMR, RB, FA324, Series O, Box 7, Folder 7, RAC.

10 KBD, "Study of the Sex Life of the Normal Married Woman, I," 173.

11 Allen, *Only Yesterday*, chap. 5; Chauncey, *Gay New York*, chap. 11; Zeitz, *Flapper*, 9, 211–12.

12 KBD, "Social Hygiene and the War," 526.

13 Sohn, *Man Who Hated Women*; and Cott, "Passionlessness."

14 KBD, *Factors*, 95.

15 KBD to JDR, April 27, 1927, OMR, RB, FA324, Series O, Box 7, Folder 7, RAC; KBD, "Happiness of Married Life—Continued," 130.

16 KBD, *Factors*, 95.

17 Raymond B. Fosdick to John D. Rockefeller, Jr., January 31, 1921, OMR, RB, FA324, Series O, Box 7, Folder 49, RAC.

18 KBD, *Factors*, 95, 284, and 376.

19 KBD, *Factors*, x and xiii.

20 Cott, "Passionlessness"; see also Catherine Cocks, "Rethinking Sexuality in the Progressive Era," *JGAPE* 5, no. 2 (2006): 93–118.

21 Report of the Activities of the Bureau of Social Hygiene, January 1, 1918, OMR, RB, FA324, Series O, Box 7, Folder 44, RAC; see also KBD to JDR, April 23, 1920, OMR, RB, FA324, Series O, Box 7, Folder 49, RAC.

22 Moran, *Teaching Sex*, 105, 111, 113, 163; see also Myers, *Fight for Sex Ed*, 38–39.

23 KBD, *Factors*, 34–35, 63–65, 341(quotation)–46.

24 KBD, *Factors*, 34–35("blood" quotation), 371 ("shameful" quotation), 384 ("leprosy" quotation), and 387 ("devil" quotation).

25 KBD, *Factors*, ix.

26 KBD, *Factors*, x. See Igo, *Averaged American*; and Peter Cryle and Elizabeth Stephens, *Normality: A Critical Genealogy* (University of Chicago Press, 2024).

27 Esther A. Coster, "Katherine B. Davis to Devote Time to Book on 'Sex Life of Normal Woman' in Retirement," Brooklyn (NY) *Eagle*, January 1, 1928, clipping, AAVC, VCSC.

28 KBD to "Dear Madam," January 20, 1921, OMR, RB, FA 324, Series O, Box 7, Folder 49, RAC; see also Cryle and Stephens, *Normality*, chap. 7.

29 On early sex studies and their methods, see Bullough, *Science in the Bedroom*, especially chaps. 1–3.

30 KBD, *Factors*, vii, ix–x.

31 KBD, *Factors*, vii; see also Bullough, *Science in the Bedroom*, 65–85, 109–11; and Crossan, "Liberals, Ground Breakers, and Graduate Students," chap. 1.

32 KBD, *Factors*, x; see also chap. 1.

33 KBD to JDR, January 18, 1921, OMR, RB, FA324, Series O, Box 7, Folder 49, RAC.

34 KBD, "Why They Failed to Marry," 462; see also Simmons, *Making Marriage Modern*, chap. 3.

35 KBD, *Factors*, xii(quotation)–xiii.

36 "Questionnaire for Married Women and Widows," in Katharine Bement Davis, [Studies of the sex life of women, ca. 1922–1927], NYAM.

37 "Questionnaire," NYAM, 1.

38 "Questionnaire," NYAM, 1.

39 KBD, *Factors*, 94–95.

40 "Questionnaire," NYAM, 4.

41 KBD, *Factors*, 96.

42 KBD, *Factors*, 96.

43 KBD, *Factors*, 297.

44 KBD, *Factors*, 246.

45 "Questionnaire," NYAM, 7.

46 "Questionnaire," NYAM, 1.

47 KBD, *Factors*, xi–xii. Stage, "What 'Good Girls' Do," 156, indicates that the initial five thousand names came from the YWCA.

48 KBD, *Factors*, xii(quotation)–xiii.

49 KBD, *Factors*, 11.

50 KBD, *Factors*, xiv.

51 KBD, *Factors*, xiii, xvi.

52 KBD, *Factors*, 209, 215–17.

53 KBD, *Factors*, 12.

54 See especially Gorton, *Icon and Idealist*.

55 KBD to MS, January 23, 1929, PP.

56 "Grandmother Files an Appeal Bond in Birth Control Case," Chicago *Tribune*, May 3, 1929, 20.

57 Mary Ware Dennett, *The Sex Side of Life* (privately printed, 1919). See also Leigh Ann Wheeler, *How Sex Became a Civil Liberty* (Oxford University Press, 2013), 40–43; and Gary, *Dirty Works*, chap. 2.

58 KBD to Morris Ernst, February 1, 1929, Ernst Papers.

59 Gorton, *Icon and Idealist*.

60 "Appeal to the Bureau of Social Hygiene from the Committee on Maternal Health," December 8, 1928, BSH Records, Subseries 3.2 (Social Hygiene), Folder 173: Committee for Maternal Health, 1926–1928, RAC; and RT File Memo, December 2, 1932, BSH Records, Subseries 3.2 (Social Hygiene), Folder 162: American Birth Control League, 1929–1930, RAC; see also BSH Records, Subseries 3.2 (Social Hygiene), Folder 174: Committee for Maternal Health, 1930–1934, RAC.

61 RT File Memo, June 3, 1932, and December 2, 1932, BSH Records, Subseries 3.2 (Social Hygiene), Folder 162: American Birth Control League, 1929–1930, RAC.

62 LBD to RT, May 22, 1929, BSH Records, Subseries 3.2 (Social Hygiene), Folder 162: American Birth Control League, 1929–1930, RAC.

63 Thorsten Sellin to LBD, November 17, 1930 ("ethnic" quotation); RT File Memo, December 3, 1932 ("Negro leaders" quotation); and RBF to LBD, May 4, 1933 ("free and clear" quotation); see also RT to LBD, December 3, 1930, January 4 and 5, 1932, June 1, 1932; RT File Memos, February

24, 1931, April 17, 1931, October 16, 1931, November 25, 1931, January 4, 1932, February 18, 1932, May 27, 1932, June 3, December 2, 1932, December 19, 1932; LBD to RT, January 7, 1932, all in BSH Records, Subseries 3.2 (Social Hygiene), Folder 162: American Birth Control League, 1929–1930, RAC. See also Gorton, *Icon and Idealist*, chap. 27.

64 Advertisement, *Birth Control Review* 14, no. 4 (April 1930): 125.

65 Untitled review, *Quarterly Review of Biology* 5, no. 2 (June 1930): 255.

66 KBD, *Factors*, 12; and Gorton, *Icon and Idealist*, 167.

67 KBD, *Factors*, 16, 21–22.

68 KBD, *Factors*, 96; File Memorandum. Subject: Request for Dr. Davis' Questionnaire—Mr. Harry G. Griswold, October 19, 1932, BSH Series 3.2, Folder 179, RAC.

69 KBD, *Factors*, 98 and 153.

70 KBD, *Factors*, 135, 164.

71 KBD, *Factors*, 147.

72 KBD, *Factors*, 167; and Bullough, *Science in the Bedroom*, 112.

73 KBD, *Factors*, 95.

74 KBD, *Factors*, 95.

75 KBD, *Factors*, 141.

76 F. W. Stella Browne, "Women Bear Witness," *New Generation* 9 (November 1930): 127–28 (quotation); see also Lesley A. Hall, "'I Have Never Met the Normal Woman': Stella Browne and the Politics of Womanhood," *Women's History Review* 6, no. 2 (1997): 157–82; and Terry, *American Obsession*, 126–35.

77 Chauncey, *Gay New York*, chap. 11; and Taylor, "Veritable Hotbeds."

78 KBD, *Factors*, 264; and Sherrie Inness, *The Lesbian Menace: Ideology, Identity, and the Representation of Lesbian Life* (University of Massachusetts Press, 1997).

79 MB Diaries, July 27, 1897; Sept. 3, 1902, and Nov. 16–22, 1914.

80 Jabour, "Out of the Closet."

81 Jabour, "Victorian Valentine's Day."

82 KBD, *Factors*, 245.

83 KBD, *Factors*, 247.

84 KBD, *Factors*, 298–99.

85 KBD, *Factors*, 238, 240.

86 Taylor, "Veritable Hotbeds," 181–82; and Arthur Garfield Hays, *Let Freedom Ring* (Boni and Liveright, 1928), 241.

87 Morris Ernst to KBD, December 7, 1928, Ernst Papers; see also Leslie A. Taylor, "'I Made Up My Mind to Get It': The American Trial of *The Well of Loneliness*, New York City, 1928–1929," *Journal of the History of Sexuality* 10, no. 2 (April 2001): 250–86, especially 264–65; and Taylor, "Veritable Hotbeds," 241–42.

88 KBD to Charles O. Heydt, December 3, 1927, and KBD to JDR, January 24, 1928, OMR, RB, FA324, Series O, Box 7, Folder 44, RAC. The chapters on contraceptive use and marital happiness appeared in the *Journal of Social Hygiene*; the chapters on masturbation appeared in the *Journal of Mental Hygiene*; and the chapters on the periodicity of sex desire appeared in the *American Journal of Obstetrics and Gynecology*. See KBD, *Factors*, Table of Contents.

89 Spaulding, "Emotional Episodes"; see also Taylor, "Veritable Hotbeds," 56–58.

90 KBD, *Factors*, 239, 246.

91 KBD, *Factors*, 241–45.

92 KBD, *Factors*, 241, 245–46.

93 Laura Doan and Jay Prosser, eds., *Palatable Poison: Critical Perspectives on "The Well of Loneliness"* (Columbia University Press, 2001); and Rebecca O'Rourke, *Reflecting on "The Well of Loneliness"* (Routledge, 1989).

94 "'It Has Made Me Want to Live': Public Support for Lesbian Novelist Radclyffe Hall over Banned Book Revealed," *Guardian*, January 10, 2019; Oral History of Jo, b.

1926, OLOHP; see also Oral Histories of Deedy, b. 1922, Dee, b. 1936, and Phyllis, b. 1920, OLOHP; Oral History of DJ, January 6, 1980 (Tape 3), Herstories; "Lesbianism in the 1920's and 1930's," draft manuscript, p. 2, VLBP, Box 259, Folder 10; and Blanche Wiesen Cook, "'Women Alone Stir My Imagination': Lesbianism and the Cultural Tradition," *Signs* 4, no. 4 (1979): 718–39.

95 KBD, *Factors*, 254.

96 KBD, *Factors*, 260–62, 271.

97 KBD, *Factors*, 279–83.

98 KBD, *Factors*, 280.

99 KBD, *Factors*, 285.

100 KBD, *Factors*, 286.

101 Cook, "'Women Alone Stir My Imagination,'" 719.

102 Oral History, Phyllis, b. 1920, OLOHP.

103 Oral History, Mattie, b. 1922, OLOHP.

104 Jeannette Foster, *Sex Variant Women in Literature* (Vantage Press, 1956), appendix C; and Joanne Passet, *Sex Variant Woman: The Life of Jeannette Howard Foster* (Da Capo Press, 2008).

105 Jeannette Foster to ACK, May 8, 1941, Kinsey Correspondence Collection, Kinsey Institute.

106 KBD, *Factors*, 287.

107 KBD, *Factors*, 295.

108 *Scientific American* 143, no. 6 (December 1930): 488; 145, no. 5 (November 1931): 350; and 147, no. 6 (December 1932): 374.

109 Thomas B. Wells to RT, June 15, 1928, BSH, Series 2, Box 2, File 85; and Agreement, Bureau of Social Hygiene and Harper & Brothers, December 14, 1928, BSH, Series 2, Box 2, File 83, RAC.

110 RT to LBD, February 15, 1930, BSH, Series 2, Box 2, File 85, RAC.

111 *The Nation* 134, no. 3473 (January 27, 1932): 122; RT to LBD, February 15, 1930, BSH, Series 2, Box 2, File 85, RAC; and Harper & Brothers, Undated Letter and Order Form, ca. 1929, Alumnae Files, VCSC.

112 "Scientific Truths About Sex," *Scientific American* 138, no. 2 (February 1928): 112–13.

113 *Journal of the Michigan State Medical Society* 28, no. 3 (March 1930): 270; and *Journal of State Medicine* 39, no. 5 (May 1931): 308.

114 *Church Management* 7, no. 10 (1931): 777.

115 *Sierra Educational News* 26, no. 8 (1930): 42.

116 "Book Notices," *JAMA* 93, no. 5 (1929): 405–6.

117 *America: A Catholic Review of the Week* 46, no. 23 (March 12, 1932): 532.

118 *American Journal of Public Health* 20, no. 7 (1930): 797 (quotations)–798.

119 "Religion's Voice," *New Outlook* 154, no. 15 (April 9, 1930): 592.

120 Lorine Pruette, "Sex and Marriage in a Modern Age," *Birth Control Review* 14, no. 3 (March 1930): 69–70.

121 M. J. Exner, "The Sex Side of Life," *The Survey*, April 15, 1930, 74–75.

122 Pruette, "Sex and Marriage in a Modern Age," 69.

123 V. F. Calverton, "Polygamous Women," *Forum* 83, no. 5 (May 1930): 272–76; see also KBD, "Letter 7," *Forum* 84, no. 2 (August 1930): 17.

CONCLUSION

1 Weidensall, *Mentality of the Criminal Woman*, 15, 25–26n4.

2 KBD, A/B.

3 Thomas B. Wells to RT, June 15, 1928, BSH, Series 2, Box 2, File 85, RAC.

4 RT to Harper & Brothers, May 24, 1929, BSH, Series 1, Box 1, File 7; and Eugene Sexton to RT, January 28, 1930, BSH, Series 2, Box 2, File 85, RAC.

5 RT to KBD, March 30, 1932, BSH, Series 1, Box 1, File 61, RAC.

6 KBD to Paul Kellogg, June 14, 1933, Survey Records, Folder 468, SWHA.

7 Lorine Pruett, "The Flapper," in V. F. Calverton and S. D. Schmalhausen, eds., *The New Generation: The Intimate Problems of Modern Parents and Children* (1930; rpt. Arno Press, 1971), 585–86.

8 Dorothy Dunbar Bromley, *Youth and Sex: A Study of 1300 College Students* (Harper & Bros., 1938), 5.

9 Helen Buckler, "Sex and the Law," *Scribner's Magazine* 90 (July–December 1931): 247.

10 Dale Carnegie, *How to Win Friends and Influence People* (Simon and Schuster, 1936), 229.

11 Alfred C. Kinsey, *Methods in Biology* (J.B. Lippincott, 1937), 204; and Havelock Ellis, *Psychology of Sex: A Manual for Students* (William Heinemann, 1933), 97, 119, 202, 208, 227, 223, 239; see also Frances Bruce Strain, *New Patterns in Sex Teaching: The Normal Sex Interests of Children and Their Guidance from Infancy to Adolescence* (D. Appleton, 1934), ix; see also Victor Robinson, *Encyclopaedia Sexualis:* Comprehensive Encyclopaedia-Dictionary of the Sexual Sciences (Dingwall-Rock, in collaboration with Medical Review of Reviews, 1936), 544; Edmund S. Conklin, *Principles of Adolescent Psychology* (Henry Holt, 1935), 29, 32, 304, 307; Winifred V. Richmond, *An Introduction to Sex Education* (J. Cape, 1936), 234; and Cyril Bibby, *Sex Education: A Guide for Parents, Teachers, and Youth Leaders* (Macmillan, 1944), 286.

12 "Interviews with Emily Harshorne Mudd," 204, Schlesinger-Rockefeller Oral History Project, Schlesinger; see also Ernest R. Groves, *Marriage* (Henry Holt, 1932), 230, 251, 360, 439, 539; M. J. Exner, *The Sexual Side of Marriage* (Norton, 1932), 13–15; Jessie Bernard, "The Distribution of Success in Marriage," *American Journal of Sociology* 39, no. 2 (1933): 195; Lewis M. Terman, *Psychological Factors in Marital Happiness* (McGraw-Hill, 1938), vi; Karl A. Menninger, *Love Against Hate* (Harcourt, Brace, 1942), 297; Ernest W. Burgess and Paul Wallin, *Engagement and Marriage* (Lippincott, 1953), 35; and Lena Levine and Davis Goldsmith Lott, *The Frigid Wife: Her Way to Sexual Fulfillment* (Messner, 1962), 203.

13 For sociology, see Edward Franklin Frazier, *The Negro Family in Chicago* (University of Chicago Press, 1932), 202; Robert Lee Sutherland and Julian L. Woodward, *Introductory Sociology* (Lippincott, 1937), 546; R. Mc. MacIver, *Society: A Textbook of Sociology* (Farrar & Rinehart, 1937), 435; and Judah Rumney, *The Science of Society: An Introduction to Sociology* (Duckworth, 1938), 97; for psychology, see Edmund S. Conklin, *Principles of Adolescent Psychology* (Macmillan, 1935), 29, 32, 304; Stanley D. Porteus, *Practice of Clinical Psychology* (American Book Company, 1941), 280–81; Elizabeth Hurlock, *Child Development* (McGraw-Hill, 1942), 429; Marian Edgar Breckenridge and Elizabeth Lee Vincent, *Child Development* (W.B. Saunders, 1943), 540; and Paul Henry Landis, *Adolescence and Youth* (McGraw-Hill, 1945), 268, 285; and for biology, see Frank Lorimer and Frederick Henry Osborn, *Dynamics of Population* (Macmillan, 1934), 255–59; and Glenn W. Blaydes, *Methods and Materials for Teaching Biological Sciences* (McGraw-Hill, 1938), 406.

14 KBD, *Factors*, xvii.

15 RT to Frank Lorimer, October 17, 1931; RT File Memorandum, October 19, 1932, BSH, Series 3.2, Folder 179, RAC; and Taylor, "Veritable Hotbeds," 99–102.

16 RLD, "Appendix VI: The Gynecology of Homosexuality," in George W. Henry, *Sex Variants: A Study of Homosexual Patterns* (Hoeber, 1948), 1069.

17 Havelock Ellis, *Sex and Marriage: Eros in Contemporary Life* (1952; rpt. Greenwood Press, 1977), 168.

18 Helmar Wessman to KBD, April 21, 1933, OMR, RB, FA 324, Series O, Box 7, Folder 44, RAC.

19 "Reading List ACK gave marriage course staff, 1938–40," ACK Collection, Box 2, Kinsey Institute.

20 Donna J. Drucker, "'A Noble Experiment': The Marriage Course at Indiana University, 1938–1940," *Indiana Magazine of History* 103 (September 2007): 231–64, quotations on 252, 260.

21 Alfred C. Kinsey, Wardell B. Pomeroy, and Clyde E. Martin, *Sexual Behavior in the Human Male* (Saunders, 1948); and Alfred. C. Kinsey, Wardell B. Pomeroy, Clyde E. Martin, and Paul H. Gebhard, *Sexual Behavior in the Human Female* (Saunders, 1953).

22 Cryle and Stephens, *Normality*, 233–34.

23 Igo, *Averaged American*, chap. 5.

24 Cryle and Stephens, *Normality*, chap. 9; Igo, *Averaged American*, chap. 6; and Irvine, *Disorders of Desire*, chap. 1.

25 ACK to RLD, July 26, 1946, Robert Latou Dickinson Collection, Box 1, Series IIC, Folder 8b; ACK to Glen Ramsey, September 20, 1940; and ACK to Lewis M. Terman, August 23, 1941, Kinsey Correspondence, Kinsey Institute. See also Drucker, *Classification of Sex*, 70, 90–96.

26 Kinsey et al., *Sexual Behavior in the Human Male*, 23–24; and Kinsey et al., *Sexual Behavior in the Human Female*, 94. See also Igo, *Averaged American*, chap. 5.

27 KBD to Paul Kellogg, June 14, 1933, Survey Records, Folder 468 (Davis, Dr. Katherine B., 1933), SWHA.

28 See for instance William L. O'Neill, *Everyone Was Brave: A History of Feminism in America* (Quadrangle, 1976), 299; Vern L. Bullough, *Homosexuality: A History* (Meridian Books, 1979), 188; Lillian Faderman, *Surpassing the Love of Men: Romantic Friendship and Love Between Women from the Renaissance to the Present* (Morrow, 1981), 326–27; Rosalind Rosenberg, *Beyond Separate Spheres: Intellectual Roots of Modern Feminism* (Yale University Press, 1982), 198–200; D'Emilio and Freedman, *Intimate Matters*, 385–87; Linda Gordon, *Woman's Body, Woman's Right: Birth Control in America* (Penguin Books 1990), 511, 522, 532; and Jonathan Katz, *Gay American History* (Meridian, 1992), 662.

29 See for example Carol Rinkleib Ellison, *Women's Sexualities: Generations of Women Share Intimate Secrets of Sexual Self-Acceptance* (New Harbinger Publications, 2000), 5, 181, 214; and Janet L. Carroll, *Sexuality Now: Embracing Diversity* (Wadworth Cengage, 2010), 37, 41, 42, 45, 57.

30 Matt Lavietes, "Florida's Not Alone: 19 Other States Eye LGBTQ School Bills," *NBC News*, April 11, 2022; Christine Hauser, "Teacher Is Fired for Reading Book on Gender Identity in Class," *NYT*, August 18, 2023; Sarah Bonner, "I Put an LGBTQ Book on My Classroom Reading List: Then Someone Filed a Police Report," *Education Week*, July 31, 2023.

31 Greg Jaffe and Patrick Marley, "A Sex Educator in Michigan Refused to Be Shamed: Then Came the Backlash," *Washington Post*, August 23, 2023; and Valeriya Safronova, "A Private-School Sex Educator Defends Her Methods," *NYT*, July 7, 2021.

32 Claire Thornton, "California Schools Join Growing List of Districts Across the Country Banning Pride Flags," *USA Today*, September 14, 2023; Ross Douthat, "How to Make Sense of the New L.G.B.T.Q. Culture War," *NYT*, April 13, 2022; and Kiberly Wehle, "He, She, They: The Pronoun Debate Will Likely Land at the Supreme Court," *Politico*, October 1, 2023.

33 Katie Barnes, "Transgender Athlete Laws by State," *ESPN*, August 24, 2023; Jere Longman, "Sport Is Again Divided over Inclusiveness and a Level Playing Field," *NYT*, June 23, 2022; Annette Choi and Will Mullery, "19 States Have Laws Restricting Gender-Affirming Care, Some with the Possibility of a Felony Charge," *CNN*, June 6, 2023.

34 David A. Graham, *The Project: How Project 2025 Is Reshaping America* (Random House, 2025), chap. 1.

35 Center for Reproductive Rights, "After *Roe* Fell: Abortion Laws by State," September 3, 2025. https://reproductiverights.org.

36 Julianne McShane, "Americans Are Stockpiling Abortion Pills . . . Just in Case," *Mother Jones*, January 3, 2024; for updates, see https://jessica.substack.com/.

37 Margery A. Beck, "Nebraska Mother Sentenced to 2 Years in Prison for Giving Abortion Pills to Pregnant Daughter," *AP News*, September 22, 2023; Sanya Mansoor, "What Nebraska's Sentencing of a Teen Who Used Abortion Pills Might Mean in a Post-*Roe* America," *Time*, July 26, 2023.

38 Erin Douglas and Carla Astudillo, "We Annotated Texas' Near-Total Abortion Ban: Here's What the Law Says About Enforcement," *Texas Tribune*, September 10, 2021; Maria Mendez, "How New Regulations Impact Abortion and Birth Control Access in Texas," *Texas Tribune*, October 11, 2023; and Eleanor Klibanoff, "Kate Cox's Case Reveals How Far Texas Intends to Go to Enforce Abortion Laws," *Texas Tribune*, December 13, 2023.

39 Remy Tumin, "Ohio Woman Who Miscarried Faces Charge That She Abused Corpse," *NYT*, January 3, 2024, updated January 11, 2024.

40 Anya Jabour, "'Childless Cat Ladies' Have Long Contributed to the Welfare of American Children—and the Nation," *The Conversation–US*, October 21, 2024; Rachel Treisman, "Why Republicans Are Calling Walz 'Tampon Tim,'" *NPR*, August 7, 2024; and Mike Wendling, "Project 2025: The Right-Wing Wish List for Trump's Second Term," *BBC*, February 13, 2025.

41 Executive Order, "Defending Women from Gender Ideology Extremism and Restoring Biological Truth to the Federal Government," January 20, 2025; Fact Sheet, "President Donald J. Trump Enforces Overwhelmingly Popular Demand to Stop Taxpayer Funding of Abortion," The White House, January 25, 2025, www.whitehouse.gov.

42 Devin Dwyer, "Supreme Court Formally Asked to Overturn Landmark Same-Sex Marriage Ruling," *ABC News*, August 11, 2025.

INDEX

Page numbers in italics indicate Figures.

ABOUT THE AUTHOR

Anya Jabour is Regents Professor of History at the University of Montana, where she teaches courses in the history of women, gender, and sexuality in the United States. Her previous books include *Sophonisba Breckinridge: Championing Women's Activism in Modern America* (2019); *Topsy-Turvy: How the Civil War Turned the World Upside Down for Southern Children* (2010), *Scarlett's Sisters: Young Women in the Old South* (2009), and *Marriage in the Early Republic: Elizabeth and William Wirt and the Companionate Ideal* (1998). Her work has been featured in *The New York Times, The Washington Post,* and other major outlets.